A

POLITICAL AND GENERAL HISTORY

OF

THE DISTRICT OF TINNEVELLY

IN THE

PRESIDENCY OF MADRAS

A

POLITICAL AND GENERAL HISTORY

OF

THE DISTRICT OF TINNEVELLY

IN THE

PRESIDENCY OF MADRAS

FROM THE EARLIEST PERIOD TO ITS CESSION TO THE ENGLISH GOVERNMENT IN A. D. 1801

ROBERT CALDWELL

GYAN

Published by

GYAN

Gyan Publishing House
5, Ansari Road
Daryaganj, New Delhi-110002
Phone: 011-47034999, 9811692060
E-mail: books@gyanbooks.com

Distribution Network
gyanbooks.com
India, USA, Canada, UK, Australia

ISBN: 978-93-6780-006-5 (HB)

First Published, 1881

2nd Impression 2024

Printed at: Gyan Press, Delhi.

A POLITICAL AND GENERAL HISTORY OF THE DISTRICT OF TINNEVELLY
Author: ROBERT CALDWELL

A POLITICAL AND GENERAL HISTORY OF THE DISTRICT OF TINNEVELLY, IN THE PRESIDENCY OF MADRAS,

FROM THE EARLIEST PERIOD TO ITS CESSION TO THE ENGLISH GOVERNMENT IN A.D. 1801.

BY

THE RIGHT REV. R. CALDWELL, D.D., LL.D., BISHOP,

HONORARY MEMBER OF THE ROYAL ASIATIC SOCIETY,
FELLOW OF THE MADRAS UNIVERSITY.

MADRAS:
PRINTED BY E. KEYS, AT THE GOVERNMENT PRESS.

1881.

TABLE OF CONTENTS.

CHAPTER I.

INFORMATION FROM WITHOUT RESPECTING THE EARLIEST PERIOD.

CHAPTER II.

FROM THE COMMENCEMENT OF THE RULE OF THE PĀṆḌYAS TO THE PERIOD OF THE SUPREMACY OF THE VIJAYANAGARA KINGS.

CHAPTER III.

From A.D. 1365 to 1731.

THE PERIOD OF THE SECOND DYNASTY OF PĀṆḌYAS AND OF THE NĀYAKAS.

CHAPTER IV.

THE PERIOD OF THE NAWAB OF ARCOT, TO MUHAMMAD YUSUF KHAN'S ADMINISTRATION.

CHAPTER V.

MUHAMMAD YUSUF KHAN'S ADMINISTRATION, TO THE CAPTURE OF MADURA AND HIS DEATH.

CHAPTER VI.

TINNEVELLY ANNALS FROM 1764 TO 1799.

PART I.

FROM THE DEATH OF YUSUF KHAN TO THE ASSIGNMENT OF REVENUE IN 1781.

PART II.

FROM THE ASSIGNMENT OF REVENUE IN 1781 TO THE COMMENCEMENT OF THE BANNERMAN-POLIGAR WAR.

CHAPTER VII.

THE BANNERMAN–POLIGAR WAR.

CHAPTER VIII.

THE LAST POLIGAR WAR, 194.

CHAPTER IX.

CONCLUSION OF THE POLIGAR WAR. CESSION OF THE CARNATIC TO THE ENGLISH GOVERNMENT.

CHAPTER X.

MISSIONS IN TINNEVELLY PRIOR TO THE CESSION OF THE COUNTRY TO THE ENGLISH, 1801.

PART I.

ROMAN CATHOLIC MISSIONS, 232.

PART II.

MISSIONS OF THE CHURCH OF ENGLAND.

APPENDICES.

APPENDIX I.

RELATIONS BETWEEN TRAVANCORE AND TINNEVELLY.

APPENDIX II.

ACCOUNT OF THE FLOODS AND PESTILENTIAL FEVER IN TINNEVELLY IN 1810-12.

APPENDIX III.

TINNEVELLY NATIVE AUTHORS.

APPENDIX IV.

SEPULCHRAL URNS IN TINNEVELLY.

APPENDIX V.

EXPLORATIONS AT KORKAI AND KĀYAL.

HISTORY OF TINNEVELLY,

FROM THE EARLIEST PERIOD TO ITS CESSION TO THE ENGLISH GOVERNMENT IN A.D. 1801.

CHAPTER I.

INFORMATION FROM WITHOUT RESPECTING THE EARLIEST PERIOD.

INTRODUCTION.—PAUCITY OF SOURCES OF HISTORY.

CHAPTER I.

Meaning of the word "history."

VERY little is known with certainty of the early history of most districts in India. It is a singular fact that the Hindūs, though fond of philosophy and poetry, of law, mathematics, and architecture, of music and the drama, and especially of religious or theosophic speculations and disquisitions, seem never to have cared anything for history. The original meaning of the word "history" is investigation, and the Hindūs never appear to have cared to investigate. There is hardly anything in the Indian Epic poems or Purānas that can be dignified by this name. The only histories, properly so called, India has produced were written in, and pertained to, regions that can only be included in the general name of India with some qualification. These are the Rājā-taranginī[1] of Cashmere and the Mahā-wanso[2] of Ceylon. These compositions, it is true, are not free from poetical exaggerations and evince much carelessness about accuracy in details, but on the whole they may be accepted as historical. Can it be that it was through the prevalence in India of a succession of dreamy philosophies that history became virtually an unknown department of literature? This may have had something to do with it, but perhaps the chief cause was the fondness of the mass

---

[1] Rājā-taranginī, stream of kings written in A.D. 1148.

[2] Maha-wanso (= Sansk. vamsa) The Great Dynasty, written between A.D. 459 and 477.

CHAPTER I.

Reasons why the Hindus cared little for historical truth.

of the people in all ages for poetical embellishment. It seemed to them a dull thing to record any event in the history of a king or a country exactly as it happened. It could be made to appear so much more interesting if the poetical narrator's fertile imagination were allowed free play. Whatever the cause may have been, the fact cannot be disputed that historical certainty with regard to the early history of any part of India, if attainable at all, is attainable not by means of any kind of historical composition in verse or prose proceeding from Indian literati, belonging to the district, but solely by means of coins and inscriptions and the statements contained in books written by persons belonging to foreign nations. Light is thrown, for instance, on the early history of the Pāṇḍyas and Chōḷas by the Singhalese Mahā-wanso, and we are indebted for some interesting items of information respecting the history of Southern India to the Greeks, to the Muhammadans of the North, and to European Christian travellers.

Historical information from without.

I may here appropriately quote a portion of my Address delivered at the Convocation of the University of Madras in 1879.

Learned Natives in Northern India have made a good beginning.

"The study of the history, ancient literature, and archæology of the country will never reach anything like completeness of development or realize results of national importance till it is systematically undertaken by educated Natives. Learned Natives of Calcutta and Bombay, trained in European modes of thought and vieing with Europeans in zeal for historical accuracy, have already made a promising beginning in this department of research. I trust that the Native scholars of the South will resolve that they will not be left behind in the race. The most important aid educated Natives can render to the study of the history of their country is by means of a search after inscriptions, many of which, hitherto unnoticed and unknown, they will find inviting their attention on the walls of the temples in almost every village in the interior. The only ancient Indian history worthy of the name is that which has been spelled out from inscriptions and coins. Popular legends and poetical myths, by whatever name they are dignified, may be discarded, not only without loss, but with positive advantage. No guide but our own intelligence is better than a faithless guide. Something has already been done in the direction of the search for, and decipherment of, inscriptions by Europeans, though less systematically in Madras than in Calcutta and Bombay, but much remains to be done, and will always remain, till educated Natives enter upon this branch of study with the zeal with which so many people in Europe have devoted themselves to it. Natives possess various facilities for this study which are denied to Europeans living in India. They have no reason to fear the sun. They can generally stop in their journeys without inconvenience and examine any antiquity they see; and whilst Europeans must be content with examining only the inscriptions on the outer walls of temples, inscriptions in the interior also can be examined by Natives. They will also be allowed to examine inscriptions on copper plates in the

Information from inscriptions and coins.

Facilities enjoyed by Natives.

possession of respectable Native families which would not readily be allowed to pass into the hands of Europeans.

Earliest Tamil works have disappeared.

A humbler, but still very important, branch of archæological work lies open to every educated Hindu in the Tamil districts in this Presidency. Let him set himself, before it is too late, to search out and discover the vernacular works that are commonly supposed to be lost. The names only of many Tamil works of the earlier period survive, and many works must have been composed at a still earlier period of which even the names have been forgotten. Tamil literature seems to have known no youth. Like Minerva, the goddess of learning amongst the Greeks, it seems to have sprung, full-grown and fully armed, from the head of Jupiter. The explanation of this is that every work pertaining to, or illustrative of, the youth of the language appears to have perished. Probably, however, a careful search made by educated Natives in houses and *maṭhas* would be rewarded by some valuable discoveries."

THE DISTRICT OF TINNEVELLY NOT ORIGINALLY DISTINCT FROM THAT OF MADURA.

Tinnevelly originally a portion of Madura.

Another difficulty under which the early history of Tinnevelly labours is that in early times this district had no separate existence, but formed merely the southern portion of the Pāṇḍya country, and this was the position it occupied under the Chōḷas, the early Muhammadans, and the Nāyakas, as well as under the Pāṇḍyas themselves. It was not till the incorporation of the kingdom of Madura, including its various districts and dependencies into the territories under the rule of the Nawab of Arcot, about A.D. 1744, that the district of Tinnevelly came to be regarded, at first for revenue purposes alone, as independent of, or at least as distinct from, the District of Madura. The only nāme in classical Tamil which looks like a name for Tinnevelly, as distinct from Madura, is Ten-Pāṇḍi, the Southern Pāṇḍya country; but this is represented as the name of one of the twelve districts in the Tamil country in which bad Tamil (Koḍun-Tamiḻ) is spoken; and it is evident that it could not have been intended that the whole of Tinnevelly should be denoted by this name. The interpretation of some persons is that by Ten-Pāṇḍi is meant that portion of Tinnevelly which lies to the south of the Tāmraparṇī river. Others are of opinion that the term denotes only Nāñji-nāḍu, the Tamil portion of South Travancore, lying to the south-west of Tinnevelly and the north-west of Cape Comorin. Tamil has always been the language of the whole of Tinnevelly, and Cape Comorin is represented in the Tamil classics as the southern boundary of the region in which Tamil is spoken. The boundary could not well be carried further south without being carried out to sea, but Tamil has always been spoken, as I know from inscriptions, in Nāñji-nāḍu.

Meaning of Ten-Pāṇḍi.

Earliest Inhabitants of Tinnevelly.

Chapter I.

The hill tribes not representatives of the earliest inhabitants of Tinnevelly.

Nothing is known as yet of the earliest inhabitants of Tinnevelly, except that whoever they were they could not have been Áryans. The hill tribes called in Malayālam Malayarasas (hill kings), and in Tamil Kāṇikkāras (hereditary proprietors of land), are not, I think, to be regarded, like the Tudas of the Nīlagiris, as surviving representatives of the earliest inhabitants of the plains; but, like the hill tribes of the Pulneys, appear to be the descendants of some Hindūised low-country people of a later period, who were driven to the hills by oppression or who voluntarily migrated thither. Probably the earliest inhabitants came to be mixed up so completely with succeeding immigrants that it will be impossible now to distinguish them. Perhaps the best representatives at present of the earliest race of inhabitants are those long-oppressed tribes that are now considered the lowest, in the social scale, the Paraiyas and Paḷḷas. We meet occasionally with traditions of a more or less reliable character respecting the arrival of most other tribes from other parts of the country. There can be no doubt, for instance, of the fact that the Brahmans came from the north. There can be no doubt also about the arrival from the north of the Nāyakas and other Telugu castes. It is commonly supposed that the Veḷḷālas came from the Chōḷa country, the Maṛavas from the Ramnad country, and the Shanars from Ceylon. Such traditions, it is true, are too uncertain to be of much ethnological value, but it is a noticeable circumstance that there is no tradition whatever of the arrival in the country at any time of the Paḷḷas and Paṛaiyas. From the silence of tradition it may therefore, perhaps, be inferred that those tribes were already in the district when other bands of immigrants, represented by the other tribes or castes we now find, arrived. The names by which they are now called are not necessarily of the same antiquity as the tribes themselves. "Paṛaiya" means a drummer; "Paḷḷa" appears to mean a man who works in low-lying lands, and both these names connect them with a somewhat developed state of society. If they were really the oldest tribes that settled in the district, they must have subsisted mainly by the chase, like the rude tribe commonly called Vēḍas, and partly by the cultivation of dry grains. The cultivation of rice by means of irrigation would seem from etymological reasons to have been a specialty of the Veḷḷālas. Veḷ, the root of Veḷḷāla, seems to be identical with Veḷ, the root of Veḷḷam, water used for irrigation.

The lowest castes probably aboriginal

The Paṛaiyas and Paḷḷas.

The Veḷḷālas.

Stone implements.

The only traces of the earliest inhabitants of Tinnevelly that survive, so far as I am aware at present, are certain stone implements that have been found near Shērmādēvī (Cheran-mā-dēvī) and Puthuguḍi. They were taken to Berlin by Dr. Jägor. These

CHAPTER I.

implements betokened some little progress in civilization, as the sides were rounded and the curves symmetrical. This would identify them with what has been called the 'neolithic age.' I am unable to regard the sepulchral urns or jars found almost everywhere in Tinnevelly as relics of the earliest period, notwithstanding the interest that attaches to them and the mystery which hangs over them. The excellence of the pottery and the circumstance that copper ornaments have sometimes been found in the urns show that the people who buried their dead in those urns, whoever they were, and at however early a period they may have lived, were a comparatively civilised race.[1]

Sepulchral urns.

Whatever relics of the oldest period still survive will be found, I think, like the stone implements referred to above, not in the valley of the Tāmraparṇī itself, which must have been too frequently covered with water and too marshy to allow of human habitations being erected upon it at the outset, but on the gravelly slopes on either side of the valley, constituting the primeval banks of the stream. One place of this description called Āditta-nallūr, near Puthuguḍi, has been found particularly rich in sepulchral urns, &c. I should not expect to find relics of the oldest period anywhere near the sea, as I consider it certain that the land has been slowly but steadily rising above the ancient sea level for ages, probably even before man made his appearance in the district. The rise of the land all through the historical period is capable, I think, of proof. Near Kulasēkharapaṭṭanam, a town and port of some antiquity, pieces of broken pottery are occasionally found imbedded in the grit stone, a marine formation abounding in sea shells of existing species, found all along the coast. I have a specimen in my possession found about a mile from the sea-shore, but I regard this as proving, not the immense antiquity of the pottery, which does not appear to differ in the least from the pottery now in use, but rather the comparatively recent origin of some portions of the grit stone.

The Tāmraparṇī River.

Attraction of the Tāmraparṇī.

If the history of the dawn of a higher civilisation in Tinnevelly could be brought to light, I have no doubt that the Tāmraparṇī, the great river of Tinnevelly, would be found to occupy the most prominent place in the picture. It must have been the facilities afforded by this stream for the cultivation of rice which attracted to its banks family after family of settlers from the north of a higher class than the rude, black aborigines. This river like the Kāvērī, but unlike most Indian streams, is fed by both monsoons—

[1] See Appendix.

CHAPTER I.

the south-western and the north-eastern—and is seen in full flood twice a year. It flows through a narrow but very rich alluvial valley, originally formed by itself, when natural forces appear to have been stronger than they are now, by the process of denudation, and then filled up by itself in later periods by the process of sedimentary deposition. It flows smoothly to the sea without torrents and along a bed which, instead of being hollowed deeper and deeper every year, and thus becoming less and less capable of being utilised for irrigation, gets silted up a little from year to year, so that at length in the lower half of its course, between Palamcotta and the sea, it has become necessary to confine it within artificial banks. Such a river would necessarily prove an attraction to settlers, if not from the very first, yet at least from the first appearance in the district of a people systematically practising agriculture and acquainted with the cultivation of rice by irrigation.

Description of the Tāmraparṇī.

ORIGIN OF THE TĀMRAPARṆĪ.—AGASTYA'S HILL.

The mountain Potigai.

The Tāmraparṇī rises on a noble conical mountain called Potigai, more commonly called Potiyam, or Potiya-mā-malai, the meaning of which is probably "a place of concealment," as will be explained below. Locally it is called Periya Potigai, the great Potigai, to distinguish it from a smaller mountain adjoining it called Aindu-talai Potigai, the Potigai with the five heads. This mountain is the highest in the Tinnevelly range of ghauts, being 6,800 feet in height, and is regarded by Native poets as the distinguishing mountain of the Pāṇḍyas, one of the titles of the Pāṇḍya king being 'lord of Potiyam.' This mountain stands back nearly ten miles from the rest of the mountains of the range, so that the Tāmraparṇī which takes its rise upon it drains a considerable extent of mountain country before it emerges into the plains. Potiyam is visible from Palamcotta, the capital of Tinnevelly, and is still more distinctly visible from Trevandrum, the capital of Travancore, on the western side of the range. It is usually called Agastyar's Hill, or by the English simply 'Agastier,' from the tradition that the great *rishi* Agastya, when he retired from the world after civilising the south, took up his abode in its inaccessible recesses. It was long supposed by all Natives to be inaccessible, on account of the force of the charms with which Agastya had fenced in his retreat, but Europeans have frequently found their way to the top, and some years ago, a meteorological observatory was erected near the top by Dr. Broun, the Astronomer of the Mahārājā of Travancore. The rainfall on the top of the mountain was found to amount to 300 inches in the year. The rainfall at Palamcotta, half way between the mountains and

'Agastier.'

Supposed to be inaccessible.

Rainfall on Agastya's hill and in the plains.

the sea, is less than 27 inches, whilst 25 inches is the general average in the Tinnevelly plains; and here we see the reason why it is that, though the plains of Tinnevelly are so parched and dry, through the excessive heat and excessive evaporation, and though the rainfall is so insignificant, the Tāmraparṇī rolls to the sea its full flood of fertilising waters twice every year, and twice every year enriches the beautiful valley through which it flows with abundant crops. In consequence of this Tinnevelly stands next to Tanjore—yet with a long interval—in regard to the amount of revenue its land assessment yields.

REFERENCES TO THE TĀMRAPARṆĪ IN INDIAN LITERATURE.

Lassen's reference to the Tāmraparṇī.

Lassen in his *Indische Alterthumskunde* (Vol. I) describes the Tāmraparṇī as "an inconsiderable stream, with a renowned name." Looking at the length of its course (only 70 miles from its rise to the sea, including windings), it may certainly be considered an inconsiderable stream, but it holds a high position amongst the Indian rivers in regard to the benefits it confers; and its name seems to have become famous in India from a very early period. It may worthily be called an "ancient river," by which I understand a river renowned in ancient song. It is mentioned amongst the rivers of India in the geographical sections of several of the Purānas, and seems to have been regarded in those times as a particularly sacred stream. It is represented as rising in the mountain Malaya, and this enables us to identify Malaya with the Southern Ghauts. The Sanskrit Malaya of course represents the Dravidian mala, a hill. The earliest and most noticeable reference to it in Sanskrit literature is in the Mahābhārata;—"Also I will remind thee, O son of Kunti (Yudhishtira, the eldest of the Pāṇḍava brothers), of the fame of the Tāmraparṇī, in the hermitage connected with which the gods, desirous of heaven, performed austerities."—Āraṇya Parva.

The Tamraparṇī in the Mahabhārata.

In the Raghu-vamsa.

There is an interesting, though probably much later, verse in the Raghu-vamsa, in which the Tāmraparṇī is mentioned. It says, "They (the Pāṇḍyas) having prostrated themselves before Raghu presented to him as their glory, the collected excellence of the pearls of the ocean into which the Tāmraparṇī flows," iv, 50. From this it appears that it was even then known that the Tāmraparṇī was in the country of the Pāṇḍyas, and that pearls were found near the place where the Tāmraparṇī fell into the ocean. The author of this poem, the celebrated Kālidāsa, is generally supposed to have lived in the century before the Christian era. Some make him several centuries later.

SACRED BATHING PLACES ON THE TĀMRAPARṆĪ.

Hindūs have still a great idea of the religious merit of bathing in this stream. Every portion of the stream is sacred; but

CHAPTER I.

bathing at the waterfalls in the upper part of its course is supposed in these times to be specially meritorious.

Falls of the Tāmraparṇī.

There are two of these waterfalls on the main stream, one called Vāṇatīrtham (from the name of an Asura called Vāṇa) on the slope of Potiyam, and another still more frequented, about 90 feet in height, at Pāpa-nāsakam (destruction of sin). The latter is commonly called Kalyāṇītīrtham, the sacred bathing place of Kalyāṇi (Pārvati), but by some Kalyāṇa-tīrtham, the wedding bathing place, that is, the place where Pārvati's marriage to Siva was exhibited to Agastya. This fall is at the place where the Tāmraparṇī leaves the mountains and enters the plains. There is another celebrated waterfall, not far from Vāṇa-tīrtham, called Pāmban-aruvi, the snake waterfall, so called on account of its long snake-like appearance when seen from a distance. It consists of two falls, the upper 500 feet in height, the lower 200 feet. This remarkable fall is not on the main stream, but on a tributary, which rises on the "five-headed Potigai."

FALLS OF COURTALLUM.

The Chittār.

The northern tributary to the Tāmraparṇī, which does not join it till near the sea, is called the Chitra-nadī, the beautiful river, vulgarly Chittār, the little river. The falls on this stream, at Courtallum, are much celebrated, and Europeans and Hindūs are equally fond of bathing in them, though for different reasons. It may be asserted without risk of exaggeration that Courtallum is the finest fresh-water bathing place in the world. Two forms of the name Courtallum are given in the Courtallum Sthala-purāṇa, one with tt, the other with RR=ttr. If the form of the word adopted be Kuttālam, the meaning will be "the wild Ātti tree" (*Bauhinia parviflora*), and the name will then signify the temple or village near the Kuttālam tree. This form of the word, Kuttālam, is said to be Sanskrit, but I can find no trace of it in any Sanskrit dictionary. If the form adopted be Kuttrālam, which is the one in common use, it will mean the ālam, destruction, literally poison, of Kuttru, sin, a meaning equivalent to that of the other great sacred bathing place along this range, viz., Pāvanāsam (properly Pāpanāśakam, annihilation of sin). Ālam is from the Sanskrit halā-hala or hāhala, "a deadly poison." This is the meaning generally attributed to the name of the place in the Sthala-purāna. This shape of the word Kuttru is not found in any dictionary, but one of the most common Tamil words for sin is Kuttram, which is substantially the same. The lowest of the three falls of Courtallum is commonly called by the Natives Vaḍa-aruvi, the northern fall. It consists of two falls, the united height of which is about 180 feet. The upper pool of this fall they call Pongumākaḍal, the boiling sea, the depth of which is 38

Meaning of the name of Kuttrālam.

Courtallum falls.

feet. The second fall is called Sembagāṭavi tīrtham, the sacred bathing place of the Sembaga forest. Sembaga is the Tamil form of the Sanskrit Champaka (the *Michelia Champaka*). The third is called Tēnaruvi, the honey fall. A poetical name of Courtallum is Trikūḍam, which may best be rendered, the three plateaus or platforms. The spices cultivated at Courtallum were introduced by Mr. Casamajor in 1800.

MOUTH OF THE TĀMRAPARṆĪ.

The early Hindūs must have been acquainted with the mouth of the Tāmraparṇī long before they knew anything of its inland course or of the falls in the mountains, so that I conclude that it was near its mouth, and probably at the place where its junction with the sea took place, that people bathed and performed austerities, as the gods are represented to have done, in the time of the Mahābhārata. It would seem probable that there also, at Korkai, was formed the first settlement of civilised men in Tinnevelly, and that it was there that the name of Tāmraparṇī, by which the river became known, was first given to it.

The first settlement of civilised men in Tinnevelly. Where?

MEANING AND ORIGIN OF THE NAME TĀMRAPARṆĪ.

'The tree with red leaves.'

The meaning of the name Tāmraparṇī, considered in itself, is sufficiently clear, but its application in this connexion is far from being self-evident. Tāmra means red, parnī, from parna, a leaf, that which has leaves, that is, a tree. Tāmraparṇī might therefore be expected to mean a tree with red leaves, but this is a strange derivation for the name of a river, and the idea naturally suggests itself that some event or legend capable of explaining the name lies beyond. It is especially worthy of notice that this very name was the oldest name for Ceylon. It was called Tāmbapaṇṇi by the early Buddhists, three centuries before Christ, in king Asoka's inscription at Girnar, and when the Greeks first visited India in the time of Alexander the Great and began to inquire, with their usual zeal for knowledge, about India, the countries and peoples it contained, and the neighbouring countries, they ascertained the existence of a great adjacent island which they were told was called Taprobane—a mispronunciation of Tāmbapaṇṇi. Lankā, the beautiful island, is the name by which Ceylon is called in the Rāmāyana, and ordinarily in the Mahā-wanso. Simhalam, however, is the name by which it was called by the later Buddhistic writers, from which came in regular succession the forms Sihalam, Sīlam, Selen-dib, Serendib, Zeelan, Ceylan, and Ceylon. [Dib is the Arabic survival of the Sanskrit dvīpa, island.] From the form Sīlam comes the Tamil Īḻam. Simha means a lion, Simhala the lion country, that is, either the country of the lion-slayers or more probably the country of the lion-like men. Tāmbapaṇṇi, or Tāmraparṇī, as the name is more correctly

Taprobane.

Later names of Ceylon.

CHAPTER I.

written in Sanskrit, is said in the Mahā-wanso to have been the name of the first settlement formed by Vijaya and his followers in Lankā, from which the name came to be applied to the whole island—see Turnour's Mahā-wanso, p. 57. This settlement seems to have been near Putlam on the western coast of Ceylon, nearly opposite the mouth of the chief river in Tinnevelly; and it may be regarded as certain that the two names had a common origin, one being derived from the other, like Boston in the United States and Boston in England. The name of the river may have been derived from the name of the settlement; or *vice versâ*, the name of the settlement may have been derived from the name of the river. The only question is, which use of the word was the earlier? It may be supposed that a colony from the mouth of the Tāmraparṇī in Tinnevelly carried the name over with it to a settlement founded by it on the opposite coast of Ceylon. Or, on the other hand, after the Āryan adventurers under Vijaya settled in Ceylon, they may have formed a settlement on the Tinnevelly coast and given the chief river on the coast the name of the town from which they came. The general and natural course of migration would doubtless be from the mainland to the island; but there may occasionally have been reflex waves of migration even in the earliest times, as there certainly were later on, traces of which survive in the existence in Tinnevelly and the western coast of castes whose traditions, and even in some instances, whose names, connect them with Ceylon. The marriage relations into which Vijaya and his followers are said to have entered with the Pāṇḍyas would also make them acquainted with Korkai at the mouth of the Tāmraparṇī, the oldest capital of the Pāṇḍyas, which must have been their capital at that time, and the river may thus have been indebted for its name to those Singhalese visitors. At all events it seems more natural that Tāmraparṇī, "the tree with the red leaves," should have been first the name of a tree, then of a town, then of a district, then of a river (it being not uncommon in India for villages to receive their names from remarkable trees), than that it should have been the name of a river at the outset. Lassen interprets Tāmraparṇī to mean "a tank with red lotuses," but this derivation seems to be quite unsupported. In Tamil poetical literature the first member of the compound is omitted and the river is called the Porunei, that is, the Parnī, alone. The English sometimes erroneously write and pronounce the name as Tāmrapoorney, but the error is derived from the old practice of writing the second part of the name Purni, instead of Parni.

Identity of the Tāmraparṇī of Tinnevelly with the oldest name of Ceylon.

Which application of the name was the earlier.

Greek Name for the Tāmraparṇī.

The Solen of the Greeks.

The Greeks in the time of Ptolemy called the river by the name of the Solen. This is a remarkable circumstance, because they had called Ceylon for several centuries by the name of Taprobane, and the name of the river being identical with this name of Ceylon, one would have expected that they would have called it also by the name of Taprobane. It might almost be supposed that Tāmraparṇī was not the name of the river in actual use when the Greek merchants arrived in Southern India, but this supposition is inconsistent with the use of the name in the Mahābhārata, for the bulk of the Mahābhārata is probably much more ancient than the commencement of Greek commercial relations with the South, which dates only from the Christian era, and there is no reason to suppose that the portion of the Mahābhārata in which the reference to the river is contained could have been inserted at a later period for sectarian purposes. The connection in which the name stands in the geographical lists in the Purāṇas is also unsectarian. It seems therefore necessary to suppose that the river, though called the Solen by the Greeks, was even then called the Tāmraparṇī by the natives, or at least by the Brahmans. How is this to be explained? Lassen supposes that the old name of the principal stream was Sylaur, which also he supposes to be the present name of the tributary stream. No such name, however, as Sylaur is, or appears ever to have been, in use. This is evidently a mistake for Sytaur, the name by which I find that the river was called by English officials as late as 1810. The mistake is only of *t* for *l*. In our times the name is generally written Chittaur, and this stands for Sittār or Chittār, which means the little river. It is evident also that the tributary river could never have been the principal stream, because it drains a much smaller extent of hill country. "Solen" has a meaning in Greek, and may therefore have been intended to be a Greek word. One of its meanings is a shell fish, and for want of a better explanation it may perhaps be held that the river was called by this name by the Greeks on account of the chanks, then as now, found in great numbers near its mouth. The chank is the *Turbinella rapa*. Up to the present time the greater number of the chanks used in commerce are found in the sea adjacent to the mouth of this river, and every field in the neighbouring country bears witness, by the chanks found imbedded in the alluvium, to the fact that they abounded here at that early period also, when the delta was being formed. Chanks seem always to have been used throughout India as instruments of music (or rather as instruments of noise?) and in Northern India they are much used as a material for making ornaments. The Greeks spoke of the Solen as taking its rise on a mountain called Bettigo, and it seems conceivable that by this name they meant to represent "Potigai," the name of the mountain on which we have seen that the Tāmraparṇī rises. This enables us to identify the Bettigo of the Greeks, like the Malaya of the Purānas, the mountain on which the Tāmraparṇī rises, with the Southern Ghauts.

The Chittār.

The chanks near the mouth of the Tāmraparṇī.

The Bettigo of the Greeks.

The Chēras, Chōḷas, and Pāṇḍyas.

Chapter I.

Legendary origin of the three Tamil dynasties.

The Tamil people, or as they are called in Sanskrit, the Draviḍas, were divided in ancient times into three great divisions, the Chēras, Chōḷas, and Pāṇḍyas. The arrangement of the names is climactic, and denotes that the Pāṇḍyas were supposed in those times to have the preeminence, a supposition which appears to be in accordance with the facts of the case. According to Tamil legends Chēran, Chōḷan, and Pāṇḍyan were three brothers who at first lived and ruled in common at Korkai, near the mouth of the Tāmraparṇī. The lands held by all three in common were at Mukkāṇi (the three properties) near Korkai. Eventually a separation took place. Pāṇḍiyan remained at home. Chēran and Chōḷan went forth to seek their fortunes and founded kingdoms of their own to the north and west. We have a similar representation, perhaps merely an echo of the Tamil tradition, in the Hari-vamśa and several Purāṇas in which Pāṇḍya, Kēraḷa, Kōla, and Chōḷa are represented as the four sons of Ākrīḍa, or of Dashyanta, the adopted son of Turvāsu, a prince of the Lunar line of Kshatriyas. Who the Kōla referred to here was is not clear. Was he supposed to be the ancestor of the Kōlas or Kōlarians of Central India? This is very improbable. Kōla is said to be identified by the Kerala Mahātmya with Kōlam, or Kōlattunāḍu, North Malabar. This derivation involves difficulties, but it is the only reasonable one I have met with.

The Pāṇḍyas.

Derivation of 'Pāṇḍya.'

The Sanskrit name Pāṇḍya is written in Tamil Pāṇḍiya, but the more completely Tamilised form Pāṇḍi is still more commonly used all over Southern India. I derive Pāṇḍya, not from the Tamil and Malayâlam Pāṇḍu, ancient, though that is a very tempting derivation, but from the Sanskrit Pāṇḍu, the name of the father of the five Pāṇḍava brothers. This very form Pāṇḍya, in the sense of a descendant of Pāṇḍu, is mentioned, as I am informed by Professor Max Müller, by Kātyāyana, the immediate successor of Pāṇini. It is evident that the kings of this race by their adoption of this name meant to claim kindred with the celebrated Pāṇḍava brothers, and the marriage of Arjuna with the daughter of the Pāṇḍya king seems to have been recorded, or invented, as an evidence of this relationship. The earliest indubitable reference to the Pāṇḍya kingdom in the records of Northern India is in one of Aśoka's inscriptions about B.C. 250.

Arjuna's intermarriage with the Pāṇḍyas.

Visit of Arjuna to Madura.

This marriage is supposed to be referred to in the Ādi-parva of the Mahā-bhārata. In the Sanskrit original, however, the king is not called a Pāṇḍya, but is merely mentioned by his name as Chitravāhana, and his city is called, not Madura, but Maṇipūra. This city is placed in Monier Williams' Sanskrit Dictionary in the Kalinga country, not in or near the country of the Pāṇḍyas. The king's daughter's name is Chitrāngadā. Arjuna marries the damsel and remains in Maṇipūra, according to his pledge, till a son is born, who is called Babhruvāhana. The Tamil prose translation of the Mahābhārata boldly identifies Maṇipūra with Madura, calls Chitravāhana a Pāṇḍya king, and also identifies him with Malayadhvaja, the second king in the Madura lists of Pāṇḍyas. This identification might be concluded to be a wholly unwarranted invention of the Tamil translator were it not for an incident related in the South Indian edition of the Sanskrit text of the Mahā-bhārata. It is therein stated (in the Sabhā-parva) that Sahā-dēva, one of the Pāṇḍava brothers, in the course of his *dig-vijaya* tour, visited Maṇipūra and greeted his sister-in-law Chitrāngadā, Arjuna's wife. In this narrative Maṇipūra is described as the residence of the *Pāṇḍya* king, and Sahā-dēva receives from the Pāṇḍya king himself valuable presents. This statement vindicates the honesty of the Tamil translator, but unfortunately the doubt is only removed a step further back, for Professor Wilson states that this incident is not contained in the northern copies of the Mahā-bhārata. It was not in his own copy, and he had five copies in Benares examined, in none of which was the incident mentioned. This seems fatal to the identification. He mentions also that in the Bhāgavata Purāna Arjuna's bride is represented as the daughter, not of the Pāṇḍya king, but of the serpent king of Maṇipūra.

Oldest Pāṇḍya Titles.

The Māran.

The Pāṇḍya dynasty may have existed before this relationship with the Pāṇḍava brothers was thought of, for Māran, not Pāṇḍiyan, appears to have been the most ancient name of the head of the dynasty. In the titles given to the Pāṇḍya king in old inscriptions I have always found "the Māran" stand at the head of the list, and I found a portion of Korkai itself called, not Pāṇḍya-Mangalam, but Māra-Mangalam, "the good fortune of the Māran." The names seem to have gone in pairs, Māra and Korkai, Pāṇḍya and Madura. Korkai-āḷi, ruler of Korkai, is a title given to Kulasēkhara, the supposed founder of the Pāṇḍya dynasty, by the author of the Vettri-vērkai, himself a Pāṇḍya king.

Intercourse of the Early Singhalese with the Pāṇḍyas.

Korkai, at the mouth of the Tāmraparṇī, must have been the residence of the Pāṇḍyas at that early period, six centuries before

CHAPTER I.

Christ, when the king of Tāmraparṇī (Ceylon) is said to have sent over ambassadors to negotiate an alliance by marriage with the Pāṇḍyas. "The Southern Madhurā" is the place where the Pāṇḍyas are said to have lived and reigned at that time, but this may have been an anachronism, the very existence of Korkai having most probably at the date of the composition of the Mahā-wanso been forgotten. The particular Pāṇḍya king who then reigned is not mentioned, and the name as written in the Pāli of the Mahā-wanso differs slightly from the form current in India. He is called sometimes Pāṇḍawo, which is evidently meant for Pāṇḍava, and Pāṇḍu, which stands either for Pāṇḍu, the father of the Pāṇḍavas, or for Pāṇḍi, the common Tamil form of Pāṇḍya. According to the story Vijaya married first a Yaksha, or demon-princess (a princess of the aboriginal Vēḍas?), but afterwards sent over to the continent for a human bride, in order that he might get himself duly inaugurated as a sovereign. The Pāṇḍya king gave him his daughter, as requested, and she was accompanied to Ceylon by a great retinue of maidens, who were given in marriage to Vijaya's companions. Vijaya, according to the story, had no son of his own, but he appointed a son of his brother to be his successor. This prince is called in Pāli Pāṇḍu-vāsa-dēva, by which we are probably to understand Pāṇḍu-vamśa-dēva, and though he is said to have come from Simhapura, the city in Northern India from which Vijaya himself came, we can scarcely err in concluding that he was really a prince of Pāṇḍya extraction. The fourth prince in the line was called Pāṇḍukābhaya, a name which evidently also betokens some connexion with the Pāṇḍyas. It is worthy of notice that it was by those two princes with Pāṇḍya names (princes from Tinnevelly?) that the three great reservoirs for which Ceylon is famous are said to have been made. May it hence be concluded that the idea of making reservoirs for irrigation was borrowed by the early Singhalese from the people of the Tinnevelly or Madura coast? Vijaya is said to have bestowed on his Pāṇḍya father-in-law annually two lakhs worth of chanks and pearls. Does this mean that at that time Ceylon was tributary to the Pāṇḍyas? This at least seems certain from these statements that it was the belief of the earliest Singhalese that the Pāṇḍya kingdom was in existence before the arrival in Ceylon of Vijaya and his colony of adventurers, that is, before the introduction into Ceylon of Āryan civilisation, which can hardly have been later than 550 B.C. This seems to carry up the era of the first introduction of Aryan civilisation into the Pāṇḍya country, probably at Korkai, to a very early period; shall we say about 700 B.C.? Ceylon was often invaded in early times by Tamilians (Damilos) from the mainland, but the invaders seem generally to have been, not Pāṇḍyas, but Chōḷas.

Vijaya's marriage.

Singhalese princes with Pāṇḍya names.

The great reservoirs of Ceylon.

Date of introduction of Aryan civilisation.

Tinnevelly in the Rāmāyaṇa.

CHAPTER I.

Mahendra.

The only place in Tinnevelly supposed to be mentioned in the Rāmāyaṇa is Mahēndra. This is generally identified by Hindus with Mahēndragiri, the loftiest mountain in the extreme southern portion of the range of ghauts, south of Agastya's hill; but as the legend connected with it represents it as the place from which Hanumān, the monkey-god, jumped over into Ceylon, the attempt to identify it with geographical accuracy with any particular place in our maps is not likely to be successful.

Greek Notices of the Pāṇḍyas.

Information collected by Megasthenes.

Megasthenes, who was sent as an ambassador from Seleucus Nicator, one of Alexander the Great's successors, to the court of Sandracottus (Chandragupta), king of the Prasii (Prāchyas or easterns) at Palibothra (Pāṭaliputra), near the modern Patna, about B.C. 302, speaks of a country in India called Pandaia, after the name of the only daughter of 'the Indian Heracles,' that is, of Krishṇa. I have no doubt that the country his informants meant was that of the Pāṇḍyas. A writer who had heard of the Calingae and Andarae (the Kalingas and Andhras) could not but have heard also of the Pāṇḍyas. He partly, it is true, misapprehended the legends related to him, but he was right in deriving the name of the Pāṇḍya country from that of its rulers and in connecting their name in some fashion, however erroneously, with the cycle of Krishṇa myths. Every thing related respecting the country by Megasthenes, especially the statement that it was there that pearls were procured, serves to identify it with the Pāṇḍya country, and especially with the southern portion of the Pāṇḍya country, Tinnevelly, along the coast of which at that time were the chief stations of the pearl fishery.

It may be interesting to give here in Megasthenes' own words, as quoted by Pliny, the strange mixture of truth and error he accepted and handed down.

The Indian Heracles.

"He" (the Indian Heracles) "had a very numerous progeny of male children born to him in India (for like his Theban namesake he married many wives), but had only one daughter. The name of this child was Pandaia, and the land in which she was born and with the sovereignty of which Heracles intrusted her was called after her name Pandaia, and she received from the hands of her father 500 elephants, a force of cavalry 4,000 strong, and another of infantry consisting of about 130,000 men. Some Indian writers say further of Heracles that when he was going over the world and ridding land and sea of whatever evil monsters infested them, he found in the sea an ornament for women, which even to this day the Indian traders who bring their wares to our

CHAPTER I.

Pearls.

markets eagerly buy up as such and carry away, while it is even more greedily bought up by the wealthy Romans of to-day, as it was wont to be by the wealthy Greeks long ago. This article is the sea pearl, called in the Indian tongue (?) *margarita*. But Heracles, it is said, appreciating its beauty as a wearing ornament, caused it to be brought from all the seas into India that he might adorn with it the person of his daughter."

Translation from Schwanbeck's Megasthenes by J. W. McCrindle, Esq., Indian Antiquary for September 1877.[1]

The exact situation of the country of Pandaia and some particulars in its administration are given in another extract from Megasthenes handed down by another Greek writer: "Heracles begat a daughter in India whom he called Pandaia. To her he assigned that portion of India which lies to the southward and extends to the sea, while he distributed the people subject to her rule into 365 villages, giving orders that one village should each day bring to the treasury the royal tribute, so that the queen might always have the assistance of those men whose turn it was to pay the tribute in coercing those who for the time being were defaulters in their payments."—*Indian Antiquary for December* 1877.

Pliny, following apparently another passage of Megasthenes, in his enumeration of Indian nations, mentions a nation called Pandae. We cannot doubt that the Pāṇḍyas, wherever he may have supposed them to be located, were the people referred to. His statement that the Pandae alone among Indian nations were ruled by women, though not correct, so far as is known, if supposed to relate to the Pāṇḍyas of Madura, may be regarded as sufficiently applicable to the peculiar social usages of the Malabar coast, where almost every inheritance still runs in the female line, and where, in Pliny's own time, at least, if not also in that of Megasthenes, the Pāṇḍyas of Madura had colonies.

Pliny expressly mentions that a portion of the western coast was in his time (A.D. 77) under the rule of king Pandion, "far away from his mediterranean emporium of Modoura;" yet he remarks that this name, with others in the same neighbourhood, was new to him. He evidently had no idea that the people of king Pandion were identical with the Pandae he had already described.

THE PĀṆḌYAS EMBASSY TO AUGUSTUS.

Porus or Pandion?

No information respecting the Pāṇḍya country in general or Tinnevelly in particular is supplied to us by the Greeks between

---

[1] Since then published separately.

CHAPTER I.

the time of the successors of Alexander and the commencement of Greek commercial intercourse with India, in the early years of the Christian era, when we begin to be supplied with information of an interesting nature. I regard it as nearly certain that the Indian king who sent an embassy to the Emperor Augustus, was not Porus, but Pandion, the king of the Pāṇḍyas, called in Tamil "the Pāṇḍiyan." The earliest account of the embassy is given by Strabo (A.D. 20). The statement generally made by the Greek and Roman historians who refer to this embassy is that it was sent by the Indi, without further explanation as to who those Indians were. Strabo says "the embassy was from king Pandion; or according to others" (whose opinion apparently he did not endorse) "from king Porus." One of those "others" was Nicolaus Damascenus, quoted by Strabo, who says he saw the ambassadors himself. The name of Porus had been known in Europe for several centuries, through the historians of Alexander's Indian campaign, and it was natural that Greeks should fall into the mistake of supposing every Indian king a successor of Porus, whereas the name Pandion was one which up to that time had never been known and could not have been invented. This Indian embassy has a place in the Chronicon of Eusebius (320 A.D.), but neither in the ordinary (defective) Greek text of the Chronicon, nor in the Armenian version, is the name of the king from whom it proceeded mentioned. Fortunately, however, the name, as written by Eusebius, appears in the Chronographia of Georgius Syncellus (A.D. 800), whose work has been used to restore or complete the Greek text of the Chronicon, and who says, under the head of the 185th olympiad, "Pandion, king of the Indians, sends an embassy to Augustus, desiring to become his friend and ally." This incident is an interesting proof of the advanced social and political position occupied by the Pāṇḍyas, probably in consequence of the foreign trade they carried on, viz., at Korkai, in connexion with the pearl fishery, and also on the Malabar coast. After the termination of the political relations that subsisted between the successors of Alexander and the princes of Northern India we thus find that the Pāṇḍyas were the only Indian princes who perceived the advantages of a European alliance.

INFORMATION ABOUT KORKAI FURNISHED BY THE GREEKS.

The Kolkhoi of the Greeks.

More is known about Korkai from the Greeks than from Native writings or traditions. It is mentioned by the author of the Periplūs Maris Erythraei, the circumnavigation of the Erythraean or Red Sea (by which we are to understand the whole Arabian Ocean from the mouth of the Red Sea to the Bay of Bengal), an intelligent Greek merchant who visited India probably about

Situation of Kolkhoi.

CHAPTER I. A.D. 80. It is mentioned also by Ptolemy the Geographer A.D. 130. By these it is called "Kolkhoi emporium." It is one of the very few places in India found in the ancient series of maps called from the name of their discoverer the Peutinger Tables. The date of these tables is unknown, but on examining the Asian segments, I came to the conclusion that the author could not have had any acquaintance with Ptolemy, and that therefore probably he lived at an earlier period. Some of the European segments seemed to me to belong to (or to have been brought down to) a later date. Both the author of the Periplus and Ptolemy agree in representing Kolkhoi as the headquarters of the pearl fishery at that time and as included in the dominions of king Pandion. Ptolemy places it immediately to the north of the River Solen. It was the first port visited by the Greeks after rounding Cape Comorin and the first place on the Tinnevelly coast whose name was recorded by them. The Gulf of Manaar was called by them from the name of this place the Colkhic Gulf, from which it may be included that Kolkhoi was considered by them a place of much importance. It is called in the Peutinger Tables Colcis Indorum, the Colcis of the Indians, to distinguish it from the better known Colchis on the Black Sea. The Tamil name of the place is almost identical with the Greek. It is Kolkai, and though this is now euphonically pronounced Korkai, through the necessary change of *l* into *r* before *k*, yet it is still pronounced Kolkai on the western coast, and I have found it written Kolkai in an old Tamil inscription in the temple at Tiruchendūr. This place is now three or four miles inland, but there are abundant traces of its having stood at one time in the sea coast and of having at a previous period been under the sea. I have found the tradition that it was once the centre of the pearl trade and the principal seat of civil government in the south still surviving amongst people in the neighbourhood. Afer the sea had retired from Kolkhoi, in consequence of the gradual elevation of the line of coast, a new emporium arose between it and the sea, which acquired great celebrity during the middle ages. This was Kāyal, a place to which I shall presently refer. This identification of Kolchoi with Kolkai is one of much importance, because, being perfectly certain, it helps forward other identifications. Kol in Tamil means to slay, kai, hand or arm. Kolkai therefore would seem to mean the hand or arm of slaughter, which is said to be an old poetical name for an army, a camp, the first instrument of government in a rude age. Kai is capable also of meaning place, *e.g.*, Poti-kai, place of concealment, the name of the mountain from which the river of Korkai takes its rise. Compare the name Coleroon, properly Kolliḍam, the place of slaughter. It is worthy of notice that in so far as the two

Korkai.

Importance of this identification.

words included in the name of Kolkai are concerned, the Tamil language does not seem to have altered from that day to this. The junction of the words has been euphonised by Sandhi, but the words themselves remain the same.

The line of coast including South Tinnevelly and South Travancore was called Paralia, by the author of the Periplus. It commenced at what they called "the red cliffs" south of Quilon, and included not only Cape Comorin, but also Korkai. Paralia is the Greek word for coast; it does not appear to me to be the Greek mode of writing a native name, for Ptolemy mentions several Paralias. The coast mentioned by this name included Ptolemy's country of the Aii, South Travancore, and that of the Kareï, South Tinnevelly. The Kareï of the one writer inhabited the Paralia of the other. Karai in Tamil means a coast, from the verbal root karai, to be melṭed down, to be washed away, and is obviously identical in meaning with the Greek Paralia. It is worthy of notice that up to the present time several portions of the Tinnevelly coast are called Karaichuttru, the coast circuit, whilst a caste of fishermen farther north are called Karaiyār, coast people. This Tamil word for coast occurs in the names of several places mentioned by Ptolemy, though the places themselves have not been identified, *e.g.*, Peringkarai. If this name had been written Perung instead of Pering, it would have been identical, letter for letter, with the Tamil of the present time. The meaning would have been "great-shore."

CAPE COMORIN AS KNOWN TO THE GREEKS.

Description of Cape Comorin in the Periplūs.

Cape Comorin is not now in Tinnevelly, but in Travancore, but as it originally belonged to Tinnevelly, being the southern extremity of the Pāṇḍya country, and as it is so near the Tinnevelly boundary and is so celebrated a place, it seems desirable that I should mention here what is said about it by the Greeks. It is called Komaria Akron, Cape Komaria, by Ptolemy, and Komarei or simply Komar by the author of the Periplūs. The latter says, "After Bakarē occurs the mountain called Pyrrhos (or the Red) towards the south, near another district of the country called Paralia (where the pearl-fisheries are which belong to king Pandion), and a city of the name of Kolkhoi. In this tract the first place met with is called Balita, which has a good harbour and a village on its shore. Next to this is another place called Komar, where is the cape of the same name and a haven. Those who wish to consecrate the closing part of their lives to religion come hither and bathe and engage themselves to celibacy. This is also done by women; since it is related that the goddess once on a time resided at the place and bathed. From Komarei towards the

CHAPTER I.

south the country extends as far as Kolkhoi, where the fishing for pearls is carried on. Condemned criminals are employed in this service. King Pandion is the owner of the fishery. To Kolkhoi succeeds another coast lying along a gulf having a district in the interior bearing the name of Argalon. In this single place are obtained the pearls collected near the island of Epiodōros."

When the writer says "it is related" that the goddess used to bathe there it seems to be implied that he had heard of the existence of some written statement to this effect. Probably however he only meant that a tradition to that effect was in existence and was believed. This monthly bathing in honour of the goddess Durgā, called also Kumārī, is still continued at Cape Comorin, but is not practised to the same extent as in former times.

Kumārī or Kumari in Indian literature.

The place has derived its name from the Sanskrit *Kumārī*, a virgin, one of the names of the goddess Durgā, the presiding divinity of the place, but the shape which this word has taken is, especially in *Komar*, distinctively Tamilian. In ordinary Tamil *Kumārī* becomes Kumari ; and in the vulgar dialect of the people residing in the neighbourhood of the Cape a virgin is neither Kumārī nor Kumari, but Kumar, pronounced Komar. It is remarkable that this vulgar corruption of the Sanskrit is identical with the name given to the place by the author of the *Periplūs* . . . Through the continued encroachments of the sea, the harbour the Greek mariners found at Cape Comorin has completely disappeared ; but a fresh water well remains in the centre of a rock, a little way out at sea.

Kumari in Tamil, Kumārī in Sanskrit, is regarded by Puranic writers as the name of a river, one of the seven great sacred rivers of India. The southern portion of the peninsula is called by the same name. It is said to be so called after the name of Kumārī, a daughter of Bharata, the first Emperor of India, who was made by her father queen of the south. The Pāṇḍya king is called Kumari(ś)-śērppan, lord of the Kumari shore, because to him the lands lying along the banks of the Kumari belonged. It might be supposed that by the Kumari river the Tāmraparṇī was meant, but this cannot have been the case, for the name Kumari is not ncluded in the classical list of the names of this river. The Native tradition is to the effect that there was originally a river at Cape

Kumari not a river, but a place on the sea coast.

Comorin, a real river—a sacred river where people went to bathe,—but that this river has been swallowed up by the sea. This might perhaps have been believed, had it not been for the explicit statement contained in the Periplus. No Native tradition goes back so far or possesses anything like such weight as this statement of an intelligent Greek. It is evident, therefore, that in ancient times, as now, it was in the sea, not in a river, that people bathed.

Besides this, the title given to the Pāṇḍya king witnesses against this idea, for sērppu denotes a coast of the sea, not the banks of a river. Kumari(ś)-śērppan means therefore lord of the Kumari sea-coast. It is certain also, that the Kumārī in whose honor people bathed at Cape Comorin was not king Bharata's daughter, but the goddess Durgā, also called Kumārī, whose special name at Cape Comorin is Bhagavatī. This little episode about Cape Comorin shows how little reliance is to be placed on Native traditions, when not corroborated by information derived from independent sources.

PAUMBEN AS KNOWN TO THE GREEKS.

Kory identified with Kōṭi.

It may not be out of place that I should mention what the Greeks said of Paumben, the island on which the celebrated temple of Rāmēśvaram stands, though that place like Cape Comorin lies beyond the boundary of Tinnevelly. Cape Comorin is in Travancore ; Paumben in the zemindari of Ramnad and district of Madura. Ptolemy describes a place called Kory as an island in the Argalic Gulf or Palk Strait. Elsewhere he describes it as a cape, and correctly, for it was both, if it is to be identified, as I have no doubt it is, with Paumben, a long narrow island terminating in a long spit of sand. The entire bay between Point Calymere and the island of Paumben is called poetically Rama's bow, and each end is called Dhanush kōṭi, the tip of the bow or simply kōṭi (in Tamil kōḍi) the tip, end, or corner. The most celebrated of these kōṭis was that at Rāmēśvaram, at the extremity of Paumben, and this word kōṭi would naturally take the shape, especially when pronounced by foreigners, of Kori. The ease with which this change might take place is shown by the circumstance that this very word kōṭi, as the name of a high number, is written and pronounced crore. It is remarkable that the Portuguese, without knowing anything of the Kory of the Greeks, called the same spit of land Cape Ramanacoru.

The Paumben channel.

The island of Paumben, "snake-like," takes its name from the channel through the "Adam's Bridge" reef, formerly tortuous, though now straight, by which ships pass from the Gulf of Manaar to Palk Strait or the Bay of Tondi. Rāmēśvaram, the name of the celebrated temple at the eastern extremity of the island, means Rama's Īśvara, Rama's Lord, that is Siva recognised and worshipped by Rama, according to the Saivas, as his lord. Īsvara at the end of a compound generally denotes Siva. A name identical with this in meaning is Rāma-nātha, Rama's Lord, the first part of Rāma-nātha-puram, the name of the capital of the Ramnad (Rāma-nātha) Zemindari, in which the island of Paumben is included. This recognition of Siva by Rama is supposed to have been made on Rama's return from Ceylon.

CHAPTER I.

Identity of Kolis and Kory.

In the various Greek and Roman geographical works prior to the time of Ptolemy, the name Kōlis occupies an important place. In Ptolemy Kolis disappears and Kory, a name previously unknown, comes up instead. I have little doubt that Kolis and Kory were identical, and that the place meant by both was the island cape of Paumben or Rāmēśvaram. This appears from the circumstance that it is stated by Pliny to be the promontory of India which was nearest Ceylon, between which and it there was only a shallow sea. As it was regarded also as the southernmost point of India, it might be supposed that Cape Comorin was meant, but in the times preceding Ptolemy Cape Comorin was not known to be a cape. Pomponious Mela described Kolis as an "angle," a meaning which corresponds to that of koṭi in the Indian languages. He supposed it to be the termination towards the east of the southern coast, which extended according to him thus far nearly due east from the Indus.

"THE PANDION" AND MADURA AS KNOWN TO THE GREEKS.

Various cities called Madura.

I have already mentioned that the Pāṇḍyan king was called Pandion by the Greeks. They called the people also Pandiones. In this they were correct, for the people have always been called by the same name as the prince. He was the Pāṇḍi, and they the Pāṇḍis. Ptolemy's name for Madura is Modoura, described by him as 'Basileion Pandionis,' the royal city of Pandion. Pliny spells the name Modura. The Sanskrit mode of spelling this name is Mathurā. It is called the Southern Mathurā in Sanskrit, to distinguish it from the original Mathurā, Krishna's birth-place in the north-west, called Methora by the earlier Greeks, "the Modoura of the gods" by Ptolemy, and Muttra by the modern English. There is another place, of the same name, Matura in the south of Ceylon, and there is a small island called Madura, in the Eastern Archipelago, which received its name from Brahman immigrants from India.

DATE OF GREEK INTERCOURSE WITH SOUTHERN INDIA.

Greek trade with the Tinnevelly Coast.

The arrival in India of the Greek merchants from whom Ptolemy and others obtained their information appears to have been contemporaneous with the conquest of Egypt by the Romans. The earliest Roman coins found in India are those of the Emperor Augustus. A large number of Roman Imperial *aurei* (gold coins) were found some years ago on the Malabar coast; upwards of thirty types of which, commencing with the earlier coins of Augustus and including some of Nero, were described by me in a paper printed at Trevandrum in 1851 by the Mahārājā of Travancore, to whom the coins belonged. The

Greek word for rice, 'oryza' dates from the time, whenever that was, when rice was first introduced into Europe, and it cannot be doubted that here we have the Tamil word '*arisi*,' rice deprived of the husk, this being the condition in which then, as now, rice was exported. Of all the places frequented by the Greeks the place from which rice was most likely to be exported to Europe was Kolkhoi, at the mouth of the Tāmraparṇī. Prior to the time of the Greeks the trade with India was mainly in the hands of the Phenicians and Persians. The oldest Tamil word found in any written record in the world appears to be the word for peacock in the Hebrew text of the books of Kings and Chronicles, in the list of articles of merchandize brought from Ophir (about 1000 B.C.) in Solomon's ships, which formed a portion of the great mercantile fleet of the Phenicians. The old Tamil *tōkai* becomes in Hebrew *tūki*. The oldest Tamil word in Greek is the name for cinnamon learned by Ctesias (about 400 B.C.) from the Persians. This is karpion, the root portion of which, karpi, is no doubt identical with the Tamil-Malayalam karuppu, kārppu, or karuvā, the common name of cinnamon.

CHAPTER I.

Phenician Trade.

I cannot quit the history of the mercantile intercourse of the Greeks with Southern India without mentioning a story illustrative of their courage and enterprise. From the time of the Phenicians onwards the voyage to Ophir had taken three years, in consequence of the vessels being always obliged in those days, when the mariner's compass was unknown, to hug the coast. The voyage from the mouth of the Red Sea to the western coast of India, though not so long as this, was still very long and tedious. At length a Grecian mariner called Hippalus, noticing how steadily the south-west monsoon blew for many months together in the same direction, committed himself to the wind, with a courage almost equal to that of Columbus, and arrived safely on the western coast, near the place he wished to reach. The rest of the seafaring Greeks gladly followed his example, and in commemoration of his exploit called the south-west monsoon the Hippalus.

Courageous act of a Greek mariner.

The latest Greek who interested himself in Southern India was Cosmas Indicopleustes, who in A.D. 535, in his book entitled Christian Topography, mentions many interesting particulars regarding Ceylon and a few respecting the Malabar coast, or "Male, from which the pepper comes," but unfortunately says nothing respecting Tinnevelly or the eastern coast.

Cosmas Indicopleustes.

CHAPTER II.

FROM THE COMMENCEMENT OF THE RULE OF THE PĀṆḌYAS TO THE PERIOD OF THE SUPREMACY OF THE VIJAYANAGARA KINGS.

Boundaries of the Pāṇḍya Country.

CHAPTER II.

Geographical stanzas.

THERE are certain geographical stanzas current in Tamil which give the boundaries and extent of the three Tamil kingdoms—the Chēra, Chōḷa, and Pāṇḍya. These stanzas are regarded by the Tamil people as classical and authoritative. According to the stanza relating to the Pāṇḍya kingdom its boundaries were the river Veḷḷāru to the north, Kumari (Cape Comorin) to the south, the sea (that is the Gulf of Manaar and Palk Strait or the Bay of Tondi) to the east, and "the great highway" to the west. Of these boundaries the eastern, viz., the sea, calls for no remark. The river Veḷḷāru, which is represented in the Pāṇḍya stanza as the northern boundary of the Pāṇḍya country, is also represented in the Chōḷa stanza as the southern boundary of the Chōḷa country. The boundary line between two such restless, bellicose nations as the Pāṇḍyas and Chōḷas must have been continually shifting. We know indeed that at one time the whole of the Pāṇḍya country was incorporated into the Chōḷa country. On some auspicious occasion, however, when both parties, having become thoroughly exhausted by continuous wars, were perhaps cementing peace by a marriage, their representatives seem to have been able to agree in fixing on the Veḷḷāru as their common boundary, which settlement having been arrived at, the poets of both sides seem to have been commissioned to perpetuate the remembrance of the boundary in verse. The Veḷḷāru, adopted as their common boundary, is not the Veḷḷāru which falls into the sea near Porto Novo, for this would exclude the Chōḷas from Tanjore, the most valuable portion of their dominions. The Veḷḷāru, referred to rises in the hills near Marungāpuri in the Trichinopoly District, takes a south-easterly course through the Native state of Puducotta, and falls into the sea in Palk Strait, south of Point Calymere. This identification of the Veḷḷāru is confirmed by the circumstance that it was an old custom prevalent amongst the Nāṭṭukkōṭṭai Chetties that their women should never be allowed to cross the Veḷḷāru, it being considered an act of bad omen for women to cross boundaries.

The northern boundary of the Pāṇḍya country.

CHAPTER II.

According to this identification, Trichinopoly belonged to the Chōḷas, not to the Pāṇḍyas, which was doubtless the case in early times, Uraiyūr, near Trichinopoly (the Orthoura of Ptolemy), having been the ancient Chōḷa capital. It was during the Nāyaka period that Trichinopoly became a portion of the dominions of the kings of Madura. Trichinopoly, indeed, not Madura, was regarded by the later Nāyaks as their capital. The southern boundary of the Pāṇḍyas was Cape Comorin. The western boundary of the Pāṇḍyas, that is, the most westerly point their dominions reached at the time the stanza was written, is called Peruvaḻi, the great highway. In another stanza the same way is called Vaḻuti-kāl,[1] that is, "the Pāṇḍya king's way." This was the pass leading into Travancore through the hills near Courtallum. The particular pass referred to was the Achchan-kōvil pass. In later times this pass came to be less frequented, and the principal pass through those hills now is that at Āriyankāvu. According to this, the whole of Nānji-nāḍu, the district in South Travancore lying to the north-west of Cape Comorin, would fall within the Pāṇḍya boundary. The entrance to the Achchan-kōvil pass is further to the west even than the town called Travancore, the little town from which the kingdom of Travancore takes its name. The accuracy of this representation is confirmed by all the Nānji-nāḍu inscriptions.

The southern and western boundaries.

The Chōḷas and Pāṇḍyas agreed as we have seen in adopting a common boundary. The Chēras and Pāṇḍyas do not seem to have been equally inclined to agree, for whilst the Pāṇḍyas represented the Achchan-kōvil pass as their western boundary, the Chēra stanza represents the eastern boundary of the Chēras to be, not the Achchan-kōvil pass, but Tenkāsi. This would make over to Travancore a considerable slice of the Tinnevelly Taluk of Tenkāsi, including Courtallum itself. It is quite possible that Tenkāsi may at some time or another have come into the possession of Travancore, but inscriptions prove that in the 15th and 16th centuries at least it belonged to the Pāṇḍyas. The adoption of Tenkāsi, instead of the Achchan-kōvil pass, as the most westerly point of the Pāṇḍya dominions, would save to Travancore the ancestral town of the dynasty, Travancore itself, but Nānji-nāḍu would remain a portion of the Pāṇḍya country as before. Another

Boundary between the Chēras and the Pāṇḍyas.

The Shenkotta boundary.

---

[1] Vaḻuti is a poetical name for the Pāṇḍya king; kāl means a way. Achchan-kōvil is the temple of Achchan, that is, of Appan, father. The father referred to is Siva. It is worthy of notice that the use of Achchan for Appan is given by the classical Tamil grammars as an illustration of the Tamil of the Kuḍa-nāḍu, the western country, that is, Travancore. Āriyan-kāvu means Āryan's guard. Āryan, or Ārya, that is, Hari-hara-putra, the common Tamil equivalent of whose name is Aiyanār, is supposed to be guardian of boundaries. Kāvu is the Malayalam equivalent of the Tamil kāval, guard.

CHAPTER II. Chēra stanza makes Shenkotta the western boundary of the Chēras. This is almost exactly in accordance with the present arrangement. The boundary between Tinnevelly and Travancore passes at present, I believe, through the town of Shenkotta. Formerly it lay a little to the eastward, so that the whole of the town belonged to Travancore. What is called the Taluk of Shenkotta, that is, the district between Shenkotta and the hills, appears to have belonged originally to the Pāṇḍyas, but has been a portion of Travancore for centuries. It was held for some time of the Nawab of Arcot by the Rājā of Travancore (see Appendix), but was finally incorporated with Travancore in 1809. Shenkotta lies about due south of the Achchan-kōvil pass, so that it would be equally suitable to be regarded as the most westerly point of the Pāṇḍya country.

The extent, that is, the area, of each of the three countries is represented in the various stanzas as follows: the Chēra country 800 miles; Chōḷa 240; Pāṇḍya 560.

Pāṇḍya Kings.

Names of the early Pāṇḍya kings unknown.

The existence of a Pāṇḍya kingdom and dynasty can be traced back, as we have seen, several centuries before the Christian era by means of the Asoka inscriptions and the notices contained in the Mahā-wanso, the Mahā-bhārata, and the writings of Megasthenes. The existence of the dynasty, however, is all that can be concluded with certainty from these notices; no name of any king has survived. We learn from the Greek geographers who wrote after the Christian era that the Pāṇḍya dynasty not only survived till their time, but rose to special importance amongst the Indian states, but still no name of any Pāṇḍya king appears. The next authentic reference to the Pāṇḍyas after the visit of the Greeks and before the composition of the Mahā-wanso, is that which is contained in the Brihat-samhitā, one of the astronomical, or rather astrological, works of Varāha-mihira, an Indian astronomer who lived in A.D. 404. (See Dr. Kern's Translation in Journal of Royal Asiatic Society.) He mentions incidentally "the Pāṇḍya king," the river Tāmraparnī, and the chank and pearl fisheries. When the Dravidas are mentioned as distinct from the Chōḷas, as they sometimes are in the Mahā-bhārata and the Purāṇas, the Pāṇḍyas must be meant. I should be delighted to be able to supplement the deficiencies of the Greeks and the early Indian authorities by supplying a list of the Pāṇḍya kings from Pāṇḍyan sources, but I regret to say that I can place no confidence whatever in the lists of Pāṇḍya kings furnished by local poets and panegyrists. I should be happy to avail myself of any information respecting the Pāṇḍyas and their affairs coming from the outside, but I believe

Indian references to the Pāṇḍyas.

Lists of Pāṇḍya kings untrustworthy.

it is the greatest possible error to trust to home-made lists of kings, in the absence of reliable contemporary information from coins and inscriptions. Any person who is curious on the subject may consult Professor Wilson's Historical Sketch of the Kingdom of Pāṇḍya and the Abstract of the Madura Sthala Purāṇa contained in Nelson's Madura Manual (Part II, p. 3), together with its lists of kings from Kulasēkhara, the supposed founder of the dynasty, to the last Pāṇḍya, Kubja or Sundara. A very cursory perusal of that composition will show that its contents are almost entirely mythical. There is a Tamil version of the Madura Purāṇa, called the Tiruviḷaiyāḍal Purāṇa, which is still fuller than the original of incredible marvels. This translation is said to have been made at the request of the poet-king Ati-vīra-rāma Pāṇḍya, and if so, this must have been some time towards the end of the 16th century A.D. I do not mean to assert that the names of all the kings in the Madura lists are to be regarded as purely inventions of later times. I mean only that until they have been verified by inscriptions, which has not yet been the case, they are of no conceivable historical value. For the present they must take rank, I fear, with the long roll of pre-Christian Caledonian kings, whose pictures ornament the walls in Holyrood Palace, Edinburgh. It seems better, therefore, that I should leave those lists for the present unnoticed. One name only in those lists has hitherto, so far as I am aware, been authenticated by a coin; that is Samara Kolāhala (din of war, a title, rather than a name), which I found on a coin belonging to Sir Walter Elliot. The date, however, is unknown; this is a department of research in which very little has yet been done.

Lists of the Madura Purāṇas.

The names of the two last Pāṇḍya kings belonging to the original line of Pāṇḍyas appear in an inscription, as I learn from Dr. Burnell, at Chillambaram (Chidambaram). These are Vikrama Pāṇḍya and his son Vīra Pāṇḍya. This Vīra Pāṇḍya was conquered by Rājēndra Chōḷa (called also Vīra Chōḷa and Kōpparakēsari Varmā). As we know that this event happened in 1064, we now know also that the two reigns of Vikrama Pāṇḍya and Vīra Pāṇḍya preceded that date, and therefore that they preceded the Chōḷa occupation of the Pāṇḍya country. Many Pāṇḍya kings seem to have borne this name of Vīra, but probably one of them was more famed than the rest, for we find the name given to various villages in the records, *e.g.*, Vīra-Pāṇḍya-paṭṭanam and Vīra-Pāṇḍya-puram. It will be seen also that there was a 'measuring rod of Vīra Pāṇḍya' used in subsequent reigns.

Two last names recorded.

THE CHŌḶA OCCUPATION.

The occupation of the entire Pāṇḍya country by the Chōḷas is not even alluded to in the Madura Purāṇa, nor is the name of any

Rājēndra Chōḷa.

CHAPTER II.

of the Chōḷa kings contained in the Madura lists. This could not have been owing to the Purāṇa having been composed and the lists completed before the Chōḷa occupation commenced, for the last king in the lists, Kubja or Sundara, reigned long after, probably 200 years after, the reign of the first Chōḷa who ruled over the Pāṇḍya kingdom, Rājēndra Chōḷa, who commenced to reign in A.D. 1064. It is uncertain whether Rājēndra Chōḷa gained the sovereignty of the Pāṇḍya country by conquest or by voluntary cession, but I think it could not have been by conquest, for in two inscriptions belonging to his reign which I found in an old temple near Cape Comorin, one dated in the fourth year of his reign, and the other in the fifth, a victory said to have been achieved by him over Āhava-Malla (a Jaina king of the Chālukya race) on the banks of the Tunga-bhadra, is recorded. I conclude, therefore, that if he had acquired his sovereignty over the Pāṇḍyas in a similar way by war and conquest, the fact would certainly have been mentioned. If some person living in the Chōḷa country had asserted that Rājēndra Chōḷa had annexed the Pāṇḍya country to his own territories, the assertion would have been of no value, for it is customary for every petty sovereign in India to be represented by his poets and panegyrists as having conquered all his neighbours. The value of the assertion, however, becomes widely different when we find it in inscriptions on temples in the conquered or annexed country itself, recorded by persons who must formerly have been subjects of the old dynasty, but who now set themselves to glorify the new.

Rajēndra Chōḷa's victory over Āhava-Malla.

It is a remarkable circumstance that the remembrance of the Chōḷa occupation of the Pāṇḍya country has entirely disappeared from the minds of the people. I have never yet met with any Native who had even heard of it. Yet it is a fact respecting which there cannot be the smallest shade of doubt. The country is full of inscriptions testifying to it. Rājēndra Chōḷa has also been shown by inscriptions to have reigned over the Kalinga country, or Northern Circars, in succession to the eastern branch of the Chālukyas. I have found inscriptions in Rājēndra's reign in every part of Tinnevelly, and also as far as Kōttār in South Travancore, which was at that time considered a portion of the Pāṇḍya country. Generally he is called simply Rājēndra Chōḷā, but in one inscription the names of both dynasties are combined, in a manner very common in subsequent reigns, viz., Rājēndra Chōḷa-Pāṇḍyan. He is supposed to have reigned 49 years. One of my Tinnevelly inscriptions is in the 30th year of his reign.

Date of the Tamil Rāmāyaṇa.

Some traditions represent Kambar, the Tamil poet, as publishing his celebrated poetical version of the Rāmāyaṇa in this reign, others as publishing it in the reign of Rājēndra's successor

Kulōtunga Chōḷa. Possibly the work may have been commenced in the former reign and finished in the latter. Supposing it were possible to depend with certainty on either of the above-mentioned traditions, it would show that the memorial verse prefixed to Kambar's Rāmāyaṇa, and which represents it as having been published in A.D. 886, could not have been authentic, this date being too early by more than 250 years. Kambar is quoted by the Buddhist Grammarian Buddhamitra, who also appears to have lived in Rājēndra Chōḷa's time—if indeed Vīra Chōḷa, to whom the grammar was dedicated, and Rājēndra Chōḷa were one and the same person, as Dr. Burnell believed. Rājēndra Chōḷa's name is identified with that of Siva in an inscription at Kōttār in South Travancore. The temple is said to have been "erected by Kulōtunga Chōḷa, in Kōttār, the good town of the triple-crowned Chōḷa, to the great divinity Rājēndra Chōḷēśvara," that is, either to Rājēndra Chōḷa considered as identified with Siva, or rather probably to Siva as worshipped by Rājēndra Chōḷa.[1]

Temple to Rājēndra Chōḷa.

I found several records of gifts in this and other temples in the south dedicated to Rājēndra Chōḷa, one of which was by Sundara Pāṇḍya, a clear proof that, Sundara Pāṇḍya lived, not before Rājēndra Chōla, but after, and therefore that as Sundara Pāṇḍya's name is in the Madura list of kings, the names of Rājēndra Chōḷa and his Chōḷa successors ought to have been there also.

Kulōtunga Chōḷa.

Kulōtunga Chōḷa appears from Chālukya inscriptions to have succeeded Rājēndra in A.D. 1112. Dr. Burnell places the commencement of his reign in 1128. He also must have had a long reign, as I have an inscription of his dated in the 44th year of his reign. The Chōḷa or Chōḷa-Pāṇḍya kings that followed appear to have been Karikāla Chōḷa, Vīra Chōḷa, Vikrama Chōḷa. Each of these is in some inscriptions styled Chōḷa-Pāṇḍya. I have found nothing which throws any light on their date, except that they were all posterior to Rājēndra Chōḷa and that they all lived before Sundara Pāṇḍya, the last king of the old Pāṇḍya line.

Karikāla Chōḷa.

Karikāla Chōḷa's name occupies an important place in Chōḷa traditions in connection with the life of Rāmānuja, the great Vaishnava teacher, but it is uncertain whether the Karikāla Chōḷa mentioned in Tinnevelly inscriptions is the same person or another person of the same name. Dr. Burnell places the Karikāla Chōḷa of Tanjore somewhere about 950 A.D. This would be too early for any successor of Kulōtunga Chōḷa, as the Karikāla of Tinnevelly seems to have been. It is also too early for the date of the Kari-

[1] Compare the Roman title, Divus Augustus, that is, Augustus regarded as deified after his death. A parallel case is that of Rāmēśwara or Rāmanātha, Siva as worshipped by Rama. I am acquainted with a temple in which Siva is called Pāṇḍyēśvara, that is, Siva as worshipped by the Pāṇḍyas.

CHAPTER II.

kāla Chōḷa by whom Rāmānuja was persecuted. Rāmānuja is said to have fled from Karikāla's persecutions to the Court of Biṭṭi Deva, the Ballāḷa king of Dwāra-samudra, whom he converted from the Jaina to the Vaishnava faith. The king on his conversion took the new name of Vishnu Varddhana, and this event has always been placed in the beginning of the 12th century. Rice in his Mysore inscriptions places it in A.D. 1117. This is one of the most important eras in South Indian history, as it gives us a date on which we can depend, and from which we can calculate backwards and forwards. For instance, as Kambar, the author of the Tamil poetical version of the Rāmāyana, refers to Rāmānuja by name in his Saḍagōpar Antādi, we learn that Kambar's date must have been subsequent to A.D. 1100, not A.D. 886, as a certain verse prefixed to the Tamil Rāmāyana states. There seems no room for a Karikāla Chōḷa in the Chōḷa country in the beginning of the 12th century. The ground seems preoccupied by Vīra or Rājēndra Chōḷa, Vikrama Chōḷa, and Kulōtunga Chōḷa, but there may have been a local prince of the name, an ardent Saiva, between Rājēndra's death and Kulōtunga's accession. Anyhow it is not a matter of much importance, for it is only tradition which gives the name of Rāmānuja's persecutor as Karikāla Chōḷa, whereas the date of Vishnu Varddhana's conversion rests on the evidence of inscriptions.

Rāmānuja's date.

Vishnu Varddhana's conversion.

Kulasēkhara Dēva.

There seems reason for placing at this period in this list of Chōḷa-Pāṇḍya kings a king called Kulasēkhara Dēva, who may possibly be the Kalēs Dēwar, who, according to the Muhammadan historians, immediately preceded Sundara Pāṇḍya, and was indeed, according to them, his father. I have seen many of Kulasēkhara's inscriptions in Tinnevelly; there is one on the walls of the Tinnevelly Temple. There are also two in Sir Walter Elliot's collection, which were found at Tiruppūvaṇam in the Madura District, but in none is he styled either Chōḷa or Pāṇḍya, but always simply Kulasēkhara Dēva. It is uncertain whether there were two princes of the name or only one. One person of the name is represented by the Singhalese as having been conquered by them about A.D. 1173, another as having conquered them and carried away the sacred tooth-relic about A.D. 1310. The impression however is left on my mind that a confusion of dates has taken place in the Singhalese records, and that there was only one prince of this name, who must have been a great prince ruling over a wide extent of territory, seeing that Sir Walter Elliot found an inscription of his in the Chālukya country. If Kulasēkhara Dēva is to be placed in the list of Chōḷa-Pāṇḍyas, it will be necessary to give a still earlier place to a Vīra Pāṇḍya, one of the many princes who seem to have been called by that name. In an inscription of Kulasēkhara's mention is made of the use in the measurement of land of 'Vīra-Pāṇḍya's measuring rod.' This makes Vīra anterior to Kulasē-

Singhalese accounts.

khara, probably for a generation or two; but whether he was a Chōḷa-Pāṇḍya or the last member of the old line of Pāṇḍyas preceding Rājēndra Chōḷa, is at present uncertain.

The Chōḷa-Pāṇḍyas.

Dr. Burnell's researches.

Dr. Burnell has kindly supplied me with the information he has collected in Tanjore respecting the Chōḷa-Pāṇḍya dynasty. In most particulars it agrees with the information I have derived from Tinnevelly and Madura sources, and the discrepancies that exist may be accounted for by the supposition, which there is every reason for believing to be well founded, that the Pāṇḍyas of the old line, the Chōḷas, and the Chōḷa-Pāṇḍyas were rival dynasties, each of which, as occasion offered, was represented by its adherents to be supreme.

The name of most importance at this period is that of Rājēndra Chōḷa, and I am happy to find that Dr. Burnell's date coincides with mine. The name itself, it is true, appears in various shapes in his inscriptions as Vīra Chōḷa, Kulōtunga Chōḷa (the first), Rāja-rājēndra Chōḷa, Rājarāja Chōḷa, Narēndra Chōḷa, and Rāja-rājanarēndra Chōḷa. He is also said to be called Koppakēsari Varma. [For this read Kō(p)parakēsari Varmā. I regard Parakēsari as a title, 'lion of foreigners,' rather than a name. I find it given to many kings. Kō means king.] Dr. Burnell considers it proved by the inscriptions at Tanjore and at the Varāha Svāmi temple at Seven Pagodas that one person only was meant by all these titles, viz., the Rājēndra Chōḷa of tradition and of the Tinnevelly inscriptions, and that his reign extended, as I have represented it, for 49 years from 1064 to 1113.

He adds the following particulars respecting this prince, Vīra or Rājēndra Chōḷa :—

Vīra Chōḷa.

"His Abhisheka took place in 1079. He must have restored Tanjore, which, according to Al-Bīrūnī, was in ruins at the beginning of the 11th century. This fact confirms the earlier Chālukya boasts of conquest and was certainly owing to them. He seems to have been a great patron of Brahmans and of Saivism, but he must have been liberal to Buddhists, for Buddhamitra, the author of a Tamil Grammar, called his work Vīrachōliyam after him."

Sundara Pāṇḍya-Chōḷa.

The next name in the list is that of Sundara Pāṇḍya-Chōḷa. He is stated to have been Rājēndra Chōḷa's brother, and to have been established by him on the throne of Madura. If so he must have been more properly regent than king. Still, I find an undated inscription in Tinnevelly in the reign of Sundara Pāṇḍya-Chōḷa, who may have been this person, though I rather think he belonged to a later period. This Sundara Pāṇḍya-Chōḷa's real name was Gangaikkoṇḍa Chōḷa or Gangaikkoṇḍān, the latter form of which name survives as the name of a village—a station on the Tinnevelly

CHAPTER II.

line of rail. He took the name of Sundara Pāṇḍya-Chōḷa, according to an inscription in Karuvūr.

Dr. Burnell's succession of Chōḷas.

Dr. Burnell makes Vikrama Chōḷa Rājēndra Chōḷa's successor for fifteen years, and places next to him Kulōtunga Chōḷa II, the Kulōtunga Chōḷa whose name appears so often in Tinnevelly inscriptions. He makes him succeed Vikrama Chōḷa in 1128, which gives an interval of fifteen years between Rājēndra's death and Kulōtunga's succession. According to the Chālukya inscriptions, as we have seen, Rājēndra was immediately succeeded by Kulōtunga.

SUNDARA PĀṆḌYA.

Sources of information about Sundara Pāṇḍya.

We have more information supplied to us respecting Sundara Pāṇḍya Dēva than any other of the sovereigns of Madura. We have not only the legendary accounts contained in two Purāṇas, the Sthala Purāṇa of Madura and the Tiruttoṇḍar Purāṇam (or Purāṇam of Siva's sacred disciples), but also accounts which profess to be historical contained in the Singhalese annals and in the Indian histories of the Muhammadan historians Wassaf, Rashiduddin, and Amir Khusru. We have also notices contained in the memoirs of Marco Polo, the Venetian traveller. Notwithstanding this apparent wealth of information, the accounts we have received are inextricably confused. It might indeed be supposed (as it has been) that there were several Pāṇḍya kings of the name, but this theory does not seem to me to be in accordance with the facts. It seems to me that there could only have been one Sundara Pāṇḍya of sufficient eminence to have the place in history he has received and to be mentioned as a reigning sovereign in so many inscriptions, and that what we have got to do is to endeavour to extract from the various statements we have before us some particulars respecting him which may safely be accepted.

Sundara Pāṇḍya's zeal against the Jainas.

1. It would appear that he was originally a Saiva, that he then became a Jaina, and that he was finally reconverted to Saivism by the miracles performed by Gnāna-sambandha, a great Saiva teacher belonging to the Chōḷa country, who was invited to Madura by Sundara's wife, who was a Chōḷa princess. On this occasion he is said to have impaled eight thousand Jainas. Before his reconversion to Saivism he was said to have been a hunch-back, and hence called Kubja or Kūn, but on his reconversion he was straightened, and hence his name is said to have been changed to Sundara, the beautiful. I find, however, from inscriptions that he was called Sundara from the commencement of his reign. Probably Kubja or Kūn was merely a nick-name.

Sundara Pāṇḍya the last in the list.

2. He seems to have been the last sovereign of the old line of Pāṇḍya or Chōḷa-Pāṇḍya kings. His name stands last in every list; and even if all the other names, or most of them, had been

inventions, it is probable that the last name would be historical. This probability is converted into a certainty by the statements of the Muhammadan historians, who show that on Sundara's death the Madura kingdom fell into the hands of Muhammadans. In this particular all native traditions are in conformity with the Muhammadan statements. Even during Sundara's life it is evident that the Muhammadans had been rising to power. Rashiduddin writes, "Within the last few years (written towards 1300) Sender Bandi was Dewar, who, with his three brothers, obtained power in different directions and Malic-al-Taki-uddin, brother of Shaikh Jumaluddin, was his minister and adviser, to whom he assigned the government of Fatan, Male Fatan, and Kail." Here, it will be seen we have Marco Polo's Sender Bandi Dewar and his brothers. "In the year 692 A.H. (A.D. 1293) the Dewar died and his wealth and possessions fell into the hands of his adversaries and opponents, and Shaikh Jumaluddin, who succeeded him, obtained, it is said, an accession of 700 bullock-loads of jewels," &c. The Persian historian Wassaf gives precisely the same account. There is a difference only as to Sundara's successor. According to Wassaf he was succeeded by his brother. This discrepancy is not serious, for both statements may in a measure be true, and the brother's accession may have been merely nominal, the minister being really ruler as before. We learn from an inscription in Nelson's "Madura Manual" that in A.D. 1573 Vīrappa Nāyaka confirmed a grant originally made by Kūn Pāṇḍi, that is, Sundara Pāṇḍya, to a mosque in Madura, from which it appears that Muhammadan influences must have been at work at Sundara's court. In those days the power of the Muhammadans was extending so rapidly on every hand that where it received an inch it would not be slow in taking an ell.

Muhammadan influences in Sundara's reign.

REASONS FOR SUNDARA PĀṆḌYA'S PATRONAGE OF MUHAMMADANS.

Sundara's war with his brother.

It would be interesting to know, however, what led to Sundara Pāṇḍya's falling so completely into Muhammadan hands that he made over to them the principal places in his kingdom even in his lifetime. A reason is mentioned by Wassaf, which would certainly be an adequate reason, if it could be accepted as historically true. The difficulty in accepting it arises from a discrepancy in point of dates, but this difficulty would be removed if we supposed Wassaf to have misapprehended his dates, whilst he was correct in regard to his main facts. His statements are very circumstantial and have about them an air of truth. According to him Kales Dēwar (probably Kulasēkhara Dēva) had two sons, the elder of whom, Sundar Pāṇḍi, was legitimate, the younger, Vīra Pāṇḍi, was illegitimate. As Vīra Pāṇḍi was remarkable for his

CHAPTER II.

shrewdness and courage his father nominated him as his successor, which so enraged Sundar that he killed his father and placed the crown upon his head. Upon this Vīra collected an army and gave battle to Sundar. At first Vīra was beaten and fell into the hands of the enemy; but at length he received assistance from Perumāḷ, the son of the daughter of Kulasēkhara, whereupon Sundar fled to Delhi, where he placed himself under the protection of Alauddin. Vīra Pāṇḍi thereupon, the historian says, became firmly established in the kingdom. The Singhalese annals give also some account of these affairs, and both accounts agree in leaving Vīra on the throne. Seeing, however, that Sundara Pāndya's name is the last on the list of the genuine Pāṇḍya kings, and that he was immediately succeeded by the Muhammadans, I conclude that Sundara must have returned from Delhi with a force of Muhammadan allies sufficient to re-establish himself on the thronē —and sufficient also to reduce his authority to a mere cipher. It would appear notwithstanding this that Vīra also continued to live and to reign, and even that he outlived Sundara, seeing that it is stated by Wassaf that on Sundara's death immense treasures "fell to the share of the brother who succeeded him," and also that "Malik-i-'azam Taki-uddīn continued prime minister as before, and in fact ruler of that kingdom." He was succeeded in that position by his son Surajuddin and his grandson Nizām-uddin.

Sundara's Muhammadan ministers.

Another Muhammadan account.

According to Amir Khusru, another Muhammadan historian, Vīra Pāṇḍya and Sundara Pāṇḍya were both kings of Ma'bar (the Coromandel Coast) when the invasion by Ala-ud-din's army took place. His account of the invasion is as follows: "Ala-uddin's army under his General Malik Naib or Malik Kafur left Delhi in November 1310, and reduced Dwāra-Samudra, the capital of the Ballāḷa kings. While on his march to Dwārasamudra, it is said that he arrived at a place called Bandrī where he stayed to make inquiries respecting the countries further on. Here he was informed that the two Rais of Ma'bar, the elder named Bīr Pāṇḍya and the younger Sundar Pāṇḍya, who had up to that time continued on friendly terms, had advanced against each other with hostile intentions, and that Bellāl Deo, the Rai of Dwāra-samudra, on hearing of this fact, had marched for the purpose of attacking their two empty cities and plundering the merchants, but that, on hearing of the advance of the Muhammadan army, he had returned to his own country. After the capture of Dwāra-samudra, it is stated that Malik Naib marched to Birdhūl, the capital of the elder of the two Rais—'the yellow-faced Bīr.' He took the city and destroyed all the temples there. From Birdhūl he advanced to Kham, and thence to Mathra (Madura), the dwelling place of the younger brother, Sundar

Malik Kafur's invasion.

Pāṇḍya. He found the city empty, as the Rai had fled with his Ranis, leaving two or three elephants behind him. These were captured and the temple in which they had been left burnt. Immediately after this Malik Kafur returned to Delhi."—Elliot's Muhammadan Historians.

When Malik Kafur's army appeared, the king of Ma'bar, according to Wassaf, hid himself in the jungles. According to Ferishta Malik Kafur conquered the whole country as far as Rāmēśvaram, where he built a mosque. No tradition, however, of his having done so survives amongst the Muhammadans of Rāmēśvaram, or Paumben.

Marco Polo's Sonder Bandi.

According to the Muhammadan historians we appear to have two rulers in Ma'bar within twenty years bearing the name of Sundara Pāṇḍya, and for this reason principally Colonel Yule was unable to accept my identification of the Sonder Bandi of Marco Polo with the Sundara Pāṇḍya of the inscriptions. In the second edition of my Dravidian Grammar I have gone fully into the whole subject again (see Introduction and Appendix), and think I have answered some of the objections that were put forward. It is clear from both the Muhammadan historians that at the close of the 13th century there reigned in Madura a Sundara Pāṇḍya who was Dēwar—that is, as they interpreted the title, lord paramount of Ma'bar, the Pāṇḍya-Chōḷa country. He was, it is true, one of four (or five) brothers who had acquired power in different directions, yet still he alone was called Dēwar, and is said to have been possessed of immense wealth. Marco Polo also, though he speaks of his brothers as "kings," yet speaks of Sonder alone as "a crowned king," and gives him distinctly the title of Bandi; so that it is evident that in some respects he was regarded as supreme. There is no trace in Sundara's inscriptions of his brothers, or of his power being in any degree shared by them, or of the position he and they held being one that they had "acquired," instead of being one that they had inherited; but these are particulars which would not be likely to make their appearance in inscriptions; and there is nothing in the inscriptions or traditions inconsistent with the supposition that he had brothers who had acquired power together with himself. All that is necessary to stipulate in order to bring the accounts into agreement is that in some sense he alone should be Pāṇḍi Dēvar, or lord paramount, so that his name only should appear in the inscriptions, and in this, as it seems to me, no particular difficulty can be involved. I finally arrive at the conclusion that, pending the discovery of a *dated* inscription in which Sundara Pāṇḍya is mentioned, I see no valid reason why we should hesitate to identify the Sundar of the Muhammadan historians both with Marco Polo's Sonder and with the Sundara or Kūn Pāṇḍya

Sundara's brothers.

Sundara's date still a *desideratum*.

CHAPTER II. of the Saiva revival. Mr. Moore gives a summary of this discussion in his Trichinopoly Manual, and adds—

"I have obtained copies of a considerable number of inscriptions in the Trichinopoly District in which Sundara Pāṇḍya is mentioned. They show clearly that he ruled over this part of the country as well as Madura, but they throw no light on the vexed question as to the time at which he lived, as they are not dated."

MA'BAR.

Origin of the term Ma'bar.

Ma'bar means literally the passage. It was the name given by the early Arabian merchants to that portion of the Coromandel Coast which was nearest Ceylon, and from which it was easiest to pass over to the island from the continent. It was afterwards taken to mean the whole coast from Quilon to Nellore, including both the Pāṇḍya and the Chōḷa kingdoms. Ma'bar is mentioned (Maparh) in the Chinese annals as one of the foreign kingdoms which sent tribute to the Emperor Kublai Khan in 1286, and Pauthier has given some very curious and interesting extracts from Chinese sources regarding the diplomatic intercourse with Ma'bar in 1280 and the following years. Among other points these mention the five brothers who were Sultans and an envoy Chamalating (Jumal-ud-din) who had been sent from Ma'bar to the Mongol Court.—Colonel Yule's Marco Polo, II, 273.

Settlement of Muhammadan Arabs on both coasts.

Muhammadan Arabs seem to have settled first on the Malabar Coast in the 9th century, and thence to have spread to the eastern coast and Ceylon. Their principal settlement on the eastern coast is Kāyalpaṭṭaṇam in Tinnevelly. Heathen Arabs, that is, the Sabæans of Southern Arabia, frequented the coasts of India long before, following the lead of the Greeks. The mixed race consisting of the descendants of those Arab merchants are called Mapillas on the western coast, Lebbies on the eastern. By the Tamil people they are generally styled Tulukkar (Turks) or Jonagar (Yavanas!). Their ordinary title is Maraikān or Marakān, a word which means steersman, implying that they were first known as sailors, which doubtless is correct. They have no acquaintance with Hindustani, but speak Tamil or Malayalam, the vernacular of the country in which they live. The Hindustani-speaking Muhammadans—Patans and others—came from Northern India and form a totally different class.

KĀYAL.

One of the most interesting events in the history of Tinnevelly during the middle ages was Marco Polo's visit to Kāyal, which took place in A.D. 1292. What and where was Kāyal?

I quote Colonel Yule's Marco Polo, Vol. II, 307 :—

CHAPTER II.

'Kail, now forgotten, was long a famous port on the coast of what is now the Tinnevelly District of the Madras Presidency. It is mentioned as a port of Ma'bar by our author's contemporary Rashid-ud-din, though the name has been perverted by careless transcription into *B'awal* and Kābal (see Elliot, I, pp. 69–72). It is also mistranscribed as Kābil in Quatremēre's publication of Abdurrazzāk, who mentions it as 'a place situated opposite the island of Serendib, otherwise called Ceylon,' and as being the extremity of what he was led to regard as Malabar (p. 19). It is mentioned as Cahila, the site of the pearl-fishery, by Nicolo Conti (p. 7). The *Roteiro* of Vasco da Gama, in the report of what was learned on his first voyage, notes it as Caell, a state having a Mussulman king and a Christian (for which read Kafir) people. Here were many pearls. Giovannī Empoli notices it (Gael) also for the pearl-fishery, as do Varthema and Barbosa. From the latter we learn that it was still a considerable sea port, having rich Muhammadan merchants, and was visited by many ships from Malabar, Coromandel, and Bengal. In the time of the last writers it belonged to the king of Kaulam (Quilon) who generally resided at Kail.

Kāyal visited by Marco Polo.

Portuguese notice of Kāyal.

'The real site of this once celebrated port has, I believe, till now never been identified in any published work. I had, like others before me, supposed the still existing Kāyal-paṭṭaṇam to have been in all probability the place, and I am again indebted to the kindness of the Rev. Dr. Caldwell for conclusive and most interesting information on this subject. He writes :—

'"The Cail of Marco Polo, commonly called in the neighbourhood old Kāyal, and erroneously named Koil in the Ordnance Map of India, is situated near the Tāmraparnī river, about a mile and a half from its mouth. The Tamil word kāyal means 'a backwater, a lagoon opening into the sea,' and the map shows the existence of a large number of these kāyals or backwaters near the mouth of the river. Many of these kāyals have now dried up more or less completely, and in several of them salt pans have been established. The name of Kāyal was naturally given to a town erected on the margin of a kāyal; and this circumstance occasioned also the adoption of the name of Punnaikkāyal, as the name of a neighbouring place, and served to give currency to the name of Kāyal-paṭṭaṇam, assumed by Sōnagar-paṭṭaṇam, both those places being in the vicinity of kāyals."'

Meaning of Kāyal.

It was during a visit I paid to Korkai in 1861 that I identified it with the Kolkhoi of the Greeks, and the interest of this identification was heightened by the conclusion at which I arrived at the same time that an insignificant place called Old Kāyal, about half way between Korkai and the sea, was to be identified with the Cael of Marco Polo, the most important city and sea port on the eastern coast of India during the middle ages. It was not however till nearly ten years afterwards, when Colonel Yule was preparing his edition of Marco Polo, that these identifications were made known to him and through him were made public.

Korkai and Kāyal.

CHAPTER II.

Both places are situated on the delta of the Tāmraparṇī, Korkai within five, Kāyal within two, miles of the sea; but each was originally on the sea coast. It seemed remarkable that the sites of two such famous places should thus have been discovered in the same neighbourhood, but a glance at the geology of the neighbourhood disclosed the reason why each had been abandoned in turn. As the silt accumulated in the sea near the mouth of the river, or as the line of coast rose, or from both causes, Korkai was found at length to be too far inland for the convenience of a sea-borne trade, and Kāyal, meaning "a lagoon" rose in its stead on the sea shore and attained probably to still greater dimensions. Kāyal has now shrunk into a petty village, inhabited partly by Muhammadans, partly by Roman Catholic fishermen, with a still smaller hamlet adjoining inhabited by Brahmans and Veḷḷāḷas.

The following is Marco Polo's notice of Kāyal—Colonel Yule II, 305, "Concerning the City of Cail:"—

Marco Polo's notice of Kāyal.

'Cail is a great and noble city, and belongs to Ashar (Īshwara ?), the eldest of the five brother-kings. It is at this city that all the ships touch that come from the west, as from Hormus (Hormuz), and from Kis (an island in the Persian Gulf), and from Aden, and all Arabia, laden with horses and with other things for sale. And this brings a great concourse of people from the country round about, and so there is great business done in this city of Cail. The king possesses vast treasures, and wears upon his person great store of rich jewels. He maintains great state and administers his kingdom with great equity, and extends great favor to merchants and foreigners, so that they are very glad to visit his city. The king has some 300 wives, for in those parts the man who has most wives is most thought of.' * * *

Trade of Kāyal.

Kāyal having been the principal port in Ma'bar, much of what Marco Polo says about Ma'bar, its trade, &c., really applies to Kāyal. The king of Kāyal was not an independent prince, but the deputy (and brother) of the real king of the whole of Ma'bar at that time, Sundara Pāṇḍya Deva, who is called by Marco Polo 'Sonder Bandi Davar,' and who ruled over both the Pāṇḍya and the Chōḷa countries. I have found inscriptions of Sundara Pāṇḍya at a place called Māra-Mangalam, just outside Kāyal. Polo continues:—

Horse trade at Kāyal.

'Here are no horses bred; and thus a great part of the wealth of the country is wasted in purchasing horses. You must know that the merchants of Kis and Hormes, Dofar (Dhafār on the Yemen Coast), and Soer (Suhār in Oman) and Aden collect a great number of horses, and these they bring to the territories of this king and of his four brothers. For a horse will fetch among them 500 saggi of gold, worth more than 100 marks of silver (that is about 2,200 rupees!), and vast numbers are sold there every year. Indeed this king wants to buy more than 2,000 horses every year, and so do his four brothers who are kings likewise. The reason why they want so many horses every year is that by the end of the year there shall not be one hundred of them remaining, for they all die off. And this arises from mismanagement, for those people do not know in the least how to treat a horse; and besides they have no farriers. The horse-merchants not only never bring any farriers with them, but also prevent any farrier from going thither, lest that should in any degree baulk the sale of horses, which brings them in every year such vast gains. They bring these horses by sea aboard ship.'—Colonel Yule's Marco Polo, Vol. II, 285.

Use of the horse by Indian soldiers.

'Rashiduddin and Wassaf have identical statements about the horse-trade, and so similar to Polo's in this chapter that one almost suspects that he must have been their authority. Wassaf says: 'it was a matter of agreement that Malik-ul-Islām Jamāluddin and the merchants should embark every year from the island of Kais and land at Ma'bar 1,400 horses of his own breed' . . . . It was also agreed that he should embark as many as he could procure from all the isles of Persia, such as Kātif, Lahsā, Bahrein, Hurmuz, and Kalhātū. The price of each horse was fixed from of old at 220 dinars of red gold, on this condition, that if any horses should happen to die, the value of them should be paid from the royal treasury. It is related by authentic writers that in the reign of Atābek Abu Bakr (of Fars) 10,000 horses were annually exported from these places to Ma'bar, Kambāyat, and other ports in their neighbourhood, and the sum total of their value amounted to 2,200,000 dinars . . . . They bind them for 40 days in a stable with ropes and pegs, in order that they may get fat; and afterwards without taking measures for training, and without stirrups and other appurtenances of riding, the Indian soldiers ride upon them like demons . . . . In a short time the most strong, swift, fresh, and active horses become weak, slow, useless, and stupid. In short, they all become wretched and good for nothing . . . . There is, therefore, a constant necessity of getting new horses annually.'—(Elliot, III, 34).

'The price mentioned by Polo appears to be intended for 500 dinars, which in the then existing relations of the precious metals in Asia would be worth just about 100 marks of silver. Wassaf's price, 220 dinars of red gold, seems very inconsistent with this, but is not so materially, for it would appear that the *dinar of red gold* (so called) was worth *two dinars*.'

Wassaf's account.

Wassaf, the Persian historian, a contemporary of Marco Polo, thus describes Ma'bar, that is, as I believe, Kāyal, the port of Ma'bar:—

'The curiosities of Chīn and Māchīn (*i.e.*, Northern and Southern China), and the beautiful products of Hind and Sind, laden on large ships which they call *junks*, sailing like mountains with the wings of the wind on the surface of the water, are always arriving there. The wealth of the isles of the Persian Gulf in particular, and in part the beauty and adornment of other countries, from Irak and Khurāsān as far as Rūm and Europe, are derived from Ma'bar, which is so situated as to be the key of Hind.'—Marco Polo, II, 269.

CHAPTER II.

Marco Polo's arrival in India.

The following is Marco Polo's description of the pearl fishery. The term Ma'bar, as used at that time both by Polo and by the Arabs, included, as we have seen, the greater part of the Coromandel Coast; but when the pearl fishery of Ma'bar is referred to we are to understand, I think, mainly the southern portion of Ma'bar, from Rāmēsvaram to Cape Comorin, constituting the eastern coast of the Gulf of Manaar, the fishery carried on on the Ramnad coast being of less importance. The port mentioned, but not named, by Polo must have been near, if not identical with, Kīḷakarai; or it may have been a place called Periya Paṭṭaṇam, the great city, a place now some miles inland, the greatness of which has entirely passed away. [Was this the place which Ibn Batuta called Fattan, that is, *the* Paṭṭaṇam?]. Marco writes :—

Pearl fishery described.

'When you leave the island of Seilan and sail westward about 60 miles, you come to the great province of Maabar which is styled India the Greater; it is the best of all the Indies and is on the mainland. You must know that in this province there are five kings, who are own brothers. I will tell you about each in turn. The province is the finest and noblest in the world. At this end of the province reigns one of those five royal brothers, who is a crowned king, and his name is Sonder Bandi Davar. In his kingdom they find very fine and great pearls; and I will tell you how they are got. You must know that the sea here forms a gulf between the island of Seilan and the mainland. And all round this gulf the water has a depth of no more than 10 or 12 fathoms, and in some places no more than two fathoms. The pearl-fishers take their vessels, great and small, and proceed into this gulf where they stop from the beginning of April till the middle of May. They go first to a place called Bettelar, and (then) go 60 miles into the gulf. Here they cast anchor and shift from their large vessels into small boats. You must know that the many merchants who go divide into various companies, and each of these must engage a number of men on wages, hiring them for April and half of May. Of all the produce they have first to pay the king, as his royalty, the tenth part. And they must also pay those men who charm the great fishes to prevent them from injuring the divers whilst engaged in seeking pearls under water, one-twentieth part of all that they take. These fish-charmers are termed ***Abraiaman*** (Brahmans?); and their charm holds good for that day only, for at night they dissolve the charm so that the fishes can work mischief at their will. These Abraiamans know also how to charm beasts and birds and every living thing. When the men have got into the small boats they jump into the water and dive to the bottom, which may be at a depth of from 4 to 12 fathoms, and there they remain as long as they are able. And there they find the shells that contain the pearls

Divers.

and these they put into a net bag tied round the waist, and mount up to the surface with them, and then dive anew. When they can't hold their breath any longer they come up again, and after a little down they go once more, and so they go on all day. The shells are

Chapter II.

in fashion like oysters or sea-hoods. And in these shells are found pearls, great and small, of every kind, sticking in the flesh of the shell-fish. In this manner pearls are fished in great quantities, for thence in fact come the pearls which are spread all over the world. And I can tell you the king of that state hath a very great receipt and treasure from his dues upon those pearls. As soon as the middle of May is past no more of those pearl-shells are found there. It is true, however, that a long way from that spot, some 300 miles distant, they are also found; but that is in September and the first half of October.'

Profits to the king.

Relics of Kāyal.

We must now return to Marco Polo's Kāyal. Unlikely as the place may now seem to be identical with the "great and noble city" described by Polo, its identity is established by the relics of its ancient greatness which are still discoverable. For two or three miles north of the present village of Kāyal and a mile and a half inland, as far indeed as Māra-mangalam, the whole plain is covered with broken tiles and remnants of pottery—evidences of the perfect truth of Marco Polo's statement regarding Kāyal and its trade and of the identity of Kāyal with the sea port of Ma'bar mentioned by the Muhammadan historians. According to those statements Kāyal was frequented by multitudes of vessels from the Arabian Coast and the Persian Gulf, and also by vessels from China—junks—in one of which Marco Polo himself arrived; and accordingly I picked up everywhere on the open plain broken pieces of Arabian pottery and of China porcelain of all shapes, colours, and qualities. I could easily, if I had chosen, have collected a cart load in a single day; but the pieces into which they had been broken by the plough and the feet of bullocks were so small that they could not be put together so as to assume the shape of a vessel. I set a band of excavators at work one day in digging up a portion of the plain at hazard. At a depth of three feet beneath the present surface they came on the chunamed floor of a house, but found nothing of importance. The extent of the site of Kāyal was so great that it would take a month, instead of a single day merely, to explore it properly. The people of Kāyal, Korkai, and the neighbourhood have forgotten the existence of any trade between Kāyal and China, though the broken pieces of China pottery which lie all about might have helped them to keep the fact in their remembrance. I found, however, that they retained a distinct tradition of the trade of Kāyal with Arabia and the Persian Gulf, probably because that trade survived to comparatively recent times. They had also a tradition of European merchants, doubtless Portuguese, having lived in the place before its final abandonment as a sea port. I have already mentioned that care must be taken not to identify Marco Polo's Kāyal with Kāyalpaṭṭaṇam, another town on the coast, a modern place, but now very large, containing about 7,000

Remains of Chinese and Arabian earthenware.

Kāyal-paṭṭaṇam a different place.

CHAPTER II. Muhammadans. There is another small port in the same neighbourhood a little to the north of Kāyalpaṭṭaṇam called "Pinnacael" in the maps, properly Punnai-k-kāyal, but this also is a place of comparatively recent origin, and many of the inhabitants, as of Kāyalpaṭṭaṇam, state that their ancestors came originally from Kāyal, subsequently to the arrival of the Portuguese.

THE MUHAMMADAN INTERREGNUM.

The Muhammadans gain the upper hand for a time.

Ibn Batuta, a Muhammadan servant of the Emperors of Delhi, visited Ma'bar in 1348-49 on his way to Quilon for the purpose of embarking there, on his master's business, in one of the Chinese junks which then visited that port annually. He found the whole of Ma'bar, including both the Pāṇḍya and the Chōḷa countries, under the government of Muhammadan kings. This subjection of the country to the Muhammadans had lasted since Kafur's invasion in 1311. The country had been governed for the Emperors of Delhi by governors deputed by them for twenty or thirty years. At length one of those governors, Jelal-ud-dīn Hasan, a Sherif or Seiad, revolted against Muhammad Toghlak and made himself independent. This circumstance is mentioned by Ferishta. The power of the Muhammadans, however, does not seem to have been very firmly established, for Ibn Batuta found that there had already been several internal revolts, and on landing in Ma'bar he found the reigning sultan at war with "the heathen," that is probably with some surviving representatives of, or sympathisers with, the expelled Pāṇḍya princes. Possibly, however, the sultan's foes may have been the Maravas of Ramnad, for as Ibn Batuta was wrecked, on his voyage across the Gulf of Manaar from Ceylon, in the shallow part of the sea, the place where he landed and near which he found the sultan must have been in the Ramnad country, the country of the Maravas, a warlike race not likely to remain long in quiet subjection to petty Muhammadan princes. This Muhammadan interregnum is mentioned in Taylor's Historical Manuscripts. It is therein said to have lasted from 1323 to 1370, viz., for 47 years. Probably this was meant to represent the period of the independent Muhammadan government. It is also said therein that the name of the Pāṇḍya king conquered and sent to Delhi by the Muhammadans was Parākrama Pāṇḍya. Ibn Batuta says that the sultan of Ma'bar reigned at Maturah (Madura). The king's palace was there. He says it was a large city and not unlike Delhi.

Ibn Batuta.

THE KINGDOMS OF DWĀRA-SAMUDRA AND VIJAYA-NAGARA.

Paramount powers.

From the commencement of the decay of the power of the Pāṇḍyas and Chōḷas in the 12th century, the kingdoms of Dwāra-samudra and Vijaya-nagara occupied the position of paramount powers in Southern India. It seems desirable, therefore, that I should mention such particulars respecting those kingdoms as seem necessary for a right apprehension of the mediæval history of Madura and Tinnevelly.

DWĀRA-SAMUDRA.

I have not met with the name of Dwāra-samudra in any Tamil inscription or composition, but it is well known that the strong Telugu dynasty of Vijaya-nagara was preceded by a strong Canarese dynasty. This is sometimes popularly called a Mysore dynasty, but the name of Mysore belongs to a much later period. It is properly, and still more commonly, called a Kannaḍa, that is, a Canarese dynasty, the English word "Canarese" being intended to represent that which pertains to Kannaḍa or Canara, an abbreviation of Karnāṭa or Karnāṭaka.[1] The later name is identical with our term Carnatic, but it denoted originally, not the country below the ghauts, as it does now, but the great tableland above the ghauts, including Mysore. The capital of this Canarese dynasty was Dwāra-samudra, a place about the centre of the Mysore country, and about 105 miles north-west of Seringapatam. Dvāra-samudra is written in all the inscriptions of the Mysore country Dora-samudra. Dora for dvāra, however, is merely a local dialectic change. The modern name of the place is Haḷebīḍu, or Haḷeyabīḍu, the old abode.[2] The kings of the Dvāra-samudra dynasty were called the Hoysalas, or more commonly the Ballāḷas, from bala, prowess, and are known to have exercised for a time some sort of paramount power over the Pāṇḍya, Choḷa, and other ancient kingdoms of the south.

Kings of Dvāra-samudra.

The first king of this dynasty who acquired sovereignty over an extensive range of districts was Biṭṭi Dēva, converted by Rāmānujāchārya from Jainism to the Vaishnava faith, and known after his conversion as Vishnu Varddhana. His conversion dated probably from 1117. Rāmānuja had fled from the persecution of Karikāla Chola, an ardent Saiva. Vishnu Varddhana became ere long the most powerful monarch of his time in Southern India, and he is expressly stated to have subdued the Chōḷas, Pāṇḍyas, and Kēralas. This statement would not perhaps go for much were it not for the traces of the supremacy of this Kannaḍa power which made themselves manifest from about this time in the south,

Ramānuja's flight to Dvāra-samudra.

[1] Karnātaka probably meant originally the black country, that is, the black cotton-soil country.

[2] The sculpture of the old temple at Haḷēbīḍu receives from Ferguson the highest praise.

CHAPTER II. as is evident especially from the statements of the Muhammadan historians.

Defeat of the Ballāḷa king.

The Muhammadans appeared in the Dekhan in 1295, when Ala-ud-din took Devagiri. The Ballāḷa dominions were invaded by a Muhammadan army under Hazardinari, commonly called Malik Kafur, the general of Ala-ud-din, the second king of the house of Khilji or second Pathan dynasty. A great battle was fought in 1311 in which the Ballāḷa king was defeated and taken prisoner. Dvāra-samudra was sacked and the enemy returned to Delhi literally laden with gold. Kafur was sent to conquer the whole of the south of India, and the capture of Dvāra-samudra, at that time considered the capital of the south, was the principal object of his ambition. After the taking of Dvāra-samudra Kafur descended upon Ma'bar, which he regarded, and which was regarded by Ferishta, the Muhammadan historian, as a feudatory dependency of the Dvāra-samudra kingdom. General Wilks could not make out what place was meant by Ma'bar, but it is now well known to have meant the Chōḷa and Pāṇḍya kingdoms, or, speaking generally, the Coromandel Coast. Another expedition sent by Muhammad III of the house of Toghlak in 1326 completely demolished the city of Dvāra-samudra. The Ballāḷa kings, however, were not totally annihilated. They removed their seat of government to a place called Tonnur, about nine miles north of Seringapatam. Even after the rise of the Vijayanagara dynasty (in 1336), the Ballāḷas were permitted to exercise some sort of authority up to the year 1387.

End of the Ballāḷa dynasty.

Thus ended the rule of this powerful line, consisting of nine chief princes, and thence called the Nava Ballāḷa; which from a very small beginning had, by the valour of its several members, subdued the whole of Karnāṭaka up to the Krishṇa, with Tuluva on the west, Drāviḍa (the Tamil country, including especially the Chōḷas and Pāṇḍyas) on the east, and part of Telingana on the north-east.—Rice's Mysore Inscriptions.

Canarese traces in Tinnevelly.

Wherever we find in Tinnevelly traces of any important position having been occupied, or any important work having been done, by a Kannaḍi or Canarese man,—instances of which we have in the "Canaḍian anicut," that is the Kannaḍa man's anicut, and the person called Pālaiyan, a Canarese man, who is said to have built the oldest portion of the fort at Palamcottah—we have reason to conclude that they belonged to the period before the commencement of the rule of the Nāyakas in Madura, when paramount authority over the south was claimed by the Kannaḍa kings of Dvāra-samudra.

The following is a list of these kings, given in Rice's Mysore Inscriptions :—

CHAPTER II.

List of Dvara-samudra Kings.

Inscriptions.	—	Channa Basavana Kālajnāna.	Kongu Desa Rājakal.
	Sala, Hoysala	984–1043	..
1039–1047	Vinayādita	1043–1073	–1068
1065	Yereyanga, Pereyanga, Vīra Ganga ..	1073–1114	..
1117–1138	Biṭṭi Deva, Vishnu Varddhana, Tribhuvana Malla	1114–1145	1099–1147
1142–1191	Vijaya Narasimha, Vīra Narasimha ..	1145–1188	1147–1174
1191–1207	Vīra Ballāḷa	1188–1233	1174
1223	Vīra Narasimha	1233–1249	–1237
1252	Soma, Vīra Someśvara	1249–1268	1237–1283
1262–1287	Vīra Narasimha	1268–1308	1283–1313
1310	Ballāḷa Deva	..	..

VIJAYA-NAGARA.

Origin of Vijaya-nagara.

Vijaya-nagara arose when Dvāra-samudra fell. This city and state, the most famous and powerful of the states of Southern India, was founded in 1336 by two refugees from Warangal (Orukallu, a single stone), a place included in the Nizam's country, after its capture by the Muhammadans in 1323. Their names were said to have been Hakka, who assumed the name of Harihara, and Bukka, and they are said to have received valuable assistance from the sage Mādhava.[1] The capital was called both Vidyā-nagara and Vijaya-nagara. Rice considers Vidyā-nagara, the city of learning, the original form, and supposes this name to have been given to it in compliment to the sage Vidyāraṇya, who was chiefly instrumental in its foundation. By a natural transition Vidyā-nagara passed into Vijaya-nagara, the city of victory, the Bijanagar of the Muhammadan historians and the Bisnagar of the early Europeans. It is also commonly known as Ānegunḍi, a Canarese name—elephant pit—which is properly a village on the other side of the river. Vijaya-nagara was erected on the banks of the Pampa or Tunga-bhadra, in what is now the district of Bellary. The beauty of the ruins of this city, near Hampi, show what the grandeur of the capital of the Rāyas must have been in the days of its prosperity.

Names of Vijaya-nagara.

The succession and dates of the Vijaya-nagara kings as traditionally handed down are much confused. The following list, Mr. Rice says, is approximately correct, based on many inscriptions he has examined :—

[1] Mādhava is generally said to have been a brother of the still more celebrated Sāyana, and is sometimes regarded as one of the authors of the great commentary on the Vēdas. By others he is identified with Sāyana and as such is said to have been surnamed Vidyāraṇya, the forest of learning.

CHAPTER II.

List of Vijaya-nagara kings.

	A.D.
Harihara, Hakka, Hariyappa	1336–1350
Bukka, Vīra Bukkanna	1350–1379
Harihara	1379–1401
Deva Rāya, Vijaya Rāya, Vijaya Bukka.	1401–1451
Mallikārjuna, Vīra Mallanna, Prauḍha Deva.	1451–1465
Virupāksha	1465–1479
Narasa, Narasimha	1479–1487
Vīra Narasimha, Immaḍi Narasinga ..	1487–1508
Krishna Rāya	1508–1530
Achyuta Rāya	1530–1542
Sadasīva Rāya (Rāma Rāja, regent, usurps the throne till 1565)	1542–1573
Srī Ranga Rāya (Tirumala Rāja, brother of Rāma Rāja, 1566)	1574–1587
Vīra Venkatapati, &c.	1587

The following is Dr. Burnell's list of the kings of the Vijaya-nagara dynasty. *See* Dravidian Palæography, p. 55.

Dr. Burnell's list of Vijaya-nagara kings.

"iv. The Rāyas of Vijayanagara; from about 1320 to 1565.

"The following is the list as I have been able to correct it from several sources (see my 'Vamcabrāhmaṇa,' p. xvi); the dates, however, are only approximate.

Sangama of the Yādava family and Lunar race ! !

Hariyappa (1336-1350).

Bukka I (1350–1379) m. Gaurambikā.

Harihara (1379–1401).

Bukka II (1401–1418) m. Tippāmba.

Devarāja, Vīradeva or Vīrabhūpati (1418–1434) Kṛishṇarāja
married Padamāmba *and* Mallāmba
Vijaya (? 1434–1454) and others ?
Prauḍha Deva (? 1456–1477)
Mallikārjuna (1481–1487)
Rāmacandra (1487)
Virūpāxa (1488–1490) Narasimha (1490–1508)

Vīranarasimha (Kṛishṇarāja (1508–1530.)
Acyuta (1534–42.)

"(Sadāçiva) made an alliance with Viceroy J. de Castro in 1546).

"(This Sadāçiva succeeded as a child: thirty years was this kingdom governed by three brethren which were tyrants, the which keeping the rightfull king in prison, it was their use every yeere once to show him to the people, and they at their pleasures ruled as they listed. These brethren were three captaines belonging to the father of the king they kept in prison, which when he died, left his sonne very young, and then they tooke the government to themselves." (C. Frederick in : "Purchas His Pilgrimes," ii., p. 1704. *cfr.* canto, Dec. vii. 5, 5 ; f. 936).

Vīrappa Nāyak.

- Rāmarāja (killed in 1565.)
- Timma (Tirumala Bōmma). (Transferred the seat of government to Pennakoṇḍa in 1567. Purchas, ii., p. 1705.)
    - Rangarāja (? 1572–1585.)
    - Venkatapati (? 1585–1614) at Chandragiri (Purchas, ii., 1746).
- Bengatre (*Sic* in Purchas). He was killed in 1565. According to Conto, Decada vii., 2, 8, his name was Venkaṭarāya.

" Vīrarāma (?). This name occurs in inscriptions, but Venkaṭapati was the last of his race.

The Nāyakas.

" The earlier kings of this dynasty had conquered all Southern India before the end of the 14th century ; but they left many of the original kings (*e.g.*, the last Pāṇḍyas) undisturbed for a time ; in the 16th century they had their deputies (called Nāyaks) at Madura (from about 1540). Tanjore and Gingee (Śinji). In the 17th century these Nāyaks acted as independent sovereigns ; the last Nāyak of Tanjore, Vīrarāghava (*e.g.*), granted Negapatam to the Dutch by a grant on a silver plate, now in the Museum at Batavia. These predatory chiefs and the rabble they brought with them are the 'Badagas' of whom the early Portuguese Missionaries complain so much. They did not reach the extreme south till about 1544."

Differences between the two lists unimportant.

It will be seen that there are many minor differences between these two lists. They both agree, however, respecting the date of the most distinguished member of the dynasty, Kṛishṇa Rāya. Each list is stated by its author to be only approximately correct.

Spread of Telugu in the south.

The Vijaya-nagara kings are always styled, not Rājās, but Rāyas, though the meaning is identical.[1] Rāya in Tamil is pluralised as Rāyar, in Telugu as Rāyalu, and the plural, as is usual in the Dravidian languages, is used honorifically for the singular. Canarese was the language of the Dvāra-samudra

[1] The Rāyas of Vijaya-nagara having long been the greatest paramount power in Southern India, Rayar is used in the Tamil New Testament as the equivalent of "Cæsar" with the meaning of emperor.

CHAPTER II.

dynasty, but the founders of Vijaya-nagara were Telugus and made Telugu the language of administration throughout their dominions. The district of country in which they established themselves, though not a portion of Mysore, was a portion of the Kannaḍa country or country in which Canarese was spoken. Right in the heart of this Canarese district a new Telugu dynasty set up a Telugu court, supported by a Telugu army, and sending forth Telugu colonies and expeditions into all parts of the south. This explains the position occupied by the Telugu lieutenants of Vijaya-nagara at Madura, and also in part the position occupied by Telugu Poligars and settlers throughout the Trichinopoly, Madura, and Tinnevelly Districts. It was during the reign of Krishṇa Rāyar that Vijaya-nagara rose to its greatest importance. He reigned from 1508 to 1530. It is certain at least that his reign fell between these two dates. The state of Vijaya-nagara was the most powerful Hindu state that ever existed south of the Krishṇa, and Krishṇa Rāyar has the reputation of having been the ablest, most enlightened, and most successful of the rulers of that state. He is celebrated as having been a munificent patron of Telugu literature. About 1520 the Muhammadans sustained from him a severe defeat, in consequence of which they were kept in check for a considerable period. After his time the kingdom began to decline. Next to him perhaps in fame, but prior to him in point of time, we have to place Narasimha, or Vīra Narasimha, Rāyar, whose reign commenced in 1487, and who is said to have been the first king of this line who extended his conquests into the Chōḷa and Pāṇḍya countries. The forts of Chandragiri and Vēlūr are said to have been built by him. By some, however, they are said to have been built by his great successor Krishṇa Rāya. It was the rise of the strong Hindu kingdom of Vijaya-nagara which opposed the first barrier to the progress southward of the Muhammadan arms, and for nearly two centuries this barrier was found effectual. After a time the Vijaya-nagara kingdom ceased to keep the power of the Muhammadans in check.

Krishṇa Rāyar.

Conquests over the Chōḷas and Pāṇḍyas.

Arrival of the Portuguese in this reign.

It was in Narasimha Rāyar's reign that the Portuguese first arrived in India. They arrived at Calicut in 1498. As in 1311 the Muhammadans found, as we have seen, the Pāṇḍya and Chōḷa kings of Ma'bar, that is, the Coromandel Coast, feudatories of the Canarese king of Dvāra-samudra, so on the arrival of the Portuguese the only kingdom that seemed to them to have any real independent existence was that of Vijaya-nagara. They described the Coromandel Coast, which they called Choramandala, as the fifth province of the Rāyar's empire; and they regarded this province as extending from Quilon to Orissa, an extent greater than that of the Ma'bar of their Arab predecessors. One of the names by which the early Portuguese denoted the whole of

Southern India was the kingdom of Narsinga, doubtless from the name of the great Rāya they found on the throne. CHAPTER II.

Barbosa in 1516 says :—

Kingdom of Narsinga.

" Beyond this river commences the kingdom of Narsinga, which contains five very large provinces, with each a language of its own. The first which stretches along the coast to Malabar is called Tulinate (that is Tulu-nādu) or the modern province of South Canara; another lies in the interior. Another has the name of Telinga, which confines with the kingdom of Orissa. Another is Canari, in which is the great city of Bisnaga ; and then the kingdom of Charamendel, the language of which is Tamul." Colonel Yule and Dr. Burnell, in *Indian Antiquary* for June 1879.

The writers state that the text of this notice has been put together from three versions of Barbosa. The Vijaya-nagara kingdom was sometimes called Karnāṭaka, the Carnatic, and sometimes by a corruption of this name, Canara.

Overthrow of Vijaya-nagara.

Whilst the Muhammadans were growing in power the Hindu states misspent their opportunities and wasted their strength in mutual wars. At length in 1564 Rāma Rāyar, the reigning king of Vijaya-nagara, whose arrogance had provoked the hostility of the Muhammadan powers to the north, was defeated and put to death by a combination of those princes. The great battle in which he fell was fought at Talikota, on the 25th of January 1565. Vijaya-nagara itself was at the same time ruthlessly destroyed. It is from this time I date the largest influx of Telugu settlers into the southern districts of the Tamil country. There are probably at least a million of people in the Tamil districts of Telugu origin, and I think it probable that the ancestors of a very large number of these fled for protection to the Telugu rulers of Madura and Tanjore to escape the oppression of the Muhammadans to which they had been exposed in their Telugu homes.

Origin of Eṭṭaiyāpuram Zemindar.

The account traditionally preserved in the family of the Zemindar of Eṭṭaiyāpuram in Tinnevelly may be taken as an illustration of the mode in which these emigrations generally originated and were carried on. The following is a summary of the statements contained in the native history of the family: —

On the defeat of Anna Dēva Rājā, king of Vijayanagaram, by Muhammad Alauddin, one Kumāramuttu Eṭṭappa Nāyaka, the ancestor of the Eṭṭaiyāpuram Zemindars, fled from Chandragiri, in company with 64 armed relations, 300 men at arms, and 1,000 dependents, with a certain number of accountants and others, and took refuge with Ati Vīra Parākrama Pāṇḍya Rājā at Madura, who appointed them to repress outrages in the country of the Kaḷḷars, and gave them some villages therein for their maintenance. This is represented to have taken place between 1423 and 1443. In process of time they moved on towards the south and became

CHAPTER II.

possessed of various villages in the Tinnevelly District, one of which, to which they gave the name of Eṭṭaiyāpuram, they made their capital.

There are some historical discrepancies in this account. Vijaya-nagara was not taken by Alauddin. The reference may be to the taking of Dvāra-samudra by Alauddin's lieutenant Kafur in 1311. The last king of Vijaya-nagara was not Anna Dēva Rājā, but Rāmarajā, who was defeated and slain by a combination of the Muhammadan princes of the Dekhan in 1565. Chandragiri was taken by the Muhammadans in 1645. The general outline only of the story can be accepted as in the main correct.

Last days of the Vijaya-nagara dynasty.

Notwithstanding the destruction of Vijaya-nagara, the dynasty was not entirely destroyed. The family had still strength enough left to establish themselves afresh in another place. For this purpose they fortified Pennakoṇḍa (or Penugoṇḍa), a steep hill 97 miles north of Bangalore, situated like Vijaya-nagara in the modern district of Bellary, and converted it into a hill fort of great strength with a fortified city at the foot, where they continued for about a century to keep up kingly state and to exercise more or less authority over other princes, south of the Krishṇa, including especially the Nāyaka rulers of Madura and Tanjore, in accordance with what they believed to be their ancestral rights. After a time those various feudatory princes made themselves independent of the feeble survivors of the Vijaya-nagara dynasty, both in reality and in name. The most important of the new independent princes that arose was the Rājā of Mysore. One of the few surviving lineal representatives of the ancient family was the Rājā of Chandragiri, and it was from the last of the Chandragiri Rājās that the English obtained a grant of the site of the town of Madras on the 1st March 1640. It was from the name of Chennappa, this Rājā's lieutenant, that the town came to be called by the natives Chennapaṭṭaṇam, Chennapa's town. The Chandragiri dynasty was finally subverted by the Muhammadans in 1645.

Grant of Madras to the English by the Rāja of Chandragiri.

SUCCESSION OF PARAMOUNT POWERS IN SOUTHERN INDIA.

Pāṇḍayas, Chōḷas.

The outline of the history of the successive dynasties that exercised supreme power in Southern India is clear enough, however doubtful most of the details may be. First the Pāṇḍyas, properly so called, who bore rule in Madura and Tinnevelly from the firs establishment of civil government to the middle of the 11th century, seem during the greater part of that time to have been the paramount power in Southern India. From about the middle of the 11th century the Chōḷas rose to the position of the paramount power and bore rule, directly or indirectly, for about two centuries and a half over the whole Coromandel Coast from Orissa to Cape

Comorin, including even the Tamil or southern portion of Travancore. During the later period of the Chōḷa or Chōḷa-Pāṇḍya rule paramount power over all the southern princes was claimed by the Ballāḷa dynasty of Dwāra-samudra, though it may be doubtful in what degree the power so claimed was really exercised or submitted to. After a short-lived subjugation of the south by the Muhammadans, from the beginning to the middle of the 14th century, the paramount power fell into the hands of the kings of Vijaya-nagara, who succeeded to all and more than all the possessions and power the Ballāḷas and Chōḷas had acquired, and who for nearly two centuries exercised the power they claimed. After the middle of the 16th century no one power can be said to have been really paramount in Southern India till the appearance on the scene of the Nawab of Arcot about the middle of the 18th century.

Paṇḍyas again, Nagakas, the Nawab.

CHAPTER III.

FROM A.D. 1365 TO 1731.
THE PERIOD OF THE SECOND DYNASTY OF PĀṆḌYAS AND OF THE NĀYAKAS.

SECOND SERIES OF PĀṆḌYA KINGS.

CHAPTER III.

THE Pāṇḍya kings, or a line of kings calling themselves by the same name, succeeded after a time in getting the better of the Muhammadans and resumed their ancient sway. The Muhammadan rule commenced in 1311, and Ibn Batuta found it still in full vigour in 1348; but I have found an inscription of one of the Pāṇḍya kings of the new line—possibly the first of the line—at Kōṭṭār (now in South Travancore, but formerly considered a portion of the Pāṇḍyan country), dated in the Śaka year corresponding to A.D. 1370, in the fifth year of Parākrama Pāṇḍi Dēva.

Parākrama Pāṇḍya.

1365 must have been the year of Parākrama's accession, and it supplies us with a date from which the commencement of the new dynasty may safely be calculated.

Whether the Pāṇḍyas received any help towards thrusting out the Muhammadans is not perfectly certain, but it may be presumed that they did. It does not seem probable that they could have achieved their independence alone, and tradition represents them as receiving help from Canarese generals. It is stated in one of the quasi-historical documents published by Mr. Taylor that in 1372 a Mysore (that is, a Canarese or Kannada) general named

Kampana Uḍaiyār.

Kampana Uḍaiyār reduced the Muhammadan invaders of Madura to submission, and it is further stated in one of the Mackenzie MSS. that this general was an agent of Bukka Rāyar, the first Rāyar of Vijaya-nagara. Bukka became king of Vijaya-nagara in 1350. It would seem, therefore, that Bukka conceived it right to claim in behalf of his new state of Vijaya-nagara some portion of the general suzerainty said to have been exercised over the various states of the south by the later kings of the preceding Canarese dynasty of Dwāra-samudra. It may be concluded, therefore, that from the outset it was in some degree, through help received from Vijaya-nagara, that the second line of Pāṇḍyas succeeded in ousting the Muhammadans and rising to power. The Muhammadans state that in 1374 Mujahid Sha overran the countries between Vijaya-nagara and Cape Comorin, and advanced, like Malik Kafur, to Rāmēśwaram. If he ever did so, which seems to me very doubtful, the invasion must have been a mere plundering expedition which left no trace behind it.

Dated inscriptions of the later Pāṇḍyas.

I have not been able to work out anything like a complete list of the Pāṇḍya kings of the second line. Fortunately, however, the custom of dating inscriptions, not merely by the year of the king's reign, but by the Śaka or some recognised era, which had almost always prevailed in Northern and Central India and in the Telugu and Canarese countries, but had been unknown in the old Pāṇḍya country, came to be acted upon during this period, so that the few particulars I have collected may be regarded as historically certain. All the inscriptions here referred to are in Tinnevelly, except the first of the line already referred to, which is in South Travancore. The next prince, after the one mentioned in that inscription, with an interval of sixty-six years still to be filled up, was Ponnan Perumāḷ Parākrama Pāṇḍi, whose reign commenced, as I find by an inscription on a pillar in Tenkāśi (the Southern Benares) opposite the temple, in the Śaka year corresponding to A.D. 1431. This inscription of Ponnan Perumāḷ Parākrama Pāṇḍi is a sort of proclamation to the effect that the work of the temple having been finished in the short period of seventeen years, it should be concluded that it was not a work of man, but a divine work! The interval may partly perhaps be filled up a tradition related by the people at Tenkāsi, who say that the Ponnan Perumāḷ Parākrama Pāṇḍi who built the temple was preceded by his father, Kāśi Kaṇḍa Parākrama Pāṇḍi, *i.e.*, the Parākrama Pāṇḍi who visited Benares. The next prince is Vīra Pāṇḍi, in whose reign I have found two inscriptions at Śrī-vaikuṇṭham on the northern bank of the Tamraparṇī. They are dated in different years of his reign, but both agree in making his reign commence in 1437. His predecessor's reign, therefore, was very short. It commenced, as we have seen, in 1431 and ended in 1437. The next prince noticed in inscriptions is another Vīra Pāṇḍi, who commenced to reign, according to the Mackenzie MSS., in 1475. He is mentioned in an inscription as reigning in 1490. The next, whose inscription I find in the temple at Courtallum, was also called Parākrama Pāṇḍi and commenced to reign in 1516. The next, probably without an interval, was Vikrama Pāṇḍi. His reign commenced in 1543. The next reign, probably without an interval, was that of Vallabha Dēva, called also Ati-Vīra-Rāma Pāṇḍya, who commenced to reign, according to an inscription in Courtallum, in 1565. This inscription was dated in his fortieth year, that is, in 1605. Another inscription of his in Tenkāśi makes his reign commence in 1562. In this inscription he is called simply Ati-Vīra-Rāma Pāṇḍya, not also Vallabha Dēva. Dr. Burnell informs me that, according to a grant in copper

Tenkāsi inscription.

Śrī-vaikuṇtham inscription.

Ati-Vīra-Rāma Pāṇḍya.

CHAPTER III.

belonging to a Maṭha in the Tanjore District, Ati-Vīra-Rāma must have died in 1610. This gives him an unusually long reign, but is not incredible. The same grant represents him as succeeded by a Sundara Pāṇḍya. Dr. Burnell has a grant of this Sundara Pāṇḍya dated in the thirteenth year of his reign. This must have been A.D. 1623. So far as appears from the inscriptions I have found in Tinnevelly itself, Ati-Vīra-Rāma seems to have been the last of his line. As, however, he was a man of learning and culture, and a poet of considerable eminence, his line may be said to have set in glory.

The last of the Pāṇḍyas.

The unreliableness of popular traditions and verbal statements regarding events belonging to the distant past, as compared with information derived from inscriptions, may be illustrated by a comparison of the dates given above with those furnished to Mr. Turnbull, a surveyor, who was making inquiries for Colonel Mackenzie about 1820. See his Geographical and Statistical Memoir of Tinnevelly printed at Palamcottah in 1877, p. 25.[1] In giving an account of the town, temple, and ancient fort of Tenkāśi, Mr. Turnbull gave the names and dates of several Pāṇḍya kings who were said to have been, directly or indirectly, connected with the place. Ati-Vīra-Rāma Pāṇḍya is represented in this account as having commenced his reign in A.D. 1099; whereas a Tamil inscription belonging to his reign, found in the temple at that very place, states that his reign commenced in 1562. A similar inscription in the Courtallum temple in Sanskrit makes his reign commence nearly at the same date, viz., in 1565. So also Ponnan Perumāḷ Parākrama Pāṇḍya, in whose reign the Tenkāśi temple was built, was stated by Mr. Turnbull's informants to have commenced his reign in 1309; whereas the inscription on the pillar opposite the temple, referred to above, places the commencement of his reign in 1431.

Value of inscriptions as compared with oral information.

Vijaya-nagara supremacy.

Throughout the greater number of the reigns of these Pāṇḍya kings of the later line, the kings of Vijaya-nagara appear to have exercised supreme authority, but I think it may be assumed that they did not interfere much in the internal affairs of the country, that they contented themselves with receiving tribute and occasionally military help, and that the principal result of their suzerainty was that the various petty states included within their nominal rule were protected from foreign invasion, and their propensity to spend their time in fighting with one another kept in check.

[1] This interesting memoir, compiled apparently about 1823, was discovered in the India Office by R. K. Puckle, Esq., formerly Collector of Tinnevelly, after it had lain there unnoticed for more than fifty years.

The Nāyakas of Madura.

Chapter III.

Sources of the history of the Nāyakas.

The history of the Nāyakas of Madura is fully related in Mr. Nelson's Madura Manual, but there are very few particulars in that history connected with Tinnevelly, and it is very doubtful how far the particulars mentioned in it on the authority of native traditions and late compilations can be regarded as trustworthy. The main facts in the history of the Nāyakas related therein may be, and doubtless are, capable of being accepted as correct, but the only incidents and dates that seem to me perfectly reliable are those for which we are indebted to the letters written at the time to their ecclesiastical superiors at home by the Roman Catholic Missionaries. This source of information, however, is of no avail prior to 1600. The narratives, for instance, of the administration of Viśvanātha Nāyaka, taken by Nelson from Taylor's Historical Manuscripts and the Mackenzie Collection, seem to me to fall beneath the level even of tradition. They seem to me little better than pure inventions, dating from the beginning of the present century, attributing to a half mythical Nāyaka the characteristics and aims of a good English Collector.

Letters of the Jesuits.

Commencement of the Nāyaka rule.

The commencement of the rule of the Nāyakas is generally said to have taken place in 1559, but this date depends entirely on very late native authority, and as at that date the power of Vijaya-nagara had sunk very low, it would seem to be more probable that the Nāyaka intervention in the affairs of Madura took place earlier than that, viz., in Krishṇa Rāyalu's reign, about 1520. Nothing can be clearer from the letters of the celebrated Francis Xavier, written in 1543, than that the "Badages," that is the Vaḍugas, or Nāyakas, had already taken possession of the whole interior of the country, and that they were then endeavouring to possess themselves of the sea coast as far south as Cape Comorin. If we suppose this state of things, as we fairly may, to have been gathering head for twenty years or so, we shall trace our way back to the reign of Kṛishṇa Rāya, viz., to about 1520.

The "Badages" of Xavier.

Origin of the intervention of Vijaya-nagara.

The Vijaya-nagara king's intervention in the affairs of the south is said to have been owing in the first instance to a request for help against a rival preferred to him by the reigning Pāṇḍya. The king of Tanjore had dispossessed the Pāṇḍya and occupied his country, whereupon the latter fled to Vijaya-nagara (as Sundara Pāṇḍya had previously fled to Delhi) and begged for protection. The king of Tanjore is called Vīra-śēkhara, the king of Madura Chandra-śēkhara. I regard these names, however, as quite uncertain. On this application, it is said, the king of Vijaya-nagara despatched a general of his, one Nāgama Nāyaka, to chastise the Chōḷa king and reinstate the Pāṇḍya on the throne of his ancestors. If this really took place, as stated, the Pāṇḍya

CHAPTER III.

prince referred to may have been Parākrama Pāṇḍi, who commenced to reign, as we have seen, in 1516.

Visvanātha Nāyaka.

Nāgama is said to have declared himself independent, whereupon his son, Viśvanātha Nāyaka, volunteered to go and reduce his father to submission. This the son is said to have succeeded in doing, and was rewarded for his loyalty by being made lieutenant or governor of Madura in the Vijaya-nagara Rājā's interest. It is not stated that he, like his father, made himself by his own act independent of his master; but the result was not dissimilar, for the power and dignity that had been conferred upon himself personally, as a mark of royal favour, descended to his posterity for fifteen generations. Viśvanātha Nāyaka seems to have been a man of energy and administrative power. It was by him that Madura is said to have been fortified. Trichinopoly was also said to have been acquired by him from the king of Tanjore, in exchange for Vallam, and incorporated in the Madura country, in which it continued to be included till the period of the supremacy of the Nawab of Arcot. He also quelled a formidable insurrection in Tinnevelly headed by five confederate chiefs, said to have been brothers, who styled themselves the five Pāṇḍavas.

Number of the Poligars.

As the number of Poligars or Pāḷaiyakāras in Tinnevelly is considerable, though not equal to what it is in Madura—(there are at present 22 zemindaries in Tinnevelly and 26 in Madura, including the two very extensive zemindaries of Ramnad and Sivaganga),—I here cite Mr. Nelson's account of the state of things in the Pāṇḍya country generally, which is said to have led to the appointment of Pāḷaiyakāras (Poligars, now Zemindars) by Viśvanātha Nāyaka on his setting himself to the task of pacifying the country:—

ORIGIN OF THE POLIGARS OF THE SOUTH.

Viśvanātha's policy.

"Whilst the settlement of the southern districts was being effected, Visvanātha found it necessary to attempt to provide for the stability of the dynasty of which he hoped to be the founder, by identifying its interests with those of the principal men of the country; and by rendering his rule equally popular with all classes of society. But the task appeared to be one of almost hopeless difficulty. He had brought with him to Madura crowds of dependents and adherents of his own caste, who had as a body proved themselves to be faithful and obedient and had done his work excellently well. These men were all of them greedily looking for their rewards: and unless provided

Parties to be conciliated.

for with lavish liberality would very soon show their teeth. Then there were the old Tamil hereditary chieftains, whom he had found possessed of considerable territories and power. Their good will it was at once most necessary and most difficult to secure. Accustomed from generation to generation to perpetually recurring periods of anarchy, they knew only too well how to draw profit from misrule:

and as they sulkily looked on at the doings of the Telugu intruder, it seemed ridiculous to expect that they would ever acquiesce in the establishment of order and sovereign power. Moreover they could not but regard with feelings of the bitterest jealousy and hatred the foreigners who surrounded the governor's person, and who seemed about to appropriate to themselves all the highest offices and emoluments in his gift. Then again there were the impoverished and discontented adherents of the Pāṇḍyas—men who could hope for everything from revolution; from peace and quiet nothing. And lastly there were the bold and turbulent Telugu and Canarese adventurers, whose ancestors had seized with a strong grip the northern and western divisions of the country; who paid no man tribute; and whose lawless tempers could ill-brook the curb and spur of a strong government. It was Visvanātha's task to reconcile the conflicting interests of all these classes, to smooth away differences, and to conciliate affection: and to do this in a strange country and with an empty purse! At last he contrived a scheme by which it seemed possible to attain success. Its object was to enrich and ennoble the most powerful of each class, and at the same time secure their and their descendants' allegiance to himself and his successors. This scheme, though possibly as good as any that could at such a time be devised, was nevertheless fraught with all the elements of danger, and in the end contributed largely, as we shall see, to the subversion of the Nāyaka dynasty. Its details were as follows. There were seventy-two bastions to the fort of Madura, and each of them was now formally placed in charge of a particular chief, who was bound for himself and his heirs to keep his post at all times and under all circumstances. He was also bound to pay a fixed annual tribute; to supply and keep in readiness a quota of troops for the governor's armies; and to keep the governor's peace over a particular tract of country. And in consideration of his promise to perform these and other services, a grant was made to him of a tract of country consisting of a certain number of villages, proportioned to his rank and the favour with which Visvanātha and Arya Nāyaka respectively regarded him, together with the title of Pālaiyakāran (Poligar). In addition to this, each grantee was presented with valuable gifts; titles and privileges were conferred upon him amid much pomp and ceremony, and nothing was omitted which could in any way add to the solemnity and importance of the governor's act. Such was the origin of the famous Madura Pālaiyakāras, of some of whom the descendants are still possessed of their ancestors' feuds, if not of their rank and power."

Viśvanātha's plan of conciliation.

Investiture of the Poligars.

It appears to me very doubtful whether all the Poligars in Madura and Tinnevelly were appointed in this manner by one Nāyaka ruler alone, whether Viśvanātha himself, the supposed founder of the dynasty, or any other. The documents on which Mr. Nelson relied seem to me to possess little or no historical value. All that can be regarded, I think, as probable is that the existence of the Poligars as a class dates from the period of the commencement

Doubtfulness of these traditions.

CHAPTER III. of the rule of the Nāyakas. Very few of the Zemindars (the principal exception is the Sētupati of Ramnad) can claim that their estates or chiefships were conferred upon them prior to the Nāyaka period by the old Pāṇḍya kings.

Etymology of "Poligar." The title of Poligar is said by General Wilks to have been given by the Vijaya-nagara kings (though he does not say by which of them) to the chiefs of the Telugu colonies planted in the neighbouring provinces for the purpose of overawing the original inhabitants. The Tamil name is Pālaiyakkāra, the literal meaning of which is the holder of a camp, secondly the holder of a barony on military tenure. But the English seem to have taken their name Poligar, not from the Tamil Pālaiyakkāra, but from the Telugu Pālegāḍu, or the Canarese Pāḷegāra, the meaning of which is identical. [Gāḍu and gāra are equivalent to kāra.] In like manner the English seem to have taken their word Pollam, a Poligar's holding, rather from the Telugu Pālem-u, than from the Tamil Pāḷaiyam. The Vijaya-nagara Poligar was held to be a lord over thirty-three villages, but there is no trace of any such rule as to number in the Tamil country. The Poligar is said to have been originally in the Kannaḍa country called an Oḍeyar (proprietor, pronounced Woḍeyar). The Tamil form of this title is Uḍaiyār, and this is often used by Zemindars in the Tamil country. I have found it sometimes in inscriptions included amongst the titles of ancient kings.

Results of the appointment. Looking at the result of the appointment of Poligars by the rulers of Madura, it can hardly be said that the idea of governing the country by means of an order of rude, rapacious feudal nobles, such as the Poligars generally were, turned out to be a happy one, for down to the period of their final subjection and submission to British authority in 1801, whenever they were not at war with the central authority they were at war with one another, and it was rarely possible to collect from them the tribute or revenue due to the central authority without a display of military force, which added greatly both to the unpopularity and the expense of the collection.

See an account of the position occupied by the Poligars at a later period in Chapter IV.

Defence of the Poligar system. Mr. Stuart in his Tinnevelly Manual, after quoting the above estimate of the results of the appointment of Poligars by the rulers of Madura, endeavours to extenuate the evils of the system. He says, "this remark would, however, apply with equal force to feudal institutions in Europe in the middle ages, and as these served their purpose in the age of the world in which they flourished, it is perhaps reasonable to suppose that protection from foreign foes and internal order and progress, though frequently accompanied by oppression and misrule, were secured by this means to an extent which would have been otherwise impossible." It is so seldom that one hears a good word about the Poligars that I quote these remarks of Mr. Stuart with pleasure. He does not question their misdeeds, but endeavours to extenuate them by a historical parallel. I fear, however, that the misdeeds of the Poligars were more systematic and audacious than those of the feudal nobles of Europe in the middle ages. Even admitting, however, the appropriateness of the parallel, not much seems to be gained by it, for, whether in Europe or in Southern India, the "foreign foes" that were most sedulously guarded against were not foreigners, properly so called, but the legitimate rulers of the country, and it was not till the Poligars of the Highlands of Scotland and of the Rhine, like the Poligars of Tinnevelly, had submitted to the dominion of the central government that "internal order and progress" were in any degree secured.

The only other incidents connected with Tinnevelly I find in the history of the Madura Nāyakas are the following :—

Krishnapuram.

Arya Nāyaka Mudali having succeeded in quieting the country, the Nāyaka ruler, Kumāra Krishṇappa (or Krishṇama), occupied himself, it is said, in building a town to the east of Palamcottah, which he called after himself Krishṇapuram. This statement, however, is not supported by local evidence. This Krishṇapuram appears to have been built by a Mudali called Mayil-ērum-perumāḷ, who being originally a Saiva became a convert to the worship of Krishṇa and afterwards a Tādar (Dāsa) or Vaishṇava devotee. The work of this temple is considered to be particularly beautiful. This new town of Krishṇappa's being a great success, he is said to have built another of the same sort to the westward called Kaḍaiyam Krishṇapuram, the Krishṇapuram which is near Kaḍaiyam. It lies between Tenkāśi and Brahmadēsam. Krishṇappa died in 1573. Nelson, p. 105.

Rebellion of Ettaiyapuram.

"During the rule of Tirumala Nāyaka, for some reason which cannot now be discovered, the powerful Poligar of Ettaiyāpuram in the Tinnevelly District put himself at the head of a confederation of Poligars and took up arms against the king. The Sētupati, the Poligar of Ramnad, being the chief of all the Poligars, was entrusted with the duty of quelling the rebellion and performed it most satisfactorily. The leader of the rebels was put to death, and the others severely punished, and in a few months tranquillity was completely restored. For this service he was rewarded by the gift of a large slice of land in the neighbourhood of Mańār koil and entrusted with the duty of protecting the pearl fishery, which yielded considerable sums of money to the royal treasury." Nelson's Madura.

The latter clause means, I think, that the pearl fishery to the north of the island of Paumben was now admitted to be the

CHAPTER III.

property of the Ramnad Sētupati, whilst the rest of the fishery, by far the largest portion of it, extending from Paumben to the neighbourhood of Cape Comorin, remained as before in the king's own hands.

Royal representatives in Tinnevelly.

"Another and much higher official (than the Collector of Customs) was the Administrator or Governor of the Tinnevelly country. When the king lived in Madura it was highly necessary to place a man of ability in charge of the southern districts and vest him with large powers ; and it became still more necessary to do this when Trichinopoly was made the capital."

There is an inscription near Sheranmādēvi in which one Vīrarāghava Mudaliār is described as the Kārya-karttā, or agent, of Vīrappa Nāyaka in the beginning of the seventeenth century.

Tirumalai's younger brother, Kumāramuttu, claimed the right of succeeding to the throne. In virtue, however, of some negotiations he consented to waive his claim and accepted in lieu of the crown the district of Sivakāsi and other territories in the Tinnevelly province.

Tigers on the sea coast.

A French Missionary's letter written in 1700 states that "for some time past a large jungle on the Tinnevelly coast had been infested by tigers to such a degree that after sunset no inhabitant of any village situated in its neighbourhood dared to move outside his door. Watch was kept in every village at night, and large fires were lighted for the purpose of scaring the monsters away. Even in the day time travelling was not quite safe ; and numbers of people had disappeared who had without doubt been seized and devoured in lonely places." This fact is noticeable, inasmuch as tigers have been for many years unknown in the Madura and Tinnevelly Districts (except in the vicinity of the mountains); and their existence in large numbers on the sea coast in 1700 would seem to show that the country was then much more sparsely populated and contained many more uncultivated tracts than at the present day.

LIST OF THE NĀYAKAS.

List of the Nāyakas of Madura.

The following is a list of the Nāyaka rulers of Madura with the dates of their accession, according to the authorities followed by Mr. Taylor and Mr. Nelson. The reader is requested, however, to remember that I have shown that the commencement of the rule of the Nāyakas is probably to be placed at least thirty years earlier :—

Name	Accession
Viśvanātha Nāyaka	1559
Kumāra Krishṇappa Nāyaka	1563
Periya Vīrappa Nāyaka	1573
Viśvanātha II Nāyaka	1573
Lingaiyā Nāyaka Viśvappa Nāyaka	1595

Muttu Krishṇappa Nāyaka	1602
Muttu Vīrappa Nāyaka	1609
Tirumalai Nāyaka	1623
Muttu Aḷakādri Nāyaka	1659
Choka Nātha Nāyaka	1662
Ranga Krishṇa Muttu Vīrappa Nāyaka ..	1682
Mangammāḷ (Queen Regent)	1689
Vijaya Ranga Choka Nātha Nāyaka ..	1704
Mīnākshi Ammāḷ (Queen Regent)	1731
Chanda Saheb's usurpation	1736

Tirumala Nāyaka.

By far the most distinguished prince of the Nāyaka dynasty was Tirumalai Nāyaka (from 1623 to 1659), a prince whose magnificent tastes are attested by the remains of the buildings he erected at Madura, especially the remains of his palace, a Saracenic structure, which is the grandest building of its kind in Southern India. What is now called the palace was originally little more than the hall of audience. He erected another palace of much smaller dimensions, but in the same style of architecture, at Srīvilliputtūr in Tinnevelly, where it is said he liked to reside occasionally. The remains of the Madura palace are now utilised for courts and other public offices. The greater part of Tirumalai Nāyaka's reign was disfigured by exhausting and impolitic wars. The next most noticeable personage in the Nāyaka line was the Queen Regent Mangammāḷ (from 1689 to 1704), who ruled as regent during the minority of her grandson. She eschewed wars and cultivated the arts of peace, and all through Tinnevelly, as well as in Madura and the adjacent districts, she achieved a reputation which survives to the present day as the greatest maker of roads, planter of avenues, digger of wells, and builder of choultries the royal houses of Madura ever produced. It has become customary to attribute to her every avenue found any where in the country. I have found, for instance, that all the avenues in the neighbourhood of Courtallum are attributed to Mangammāḷ. Having done so much she is supposed to have done all.

Buildings erected by him.

Mangammāḷ.

Nāyaka Titles.

The Nāyakas did not style themselves kings.

It is worthy of notice that the Nāyakas never called themselves kings of Madura. They professed to be lieutenants of the great Rāyalu of Vijaya-nagara and nothing more; and even when they refused the tribute due to their lord paramount or waged war against him, they do not seem to have cared to clutch at a higher title. They assumed all the state and wielded all the power of kings, but seem to have been deterred by some feeling of hereditary loyalty from assuming the name. We have seen also that there were Pāṇḍya kings surviving and nominally reigning in the

CHAPTER III.

Madura country at least down to 1605, notwithstanding the contemporaneous existence of the Nāyakas. Nāyaka in Sanskrit means a leader, a chief, but as used in Southern India it is the hereditary title of certain Telugu castes. In Telugu the masculine singular is written Nāyuḍu, in Tamil Nāyakkan. There are several divisions among the Nāyakas, and it is said that the Madura royal dynasty belonged to the division of the caste called Vaḍuga-Nāyakas, commonly called simply Vaḍugas, the Badages of Xavier. The ordinary name by which the Nāyaka rulers of Madura are styled in the Tamil country, at least in the south, is the "Karttākkaḷ." People speak of such and such an event as happening in the days of the Karttākkaḷ. This is the Tamil plural of the Sanskrit Kartā, a doer, an agent, a representative. This title seems to have been chosen as being one that involved less assumption than the title of king, and yet had more of a royal sound than Nāyaka, which after all was only a caste title. Perhaps the best rendering of the title of Kaṛttā in this connection would be "High Commissioner."

The Karttākkaḷ.

CHARACTERISTICS OF THE NĀYAKA RULE.

Reputation of the Pāṇḍyas as rulers.

It is unfortunate for the reputation of the Nāyakas as rulers that so much more is known about them and their proceedings than about their Pāṇḍya and Chōḷa predecessors. The Pāṇḍyas and Chōḷas left behind them few or no records of their rule. It is often, therefore, taken for granted that their rule must have been characterised by an unfailing respect for justice. The age in which they lived has become the patrimony of the poets, who describe it as a golden age of light taxes, of freedom from oppression, of rain three times a month, and of universal happiness. On the other hand the Nāyakas lived and ruled at so recent a period, and so much was written about them at the time by European Missionaries residing in their territory, that the entire public and private character of most of them stands exposed to "that fierce light which beats upon a throne." Judged therefore not merely by modern European standards of right and wrong, but even by the standards furnished by Hindu and Muhammadan books of authority, the Nāyakas must be decided to have fallen far short of their duty as rulers. Their reigns record little more than a disgraceful catalogue of debaucheries, treacheries, plunderings, oppressions, murders, and civil commotions, relieved only by the factitious splendour of gifts to temples, idols, and priests, by means of which they apparently succeeded in getting the Brahmans and poets to speak well of them, and thus in keeping the mass of the people patient under their misrule.

Reputation of the Nāyakas.

Misrule hidden by shows.

Works of public utility almost unknown.

As we have no reason to suppose the Nāyakas worse than the dynasties that preceded them, we cannot safely form a higher estimate of the characteristics of the administration of the Pāṇḍya and Chōḷa kings. Neither during the period of the Pāṇḍyas and Chōḷas nor during the Nāyaka period were any roads in existence. What were called roads were merely cross-country tracks, sometimes lined with trees. Bridges appear to have been unknown. There were no magistrates or judges, except at the capital, where the king himself sat in judgment, assisted by Brahman advisers. There were no schools, except for Brahmans. Trade was unprotected, and merchants did not dare to appear to grow rich. Hospitals were unknown. When any question came up for decision, every thing was determined in accordance either with the caprice of the monarch or the iron code of custom and caste; and it does not seem to have entered into the mind of any person that it was possible for him to become freer, better, or happier than his ancestors. It was not until the British Government appeared on the scene that any serious attempt was made to lift the mass of the people to a higher level. The only public works then carried on were works of irrigation, and it must freely be admitted that they were generally carried on with exemplary vigour and marked success, not however, so far as appears, by the rulers, but by the people themselves. Anicuts, or weirs, were thrown across the principal rivers, especially the Tāmraparṇī, and the open country was covered with a net-work of tanks.

Administration of laws.

Anicuts on the Tāmraparṇī.

Anicuts on the Tāmraparṇī.

There are eight anicuts [1] on the Tāmraparṇī, seven of which were constructed before the arrival of the English in Tinnevelly.

1. The highest of these is rather a dam than an anicut. It is called, however, by the Natives talaiyaṇai, the head or first anicut. The river after descending the Pāpanāsam falls passes through a narrow gorge, which is partially blocked up by huge boulders and a reef of rock. In the rock holes have been cut in which posts, for the most part of palmyra trees, have been inserted, and against these cross bars with brushwood have been placed. Water is thus supplied for the channels leading off from either bank.

2. Probably the most ancient of the anicuts, properly so called, is that styled the Nadiyuṇṇi anicut, about a mile and a half above Ambāsamudram. It is made of large uncemented stones. Nadiyuṇṇi means "that which drinks up the river." An inscription on a stone belonging to this anicut now in the bed of the stream represents it as having been made at a comparatively recent time. "This Nadiyuṇṇi aṇai was made," says the inscription, "as a

---

[1] Aṇaikkaṭṭu is the equivalent Tamil, from aṇai a dam, and kattu a construction.

CHAPTER III. charitable work by Khan Saheb, in the years of the Śālivāhana and Quilon eras answering to A.D. 1759." Khan Saheb means the celebrated Muhammad Yusuf Khan, who was in power at that time and about whom we shall hear much in the sequel. The natives in the neighbourhood say with much probability that the anicut was originally made by the ancient Pāṇḍya kings, but repaired and strengthened by Khan Saheb.

Legend of the Kannaḍian Aṇai.

3. The most famous of the anicuts is that which is called by the English the Caṇadian anicut. "Canadian" stands for Kannaḍiyan, and the meaning is the anicut made by the Kannaḍi or Kannaḍiyan, that is, by the Canarese man. This is opposite Ambāsamudram. Of the many legends current respecting this Kannaḍiyan one is to the effect that he was placed in possession of immense wealth by a local divinity, who ordered him to devote this wealth to the construction of an anicut. One form of the legend is that all the anicuts were made by the same person. A cow, it seems, was sent forth as a guide, and wherever the cow lay down an anicut was to be constructed. The cow lay down six times between Ambāsamudram and the sea, and accordingly six anicuts were made by the Kannaḍi out of the same supernatural supply of funds. Another and milder form of the legend is that only this one anicut which bears his name was made by the Kannaḍi, and that the cow was commissioned only to mark out the channel leading from this one anicut. Wherever the cow went a channel was to be dug, and wherever she lay down they were to make a tank. The only particular in these legends which seems likely to be true is that the maker of the anicut was some public-spirited Kannaḍi or Canarese man, probably a representative of the Madura government for the time being.

Date of this anicut.

The date of the construction of this anicut is unknown, but it may be placed any time between the commencement of the fourteenth century and the close of the sixteenth. There are inscriptions in a temple near the channel, one of which is dated in the beginning of the seventeenth century. There is a little temple near the anicut itself, where a sacrifice is offered yearly to the local divinity, on the 5th of June, on which occasion the sluice is ceremonially opened and the water allowed to enter the channel. There is a choultry at Shermadēvy (Chēran-mā-dēvī) said to have been built by the same Kannaḍi.

Another form of the legend.

Another form of the legend is given in Shungoonny Menon's History of Travancore.

" It would seem that a Telugu (?) Brahman, commonly known by the name of Kunnaḍia, received a donation of a large number of gold coins from the Mahā Rājāh Prathāpa Rudra of Veloor; that this Brahman, by the advice of the sage Agastyar, who resided on a hill in Thiruadi Dēsam (Travancore), built an anicut (still in existence) across the Thambraverni river, and opened an irrigation canal from that spot to the extent of about twenty-one miles; that with the surplus money he built a sathram at Chēra Mahā Dēvi for feeding a certain number of Brahmans daily; and that he appointed the holder of the copper plate as the perpetual manager of that institution."

The writer quotes the substance of the language of the plate itself:—

"A copy of the copper sasanum in question was procured by us. It purports to have been executed by Narayanappaya of the Kuṇṇaḍian family of Bharadwaja Gothram (line) of Brahmans, professing the Rig Veda, and who received a donation called Kalapurusha Danum from Mahā Rājāh Gajapathi Prathāpa Rudra Rayer, who reigned at Veloor; that he, the recipient, resolving to perform some charity with the money proceeded to Thrippathi, and on invoking Vencatachala Swamy obtained that deity's blessing, and in accordance with the commands of the swami he repaired to the southern kingdom called Thiruadi Dēsam (Travancore country) where on the Malayachala mountain, he met the sage Agastyar by whose order he excavated an irrigation canal for the benefit of the Brahmans: with the surplus money he resolved to institute a sathram for the daily feeding of Brahmans and accordingly constructed a building on the southern banks of the Thambraverni and on the western side of Chera-Maha Devi Alakiyappen Swamy Kovil; Narayana Pillay, the son of Gopala Pillay, Brahman of Sreevatsa Gothram (line), professing the Yajur Veda, and residing in the old village or Brahman hamlet, built by Cheren Perumal Rajah, was entrusted with the management of this sathram, a perpetual grant being made to Narayana Pillay by this copper plate document, executed on Thursday, Shrawana asterism, Punchami Aushada month, Sowmmya Nama year of Kali 3342 (242 A.D.) for the maintenance of the sathram of certain lands purchased for 2587 Kali Yuga Ramen [1] Madura vella fanams, together with nine slaves of the soil at the rate of one hundred and thirty-five fanams, accompanied by a scale of the daily expenditure to be made and mentioning a fixed sum as remuneration to the Superintendent Narayana Pillay.

"To this sathram, pepper was to be supplied from Travancore, as that spice was a produce of that country and could not be obtained without the king's permission. It was given gratis, and in the year 970 M.E. (1795 A.D.), three years previous to his death, the old Rama Rajah ordered a commutation price of one hundred and eighty Kali fanams to be paid to the sathram, which sum is paid to the present time."

This account of the origin of the anicut is evidently as legendary and as little trustworthy as the others. It throws light, however, on the personality of the Kannaḍiyan. It may be regarded as certain from the plate that he was a Brahman. The date assigned to the transaction in the plate, viz., A.D. 242, is of course a

[1] "One Kali Yuga Ramen fanam is still the currency of Travancore."

CHAPTER III. pure invention. I have never found the use of the year of the Kali yuga era or of the year of the cycle of Jupiter in any inscription in Tinnevelly older than the fifteenth century A.D. But the date is contradicted by a statement contained in the plate itself. The king from whom the Kannaḍi or Canarese Brahman received this donation was not one of the ancient Pāṇḍya, Chōḷa or Chēra kings, but a monarch of comparatively modern times, a member of the Vēlūr branch of the Rāyars. When the Vijaya-nagara empire was overthrown by the Muhammadans in 1564 various princes belonging to the defeated but still powerful Rāyar family established themselves in various places, one of which was Vēlūr. Tirumalai Nāyaka, the greatest of the Nāyakas of Madura (from 1623 to 1659) acknowledged the Rāyar of Vēlūr as his feudal superior. Pratāba Rudra was a common name amongst the Telugu dynasties. The date of the construction of the anicut is thus brought down within the range of probability.

Ariyanāyakapuram anicut.

4. The next anicut is that of Ariyanāyakapuram. It will be remembered that Ariya-nāyaka was a person of great importance in the earliest period of Nāyaka history. It does not follow however that this Ariya-nāyaka had anything to do with the erection of this anicut, which receives its name from the name of the village nearest to it.

Suttamalli anicut.

5. The fifth anicut is that of Suttamalli. This important anicut supplies water of irrigation to the town of Tinnevelly and the neighbourhood.

Paḷavūr anicut.

6. The sixth is at Paḷavūr and supplies Palamcottah and the neighbourhood. The channel leading from the latter is called Pāḷaiyan's channel, and is attributed, with the original fort of Palamcottah, to one Pāḷaiyan, who was also a Kannaḍi. The latter Kannaḍi is said to have been a descendant of the former. Paḷavūr is on the left bank of the river, though the channel which leads from it runs along the right bank.

Marudūr anicut.

7. Of all the anicuts on the Tāmraparṇī the one which supplies the largest extent of paddy cultivation is that at Marudūr, some miles to the east of Palamcottah. This anicut was almost wholly rebuilt in 1792, during the Collectorship of Mr. Torin (as an inscription testifies), and great improvements were again made in it in 1807 by Colonel Caldwell.

Puthugudi anicut.

8. The last of the eight anicuts, the one that is nearest to the sea, between Puthugudi and Srīvaikuṇṭham, was constructed only a few years ago by Lieutenant Shepherd. The river is here 800 yards broad. The anicut cost eleven lakhs. This is the only anicut on the Tāmraparṇī wholly constructed by the British Government. All the anicuts, however, have been strengthened and improved since the country came under British rule.

The Portuguese on the Coast of Tinnevelly.

Chapter III.

Vasco da Gama's information.

The Portuguese arrived at Calicut on the 20th of May 1498. They came in three small vessels under the command of Vasco da Gama, the first European mariner who found his way to India by doubling the Cape of Good Hope. He returned to Europe the following year, when he presented to his sovereign a summary of the events of his voyage and of his discoveries. He therein mentioned a place on the Tinnevelly coast, Cael (Kāyal), where he was told that pearls were found, and which he was informed was under a Mussulman king. Not long after we find a king of Quilon living at Kāyal, but it may have been true that in Vasco da Gama's time the ruler of the place was a Muhammadan, for it was from the Muhammadans that the Paravas shortly after asked to be protected; we know from other sources that the Muhammadans were numerous and powerful along the coast at that time, and I have found in Kāyal itself a tradition that the last king of the place was a Muhammadan.

The Portuguese at Cochin.

The first settlement of the Portuguese in India was at Cochin, where they established a factory in 1502. In the following year they erected a fort there. From that time they became virtually masters of the whole sea coast of India, and ere long drove all Moorish, that is, all Muhammadan, vessels from the sea, except those that consented to receive Portuguese passes. Barbosa, a Portuguese Captain, who visited many places in the east shortly after, relates that in 1514 he found Cael (Kāyal) belonging to the king of Quilon, who generally resided there. By the king of Quilon we are to understand the sovereign who at a later period was styled, as now, the king of Travancore. Marco Polo in 1293 distinguished between the kingdom of Quilon and the kingdom of Travancore, the latter of which he called the kingdom of "Comari." At the time, however, of the arrival of the Portuguese Travancore was found to have absorbed Quilon. If we are to suppose that the king of Quilon found by Barbosa at Kāyal was the reigning king of Travancore himself, he must, according to Travancore authorities, have been Srī Vīra Ravivarmā. It does not seem certain however that it was the reigning Rājā himself, for each of the Rājā's brothers is commonly called Rājā, and a little later on, in Xavier's time, we find that it was a relative of the king who was residing at Kāyal. However this may be, it is clear that Kāyal was regarded by the earliest Portuguese as belonging to Travancore, and that the king of Travancore was regarded as the legitimate sovereign of the whole of the south of Tinnevelly. This is quite in accordance with Tinnevelly traditions and inscriptions, and in particular with the records contained in the temple at Trichendūr. At that time the Pāṇḍya Rājās had sunk into insignificance, and the Nāyakas of

Barbosa's information.

The king of Travancore at Kāyal.

CHAPTER III.

Madura had not yet consolidated their power. It was natural therefore that the king of the adjacent territory of Travancore should take the opportunity of bringing at least the southern portion of Tinnevelly under his rule.

In 1517 the Portuguese established a settlement, with a fort, at Colombo in Ceylon; and in 1522 they sent a commission from Cochin to Mailāpūr, or Saint Thomé, near Madras, to search for the body of Saint Thomas, which was supposed to have been preserved in the church at a place called the Little Mount. We cannot doubt that long ere that date they had explored the whole of the Tinnevelly coast, and made themselves acquainted with the lucrative pearl fishery to which their attention had been called by Vasco da Gama, and which had been carried on along that coast from the beginning of the historical period to that time.

THE FIRST EXPEDITION OF THE PORTUGUESE.

Embassy of the Paravas to Cochin.

The first recorded appearance, however, of any Portuguese expedition on the Tinnevelly coast was in 1532, when a deputation of Paravas, people of the fisher caste, came to Cochin for the purpose of obtaining the aid of the Portuguese against the Moors or Muhammadans. The chief place along the coast then as now inhabited by Muhammadans was Kāyalpaṭṭaṇam, a town not to be confounded, as it has often been, with Kāyal, now called Old Kāyal. The deputation to Cochin is said to have comprised seventy persons. They were successful in their application, and an expedition was fitted out. Father Michael Vaz, the Vicar-General at Cochin, accompanied the fleet with some priests, and is described by Xavier some years afterwards as "the true father of the Comorin Christians." The application of the Paravas to the Portuguese at Cochin and the plan they adopted of securing their help by promising to embrace their religion were owing, it is said, to the advice given them by a native, himself a recent convert, called Joam de Cruz. The members of the deputation were baptised at Cochin by Father Vaz, and on his arrival on the coast, after the overthrow of the Muhammadans, 20,000 Paravas, inhabiting thirty villages, are said to have been baptised. Looking at these circumstances I think we cannot err in setting down 1532 as the date of the commencement of the Portuguese power on the Tinnevelly coast. Xavier writes that the chiefs of the Saracens (Muhammadans) were slain and that their power was utterly broken. By 1542, when he first visited the coast, the pearl fishery had fallen entirely into Portuguese hands. The places where the Portuguese had established themselves in Xavier's time were Maṇapāḍu, Punnaikāyal, Tuticorin, and Vēmbār, but it will appear afterwards, from notes from early Portuguese writers

The Portuguese in power along the coast.

communicated to me by Dr. Burnell, that till about 1582 Punnaikāyal was their principal settlement and Tuticorin a place of less importance.

INROADS OF THE "BADAGES."

Ravages of the Badages.

Between 1532, the date of the expedition against the "Moors", and 1542, the first year of Xavier's residence on the coast, a new enemy came upon the scene, an enemy much more formidable than the Moors, and one with which even the Portuguese found it more difficult to deal. These were the "Badages" whose ravages are so frequently described and so pathetically deplored in Xavier's letters. Xavier represents them as lawless marauders; by another writer, as we shall see, they are described as tax-gatherers; and doubtless both representations were correct, for this extraordinary combination of the characters of tax-gatherer and marauder continued to be common in the south till the cession of the Carnatic to the East India Company. In one village near Cape Comorin Xavier himself was a witness of the horrors the Badages had inflicted, and it will presently be seen that even the Portuguese settlements themselves were not safe.

Who were they?

Who were these Badages? I have already mentioned that "Badages" stands for Vaḍugas, that is, Nāyakas. The Canarese form of the name is Baḍaga, the literal meaning is northern, and the Nāyakas are so called in the Tamil country because being Telugus they came from the north. The division of the Nāyakas called Vaḍugas is that of Tirumalai Nāyaka's caste. Their title as a caste is Nāyaka or Nāyuḍu, but the name by which they are ordinarily called and by which they are distinguished from other Nāyakas is Vaḍugas. A Jesuit writer of that time describes the Badages as "the collectors of the royal taxes, a race of overbearing and insolent men, and commonly called Nairs." Here the writer, who resided on the western coast, inaccurately uses the Malayâḷam term Nair (Nāyar) instead of the corresponding Tamil Naik, or Nāyaka. In other respects his definition is correct. One expression he uses is noticeable—"the royal taxes." This meant the taxes claimed by the Rāyas of Vijaya-nagara (or the kings of Narsinga, as they were generally called by the Portuguese), which were exacted through their lieutenants at Madura and elsewhere, who had not yet succeeded in making themselves independent of their masters. Xavier used a variety of means for protecting the Christian villages, that is, the villages of the Paravas along the coast, from the violence of the Badages, one of which was his intercession in their behalf with the king of Travancore. He calls this king by the strange name of "Iniquitribirimus." The only portion of this name which seems capable of explanation is

Collectors of the Vijaya-nagara taxes.

Xavier's appeal to the king of Travancore.

CHAPTER III.

the last, birimus, which probably stands for Varmā, the Kshatriya title affixed to the personal name of each Travancore king. According to the Travancore lists the king at that time was called Udaya Mārtānda Varmā who reigned from 1537 to 1560. No name in the list and no Hindu name I know seems to bear any resemblance to Iniquitri. The copier of Xavier's letter probably mistook his writing. Can the name have been intended for that of a king of Travancore who reigned some time previously, Vīra Ravi ?

Power of the Travancore king.

Xavier describes this king as " the great king of Travancore " and speaks of him as having authority over all South India. Again he speaks of the oppressed Paravas as the king's subjects. He mentions that a near relative of the king resided at Tael[1] (that is Cael = Kāyal). It is evident, however, that the power of the king of Travancore along the Tinnevelly coast had become at that time little better than nominal. He gave his sympathy, but apparently was unable to render any real assistance ; and the following year we find that Travancore itself was invaded by the " Badages " in greater force and better armed than when they went against the poor fishermen of the coast. According to some accounts the Rājā was more indebted to Xavier than to his force of Nairs for deliverance from this danger, a panic having, it is said, been produced in the ranks of the Badages by Xavier's sudden appearance in the front of their host. The Badages failed in their attempt to conquer Travancore, but from that time forward we hear no more of the power of the king of Travancore in Tinnevelly, and from time to time we find the Nāyaka rulers of Madura claiming the right of levying tribute on Travancore itself. It is admitted, however, that the king of Travancore paid them tribute only when compelled. At the time these conflicts were occurring between the Badages and the Paravas the Pāṇḍya kings of the second series still professed to reign over the whole country. The Pāṇḍya of that time, according to an inscription of mine, was Vikrama Pāṇḍya. But nobody seems to have cared about him or taken any notice of him.

Designs of the Nāyakas on Travancore.

Motives of the " Badages."

What can have been the motive of the special hostility of the " Badages," that is, of the Nāyaka emissaries and representatives of the Vijaya-nagara Rāyas and their Madura deputies against the unwarlike Parava fishermen along the coast of Tinnevelly ? They were said to have expressed " their determination to expel the

---

[1] The name of this place is written Tael, Tale or Tala. As it is said to have been two leagues from Maṇapāḍu, Tāḷai, a fishing village on the coast, would appear to have been meant. It is difficult, however, to suppose that a relation of the king of Travancore would be living at a poor fishing village, when it was so much more natural for him to live at Kâyal where Barbosa not long before found the king himself. Cael would easily have been written by mistake Tael.

Christians, both natives and foreigners, from the coast." Whence this determination? The Nāyaka rulers of Madura tolerated Robert de Nobili and his Christian converts at Madura itself some time later. Why were they not equally willing to tolerate the Christian Paravas? The reason is that the Paravas had changed their nationality as well as their religion. Xavier in one of his letters to a colleague speaks of the Paravas as "subjects of His Portuguese Majesty," and nothing can be more evident from all the letters written by him and others during his two years' stay than that the entire civil and criminal jurisdiction of the fishery coast had been seized upon by the Portuguese, and that all dues and taxes, including the valuable revenue arising from the pearl fishery, had been assumed by the governors appointed by the Portuguese Viceroy. The Portuguese had not asked any native potentate's consent to the formation of their settlements. They seized possession of the whole fishery coast, established settlements wherever they pleased, and conferred on the Paravas the somewhat dangerous privilege of being Portuguese subjects. Hence the repeated violent efforts of the Badages, or representatives of the Madura Nāyakas, to compel the Paravas to pay tax and tribute, not to the Portuguese, but to themselves. It will be noticed that amongst the expedients adopted by Xavier for the purpose of protecting his flock from the violence of the Badages, that of advising them to pay the taxes demanded of them and submitting to the authority of Madura had not a place.

Explanation of the hostility of the Badages.

The policy of the Portuguese.

The coast was generally called by Xavier the Comorin Coast, the villages along the coast amongst which he itinerated the Comorin villages, and the Christian converts the Comorin Christians. Later on, however, the coast was commonly called the Pescaria, the fishery, by which the pearl fishery was denoted, and the principal functionary amongst the Portuguese on the coast was styled the Captain of the Fishery. The Portuguese, at least in that early period, were more fortunate in relation to the profits of the pearl fishery than the Dutch were afterwards, for whilst the Dutch had always to pay a share of the profits of the fishery to the Nāyakas of Madura or the Sētupati of Ramnad, the Portuguese found themselves for a time strong enough and the Native rulers weak enough (or distant enough) to allow of their appropriating the whole of the profits to themselves. When the Portuguese grew weaker and the Nāyakas stronger, a different arrangement had to be submitted to.

Government of the coast.

Profits of the pearl fishery.

In Guerrero's "Relation" of the Missions on the coast (1604) the Nāyaka is spoken of as "Lord of those lands," and as holding his court in Madura, from which it is evident that the sovereignty over the coast had ceased to be claimed by the Portuguese. I

Portuguese claim abandoned.

CHAPTER III. find also from another authority that in 1609 the Paravas paid their dues, not to the Portuguese, but to the representatives of the Madura Government. Bishop Barretto in 1615 complains that the people were much oppressed by the Nāyaka of Madura.

Punnaikayal. The principal settlement of the Portuguese for about fifty years after their arrival seems to have been Punnaikāyal. Punnai means the Indian laurel, Kāyal a lagoon opening into the sea. Old Kāyal is situated to the north of the Tāmraparṇī river, Punnaikāyal to the south, very near the mouth and right on the seashore. It is now only a fishing village, but some traces remain of its former greatness. The foundations of some European bungalows and warehouses are still seen, with a portion of an encircling wall; and a distinct tradition survives of the existence of a fort during the Portuguese period, of a siege, a battle, and a defeat. This it will be seen is quite in accordance with the historical notice which will be found beneath under the head of 1552. There is also a tradition of the death by the hands of the enemy of Father Antonio (Antonio Criminalis), Xavier's successor.

For the following items of information about Punnaikāyal subsequently to Xavier's time, I am indebted to Dr. Burnell, who has taken them from early Portuguese writers, especially DeSousa:—

Annals of the Portuguese on the coast.

1551. Two hospitals and a seminary founded at Punicale.

1552. At Punicale, the chief place on the coast, there was a mud fort. This fort was taken by the Badages, Countinho, Captain of the Fishery, being defeated.

1553. Punicale retaken by the fleet from Calicut.

1560. There was a garrison at Punicale of fifty men.

1563. Shortly after 1563, when Cæsar Frederic visited the coast, the fishers for pearls still continued to pay for permission to the representative of the King of Portugal. The Madura Nāyakas had, therefore, not yet succeeded in gaining supreme power.

1570. Great famine on the fishery coast. Father Henriquez established famine relief houses, in some of which fifty persons were daily fed.

Don Sebastian limits to the Christian fishermen the tithes on pearls.

1578. DeSousa states that in 1578 Father João de Faria cut Tamil types and printed certain religious books the same year on the Pescaria coast, that is, on the coast of Tinnevelly. The books were the Doctrina Christiana, the Flos Sanctorum (an epitome of the lives of the Saints), and some others.

Printing introduced.

Printing at Cochin.

Paulinus a Sancto Bartolomæo seems to make the same statement with reference to Cochin. He says that at Cochin in 1577 a lay brother, Joannes Gonsalves, cut Malabar-Tamil types and printed a Doctrina Christiana, and that the next year a Flos Sanctorum followed. It certainly looks very much as if the same incident were referred to by both writers. If one of these narratives is to be accepted and the other rejected, the one which has the best claim to be accepted is the one which relates to Tinnevelly, as DeSousa compiled his book from MSS. in Goa in the seventeenth century, a century before Paulinus. This is an interesting incident, as being the first introduction of printing on the Coromandel Coast. It does not seem to have been carried on any further. The next Tamil printing we hear of is at Ambalakāḍu in the Cochin country in 1679.

The Pearl Fishery.

I subjoin here Cæsar Frederic's description of the pearl fishery as carried on in his time. It seems probable that his observations were made at Kāyal (or Punnaikāyal), that being the only place on the coast he mentions. Cæsar Frederic was a Venetian merchant, a fellow-countryman of Marco Polo. He spent eighteen years in India between 1563 and 1581, and his visit to Tinnevelly and the scene of the pearl fishery must have been in or soon after 1563 :—

"Of the Pearl Fishery in the Gulf of Mannar.

"The sea along the coast which extends from Cape Comorin to the low land of Kāyal and the island of Zeilan (Ceylon) is called the pearl fishery. This fishery is made every year, beginning in March or April, and lasts fifty days. The fishery is by no means made every year at one place, but one year at one place, and another year at another place; all however in the same sea. When the fishing season approaches, some good divers are sent to discover where the greatest quantity of oysters are to be found under water; and then directly facing that place which is chosen for the fishery a village with a number of houses, and a bazaar, all of stone, is built, which stands as long as the fishery lasts, and is amply supplied with all necessaries. Sometimes it happens near places already inhabited, and at other times at a distance from any habitations. The fishers or divers are all Christians of the country, and all are permitted to engage in this fishery, on payment of certain duties to the king of Portugal and to the churches of the Friars of Saint Paul on that coast. Happening to be there one year in my peregrinations, I saw the order used in fishing which is as follows :—

"During the continuance of the fishery, there are always three or four armed foists or galliots stationed to defend the fishermen from pirates. Usually the fishing boats unite in companies of three or four together. These boats resemble our pilot boats at Venice, but are somewhat smaller, having seven or eight men in each. I have seen of a morning a great number of these boats go out to fish, anchoring in 15 or 18 fathoms water, which is the ordinary depth along this coast. When at anchor, they cast a rope into the sea, having a great

CHAPTER III. stone at one end. Then a man having his ears well stopped, and his body anointed with oil, and a basket hanging to his neck or under his left arm, goes down to the bottom of the sea along the rope, and fills his basket with oysters as fast as he can. When that is full, he shakes the rope, and his companions draw him up with the basket. The divers follow each other in succession in this manner till the boat is loaded with oysters, and they return at evening to the fishing village. Then each boat or company makes their heaps of oysters at some distance from each other, so that a long row of great heaps of oysters are seen piled along the shore. These are not touched till the fishing is over, when each company sits down beside its own heap, and falls to opening the oyster, which is now easy, as the fish within are all dead and dry. If every oyster had pearls in them it would be a profitable occupation, but there are many which have none. There are certain persons called Chitini (Chettis) who are learned in pearls; and are employed to sort and value them according to their weight, beauty, and goodness, dividing them into four sorts. The first sort which are round are named *aia* of Portugal, as they are bought by the Portuguese. The second, which are not round, are named *aia* of Bengal. The third, which are inferior to the second, are called *aia* of Canara, which is the name of the kingdom of Bijanagur or Narsinga, into which they are sold. And the fourth, or lowest kind, is called aia of Cambaia,[1] being sold into the country. Thus sorted, and prices affixed to each, there are merchants from all countries ready with their money, so that in a few days all the pearls are bought up according to their goodness and weight."

The author of the Report on the Tinnevelly Census, in which the above is included, observes of this description of the pearl fishery that it is "as applicable to the method of procedure at the present day, as when it was written nearly 300 years ago, except that from some causes but little understood the banks of recent years have unfortunately ceased to furnish a supply of the valuable oysters yielding the pearl of commerce."

TUTICORIN UNDER THE PORTUGUESE.

The first appearance of the Portuguese in force in Tuticorin was in 1532, when the fleet despatched from Cochin broke the power of the Muhammadans along the coast and the Paravas were baptised by Father Michael Vaz and his assistant priests. The number said to have been baptised was, as has been said, 20,000 inhabiting thirty villages from Cape Comorin northwards. Of these

[1] It is not clear what word was meant by *aia*. Haya, horse, was the title of the first of eight varieties of pearls sent by king Devenipiatissa in B.C. 306 to King Asŏka. See Emerson Tennent's Ceylon. Each of Cæsar Frederic's varieties, however, was called the *aia* of such and such a kingdom. Can the ordinary word aya (in Tamil ayam), which means "tax" have been intended? This is the impression of the Tuticorin traders, as they say the tax to the Portuguese, &c., was paid in pearls.

villages Tuticorin was one, but it is uncertain when a regular settlement was formed there by the Portuguese. In 1543, when the celebrated Xavier arrived, Tuticorin had a Portuguese Governor. The establishment of the settlement there must, therefore, be placed somewhere in the ten years between 1532 and 1542, but from 1532 for some fifty years the inhabitants of Tuticorin were regarded, like the rest of the baptised Paravas, as Portuguese subjects.

Date of the establishment of the Portuguese in Tuticorin.

Tuticorin is the European equivalent of the Tamil name of the place Tūttukkuḍi. The cerebral ḍ of Tūttukkuḍi became r in the mouth of Europeans by that rule of mispronunciation by which Maṇappāḍu, another place in the neighbourhood, became Maṇapār. The final n in Tuticorin was added for some such euphonic reasons as turned Kochchi into Cochin and Kumari into Comorin. The meaning of the name Tūttukkuḍi is said to be the town where the wells get filled up; from tūttu (properly tūrttu), to fill up a well, and kuḍi, a place of habitation, a town. This derivation, whether the true one or not, has at least the merit of being appropriate, for in Tuticorin the silting up of old wells and the opening out of new ones are events of almost daily occurrence. Tuticorin was not only a village, but appears to have been a place of some little trade, before the arrival of the Portuguese; but the Portuguese were especially attracted to it by the advantages offered by its harbour, which is the only place that can be called a harbour along the entire Coromandel Coast. The harbour is well sheltered from every wind by islands and spits of sand. Unfortunately it is so shallow that only vessels of sixty tons' burthen can load in it. Had it not been for this disadvantage Tuticorin might have eclipsed Madras. The Portuguese, as we have seen, made Punnaikāyal their chief station for a time, but as there is only an open road-stead there, without any thing that could be called a harbour, they made Tuticorin their chief settlement from about 1580. Probably the vessels used by the early Portuguese, though built in Europe, were not much larger than good-sized country craft, so that they would be able to load and unload inside the harbour. Probably also the harbour was a few feet deeper then than it is now. This indeed may be regarded not as a probability, but as a certainty, for there is abundant evidence to prove that the whole coast has been steadily rising little by little out of the sea for ages.

Meaning of the name of Tuticorin.

Tuticorin harbour.

The principal island, that on which the light-house stands, is called Pāṇḍiyan-tīvu, the island of the Pāṇḍyan. Coral, called in Tamil nurai-kal, foam-stone, is formed abundantly in the shallow water outside the islands. Whenever people dig in the town of Tuticorin they find about two feet beneath the surface a thin layer, generally only a few inches in thickness, of a fine-grained grit-

Coral.

CHAPTER III. stone, called by the natives uppukal, salt-stone, formed by the induration of the upper surface of the sea bed when the sea covered the place. Underneath this stratum we find sea sand, the larger grains above, the smaller below, as is usual in sedimentary depositions. Sea sand and shells, including deep sea shells, are found lying on the surface of the ground or a few inches beneath the surface, as far inland as Kōrampaḷḷam, at the fifth milestone on the road to Palamcottah. The grit-stone formation lies beneath, as elsewhere, all along the coast, and is found half a mile further inland. It also is full of recent shells; but with this difference that the shells in the grit-stone are fossilised and very much comminuted. The shells lying on the surface are not fossilised, many of them are nearly perfect, and some retain traces of their original colour. I found the open country near the Kōrampaḷḷam tank covered with deep sea shells, such as chanks, pectens, oysters, and a few pearl-oysters. I found in places also large quantities of sea shore shells. The place in the vicinity of the Kōrampaḷḷam sluice, where I found these chanks, &c., is 11 feet above the present level of the sea at Tuticorin. Chanks are usually found in 7-fathom water, but we may take a minimum depth of 5 fathoms, and reckon 30 feet for the depth of their habitat. This added to 11 gives us about 40 feet, as the depth of the sea which swept over Tuticorin at that early period when these shell fish were living in the sea bottom at Kōrampaḷḷam. The natives of Tuticorin confirm this conclusion by a so-called tradition. They say that it was at Kōrampaḷḷam, when the sea came up to that place, that Tuticorin first began to be built, and that as the sea retired they built their houses further and further to the eastward, till they reached the place where Tuticorin now stands, and where it has stood ever since the arrival of the white men. This seems to me a tradition invented to account for the fact which people could not help observing, that sea shells were found lying on the surface of the ground at Kōrampaḷḷam. I do not think it probable that the date of the commencement of the elevation of the land was so recent as this tradition would make us believe, though probably it was after Tinnevelly began to be inhabited. *See* Appendix IV.

Grit-stone.

Deep sea shells found inland.

First Reliable Notices of Tuticorin.

Governor of Tuticorin.

The first reliable notices of the Portuguese settlement at Tuticorin I find in Xavier's letters, which were written on the spot, or in the neighbourhood, in 1542–44. Tuticorin had then a Portuguese Governor, who was probably also the Governor of the other settlements on the coast, for in his letters to his assistant, Francis Mancias, Xavier always speaks of the Governor in the singular. It is probably that it was the same functionary who was afterwards called Captain of the Fishery. The principal letter relating to Tuticorin is one which records a disaster. It was dated at Alendale (a small Parava village three miles south of Trichendūr, properly Ālandulai), 5th September 1544. An attack had been made by the dreaded Badages (Nāyakas from Madura) on the Governor of Tuticorin. Xavier's letter on the subject was addressed to Mancias at Punnaikāyal. He says: "I have just received the most terrible news respecting the Governor (of Tuticorin), that his ship has been burnt, and his house on shore also destroyed by fire; that he has himself been robbed of every thing, and has retired to the islands in broken spirits and utter destitution. Fly to his relief, I conjure you in the name of charity; carry with you as many as you can get together of your people at Punicale, and all the boats which are there, filled with provisions, and especially with a supply of fresh water. Use the utmost despatch, for the extremity of the man's distress admits of no delay. I am writing to the Patangats[1] (headmen) of Combutur and Bembare[2] in the most urgent terms, to render you every possible assistance in discharge of their bounden duty to their Governor. Let them load as many boats as are fit for the service with provisions and fresh water, for it is well known that they are deficient in that necessary. I wish many boats to be sent, that these may be the means of carrying over to the mainland the crowd of all ages, who were driven to take refuge in these inhospitable rocks by the same incursion as drove the Governor thither." He adds: "The same calamity has overwhelmed very many Christians also." This calamity came to an end ere long, but by what means does not appear.

Tuticorin taken by the Badages.

Xavier's efforts for its relief.

Boats sent to the islands.

Two months later Xavier writes to Mancias again: "Tell N. Barbosa (the Governor or Captain of the Fishery) from me not to employ any person in the pearl fisheries at Tuticorin, who have taken possession of the houses of the Christian exiles; as the King and the Viceroy have given me authority in this matter, I positively forbid it." To understand the style of language employed by Xavier it is necessary to remember that he had been made a Royal Commissioner with extraordinary powers. About the same time he obtained an order from the King of Portugal that the pearl fishery should be entirely in the hands of the Christians.

Xavier's authority.

For the following particulars respecting Tuticorin I am indebted as before to Dr. Burnell.

---

[1] Patangat means Paṭṭangkaṭṭi (title-wearer), the title of a headman amongst the Paravas.

[2] Bembare is easily identified with Vēmbār, but it was a long time before I discovered that by "Combutur" (confounded by some with far-off Coimbatore) we are to understand Kombukireiyūr, a small fishing village near Kāyalpaṭṭaṇam.

CHAPTER III.

Correa, writing about 1560, says that in 1544 (when as we have seen Xavier himself was on the coast) the places in which there were most Christians were Tuticorin and Maṇapāḍu.

Later notices of Tuticorin.

A church was built at Tuticorin in 1582 (DeSousa). It was dedicated to "Nossa Senhora da Piedade," and 600 persons communicated at the first mass said in it. This name is supposed to be an error—See in the chapter on Roman Catholic Missions a quotation from Guerrero in 1600 relating to the name of this church.

In Lunchoten's map (1596) Cael appears, but not Tuticorin. He only mentions a Captain of the Fishery.

I find the following names of places on or near the coast mentioned in Xavier's letters:—Tuticorin, Maṇapāḍu, Punnaikāyal, Kombukiraiyūr, Ālandulai, Kāyal, Tāḷai, Vīrapāṇḍiyanpaṭṭaṇam, Vēmbāru, Pudicurim (Pudukuḍi), Trinchandour (Tiruchendūr), Paṭṭanam.

Tuticorin taken by the Dutch.

Baldæus mentions that the Dutch took Tuticorin from the Portuguese in 1658. He mentions the existence of churches along the coast, but says nothing of Portuguese settlements. It may be assumed that by that time Tuticorin was the only place on the coast where the Portuguese continued to bear rule. Baldæus says that Tuticorin was not fortified, and this appears from his view. It will be seen that a fort was erected in Tuticorin by the Dutch shortly before 1700. Prior to that, however, the portion of the town which is now inhabited by the higher Hindu castes was called Vāḍi, the enclosure. Both during the Portuguese period and during that of the Dutch the chief trade of Tuticorin was with Ceylon.

Relics of the Portuguese time.

In addition to the Goanese Church at Tuticorin the only other relic of the Portuguese period I have seen is a tomb-stone of a Native Roman Catholic female with a Portuguese name, dated 1618. The oldest thing in Tuticorin appears to be a great Baobab tree, near the church, probably planted there by some early Arab merchants and said by tradition to have been standing there before the church was erected. The Baobab is the Adansonia Digitata, an African tree, called the monkey-bread by the Negroes. The natives of Tuticorin call it "the tree without a name."

TUTICORIN UNDER THE DUTCH.

The first mercantile expedition despatched by the Dutch to the east was in 1595. In 1602 the first Dutch ship was seen in Ceylon, from which period till 1658, when the Portuguese were expelled from Ceylon and the Coromandel Coast, the Dutch and the Portuguese were incessantly at war. Colombo was taken by the Dutch in 1655, three years before the capture of Tuticorin.

CHAPTER III.

Dutch factories.

The Dutch had factories also at Vēmbār, Vaipār, Punnaikāyal, Old Kāyal, Maṇapāḍu, and Cape Comorin. They had several trading out-stations also in places in the interior as at Alvār Tirunagari. At Tuticorin they had latterly a Resident, a more important functionary than Governor. The Dutch did not, like the Portuguese, claim civil authority over the Paravas, the caste of fishermen along the coast, but they professed themselves to be their patrons and protectors, and it was to the interest of the Paravas to keep on terms of amity with their Dutch neighbours, as they thereby gained protection from the exactions and oppressions of the Hindu and Muhammadan rulers of the interior. Before the arrival of the Dutch the residence of the "Jāti-talaivan," the head of the (Parava) caste, is said to have been at Vīrapāṇḍiyanpaṭṭaṇam, but as the Dutch wanted to avail themselves of his local influence, they induced him to take up his abode in Tuticorin.

Head of the caste.

A letter written by a French Missionary, Father Martin, in 1700, quoted in Lockman's Travels of the Jesuits, describes Tuticorin as a flourishing town of more than 50,000 inhabitants. I am very doubtful about the accuracy of this estimate of the population. It is now one of the most flourishing towns on the coast, is a railway terminus, and is governed by a municipality, yet its population, when the census of 1871 was taken, was under 11,000. The same writer describes the natural harbour of Tuticorin as the only one on the coast in which a European vessel could attempt to pass the stormy season, from which it would appear that, in consequence either of the harbour being deeper then than it is now, or of the smaller size of the European vessels, or from both causes, it was possible for European vessels at that time (in 1700) to ride inside the harbour. The writer says: "Tuticorin appears a handsome town to those who arrive at it by sea. We observe several buildings which are lofty enough in the two islands that shelter it; likewise a small fortress built a few years since by the Dutch, to secure themselves from the insults of the idolaters who came from the inland countries; and several spacious warehouses built by the water side, all which look pretty enough. But the instant the spectator is landed, all this beauty vanishes; and he perceives nothing but a large town built mostly of hurdles. The Dutch draw considerable revenues from Tuticorin, though they are not absolute masters of it. The whole fishery coast belongs partly to the king of Madura, and the rest to the prince of Marava, who not long since shook off the yoke of the Madura monarch, whose tributary he was. The Dutch attempted some years since to purchase of the prince of Marava his right to the fishing coast and all the country dependent on it; and for this purpose sent him a splendid embassy with magnificent presents.

Population of Tuticorin.

Appearance of Tuticorin.

The fishery.

CHAPTER III. The prince thought fit to receive the presents, and promised fine things, but has not yet been so good as his word.

Dutch monopoly in the fishery.

The Dutch had already obtained from the king of Madura the monopoly of the fishery of the Tinnevelly coast, and drew a considerable revenue from licenses to fish, which they granted to all applicants at the rate of sixty *ecus*[1] and occasionally more for each vessel employed, the number of licensed vessels amounting often to as many as six or seven hundred. The conch-shell fishery was also theirs within the same limits as the pearl fishery, and yielded a considerable profit. Their ordinary trade was in cloths manufactured at Madura, for which they gave in exchange Japan leather and Molucca spices. The Jesuit Missionary, from whose letters these particulars have been obtained, furnishes an account of the manner in which the pearl fishery was carried on by the Dutch in 1700. Though I have already quoted the descriptions of Marco Polo and Cæsar Frederic, I cannot forbear quoting this description also, which is particularly full and clear:—

MARTIN'S ACCOUNT OF THE PEARL FISHERY IN 1700.

"In the early part of the year the Dutch sent out ten or twelve vessels in different directions to test the localities in which it appeared desirable that the fishery of the year should be carried on; and from each vessel a few divers were let down, who brought up each a few thousand oysters, which were heaped upon the shore in separate heaps of a thousand each, and opened and examined. If the pearls found in each heap were found by the appraisers to be worth an ecu or more, the beds from which the oysters were taken were held to be capable of yielding a rich harvest; if they were worth no more than thirty sous, the beds were considered unlikely to yield a profit over and above the expense of working them. As soon as the testing was completed, it was publicly announced either that there would or that there would not be a fishery that year. In the former case enormous crowds of people assembled on the coast on the day appointed for the commencement of the fishery; traders came there with wares of all kinds; the roadstead was crowded with shipping; drums were beaten and muskets fired; and everywhere the greatest excitement prevailed, until the Dutch Commissioners arrived from Colombo with great pomp and ordered the proceedings to be opened with a salute of cannon. Immediately afterwards the fishing vessels all weighed anchor and stood out to sea, preceded by two large Dutch sloops, which in due time drew off to the right and left, and marked the limits of the fishery; and when each vessel reached its place, half of its complement of divers plunged into the sea, each with a heavy stone tied to his feet to make him sink rapidly and furnished with a sack in which to put his oysters, and having a rope tied round his body, the end of which

[1] The writer being a Frenchman mentions a French coin then current. The *ecu* contained five francs. The name is now obsolete.

was passed round a pulley and held by some of the boatmen. Thus equipped the diver plunged in, and on reaching the bottom filled his sack with oysters until his breath failed ; when he pulled a string with which he was provided, and the signal being perceived by the boatmen above, he was forthwith hauled up by the rope, together with his sack of oysters. No artificial appliances of any kind were used to enable the men to stay under water for long periods : they were accustomed to the work from infancy almost, and consequently did it easily and well. Some were much more skilful and lasting than others, and it was usual to pay them no proportion to their powers—a practice which led to much emulation and occasionally to fatal results. Anxious to outdo all his fellows, a diver would sometimes persist in collecting until he was too weak to pull the string ; and would be drawn up at last half or quite drowned. And very often a greedy man would attack and rob a successful neighbour under water : and instances were known in which divers who had been thus treated took down knives and murdered their plunderers at the bottom of the sea. As soon as all the first set of divers had come up, and their takings had been examined and thrown into the hold, the second set went down. After an interval the first set dived again, and after them the second ; and so on turn by turn. The work was very exhausting, and the strongest man could not dive oftener than seven or eight times in a day ; so that the day's diving was finished always before noon.

"The diving over, the vessels returned to the coast and discharged their cargoes : and the oysters were all thrown into a kind of park and left for two or three days, at the end of which time they opened and disclosed their treasures. The pearls having been extracted from the shells and carefully washed, were placed in a metal receptacle containing some five or six colanders of graduated sizes, which were fitted one into another so as to leave a space between the bottoms of every two, and were pierced with holes of varying sizes ; that which had the largest holes being the topmost colander, and that which had the smallest being the undermost. When dropped into colander No. 1 all but the very finest pearls fell through into No. 2, and most of them passed into Nos. 3, 4, and 5 ; whilst the smallest of all, the seeds. were strained off into the receptacle at the bottom. When all had staid in their proper colanders, they were classified and valued accordingly. The largest or those of the first class were the most valuable : and it is expressly stated in the letter from which this information is extracted that the value of any given pearl was appraised almost exclusively with reference to its size, and was held to be affected but little by its shape and lustre. The valuation over, the Dutch generally bought the finest pearls. They considered that they had a right of preemption : at the same time they did not compel individuals to sell if unwilling. All the pearls taken on the first day belonged by express reservation to the king or to the Sētupati, according as the place of their taking lay off the coasts of the one or the other. The Dutch did not, as was often asserted, claim the pearls taken on the second day.

CHAPTER III.

They had other and more certain modes of making profit, of which the very best was to bring plenty of cash into a market where cash was not plentiful and so enable themselves to purchase at very easy prices. The amounts of oysters found in different years varied infinitely. Some years the divers had only to pick up as fast as they were able, and as long as they could keep under water; in others they could only find a few here and there. In 1700 the testing was most encouraging, and an unusually large number of boat-owners took out licenses to fish; but the season proved most disastrous. Only a few thousands were taken on the first day by all the divers together, and a day or two afterwards not a single oyster could be found. It was supposed by many that strong under-currents had suddenly set in owing to some unknown cause and covered the oysters with layers of sand. Whatever the cause, the results of the failure were most ruinous. Several merchants had advanced large sums of money to the boat-owners on speculation, which were of course lost. The boat-owners had in like manner advanced money to the divers and others, and they also lost their money. And the Dutch did not make anything like their usual profit."

Failures in the pearl fishery.

In the earlier period described by Marco Polo and Cæsar Frederic the pearl fishery seems never to have proved a failure. It was successfully carried on on some bank or another off the coast year after year; but in later times failures frequently occurred. The first of these failures I find mentioned took place about thirty years after Cæsar Frederic's visit and lasted for an entire generation. I have learnt from Dr. Burnell that Barretto, Bishop of Cochin, in an account of the Missions published in 1615, says that the pearl fishery along the coast, of which he gives a description, had failed for thirty-four years. It commenced again, he says, four years ago. This appears to have been the commencement of those frequent failures which have formed the principal characteristic of the fishery in modern times. In 1700 we see Father Martin's account of the failure that year. The first time the fishery was conducted under the East India Company's Government was in 1784, Mr. Irwin being then "Superintendent of Assigned Revenue," or Collector, and this proved a failure. The cause of these failures is, I understand, still involved in mystery.

The earliest date I have found on a Dutch tomb-stone in Tuticorin is 1706.

Dutch alliance with Poligars against the English.

The only reference to the Dutch in Tuticorin contained in Orme will be found further on in connexion with the events of 1760. It would appear that the Poligars were frequently receiving encouragement and assistance from the Dutch.

Later on we learn from Colonel Fullarton that the Dutch entered into a regular alliance with the refractory Poligars of Tinnevelly against the English; nor was this an empty suspicion on the part of the English of that time, founded on national jealousy, for on the capture of Pānjālamkurichi by Colonel Fullarton in 1783 the original of a treaty between the Dutch Government of Colombo and Kaṭṭaboma Nāyaka was found in his fort.

Dates relating to Tuticorin.

I append the principal epochs in the history of the occupation of Tuticorin, though some of these come down to a later date than that at which it was intended that this narrative should terminate.

1. The Dutch took Tuticorin from the Portuguese in 1658.
2. It was taken from the Dutch by the English in 1782.
3. It was restored by the English to the Dutch in 1785, in consequence of the treaty of 2nd September 1783.
4. It was taken again by the English in 1795.
5. And was again given back to the Dutch on the 9th February 1818.
6. It was finally ceded peacefully by the Dutch to the English on the 1st June 1825.

Tuticorin during the Poligar war.

During the last Poligar war Tuticorin was taken from the English and held for a short time by the Poligar of Pānjālamkurichi. This was in the beginning of 1801. A young subaltern was in command of the fort of Tuticorin with a company of sepoys. Unfortunately, while he was defending the fort on one side the native officer under him capitulated and admitted the enemy on the other. The rebels disarmed the sepoys and then set them at liberty, and permitted the English officer to embark in a fishing boat for an English settlement. They found an Englishman, Mr. Baggott, who was Master Attendant of Tuticorin, and carried him off a prisoner. His wife followed him into the fort where the Poligar had taken up his headquarters and petitioned for her husband's life, whereupon the Poligar set him at liberty and restored to him his property. There were many Dutch residents in Tuticorin, but these were unmolested by the Poligar. He considered them neutrals, or indeed friends, for the sympathies of the Dutch all through the troubles in Tinnevelly were rather on the side of the enemy than on ours. A son of this Mr. Baggott was well known in Tuticorin in connection with the cotton trade many years afterwards.

Introduction of cotton screwing.

I have the pleasure of adding here (though they belong to a later period) some particulars respecting the introduction of the screwing of cotton into Tuticorin, kindly furnished me by the gentleman by whom it was introduced, C. Groves, Esq., of Liverpool, now of New Brighton, Cheshire. This was in 1831, nearly fifty years ago. Mr. Groves, who, with his brother, had then a house in Colombo, came across to Tuticorin for the purpose of seeing whether cotton could not be screwed there and shipped directly to England. Up to that time Tinnevelly cotton was either sent unscrewed to Madras, or it was partially screwed in Palamcottah and then sent from Tuticorin to Madras to be properly screwed. Mr. Groves landed at Tuticorin on

CHAPTER III.

the 1st March 1831 and went immediately to Palamcottah to see Mr. Hughes (about whom we hear much in connection with the Poligar wars), who at that time had all the cotton business in his hands. He bought 200 bales of him, and after he left his agent in Colombo sent a vessel to Tuticorin to take these bales to London. This was the first shipment of cotton ever made directly from Tuticorin to Europe, and it answered well financially. The following year, in 1832, Mr. Groves had the first cotton screw erected in Tuticorin in connection with his Colombo business. Afterwards other screws were erected by Madras merchants and others. At first Mr. Baggott, who succeeded his father as Master Attendant in Tuticorin, acted as Groves and Co.'s agent, but after they withdrew he carried on the cotton screwing business on his own account.

Some relics of Mr. Hughes's screw may still be seen lying about near the Court House in Palamcottah.

Tuticorin in 1801.

At the end of 1801, on the termination of the Poligar war, General (then Captain) Welsh was sent to command Tuticorin and superintend the transportation to Penang of seventy of the principal rebels. He describes it as having a large fortified factory, washed by the sea and as a neat little town, the front street of which, on the sea-shore, had some good houses in it. The native inhabitants were about five thousand in number. From this place, he says, the passage by sea to Colombo is performed in one or two days, the gulf always having strong winds blowing, either up or down, which are equally available going or returning. He describes the Factory-house, inhabited by the Dutch Governor, as a very roomy, well-furnished, and very cool habitation, besides which he had a garden house about three miles inland. The Tuticorin fort was destroyed by the English in 1810.

Tuticorin at present.

I may add that the Tuticorin of the present is not only the chief seaport in Tinnevelly, but the principal emporium of the cotton trade in Southern India. It was always a thriving place, but it has recently received a great impetus from being made the southern terminus of the railway connecting Tinnevelly with Trichinopoly and Madras. It is one of the few towns in Tinnevelly which are under municipal government, and had a population in 1871 of nearly 11,000.

CHAPTER IV.

THE PERIOD OF THE NAWAB OF ARCOT, TO MUHAMMAD YUSUF KHAN'S ADMINISTRATION.

END OF THE RULE OF THE NĀYAKAS OF MADURA.

CHAPTER IV.

WE must now return to the closing period of the Nāyaka administration. I must content myself, however, with a brief record of facts, as Trichinopoly had now become the capital of the Nāyaka dominions, instead of Madura, and, this place being still more remote than Madura from Tinnevelly, hardly any reference to Tinnevelly affairs appears in the records of the time. It was not until the contest for the Nawabship of Arcot arose between Chanda Saheb, the *protégé* of the French, and Muhammad Ali, the *protégé* of the English, that Tinnevelly seems to have been regarded as a district of any importance.

In 1731, the last of the Nāyaka kings, Vijayaranga-chokka-nātha, died without issue, and was succeeded by his queen Mīnākshi, who adopted, as heir to the throne, the son of a member of the royal family, in whose name she ruled as regent. A party, however, arose who endeavoured to depose Mīnākshi and set up instead Vangāru Tirumalai, the father of the boy she had adopted. Mīnākshi remained in possession of the fort of Trichinopoly, its palace and treasures, whilst most of the country outside Trichinopoly fell away to her rival.

CHANDA SAHEB AT TRICHINOPOLY.

Hearing of these disputes the Nawab of Arcot sent an army, in 1734, under the command of his son Safdar Ali and his relation and Dewan Chanda Saheb, nominally for the purpose of collecting tribute, but really to seize any opportunity that might offer for getting possession of Trichinopoly. Chanda Saheb after having taken an oath, it is said, on the Koran that he would do nothing to the queen's detriment, was admitted with a body of troops into the city, whereupon he soon succeeded in usurping the entire government, first of the portion of country which remained in the queen's possession, then of Madura and the districts which adhered to Vangāru Tirumalai.

Chanda Saheb's treachery.

Chanda Saheb now threw off the mask and showed himself in his true colours. His schemes had all succeeded; the Madura

CHAPTER IV.

kingdom, or at all events the greater and more important portion of it, was held by his troops; Vangāru Tirumalai was a refugee; and Mīnākshi was a helpless woman, living in a building which he could at any moment seize and turn into a prison. Accordingly, in 1736, he openly proclaimed himself to be the ruler of the Madura kingdom, and, locking up the queen in her palace, assumed to himself all the power and dignity of a sovereign prince. And thinking after awhile that the queen might find means to do him harm, and that she was an expense to him, and finding perhaps that the presence of the poor woman in the palace was productive of unpleasant action on the part of what he supposed to be his conscience, he began to take into consideration the advisability of murdering her. But he was saved the trouble of committing this fresh crime. Her misfortunes were more than Mīnākshi could endure, and, weary of her life, she took poison and placed herself beyond the reach of her betrayer.—Nelson, III. 260.

Chanda Saheb seizes the kingdom.

Mahrattas at Trichinopoly.

The next turn of fortune brought the Mahrattas, for the first time, into the ancient Pāṇḍya kingdom. According to Nelson's account, which seems to be more reliable here than Orme's, Vangāru Tirumalai found that his only chance was to call to his aid a power stronger than that of Chanda Saheb. He therefore begged the Mahrattas of Sattara to come and help him. Accordingly, in 1739, Rāghuji Bhonslai and Futta Singh, the Mahratta generals, marched southward at the head of a large body of cavalry, and after defeating the Nawab of Arcot, Daust Ali, laid siege to Trichinopoly. They were assisted by the King of Tanjore and the other Hindu princes in the neighbourhood, who were anxious to see the Muhammadans expelled. The fortress was on the point of being taken when Chanda Saheb surrendered it, with himself, to the Mahrattas, by whom he was sent a prisoner to Sattara. This took place in March 1741, and the capture of Chanda Saheb had been already preceded by the death of his brother Bada Saheb, who had been appointed Governor of Madura. After taking Trichinopoly the Mahratta leaders appointed Morari Rau to be Governor temporarily, and the latter appointed Appāji Rau to be the Governor of the less important fortress of Madura. The Governor of Madura was doubtless nominally Governor also of Tinnevelly, but there is nothing to show that he was actually in possession of Tinnevelly or any part of it, though he may have made incursions into it, and it may be assumed without hesitation that the Poligars paid very little attention to his commands.

Arrival of the Mahratta army.

Mahrattas in possession of sovereign power.

Sir Mādhava Rau, in his History of Travancore (which I have only seen in the vernacular), mentions some additional particulars (which are repeated in Shungoonny Menon's History of Travancore), respecting the doings of Chanda Saheb and Bada Saheb in the southern districts prior to the siege of Trichinopoly by the Mahrattas. He states that Daust Ali, in order to obtain a kingdom for his eldest son Safdar Ali, sent Chanda Saheb and his brother Bada Saheb to seize upon the Hindu kingdoms in the south. In carrying out this design he states that they attacked Travancore, a circumstance which is not mentioned by any other writer, but in a matter of this kind we may safely trust a local historian in possession of local records. He says that the army of the two Sahebs entered Travancore by the Aramboly Pass in February or March 1740. They returned on hearing of troubles in their own country, and also because the King of Travancore sent them presents. The troubles they heard of were doubtless those that were owing to the approach of the Mahrattas to Trichinopoly.

Muhammadan invasion of Travancore.

Commencement of the Rule of the Nawab of Arcot.

Approach of the Nizam.

In 1743 the Nizam himself entered the Carnatic with a great army, whereupon Trichinopoly and Madura were at once surrendered to him, the Mahrattas not being able to cope with so formidable an antagonist. About this time Vangāru Tirumalai died, and his son retired to Veḷḷaikurichi, in the Sivagangai country, where, it is said, his descendants still live in peaceful obscurity.

Anwar u-din

From the time of the expulsion of the Mahrattas by the Nizam in 1744 until 1747 or 1748 the Madura country appears to have been held by officers commissioned by Anwar-u-din who had been appointed Nawab of Arcot by the Nizam in 1744, and his son Muhammad Ali, who succeeded him in 1749. We may therefore take 1744 as the commencement of the rule of Nawab of Arcot in the districts heretofore held by the Nāyakas, that is, in Trichinopoly, Madura, and Tinnevelly, though it will be seen that till the appearance of the English upon the stage as the Nawab's allies and helpers his rule was little better than nominal. In 1748 Chanda Saheb regained his liberty, and was acknowledged as the Nawab of Arcot by the French, whilst the cause of Muhammad Ali was espoused by the English, and in every district in the south the rival claims of these two princes led to conflict and confusion. We now come, for the first time, in the course of these events to a portion of the history of Tinnevelly in which we shall be able to avail ourselves of Orme's valuable help. Before commencing this portion of the history, however, it will be desirable to mention some particulars respecting the town of Tinnevelly and the fort of Palamcotta, to each of which reference will have to be made from time to time.

The rival Nawabs.

CHAPTER IV.

TOWN OF TINNEVELLY.

The town of Tinnevelly was the more ancient capital of the district, as Palamcotta is the more modern. It is uncertain whether Tinnevelly was anything more than one of the principal towns in the district during the time of the Pāṇḍya kings, but it seems to be certain that during the greater portion of the period of the rule of the Nāyakas at Madura it was regarded as the capital of the southern portion of their dominions. Its only rival in importance was Strivillyputtoor (Srīvillipputtūr), where some of the Nāyaka rulers liked occasionally to reside. It is strange that, though the capital of a district, and the rich centre of a rich neighbourhood, it seems never to have been fortified. Probably there was always a stronghold at Palamcotta, only about three miles off, and this may always have been regarded as a sufficient protection, as we know it was at a later period, to the town of Tinnevelly and the towns and villages in the neighbourhood. Tinnevelly should be written Tiru-nel-vēli, and the meaning of this name is "the sacred rice hedge," from tiru (the Tamilised form of the Sanskrit śrī), sacred; nel, paddy, rice in the husk; and vēli, hedge. The Sthalapurāṇa of the Tinnevelly temple represents nel as meaning "bambū," as well as rice or paddy. Hence it gives also the meaning, the sacred bambū hedge. This meaning would be a very appropriate one, but I can find no trace of nel having the meaning of paddy in any dictionary. The absence of this meaning in the dictionary does not quite settle the matter, but it renders this derivation somewhat doubtful. The ordinary legendary derivation of the name is founded, not on any reference to a bambū, but on the ordinary meaning of nel, paddy, rice in the husk. The story goes, that a man belonging to this place (which then must have had a different name, bambū hedge ?) went to the river to bathe, having previously spread out a quantity of paddy near his house to dry. Whilst he was bathing a heavy shower of rain came on. He left the river and ran home expecting to find his paddy wet and spoiled, when, behold ! he found that the rain had fallen all round the paddy, but not a drop on the paddy itself. Hence he praised Siva as he who had made a hedge round his paddy, and built a temple to his honour, whereupon the name of the place was altered to Tiru-nel-vēli, the sacred rice hedge. The Sthalapurāṇa gives both meanings and gives the legend quoted above in confirmation of the second. It identifies Tiru-nel-vēli with Dārukāvana, where the rishis, who were Siva's opponents, performed sacrifice, and the linga here with the linga that grew there out of a bambū. Hence at a certain festival a young bambū plant is made to appear to be growing beside the linga. Siva's consort, as worshipped in the Tinnevelly temple, is called Kāntimatī (fem. of Kāntimat), the lovely one. The town of Tinnevelly is now a municipality, with a population of 20,000.

Town of Tinnevelly always a place of importance.

Meaning of "Tiru-nel-vēli."

PALAMCOTTA.

Palamcotta, the present capital of the district of Tinnevelly, is a municipality, with a population of about 18,000. It is situated about a mile to the south of the Tāmraparṇī, whilst Tinnevelly lies two miles to the north. Intercourse and traffic between the two towns have been facilitated since 1844 by a beautiful bridge over the Tāmraparṇī, erected by Colonel Horsley at the sole expense of a wealthy native, Sulochana Mudaliyār. Few traces now remain of the fortifications of Palamcotta, most of which have been removed as no longer necessary, but when the English first arrived in Tinnevelly they found it the strongest fort south of Madura. It was a fortified town, as well as a fort, and was defended by a double system of fortifications, the outer line lower than the inner, with a complete set of bastions and strongly fortified gates. The whole of the fortifications were cased with cut stone. It was the only stone-built fort in the Tinnevelly District. Madura was frequently taken and retaken, but Palamcotta lay so far to the south that it was never exposed to any attack from Europeans, and never sustained any serious assault from natives. If Tippu Sultan had succeeded in taking the northern Travancore lines in 1789 and bringing his forces round by Tinnevelly and Madura for the purpose of taking the English in the rear, as he hoped to do, the strength of the fort of Palamcotta might have been put to the test.

Palamcotta the strongest fort south of Madura.

Tippu's designs.

Palamcotta is in Tamil Pāḷaiyangkōṭṭai, which means camp-fort, from pāḷaiyam, originally a camp, secondarily an estate held on military tenure, and kōṭṭai, a fort. The Telugu form which corresponds to pāḷaiyam is pālem (u), from which it might be concluded that the early English got their pronunciation and spelling of the word from their Telugu followers. The derivation I have here given is that which accords best with the spelling of the name in actual use, but the derivation of the name almost universally accepted by natives requires it to be written, not Pāḷaiyangkōṭṭai, but Pāḷaiyankōṭṭai. They represent Pāḷaiyan as a man's name, admitting however that it may have originally been a title. As a title it would mean the holder of a camp. This would virtually be identical with the more common title Poligar, and it is noticeable that tradition represents this Pāḷaiyan as a Canarese man, and that the ordinary title of a Poligar in Canarese is Pāḷeya, *i.e.*, Pāḷaiyan. This derivation is confirmed by the circumstance that the water channel which brings water of irrigation from the Pāḻavūr anicut to Palamcotta and the neighbourhood is always called Pāḷaiyan-kāl, that is, Pāḷaiyan's channel. The native idea is that the fort of Palamcotta, that is, the old fort, or the oldest portion of the more recent fort, was built by this Pāḷaiyan about 200 years ago. This of course is a very vague estimate. It would place the erection of

Meaning and origin of the name.

the fort in the time of the Nāyakas of Madura, whereas if the founder of the fort and the excavator of the channel were really, as tradition invariably states, a Kannaḍi, which there is no reason to doubt, it would appear probable that he lived in the still earlier period when the Kannaḍi kings of Dwāra-samudra held supreme power. Two reasons may be adduced, on the other hand, for adhering to the derivation which accords with the ordinary spelling and consequently regarding the first part of the name of Palamcotta as denoting a camp. One is that Palamcotta is called, it is said, in some old documents Vilangkuḷam Pālaiyam, the camp of Vilangkuḷam; another is that there is a large village to the westward called Mēlapāḷaiyam, the western camp. Pāḷaiyam, however, in the latter case may mean merely a suburb.

Age of the founder.

A poetical name for Palamcotta is Mangai-nagaram, the city of the maiden, but who this maiden was is at present unknown. A tradition survives of the existence of a town in ancient times on the site on which the fort of Palamcotta was subsequently built. A petty king lived there, it is said, called Prānda Rājā, who has given his name to various places in and about the fort, including a tank.

It had always been noticed that many of the stones in the walls of the Palamcotta fort had previously been portions of some Hindu temple, and this is clearly proved by the carvings and inscriptions that remain. These temple stones were found not only in the outer fort, which was undoubtedly built in the Nawab's time, but also in the walls of the inner fort, which is said to have been erected by a Hindu. One explanation of this, given by natives, is that Pāḷaiyan, though a Hindu, did not scruple to avail himself of the stones of abandoned temples, and in particular that he made use of the stones of a great wall which formerly surrounded the temple at Muttukrishṇapuram, a place about five miles east of Palamcotta, a temple which had been erected about a hundred years before the fort by one Mayilērum Perumāḷ Mudali, a convert from the Saiva to the Vaishṇava religion. Another and more probable explanation is that, not only was the outer fort wholly built by the Muhammadan commandant during the period of the Nawab's rule, but that the wall of the inner fort also was completed and strengthened by him, when he not only made use of the stones of dilapidated temples, but also, it is said, pulled down some temples for the purpose. One of the temples said to have been appropriated in this manner was that at Mūrttiyāpuram, a place on the banks of the river near Palamcotta. The outer and lower fort used to be called the Piḷḷaikkōṭṭai, or child fort. This name was probably given to it on account of it being the smaller of the two, but some natives assert that it meant the fort of the Piḷḷai, that is, of Muhammad Yusuf Khan, commonly called

Construction of the fort.

Outer and inner forts.

simply Khan Saheb, who was often called "the Piḷḷai," in consequence of his having originally been, not a Muhammadan, but a Veḷḷala Hindu, a caste to which the title Piḷḷai pertains. CHAPTER IV.

During the time the East India Company carried on trade they had a Commercial Agent in Palamcotta. They had a warehouse for their goods, and also a cotton-screw near the Agent's house on the banks of the river. See in page 83 the account of the first introduction of cotton screwing into Tuticorin. The first reference to Palamcotta in Orme is in 1756, in which it was stated that the ramparts of the fort were in ruins, and only capable of resisting an enemy which had no battering cannon. Muhammad Yusuf Khan was appointed to command the troops and carry on the revenue administration in Madura and Tinnevelly in the same year, soon after which doubtless he commenced to make the fort of Palamcotta a place of greater strength. It appears to have been garrisoned by the English from 1765. The first reference to it in the journals of Swartz, the eminent missionary, is in 1771, when he speaks of it as a fort belonging to the Nawab, but having an English garrison. The earliest date in the English churchyard in Palamcotta is 1775.

English garrison.

FIRST HELP RENDERED BY THE EAST INDIA COMPANY TO THE NAWAB'S GOVERNMENT IN TINNEVELLY, AND FIRST ENGLISH EXPEDITION INTO TINNEVELLY.

ORME, Vol. I.—"The countries lying between the Coleroon and the extremity of the peninsula did not openly throw off their allegiance to Muhammad Ali, but were lukewarm in his interests: he therefore (in 1751) sent 2,500 horse and 3,000 peons, under the command of his brother Abdul-rahim, together with a detachment of 30 Europeans, to settle the government of Tinnevelly, a city lying 160 miles to the south of Trichinopoly, and capital of a territory which extends to Cape Comorin. Abdul-rahim met with no resistance from the people of the country, but found it difficult to restrain his troops from revolt; for most of the officers being renters, were indebted to their prince as much as he was indebted to their soldiers, and expected as the price of their defection that Chanda-saheb would not only remit what they owed to the Government, but likewise furnish money for the pay of their troops. However, great promises, and the vigilance of Lieutenant Innis,* who commanded the English detachment, prevented them from carrying their schemes into execution; but the same spirit of revolt manifested itself more openly in another part of Muhammad Ali's dominions.

The first Englishman in Tinnevelly.

"Aḷam Khan, a soldier of fortune, who had formerly been in the service of Chanda-saheb, and afterwards in that of the King of Tanjore, had lately left this prince and came to Madura, where his reputation

* Probably the first Englishman who was ever seen in Tinnevelly.

CHAPTER IV.

as an excellent officer soon gained him influence and respect, which he employed to corrupt the garrison, and succeeded so well, that the troops created him governor, and consented to maintain the city under his authority for Chanda-saheb, whom he acknowledged as his sovereign.

Importance of Madura.

"The country of Madura lies between those of Trichinopoly and Tinnevelly, and is as extensive as either of them. The city was in ancient times the residence of a prince who was sovereign of all the three. Its form is nearly a square 4,000 yards in circumference, fortified with a double wall and a ditch. The loss of this place, by cutting off the communication between Trichinopoly and the countries of Tinnevelly, deprived Muhammad Ali of more than one-half of the dominions which at this time remained under his jurisdiction. On receiving the news, Captain Cope offered his services to retake it. He was unsuccessful and had to march back to Trichinopoly with a greatly diminished force. This occurred in 1751. In 1755, we reach events in the history of Tinnevelly of greater interest and importance.

Mahfuz Khan's expedition.

"At the request of the Nawab a force of 500 Europeans and 2,000 sepoys was, in 1755, ordered to proceed into the countries of Madura and Tinnevelly to assist in reducing them to his obedience. Mahfuz Khan (the Nawab's elder brother) was appointed by the Nawab his representative in those countries, but from first to last was found to be either a lukewarm, useless friend, or an open enemy. The Nawab himself accompanied the expedition as far as Manapar (Maṇa-pārai), a place in the hands of a rebellious Poligar, a little to the south of Trichinopoly, and then returned. The whole force was commanded by Colonel Heron, an English officer recently arrived in the country, whilst the sepoys were under the special command of a native."

COLONEL HERON'S EXPEDITION AND MUHAMMAD YUSUF KHAN.

The commander of the native force under Colonel Heron was a distinguished native soldier called Muhammad Yusuf Khan. I give here some particulars respecting this person not mentioned by Orme.

Career of Muhammad Yusuf Khan.

For some time prior to 1754 Yusuf Khan had been employed as Commander of the Company's Native troops, in which capacity he showed so much ability and zeal and gave such entire satisfaction to his European superiors, that at the recommendation of General Lawrence, then Commander-in-Chief, the Government, on the 25th March 1754, conferred upon him a regular commission as the "Commander of all the Company's Sepoys," and at the same time presented to him a gold medal as a mark of their favour.

We have seen that Yusuf Khan led a force into Tinnevelly in 1756 for the purpose of restoring order. The Government issued their instructions to him through Captain Calliaud on the 14th March that year, from which it appeared that he was entrusted, not only with the command of the forces, but with the collection of the revenue and the settlement of all difficulties connected therewith. The only condition was that he was to report his proceedings from time to time to Captain Calliaud and to remit all moneys to him. His success as civil administrator from that time till 1763 appears from Mr. Lushington's statements, which will be quoted hereafter. He is well remembered by the people by the name of Kānsā, a local corruption of Khan Saheb. His time is commonly spoken of as "the days of Kānsā."

The Rāja of Ramnad's proposals.

"Colonel Heron's force took Madura without opposition, and whilst there they received an important deputation from the Poligar Marawar (that is, from the Setupati, the Poligar or Rājā of Ramnad) whose country adjoins the north-eastern portion of Tinnevelly. The Poligar apologized for his conduct during the war in siding with Chanda-saheb and the Mysoreans, desired to be pardoned for that offence, and intreated to be received into alliance with the English, under whose protection he promised to remain faithful to the Nawab. As a proof of the sincerity of his intentions, he offered to give the Company two settlements on the sea-coast of his country, opposite to Ceylon, which, as he justly observed, would greatly facilitate their future communications with Tinnevelly, for they had at present no other way of approaching that city but by a tedious and difficult march of several hundred miles; whereas reinforcements might come by sea from Madras or Fort St. David in four or five days to the settlements he intended to give, from which the march to Tinnevelly was no more than fifty miles. These offers Colonel Heron deemed so advantageous, that without consulting the Presidency, he entered into an alliance with the Poligar, and, as a mark of the English friendship, gave his deputies three English flags, with permission to hoist them in their country, wheresoever they should think proper. After the business was concluded Colonel Heron took Kovilgudi, a fortified temple where the fugitive Governor of Madura had taken refuge, and from which the English soldiers unthinkingly carried off with other plunder those little copper idols, which brought upon them so much trouble in the Nattam Pass on their way back.

Idols carried off.

"The army arrived at the town of Tinnevelly about the middle of March. The renters, both of the capital and of the open country, acknowledged the Nawab without hesitation, but many of the neighbouring Poligars made pretences to evade the payment of the tribute due from them. The most considerable of these was Catabomonaig, whose country lies about fifty miles north-east from Tinnevelly, and it being imagined that the inferior Poligars would not hold out long after he should have submitted, a detachment of 200 Europeans and 500 sepoys, with two field pieces, was sent to reduce him."

The Poligar Kaṭṭaboma Nāyaka.

This Catabomonaig (properly Kaṭṭaboma Nāyaka) was the Poligar of 'Panialam crutch' (properly Pānjālam kurichi) a fort near the present taluk town of Ōṭṭapiḍārum. This was the first of many expeditions sent against this place, the last expedition,

CHAPTER IV.

and the only one perfectly successful being in 1801. Each of the later Poligars was also called Kaṭṭaboma Nāyaka, this name being the family title. The chieftain of Colonel Heron's time was Jagavīra Kaṭṭaboma Nāyaka. He died in 1760. His successor, who died in 1791, was still more decidedly hostile to the English, and this hostility culminated in the next two, one of whom was hanged by Major Bannerman in 1799 and the other by Colonel Agnew, together with the Sivagangai Poligar, in 1801. The expedition sent by Colonel Heron against Pānjālam kurichi came to nothing, as his whole force was almost immediately recalled to Trichinopoly.

Fate of his successors.

"Some days after the despatch of that expedition another detachment, consisting of 100 Europeans and 300 sepoys, with two field pieces, was sent to attack the fort of Nelli-kotah, situated forty miles to the south of Tinnevelly. These troops set out at midnight, and performed the march in eighteen hours: the Poligar, startled at the suddenness of their approach, sent out a deputy, who pretended he came to capitulate, and promised that his master would pay the money demanded of him in a few days; but suspicions being entertained of his veracity, it was determined to detain him as a pledge for the execution of what he had promised, and he was delivered over to the charge of a guard. The troops were so much fatigued by the excessive march they had just made, that even the advanced centinels could not keep awake, and the deputy perceiving all the soldiers who were appointed to guard him fast asleep, made his escape out of the camp, and returned to the fort, from whence the Poligar had sent him only to gain time in order to make the necessary preparations for his defence. This being discovered early in the morning, it was determined to storm the place, of which the defences were nothing more than a mud-wall with round towers. The troops had brought no scaling ladders, but the outside of the wall was sloping, and had many clefts worn in it by the rain, so that the assault, although hazardous, was nevertheless practicable. It was made both by the Europeans and sepoys with undaunted courage in several parties at the same time; each of which gained the parapet without being once repulsed, when the garrison retired to the buildings of the fort, where they called out for quarter; but the soldiers, as usual in desperate assaults, were so much exasperated by a sense of the danger to which they had exposed themselves, that they put all they met to the sword, not excepting the women and children, suffering only six persons out of four hundred to escape alive. Sorry we are to say, that the troops and officers who bore the greatest part in this shocking barbarity were the bravest of Englishmen, having most of them served under Colonel Lawrence on the plains of Trichinopoly: but those who contemplate human nature will find many reasons, supported by examples, to dissent from the common opinion, that cruelty is incompatible with courage."

Capture of Nellicotah.

Massacre of the defenders of the fort.

For many years I was unable to find any trace of this Nellicotah, which from another statement seems to have been near Kaḷakāḍu, nor any tradition of its sanguinary capture. I began to be inclined, therefore, to hope that this story was not altogether true. At length I discovered the place—a ruined fort in a lonely situation, about 36 miles to the south-west of Palamcotta and 6 to the east of Aramboly. The correct name was Nattakōṭṭāi, not Nellikōṭṭai, but with this unimportant exception the traditions of the place agree with Orme's account. The owner of the fort seems to have been a person of some importance, as he is traditionally styled a Rājā, and the site of his residence in the fort is still called "The Palace Mound." The survivors are said to have taken refuge in a place called Panjalingapuram in Travancore.

"The revenues which had been collected during this expedition did not amount to the expenses of the army: part of the tributes were embezzled by Mahfuz Khan, and part was likewise diminished by the presents which Colonel Heron, with too much avidity, consented to receive from those who had accounts to settle with the Government. In the meantime Mahfuz Khan, in concert with Colonel Heron's interpreter, contrived every means to make the state of the province appear less advantageous than it really was; and then made an offer to take the farm of the Madura and Tinnevelly countries together at the yearly rent of 15,00,000 rupees: this proposal was seconded, as usual, by the offer of a considerable present, which Colonel Heron accepted, and gave him the investiture of the countries.

Colonel Heron's dishonourable conduct.

"The detachment which had been sent against Kaṭṭaboma Nāyaka had been as far to the north-east as Shillinaikenpettah, the principal fort of the Poligar (by which I supposed 'Yellanāyakkanpaṭṭi must be meant). The Poligar on their appearance entered into a negotiation, paid some money in part of the tribute due from him, and gave hostages as security for the rest: some money was likewise received from several inferior Poligars, but the whole collection did not exceed 70,000 rupees. As soon as the troops received the orders to return, they summoned Kaṭṭaboma Nāyaka to redeem his hostages; but he, knowing that they would not venture to stay any longer in his country, made some trifling excuses, and without any concern suffered them to carry the hostages away with them. On the 2nd of May Colonel Heron quitted Tinnevelly, but, instead of proceeding directly to Trichinopoly, suffered himself to be persuaded by Mahfuz Khan to march against Nellitangaville, a fort situated about thirty miles to the west of Tinnevelly, belonging to a Poligar who had with much contumacy refused to acknowledge the Nawab's authority. On the march he was joined by the detachment from the north-east."

Colonel Heron's fruitless delay.

Thus far Orme. By Nellitangaville, a name which occurs very frequently in the accounts of these times, we are to understand Nerkaṭṭansevval (Nel-kaṭṭam-sevval) the head-quarters of the "Pulitaver," that is, the Pūli-dēvar, the hereditary title of the Poligar of Avuḍeiyārpuram, in what is now the Sankaranainār Kovil Taluk, a chief whose territories were of small extent, but

CHAPTER IV.

whose influence at that time throughout the whole of the western part of Tinnevelly, through the fame of his abilities, was immense.

The Pūli Dēvar's fort.

"It was the misfortune of Colonel Heron to place the utmost confidence in his interpreter, and to be constantly betrayed by him; for before the army arrived in sight of the fort, this man had informed the Poligar that they had no battering cannon, and that they would not remain long before the place: the Poligar, therefore, secure in his fort, which was built of stone and very strong, answered the summons with insolence; upon which the field pieces and two cohorns fired smartly upon the walls for several hours; but this annoyance producing no effect, another message was sent, offering that the army should retire, provided he would pay 20,000 rupees. The Poligar relying on the information which he had received from the interpreter, and encouraged by this relaxation in the terms which were at first proposed to him, answered with great contempt, that such a sum could not be raised in his whole country, and that he knew the value of money too well to pay a single rupee. By this time the army were much distressed for provisions of all kinds, and the sepoys ready to mutiny for want of pay; both which Mahfuz Khan had promised, but had neglected to supply. It was therefore determined to march away to Madura, where they arrived, accompanied by Mahfuz Khan, on the 22nd of May."

Colonel Heron's fate.

As Colonel Heron now disappears from the history of Tinnevelly I must take this opportunity of adding that he was soon after recalled to Madras, tried by a court-martial, and dismissed the service.

RENEWED CONFLICTS.

"It soon appeared that whatsoever submissions had been made in the provinces of Madura and Tinnevelly during the expedition of Colonel Heron had proceeded entirely from the dread of the English troops, whose intrepidity as well as the efficacy of their arms far exceeded the modes of any warfare which had ever been seen in these countries; and they were no sooner departed than the Colleries swarmed abroad again into all the subjected districts that lay exposed to their depredations, whilst their chiefs confederated to prevent by more effectual means the establishment of Mahfuz Khan's authority. From this time, these countries became a field of no little conflict, and continued so for several years, which renders it necessary to explain the various interests which produced the present confusions, fertile afterwards of more.

Three Patan leaders.

"When Alam Khan, in the beginning of the year 1752, marched from Madura to the assistance of Chanda-saheb, then besieging Trichinopoly, he left the countries of Madura and Tinnevelly under the management of three Patan officers, named Muhammad Barki, Muhammad Mainach, and Nabi Cawn Catteck (Nabi Khan Kattak); the first of these was generally known by the appellation of Mianah, the second of Moodemiah (Mohi-ud-din Mian?), but Nabi Khan Kattak by his own proper name. They appear afterwards to have acknowledged the sovereignty of the Nawab, but it is certain that notwithstanding that acknowledgment they continued to act only for themselves; granting immunities, remitting tributes, and even selling forts and districts for presents of ready money. This venality, coinciding with the spirit of independence and encroachment common to all the Poligars, procured them not only wealth, but attachments. In this mode of licentious government, they continued agreeing amongst themselves in the division of the spoil, and ruling with much power, until the expedition of Colonel Heron; when Mianah, who commanded in the city of Madura, abandoned it, and took refuge with the neighbouring Poligars of Nattam; Moodemiah and Nabi Khan Kattak retired from Tinnevelly to the Poligar of Nellitangaville, better known by the name of Pūli Dēvar. All the three only waited for the departure of the English troops to dispute the dominion with Mahfuz Khan when left to himself. Amongst other alienations, Moodemiah had sold to the King of Travancore a range of districts extending thirty miles from Kaḷakāḍu to Cape Comorin, and lying at the foot of the mountains which separate Travancore from Tinnevelly. The fort of Kaḷākaḍu with several others of less defence were sold with the districts. With the assistance of a Flemish officer, named De Lanoy, the King of Travancore had disciplined in the method of European infantry a body of 10,000 Nairs, the military tribe of Malabar Coast, and besides these Nairs maintained 20,000 other foot of various arms."

CHAPTER IV.

Their misgovernment.

Travancore army.

The Travancore King to whom the Nawab's agent Moodemiah is said to have sold a portion of Tinnevelly near Kaḷakāḍu, in or about 1752, was Mārtāṇḍa Varmā, who succeeded to the throne in 1729 and lived till 1758.

"The districts which the king had purchased of Moodemiah were maintained by about 2,000 of his irregular foot, who, having no enemies to oppose, were sufficient for the common guards and military attendance, which in Hindustan always support the authority of the government in the collection of the revenues. But these troops on the arrival of the army with Colonel Heron at Tinnevelly were so terrified by the reports of their exploits, and especially by the sanguinary example in their neighbourhood, at the sacking of Nellicotah, that they abandoned, not only their districts, but the fort of Kaḷakāḍu likewise, which were soon after taken possession of by a detachment of 300 horse and 500 foot sent by Mahfuz Khan from Tinnevelly. As soon as the English troops retired from before Nellitangaville, and it was known that they were recalled to Trichinopoly, Moodemiah went to Travancore in order to encourage the king to recover the districts which his troops had abandoned; at the same time the Pūli Dēvar, besides letting loose his Colleries to plunder, formed a camp ready to move and join the Travancores as soon as they should arrive. Mahfuz Khan received intelligence of these schemes and preparations on his return from Nattam and Madura, and immediately proceeded to Tinnevelly.

Travancore troops retire.

"Besides the 1,000 sepoys belonging to the Company which were left with him by Colonel Heron, he received 600 more raised and sent

CHAPTER IV.

Mahfuz Khan's policy

to him by the Nawab; but these were in no respect equal to the Company's, who had been trained in the campaigns of Trichinopoly; and Mahfuz Khan himself, having no military ideas, excepting that of levying troops, had augmented the force he brought with him from the Carnatic to 2,500 horse and 4,000 foot. Five hundred of the horse and a 1,000 of the foot were left to defend the city of Madura and its districts; but the Company's sepoys proceeded with him to Tinnevelly. Before he arrived there, Moodemiah had returned with 2,000 Nairs, and the same number of other foot, which the King of Travancore had entrusted to his command. They were joined by the forces of the Pūli Dēvar near Kaḷakāḍu; where the troops stationed by Mahfuz Khan in these parts assembled, gave battle, and were routed. Three hundred of the Nawab's sepoys were in the action, who, to lighten their flight, threw away their muskets, which were collected by the Pūli Dēvar's people, and regarded by them as a very valuable prize. Immediately after this success, the enemy invested the fugitives in the fort of Kaḷakāḍu; but before they could reduce it, the troops of Travancore returned home, pretending they were recalled by the emergency of some disturbances in their own country; however, it is more probable, that they retreated from the dread of encountering the army, and more especially the cavalry of Mahfuz Khan, which were approaching. Moodemiah went with them, and the Pūli Dēvar retired to his fort and woods, against which Mahfuz Khan proceeded, and encamped near the fort, which he could not take; but in this situation repressed the incursion of the Pūli Dēvar's Colleries into the districts of Tinnevelly, and content with this advantage, gave out with ostentation that he had settled the country. These vaunts were soon contradicted. In the month of September, Moodemiah returned from Travancore, with a large body of troops, and again defeated those of Kaḷakāḍu, who in this battle suffered more than in the former; for 200 of their horse and 500 sepoys were made prisoners; and, what aggravated the loss, it was the time of harvest, when the rents are collected, of which the Travancores took possession, and maintained their ground. Mahfuz Khan, nevertheless, continued before the Pūli Dēvar's place; whose troops in the month of November cut off a detachment of two companies of sepoys which had been sent to escort provisions. They were of those belonging to the Company, and the commanders of both were killed.

Defeat of Mahfuz Khan's troops

Another defeat.

"Mahfuz Khan, after loitering before the Pūli Dēvar's place until the middle of November, returned to Tinnevelly, in order to borrow money for the payment of his troops, which could only be obtained by giving assignments of the land to the lenders. Meanwhile the Pūli Dēvar with Moodemiah and Nabi Khan Kattak, encouraged by their late successes extended their views. The Pūli Dēvar, more from the subtilty and activity of his character, than the extent of his territory and force, had acquired the ascendance in the councils of all the western Poligars of Tinnevelly. Of these, the most powerful was the Poligar of Vadagherri (Vaḍagarai). The Vaḍagarai Pollam was identical with that of Chokkampatti, whose districts adjoin on the west to the Pūli Dēvar's, and exceeded them in extent and inhabitants. He

Western Poligars.

nevertheless conformed to whatsoever the Pūli Dēvar suggested, and sent his men on every call. The Poligars to the eastward of Tinnevelly were under the direction of Kaṭṭaboma Nāyaka. The Pūli Dēvar proposed a union between the two divisions; but Kaṭṭaboma Nāyaka, as well as his dependent of Eṭṭaiyāpuram, having given hostages to Colonel Heron, who were in prison at Trichinopoly, feared for their safety, and refused. The Poligars of Madura, whose districts lie along the foot of the mountains to the west, were solicited with more success, and promised their assistance. Mianah, the fugitive colleague of Moodemiah, and Nabi Khan Kattack, at the same time spirited up the Poligars of Nattam to join the league, of which the immediate object was nothing less than to get possession of the city of Madura. Such an extensive confederacy could scarcely be kept a secret. The Presidency of Madras received intelligence of it from Captain Calliaud, who commanded in Trichinopoly, and the Nawab from the Governor of Madura. They were, and with reason, greatly alarmed; for Madura, by its situation, extent, and defences, is the bulwark both of its own and the territory of Tinnevelly, over neither of which Trichinopoly could maintain any authority, if Madura were wrested from its dependence. The Presidency, although from the first convinced of Mahfuz Khan's incapacity, had hitherto, from deference to the Nawab, treated him with indulgence and respect: but seeing now the whole brought into risk by the successes and designs of the Poligars, they determined to take the administration of these countries into their own hands.

CHAPTER IV.

Eastern Poligars.

Fears for Madura.

"A native of Tinnevelly, named Moodilee (Mudali) came about this time to Madras, and made proposals to take the whole country at farm; but it required time to gain the knowledge necessary to adjust the terms." [Mudali is not a personal name, but a caste title. The person referred to was one of the Daḷavāy Mudalis, a family by which this office was held for a long series of years. His own name was probably Tīttārappa (properly Tīrttārappa) Mudali. Daḷavāy is a hereditary name in the family]. "Meanwhile it was immediately necessary to provide for the defence of the country; but as no part of the European force could be spared from the services of the Carnatic, it was resolved to send a 1,000 sepoys, which were to be joined by those left with Mahfuz Khan, as well as those belonging to the Nawab, and to put the whole of this body under the command of Muhammad Yusuf Khan. Yusuf Khan proceeded to Trichinopoly soon after the English army returned from Vellore; and Captain Calliaud was instructed to send him forward with the appointed force and equipments.

A Mudali's proposals.

Madura to be defended.

"Meanwhile the Pūli Dēvar, Nabi Khan Kattak, and Moodemiah with their allies had proceeded to action, and in the middle of February entered the districts of Nadamundulum (Naḍumaṇḍalam)* which occupy a considerable extent, about midway between the city of Madura and the Pūli Dēvar's place. The fort which commands these districts is called Chevelpetore (Srīvilliputtūr), and is situated at the

Srivilliputtūr.

* Naḍumaṇḍalam, the middle circuit, denoted what is now the Taluk of Srivilliputtūr.

CHAPTER IV.

foot of the western mountains, about 45 miles south-west of Madura. The troops stationed for the defence of the fort and districts were under the command of Abdul Rahim, a half-brother to the Nawab and to Mahfuz Khan, the same with whom Lieutenant Innis marched into those countries in the year 1751, and of Abdul-mally, another relation to the family. The foot, excepting 200 sepoys, were the usual rabble allotted to the guard of villages; but there were 500 horse, esteemed the best in Mahfuz Khan's service, who, proud of their prowess, and their quality of Muhammadans, held the enemy, as Indians and of no military reputation, in utter contempt, and encouraged their own commanders to risk a battle; in which they were surrounded, but with sufficient gallantry and considerable loss cut their way through, and retired to Srīvilliputtūr. Here Abdul Rahim and Abdul-mally intended to maintain themselves until succours should arrive, either from Madura or Tinnevelly; but the men of the cavalry, dissatisfied for want of pay, and fearful of losing their horses through want of provisions during the siege, marched away, and many of them joined the enemy: the fort was immediately invested and soon after reduced, but the two commanders escaped again.

The cavalry beaten.

"This success encouraged the Madura Poligars, who had hitherto only looked on to join according to their promise; and the whole camp now consisted of 25,000 men, of which 1,000 were cavalry. Their chiefs, animated by this superiority of numbers, determined to give battle to Mahfuz Khan at Tinnevelly, before they attacked the city of Madura. By this time Mahfuz Khan had prevailed on Kaṭṭaboma Nāyaka, by the cession of some districts and the promise of other advantages to join him with the forces of the eastern Poligars, and had likewise levied all the horse and foot of whatsoever kind which could be procured; but his principal strength was the 1,500 horse he had before, and the body of 1,000 sepoys belonging to the Company under the command of Jemaul Saheb, whose losses had been recruited with effective men. The battle was fought on the 21st of March, within seven miles of Tinnevelly, and was maintained with more obstinacy than usual in the fights of this country, until Moodemiah fell; he was cut down charging bravely with his cavalry. The rout then became general; 2,000 Colleries were slain, and 300 horse, with all the cannon and elephants, were taken. This victory saved Madura, for it entirely broke the army of the confederates, all of whom, and the Pūli Dēvar with as much terror as any, hurried from the field to the shelter of their respective homes."

Mahfuz Khan's victory near Tinnevelly.

MUHAMMAD YUSUF KHAN'S ADMINISTRATION.

Yusuf Khan's approach.

"The news of the victory was brought to Trichinopoly on the 24th of March, by which time Muhammad Yusuf was ready to proceed. His detachment consisted of 1,200 sepoys, 100 Caffries, 150 Colleries, and 4 field pieces, with an 18 pounder managed by Europeans. For some time before the departure of the detachment, Kaṭṭaboma Nāyaka and the Poligar of Eṭṭaiyāpuram had been treating with Captain Calliaud for the redemption of their hostages, and it was agreed that the money should be paid on their being delivered to Tondiman. Muhammad Yusuf, therefore, took the hostages with him, and directed his march to Puducottah, the principal town belonging to Tondiman, to whose care they were surrendered. On the 6th May 1756 he arrived at Madura, from whence having employed some days in refitting his carriages and stores, he proceeded to the fort of Srīvilliputtūr, which, notwithstanding their late defeat, remained in the hands of the enemy; but they abandoned it on his appearance. Leaving a sufficient garrison to defend it in future, he proceeded across the Nadamundulum (Naḍumanḍalam) country to Cayetar (Kāittār) a town about 25 miles (18 miles) north of Tinnevelly, where Mahfuz Khan was waiting for him with his victorious but inactive army.

Yusuf's want of money.

During this progress Muhammad Yusuf had not been able to collect any money from the revenues for the maintenance of his troops, because the ravages of the Poligars had ruined most of the villages and cultivated lands of the country through which he passed; and the real detriment of these devastations was increased by the pretences they furnished the landholders to falsify their accounts, and plead exemptions for more than they had lost. He found Mahfuz Khan in greater distress than himself, unable either to fulfil the stipulations at which he had rented the country from Colonel Heron, or to supply the pay of the Company's sepoys left with him under the command of Jemaul Saheb, or even to furnish enough, exclusive of long arrears, for the daily subsistence of his own troops. This distress naturally deprived him of the necessary authority over the Jamadars, or officers of his cavalry, who in Hindustan, as the ancient mercenary Captains of Italy, hire out their bands and gain not a little by the bargain. Every kind of disorder likewise prevailed in all the other departments of his administration, at the same time that the indolence and irresolution of his own character confirmed all the evils which had been introduced into his government.

Mahfuz Khan's misgovernment.

Kaṭṭaboma Nāyaka procrastinates.

From Kaittār, Mahfuz Khan and Muhammad Yusuf moved with the whole army to the woods of Eṭṭaiyāpuram, which lies about 30 miles to the east of Kaittār. Kaṭṭaboma Nāyaka and the Poligar of Eṭṭaiyāpuram were in the camp. The former had by his agents redeemed his hostages at Puducottah, but the other still delayed; and this motion was made to excite his fears, although no threats were used. He nevertheless still procrastinated, and his alliance was at this time deemed too valuable to compel him by the exercise of hostilities. From Eṭṭaiyāpuram they crossed the country to Coilorepettah (Kollārpaṭṭi, commonly called Kollāpaṭṭi) a strong fort situated near the great road. It belonged to a Poligar named Condam-Naigue (Kaṇḍama Nāyaka) who on the first summons promised without hesitation to pay the tribute demanded of him; but continued day after day to send pretences and excuses instead of the money. At length Muhammad Yusuf, finding himself trifled with, battered and then stormed the fort. It was well defended. The serjeant of the Coffres, and eight of that company were killed, and 65 were wounded: the Colleries suffered

Capture of Kollarpaṭṭi.

CHAPTER IV. still more, and all who were not killed were made prisoners, amongst whom the Poligar himself. From Kollārpaṭṭi, the whole army proceeded to Srīvilliputtūr, and encamped under this fort on the 10th of June, where most of the neighbouring Poligars, terrified by the example of Kollārpaṭṭi, made their submissions either in person or by their agents. Even the Pūli Dēvar with his usual duplicity sent one with proposals of reconciliation, and the Poligar of Ēḷāyirampaṇṇai, whose place lies between Kollārpaṭṭi and Srīvilliputtūr, redeemed his hostages. But the Poligar of Calancandan (Kollamkoṇḍān, now included in the Sēttūr Zemindary), which lies 13 miles north-east of Srīvilliputtūr, paying no regard to the usual summons, Muhammad Yusuf marched and attacked his fort, which was abandoned after a slight resistance."

THE POLIGARS.

It is desirable, before going further, to take this opportunity of explaining a little more particularly the position occupied by the Poligars and why they proved themselves on all occasions so troublesome. See also the account of the first introduction of this class into Tinnevelly in Chapter III.

A pāḷaiyam or pollam, as the English wrote it, was not merely a jaghire or zemindary. It was a district conferred by the sovereign on a chief, the holder of which, the Pāḷaiyakaran or Poligar, was bound, not only to pay his lord annually peishcush or tribute, but also to help his lord in his wars. Pāḷaiyam literally means a camp, Pāḷaiyakaran (as has been shown in p. 58) means the chief of a camp. It may, therefore, be concluded that originally the Poligar was the leader of a body of armed men, who placed his services at the disposal of his sovereign, and who held the district he received in return for his services by a military tenure. He was always to consider his territory, not as a nāḍu, a country, but as a pāḷaiyam, an encampment. Hence, though the sovereign may have exercised civil and criminal rights in the portion of country that remained in his own direct possession, he does not seem to have attempted to exercise, or even to have claimed, the right of exercising any civil or criminal jurisdiction whatever within the limits of his Poligars' domains. If his tribute were paid and his feudatory sent him assistance in his wars his demands were satisfied. A very considerable portion of Southern India, south of Trichinopoly, had passed into the hands of Poligars. In Madura and Dindigul hardly any thing remained in the sovereign's possession; and in Tinnevelly the greater part of the country north of the Tāmraparnī river was in the possession of Poligars.

Origin of the Poligars.

Relation of the Poligar to his lord.

When the English first made their acquaintance with Tinnevelly they found the whole country, whether in the hands of the Poligars or nominally in the hands of the central government, in a state of anarchy and misery, of which it is scarcely possible in these times to form any conception. This lamentable condition of things was partly owing to the feebleness and corruption of the Nawab's Government, and partly to the chronic lawlessness and incessant wars and rebellions of the Poligars. At the time referred to, when the Nawáb at last determined to call in the help of the English, there were thirty-two of these hereditary chieftains in Tinnevelly, each of whom had entrenched himself in a fort and surrounded himself with a large body of armed retainers. The constant endeavour of each was to encroach on the domains of his neighbours, and especially to swallow up any villages, revenues, or rights that still remained in the possession of the central government.

Anarchy of the Poligar districts.

The armed retainers of the Poligars are generally called "Colleries" by Orme and the writers of that period. This word had its origin in Trichinopoly and Tanjore, the tribe or caste of freebooters living in that neighbourhood, with whom the English frequently came into contact, being called Kaḷḷars, which literally means "thieves." The English rendering of this word was sometimes "Colaries," more frequently "Colleries," sometimes "Collieries;" and wherever a similar class of people were found they were usually called by the English by the same name, though in Tinnevelly the armed retainers of the Poligars, who manned their forts and went on their marauding expeditions, did not belong to the Kaḷḷar caste properly so called, but were generally either Maravas or Nāyakas. Where the Poligar was a Nāyaka, as the Poligar of Pānjālamkurichi, his retainers were doubtless mostly Nāyakas; where he was a Marava, like Pūli Dēva (Dēva is the caste title of the Maravas) his retainers were chiefly Maravas. The English do not seem to have recognized any distinction between these various castes or classes of "Colleries," but they were deeply impressed with the manliness and audacity of all they encountered. Orme describers the "Colleries" of the western districts of Tinnevelly near the mountains thus—

Who were the "Colleries?"

"The Colleries of this side of the Tinnevelly country possess nothing of the ugliness or deformity which generally characterize the inhabitants of the hills and wilds of India. They are tall, well-made, and well-featured. Their arms are lances and pikes, bows and arrows, rockets and matchlocks, but whether with or without other weapons, every man constantly wears a sword and shield. In battle the different arms move in distinct bodies; but the lancemen are rated the most eminent, and lead all attacks. This weapon is eighteen feet long. They tie under the point a tuft of scarlet horse-hair, and when they attack horse, add a small bell. Without previous exercise, they assemble in a deep column, pressing close together, and advance at a long, steady step, in some degree of time, their lances inclining forward, but aloft, of which the elasticity and vibration, with the

Description of armed Colleries.

CHAPTER IV. jingle and dazzle scare the cavalry; and their approach is scarcely less formidable to infantry not disciplined with fire-arms."

The lance referred to is called in Tamil a "Vallaiyam." The name survives, but it is scarcely possible to see a specimen of this formidable weapon now.

KĀVAL.

The claim of *kāval* was a favourite device employed by the Poligars for the purpose of extending their power. Every village from time immemorial had its Kāval-kāras (written by the English Cauwalgars) or watchmen, who were remunerated for their services by a small fee. The right of exercising this function and of levying a still heavier fee was in time claimed by the Poligars and their dependents, and this claim had been so generally submitted to that Mr. Lushington found in 1799 that out of 2,113 villages in Tinnevelly the *kāval* of 1,635½ was in the hands of the Poligars. Another step in advance was taken when the Poligars, wherever they found they could not appoint their own dependents to the *kāval* of a village, rigorously levied an annual contribution on the Kāval-kāras appointed by others. But a still more formidable engine of oppression was the *disai-kāval*, or district watch, erroneously called *dēśa-kāval* by the Europeans which the Poligars managed in time to add on to the village *kāval*. This may originally have only been a fee for the exercise of a wider guardianship, especially over roads and wastes, than the village watchmen were able to undertake. Probably also the amount claimed was originally insignificant and was paid willingly. Mr. Lushington said in 1799, it was originally only one-tenth of the amount which was claimed in his time, but it had been arbitrarily increased, especially between 1740 and 1760, when the province of Tinnevelly was convulsed by the struggle of contending interests. This contribution was levied by the Poligars from the defenceless villagers as the price of their forbearing to plunder them, and was confirmed by the strength of the Poligars and the inability of the Nawab's Government to enforce a due authority over them. Mr. Lushington adds, that "when this contribution is not quietly submitted to, torture and the whip are applied, the whole people of the village put into confinement, every occupation interdicted, the cattle pounded, the inhabitants taken captive to, and not unfrequently murdered in, the pollams (the Poligar's own domains), and in short every outrage of violence and cruelty is committed until their purposes are obtained.

Different kinds of kaval.

Miscellaneous exactions.

"The influence of the Poligars is also used in calling upon the inhabitants for additional assessments on various pretences, such as hunting batta, marriage expenses, presents for vakeels, &c., undefined and unlimited; and such is the dread which they have inspired into the cultivators of the circar lands by remaining armed in the midst of a country otherwise in profound peace, that these requisitions are never resisted."

I add here from the "Tinnevelly Manual" Mr. Stuart's account of the Poligars and their system of kāval :—

"The Maravar or Vannian caste peculiar to Southern India has a history of its own of considerable interest. To this class belonged most of the Poligars or feudal chieftains who disputed with the English the possession of Tinnevelly during the latter half of the last and the first years of the present century; as feudal chiefs and at the same time heads of a numerous caste or class of the population, and one whose characteristics were eminently adapted for the role of followers of a turbulent chieftain, bold, active, enterprising, cunning, and capricious, this class constituted themselves, or were constituted by the peaceful cultivators, their protectors in times of bloodshed and rapine when no central authority capable of keeping the peace existed.

Explanation of kaval payments.

"Hence arose the systems of dēsha (disai) and stalam kaval, or the guard of a tract of country comprising a number of villages against open marauders in armed bands, and the guard of separate villages, their houses and crops, against secret theft. The feudal chief received a contribution from the area around his fort in consideration of protection afforded against armed invasion. His servants of the same caste, spreading themselves among the villages, received fees and sometimes rent-free land for undertaking to protect the property of the villagers against theft, or to restore an equivalent in value for anything so lost. Claims to dēsha kaval fees as well as to village kaval fees are of common occurrence to the present day."

It will be interesting now to quote and compare Mr. Stuart's account of the Zemindars of the present time :—

"The condition of the tenants under the different zemindars, or the mittahs into which some ancient zemindaris have been divided by sale owing to improvidence and misfortune, is by no means so satisfactory as that of the ryots in Government taluks. The assessments are heavier everywhere, and, as a rule, the system of dividing the crop prevails for the wet lands, a system much less advantageous to the cultivators than that of fixed money-rents universal in Government taluks, as these are sufficiently moderate to leave the ryots ample encouragement to improve their lands.

Relation of Zemindars to their tenants.

"In the main, however, the tenants of the zemindaris are fairly off, and, especially in the cotton lands, many of them are substantial farmers well out of reach of poverty. The exchange of puttas and muchilkas has been strictly enforced by the Courts of late years, and has introduced much stability and independence as well as a good deal of frivolous and vexatious litigation between landlord and tenant. Money-rents are universally assessed upon dry lands, but numerous vexatious cesses are still a fruitful source of dispute between the zemindars and their ryots.

Number of Zemindaries.

"Of the whole district 27 per cent. is zemindari. There are twenty zemindaris proper and thirty-six mittahs, most of them portions of

CHAPTER IV. zemindaris broken up by the improvidence and misfortunes of ancient zemindars, sold for debts and purchased by rich Vellalars, Natukottai Chetties, and other moneyed native gentlemen.

"The twenty zemindaris vary in size from 863 acres, with a peishcush of 25 rupees, to 337,581 acres, assessed at a peishcush of 88,376 rupees.

"The thirty-six mittahs, in like manner, vary from 234 acres, assessed at 213 rupees, to 18,716 acres, paying Rupees 6,423 to Government.

"The principal Zemindar of Ettiapuram is by caste a Tottian. His ancestors supported the British Government in the wars with the Poligars, and received in recompense, besides other gifts, a large share of the confiscated lands of the principal Poligar rebel chief of Panjalamkurichi. This zemindari is situated to the north-east of the district, and consists chiefly of black cotton plains sufficiently fertile and populous, yielding a revenue to the zemindar of about three lakhs of rupees.

"The Zemindaris of Sevagiri and Setur come next, and are situated at the foot of the Western Ghauts in the north-west portion of Tinnevelly. They contain a considerable area of well-irrigated land supplied by streams from the mountains, but the dry lands are of the red and sandy series, and, except under wells, are of little value.

"These zemindars, as well those of Uttumalai, Singampatti, and Arkad (the two latter under the Court of Wards) are all of the old Poligar Maravar families. Their estates are carefully managed and their ryots in the main contented. Some of the finest of the ghaut forests of Tinnevelly are claimed as the property of the Zemindaris of Sevagiri, Setur, and Singampatti, but these mountain boundaries are mostly in dispute with the Government.

"The ancient Zemindari of Chokampatti, having a peishcush of Rupees 25,550, came under the hammer in 1868, and fell in eighteen lots to various persons who are now known as Mittahdars."

Mr. Stuart then gives a list in detail of the various zemindaris and mittahs in Tinnevelly, with their area, population, and peishcush.

COLONEL FULLARTON'S DESCRIPTION OF TINNEVELLY.

I cannot do better than give here the description of the condition of Tinnevelly written in 1783, at the time when misrule was at its height, by Colonel Fullarton. This account derives additional interest from the fact that it is the first description of Tinnevelly, as far as I am aware, which ever saw the light. By inserting this account here, I may seem somewhat to anticipate events, but I think it will be found that the narrative, especially in connexion with the affairs of the Poligars, will henceforth be more intelligible.

"The last, but not the least, considerable of your southern territories is Tinnevelly. It is a hundred and fifteen miles in length and seventy miles in breadth. A ridge of inaccessible mountains divides it on the north from the wild valleys of Watrap and Outumpollam, belonging to Tipoo Sultan. It stretches to the confines of Madura and Ramnad on the north-east and east, reaches to the sea upon the south, and borders on the west with the Rājāhship of Travancore, both terminating near Cape Comorin. Nature has been bountiful to this province. Its surface is generally flat, from the sea-coast, till it approaches the mountains on its northern boundary. The rivers by which it is intersected ensure luxuriant crops of rice, and the driest parts yield cotton in abundance. The productions of the neighbouring Island of Ceylon would flourish here, and thus render us the rivals of the Dutch in the cinnamon trade; but the peculiar tenure under which the country has been held, the convulsions it has endured from the first intrusions of the Musselmen in the course of this century, and the depravity of its rulers, have counteracted the benefits of nature. Even when a native rājāh governed Tinnevelly, the flat and open country only was reduced. This was let for specific sums to great renters, who were invested with despotic powers, and harassed the peaceful subjects; while various leaders, who possessed considerable territory, maintained armed forces, and withheld their stipulated tribute on the first appearance of disturbance. These chiefs, as well as their subjects, are called Poligars; they amount, at present, to thirty-two, capable of bringing thirty thousand brave, though undisciplined, troops into the field. They have also fortified towns and strongholds in the mountains, whither they retire in cases of emergency. Besides the territory that these Poligars possess under the range of hills that form the northern boundary of Tinnevelly, many of them hold ample tracts in the flat and cultivated country. Adverse to industry, they suffer their own possessions to remain waste, while they invade each other, and plunder their industrious neighbours. Such is the dread of these ravagers, that every district in the province has been forced to purchase their forbearance by enormous contributions. In this situation you have rather cause to wonder that your Superintendent, Mr. Irwin, should have been enabled to procure so large an increase of revenue, than that its produce should, in no recorded period, have borne any proportion to its natural advantages."

Productiveness of Tinnevelly.

Bad government neutralises its advantages.

Plundering habits of the Poligars.

It would be unfair, however, even to the Poligar if I allowed his rival in oppression, the "renter," to pass unnoticed, and here I must avail myself again of Colonel Fullarton's graphic and vigorous description. The Poligar survives to our time, though only in his peaceful descendant, the Zemindar, but the "renter," who in Colonel Fullarton's time, as all through the period of the Nawab's government, was such a formidable reality, has left behind him no representative, and has passed entirely into oblivion.

The "Renter's" oppressions.

"It was not possible for the English Government entirely to repress the misconduct of inferior instruments* who are eager to perpetuate

* "The black agents who manage the whole detail of collection in the different districts."—*Colonel Fullarton's Note.*

CHAPTER IV. oppression and to enforce unusual measures by unprecedented means. The situation of the country rendered it necessary to continue the practice of renting extensive districts to the highest bidder; although every precaution was adopted to prevent the abuse of power, still the collections could not be enforced unless an unrestrained authority were vested in the renter. His object, too, frequently is, to ransack and embezzle, that he may go off at last enriched with the spoils of his province. The fact is, that in every part of India where the renters are established, not only the ryot and the husbandman, but the manufacturer, the artificer, and every other Indian inhabitant, is wholly at the mercy of those ministers of public exaction.

The farmer's proportion.

"The established practice throughout this part of the peninsula has for ages been to allow the farmer one-half of the produce of his crop for the maintenance of his family, and the recultivation of the land; while the other is appropriated to the Circar. In the richest soils, under the cowle of Hyder, producing three annual crops, it is hardly known that less than forty per cent. of the crop produced has been allotted to the husbandman. Yet renters on the coast have not scrupled to imprison reputable farmers, and to inflict on them extreme severities of punishment, for refusing to accept of sixteen in the hundred, as the proportion out of which they were to maintain a family, to furnish stock and implements of husbandry, cattle, seed, and all expenses incident to the cultivation of their lands. But should the unfortunate ryot be forced to submit to such conditions, he has still a long list of cruel impositions to endure. He must labour week after week at the repair of water-courses, tanks, and embankments of rivers. His cattle, sheep, and every other portion of his property is at the disposal of the renter, and his life might pay the forfeit of refusal. Should he presume to reap his harvest when ripe, without a mandate from the renter, whose peons, conicopolies, and retainers attend on the occasion, nothing short of bodily torture and a confiscation of the little that is left him could expiate the offence. Would he sell any part of his scanty portion, he cannot be permitted while the Circar has any to dispose of; would he convey anything to a distant market, he is stopped at every village by the collectors of Sunkum or Gabella (transit duties), who exact a duty for every article exported, imported, or disposed of. So unsupportable is this evil, that between Negapatam and Palghautcherry, not more than three hundred miles, there are about thirty places of collection, or, in other words, a tax is levied every ten miles upon the produce of the country; thus manufacture and commerce are exposed to disasters hardly less severe than those which have occasioned the decline of cultivation.

Helplessness of the ryot.

Extraordinary powers of the renter.

"But these form only a small proportion of the powers with which the renter is invested. He may sink or raise the exchange of specie at his own discretion; he may prevent the sale of grain, or sell it at the most exorbitant rates; thus, at any time he may, and frequently does, occasion general famine. Besides maintaining a useless rabble, whom he employs under the appellation of peons, at the public expense, he may require any military force he finds necessary for the business of oppression, and few inferior officers would have weight enough to justify their refusal of such aid. Should any one, however, dispute those powers, should the military officers refuse to prostitute military service to the distress of wretched individuals, or should the Civil Superintendent [the 'Superintendent of Assigned Revenues,' the Collector of that time] remonstrate against such abuse, nothing could be more pleasing to the renter; he derives, from thence, innumerable arguments for non-performance of engagements, and for a long list of defalcations. But there are still some other not less extraordinary constituents in the complex endowments of a renter. He unites, in his own person, all the branches of judicial or civil authority, and if he happens to be a Brahmin, he may also be termed the representative of ecclesiastical jurisdiction. I will not enlarge on the consequences of thus huddling into the person of one wretched mercenary of those powers that ought to constitute the dignity and lustre of supreme executive authority."

CHAPTER V.

MUHAMMAD YUSUF KHAN'S ADMINISTRATION, TO THE CAPTURE OF MADURA AND HIS DEATH.

Further Operations of Muhammad Yusuf Khan.

Chapter V.

We must now return to Orme and to 1756.

"Yusuf Khan with Mahfuz Khan, and their respective troops, remained at Srīvilliputtūr during the months of June and July till all the adjoining Poligars had either made their submissions or seemed willing to be quiet. He then requested Mahfuz Khan to march out of the country, and proceed with his troops to Arcot, according to the injunctions of his brother the Nawab, who would be ready to settle accounts with him, and pay what arrears might be due to his soldiery. He then allotted six companies to garrison Srīvilliputtūr, and guard the adjacent country; and with the rest, about 2,000, in which were included those levied by the Nawab, and sent to Mahfuz Khan, he proceeded from Srīvilliputtūr on the 1st of August, and on the 10th arrived at the town of Tinnevelly.

Financial value of Madura.

"By this time the Presidency of Madras had made arrangements for the management of these countries, and concluded an agreement with Mudali, the native of Tinnevelly, who came to Madras on this purpose in the month of April. The district of Madura proper was then considered exceedingly unproductive. It had shrunk into very small dimensions through the encroachments of the territories of the Poligars, and what remained hardly repaid the cultivation. From these detriments and defects, the annual revenue of the whole territory seldom exceeds 1,20,000 rupees; at the same time that the maintenance of the city, its garrison, and other military posts in the country raise the expenses to triple this sum. On the other hand, the country now rated under Tinnevelly is of much greater extent and fertility, commonly yielding a revenue from 11 to 12,00,000 rupees a year; but should Madura and its districts be in the hands of an enemy, the country of Tinnevelly would be constantly exposed to the most ruinous attacks, and could receive no support from Trichinopoly; which renders it necessary to maintain the one at a certain loss, as the only means of securing the advantages which may be derived from the other. The family of Mudali, having for 100 years been employed in farming districts in both countries, had in this long course of time rented every part, and knew the properties of each. He accordingly refused to undertake the districts of Madura, but offered to rent the country of Tinnevelly for three years, at the annual rent of 11,00,000 rupees, clear of all expenses, to be paid at three periods in each year; for which purpose he was to be invested with the usual authorities of jurisdiction, civil and criminal. He obliged himself to maintain not less than 1,000 of the Company's sepoys, under the command of such officers as the Presidency should appoint; and engaged to produce, within three months from the contract, the security of substantial *shroffs*, or money-changers, for the regular payment of the stipulated sums. The agreement was concluded in the beginning of July; immediately on which Mudali appointed agents, and sent orders to place flags with the Company's colours, in the cultivated lands; and soon after proceeded himself to administer his office in person. Muhammad Yusuf, on his arrival at Tinnevelly, found that the agents of Mudali had, in the beginning of their occupations, been over-ruled and insulted by Meir Jaffier, who had hitherto managed the country for Mahfuz Khan. The dispute indeed had ceased, but the grudge still remained: and to prevent any farther effects, Muhammad Yusuf ordered Meir Jaffier to depart immediately to Madura, but permitted him to take three field pieces which belonged to him, and whatsoever retinue he chose; he at the same time detached five companies of sepoys to reinforce the garrison of Madura and ordered them to protect and watch Meir Jaffier and his people on the road. In the meantime a sort of revolution took place in the fort of Madura in the interest of Mahfuz Khan, who thought himself injured by the appointment of another renter. On the 13th September the renter Mudali arrived in the camp with two companies of sepoys which had escorted him from Trichinopoly through the countries of the two Maravars, and the next day he continued his journey towards Tinnevelly.

Financial value of Tinnevelly.

Agreement with the Mudali.

Meir Jaffier's behaviour.

"The family of Mudali by their occupation of renting the countries had formed connections with most of the Poligars dependent on Tinnevelly, more especially with the Pūli Dēvar and Kaṭṭaboma Nāyaka; and on his invitations the Pūli Dēvar and several others met him on the road. Kaṭṭaboma Nāyaka and others sent their agents; all came, as usual, with considerable retinues, and in the midst of this multitude Mudali entered the town of Tinnevelly on the 27th of September and proclaimed his commission. But the colleries of the Poligars, whom no consideration can restrain from thieving, committed night robberies in the town and adjacent villages. Several of them were taken and punished by the Company's sepoys, on which others stole the effects of the sepoys themselves, who, irritated as much by the insult as the loss, transferred their resentment on Mudali, because he suffered the Poligars to remain in the town, and continued to treat them with civility. At the same time the troops of Travancore renewed their incursions into the districts about Kaḷakāḍu; and Nabi Khan Kattak, who had concealed himself ever since the defeat in which Moodemiah was killed, now appeared again, made overtures of reconciliation to Mahfuz Khan, which were accepted; and having enlisted 400 of the horse which Mahfuz Khan had disbanded, kept traversing the country between Madura and Tinnevelly.

Influential position of the Mudali.

Nabi Khan Kattak.

CHAPTER V.

"Meanwhile, the dissension between the Company's sepoys and their renter at Tinnevelly had increased, and had produced evil consequences. Mudali by his contract was only obliged to furnish the pay of the sepoys employed by himself; but Muhammad Yusuf, by a wrong interpretation, imagined that Mudali was obliged to maintain the whole number wheresoever employed; and moreover to discharge the arrears of their pay, of which two months were due on his arrival in the country. In consequence of this mistake, Jemaul Saheb, who commanded the sepoys in Tinnevelly, demanded the amount, and on Mudali's refusing to pay it, confined him under a guard for several days, during which he ordered the Pūli Dēvar and the other Poligars to quit the town with threats of severe punishment if they remained any longer. They departed immediately; but, instead of returning to their homes, the Pūli Dēvar went to Nabi Khan Kattak and offered him his assistance, both in men and money; and by their united representations, Kaṭṭaboma Nāyaka was induced to join their league. At the same time the troops of Travancore kept their ground, and continued their depredations in the districts dependent on Kaḷakāḍu. The hopes of the advantages which might be derived from these confusions were much more agreeable to the disposition of Berkatoolah (Barakat-ulla) than the success of his negotiation with the English, by which he was to obtain nothing more than the pardon of his offences; and in the middle of November, as soon as the ground was sufficiently dry to march, he went from the city and put himself at the head of the 500 horse, which had gone out before, and were now joined to those of Nabi Khan Kattak and the troops of the Poligars. The whole force amounted to 10,000 men, of which 1,000 were horse. They were assembled about forty miles to the south of Madura, and instead of proceeding directly to the south, in the open country, struck to the east into the districts of Kaṭṭaboma Nāyaka, a part of whose woods extends within a few miles of the town of Tinnevelly. Issuing from thence at night, before their approach was known, they entered the town at daybreak by several avenues, which were weakly guarded; for Mudali a few days before had marched with the greatest part of the sepoys and his other force about twenty miles to the south-east, in order to protect the districts of Alwar Tinnevelly (Aḻvār Tirunagari), against which he had been led to believe the enemy designed to bend their attack.

The Poligars ordered out of Tinnevelly.

Fort of Palamcotta.

"The enemy remained two days in Tinnevelly, plundered much, but committed no cruelties; and during this delay Mudali regained the fort of Palamcotta, which stands on the other side of the river about three miles from the town. The fort is spacious, but the ramparts were in ruins, nevertheless capable of resisting an enemy, which had no battering cannon. Matchlocks and musketry were fired without any mischief for two days, during which the cavalry ravaged the country round. Muhammad Yusuf, who still continued at Secunder maly (Skandar malai), before Madura, received no certain intelligence of the enemy's design until four days after they were in motion; he immediately struck his camp and proceeded towards Tinnevelly, and they hearing of his approach collected all their parties and advanced to give him battle. The two armies met on the 1st of December at

Battle at Gangai koṇḍan.

CHAPTER V.

Gangadoram* (Gangai koṇḍān) about twenty (twelve) miles north of Tinnevelly. The inferiority of numbers was much more than compensated by superior skill; the Company's sepoys faced the enemy on every side with advantage of situation and discipline, and the field pieces were fired with much execution against the cavalry, whose fortunes depending on the preservation of their horses, they quitted the contest and the field. The next day Muhammad Yusuf proceeded to Tinnevelly, and from thence marched into the desolated districts, in order to give heart to the inhabitants, and recall them to their occupations.

Self sacrifice of a Brahmin at Srīvilliputtūr.

"The Poligars returned to their woods, and Barakat-ulla with his cavalry to Madura; but Nabi Khan Kattak went to Srīvilliputtūr, and not having means to attack the fort, in which were some sepoys, attempted to escalade the pagoda in the town, on which one of the Brahmins went to the top of the high tower over the gateway, and after a short but loud prayer of execration, threw himself headlong to the pavement, which dashed out his brains; the enemy, although Muhammadans, were so much afraid of incurring the general detestation of the country, if their attempts against the pagoda should incite any more acts of such enthusiastic devotion, that they immediately retreated out of the town.

Captain Calliaud's plans.

"In the meantime, Captain Calliaud, whilst regulating the affairs of the renter at Tinnevelly, acquired intelligence that the confederates were treating with the Mysoreans at Dindigul for aid against the English and their adherents, the Pūli Dēvar offering to pay down 5,00,000 rupees, and the Jamadars of Mahfuz Khan to give up the districts of Sholavandān, in which are comprised a strong pass and the only road between Madura and Dindigul. Nevertheless it was not intended that the country, when conquered, should be given either to the Mysorean or Mahfuz Khan. It was to be restored to a descendant of the ancient kings, who lived in concealment in the country of the greater Maravar: and Mahfuz Khan was to have a suitable establishment in Mysore. This news increased the necessity of attacking Madura as soon as possible; but the arrangements at Tinnevelly were not finished until the 10th of April, on which day Captain Calliaud began his march from thence with 180 Europeans, 2,500 sepoys, six field pieces, and 500 horse: Muhammad Yusuf commanded the sepoys, and Mudali what horse were levied by himself. Six companies of sepoys were left for the defence of Tinnevelly, and the same number in the fort of Palamcotta.

"A few days after, Barakat-ulla and Nabi Khan Kattak went with 500 horse to the Pūli Dēvar's place. The Commander Muhammad

* Gangadaram. This stands for Gangai koṇḍān, commonly called Genguṇḍān, a village on the Chitra-nadi, or Chittar, near which is a railway station. Gangai koṇḍān, receiver of the Ganges, is a name of Siva, and the popular notion is that as Siva is worshipped there under that name the Ganges reappears in that place as in so many other places in various parts of India. The Sanskrit form of this name is Gangādhara, which Orme's informants seem to have followed, instead of the Tamil, perhaps because there is a town of that name in the Tanjore country. There was a Chōḷa prince of the name of Gangai koṇḍān, who is said to have been made king of the Pāṇḍyas, with the title of Sundara Chōḷa Paṇḍya.

CHAPTER V.

Lieutenant Rumbold's movement.

Yusuf, on receiving the summons of Lieutenant Rumbold, had returned from the districts he was visiting to Tinnevelly, where leaving as before 1,000 sepoys, he proceeded with the rest, about 1,800, towards Madura. The renter Mudali, naturally timorous, resolved to accompany the greater force, and besides his usual retinue was attended by 100 good horse which he had lately levied. They arrived on the 16th of December at Gangādaram, where Muhammad Yusuf, hearing of Lieutenant Rumbold's departure from Madura, halted to observe the motions of the enemy, and remained there until he received information that Nabi Khan Kattak and Barakat-ulla had passed to the Pūli Dēvar's, on which he proceeded te Srīvilliputtūr, and encamped there, in order to awe the Poligars in this part of the country from joining the enemy. During the march Mudali sent one of his relations named Aḷgapa (Aḷagappa) to negotiate a reconciliation with the Pūli

Pūli Dēvar's character.

Dēvar, and offer some districts as the fee of his alliance. The Pūli Dēvar, who never refused or kept his word on any occasion, sent an agent with Aḷagappa to the camp at Srivilliputtūr, and at the same time sent his troops to join Barakat-ulla and Nabi Khan Kattak. The agent, under the usual pretext of doing honour to his embassy, was accompanied by two or three hundred of colleries. Muhammad Yusuf entirely disapproved of the intercourse, as he knew the Pūli Dēvar's character, and that some of his people were at this very time plundering to the westward of Tinnevelly. Unfortunately during this mood of indignation five of the agent's colleries were taken steal-

Yusuf's excessive severity.

ing horses and oxen belonging to the camp, and being brought to Muhammad Yusuf he immediately put them to death by blowing them off from the mouth of a cannon—a sanguinary execution, not

Pūli Dēvar's dealings with Mahfuz Khan.

infrequent in Hindustan, and in this case atrocious. The agent, with all his retinue of colleries, immediately ran away from the camp; and their injury determined the Pūli Dēvar, perhaps for the first time in his life, to act with some good faith toward those with whom he was connected. But knowing the irresolution of Mahfuz Khan, he, with his usual cunning, was afraid of trusting him in Madura exposed to the overtures and negotiations of the English, and insisted that he should come from thence to Nellitangaville and remain at all times under his own ward. In consequence Barakat-ulla, who was with the Pūli Dévar, sent for Mahfuz Khan, who in the end of December went from the city with 500 horse."

It would be tedious and unprofitable to record in detail every incident that occurred from month to month. It will be better to content myself with mentioning anything that occurred which seemed to have some special features of interest.

"Barakat-ulla and Nabi Khan Kattak set off from Nellitangaville with 500 horse, leaving Mahfuz Khan with the Pūli Dēvar. Skirting

The Poligar of Sivagiri.

along the hills they halted one evening at the fort of the Poligar Vaniah of Shevagherry ["Vaniah" stands here for Vanniya, the caste name or title of a branch of the Marava caste, to which the Sivagiri Poligar belonged. The Ēḷāyiram paṇṇei Poligar was also a Vanniya]. The Sivagiri Poligar having been gained over by Muhammad Yusuf sent out his colleries, who, in the middle of the night, fell upon this body of cavalry, and with their screams and fireworks dispersed the whole and took 40 of their horses. CHAPTER V.

Mahfuz Khan takes the field.

"The rebellious Jamadars who had seized and retained possession of Madura expected assistance from Mahfuz Khan with the western Poligars of Tinnevelly, but were doomed to be disappointed. Five hundred horse and a thousand foot remained with Mahfuz Khan at Nellitangaville, when Barakat-ulla left him and came away to defend Madura, which Calliaud at the same time was marching to attack with the main body of the English troops from Tinnevelly. As soon as Calliaud was out of sight, Mahfuz Khan and the Pūli Dēvar took the field, and were joined by other Poligars, which all together made up a camp of ten thousand men. This army marched from Nellitangaville in the latter end of April, and advanced beyond Āḷvār Kurichi within fifteen miles of Tinnevelly, but were deterred by the sepoys left there from attempting the town; nor did they immediately plunder or terrify the inhabitants of the open country, because the harvest, from which they intended to collect money, would not be reaped until the middle of June; however, they published their mandates that all who were accountable to the renter Mudali should then become accountable to them. In the meantime Mahfuz Khan negotiated with the King of Travancore for assistance, with the proffer of Kaḷakāḍu and all the other districts to which the king had ever made any pretension; but lest this should fail he, with his usual uncertainty, renewed his negotiations with the English, and sent off an agent with letters to Calliaud, proposing to rent the country from them on the security of substantial shroffs. Lieutenant Rumbold received the offers, whilst Calliaud was returned to the relief of Trichinopoly, and thinking them worth attention, sent a Jamadar of Sepoys named Ramanaig, with an intelligent Moorman, to confer with Mahfuz Khan in his camp. They were accompanied by an escort of fifty sepoys; but just before their arrival, Mahfuz Khan had received information that six companies of sepoys of the twelve left at Tinnevelly and Palamcotta were ordered to join the camp at Madura; which changed his schemes and, instead of negotiating, he surrounded the two deputies and their escort with his horse, and threatened to put them all to the sword, if they did not send an order to the sepoys in garrison at Palamcotta to deliver the fort to him. The deputies with their escort stood to their arms, and said they would rather die; but just as the fight was going to begin one of Mahfuz Khan's Jamadars named Alli Saheb declared his detestation of the treachery and joined the sepoys with the horse of his command, on which the rest recollected themselves and retired; but Alli Saheb having still some suspicions for the safety of the deputies and their escort marched with them to Palamcotta and delivered them safe into the fort.

Mahfuz Khan's attempted treachery.

"Soon after the six companies of sepoys began their march from Tinnevelly to Madura, and the harvest began on which the enemy's army entered the town, where Mahfuz Khan proclaimed his dominion which his agents and dependants exercised with much violence and

Mahfuz Khan's exactions.

CHAPTER V.

injustice. Even the shroffs, or bankers, did not escape, although the necessity and neutrality of their occupation protects their persons and property throughout Hindostan from the violence either of the despot or the conqueror. The main body of his army invested the fort of Palamcotta, which the sepoys within easily defended, and with loss to the enemy; but there was danger from scarcity of provisions; to prevent which Basappa Nāyaka, the commander of the sepoys, solicited the assistance of the Poligar Kaṭṭaboma Nāyaka, who stipulated the cession of some lands convenient to his districts, which

Siege of Palamcotta.

being promised, he took the field with his own troops and those of his dependant of Eṭṭaiyāpuram. On their arrival the garrison sallied and in a slight skirmish obliged the enemy to raise the siege; after which the two Poligars returned to their homes, and Kaṭṭaboma Nāyaka from his came and joined the English camp before Madura. Mahfuz Khan continuing at Tinnevelly, neither sent money nor troops to the Jamadars, but suffered the incomes to be dissipated, notwithstanding Barakat-ulla had continually represented to him that the scarcity of provisions in Madura was daily increasing from the want of money to pay for them and of parties in the field to facilitate their

Surrender of Madura.

importation. Shortly after the Jamadar surrendered Madura to Captain Calliaud for a sum of money claimed by them of Mahfuz Khan's arrears of pay.

"Muhammad Yusuf, returning from Madura, sent invitations to the cavalry with Mahfuz Khan and whatsoever other bodies were acting as plunderers in the Tinnevelly country. Passing along the districts of Eṭṭaiyāpuram, the Poligar redeemed his hostages which were in

Submission of the Eṭṭaiyāpuram Poligar

the camp, paying 18,700 rupees, the balance of his fine. The army arrived at the town of Tinnevelly about the middle of November, from whence Mahfuz Khan on their approach had retired to Nellitangaville. He had during his residence there made various attempts to get possession of the fort of Palamcotta, but had taken Kaḷakāḍu and given it to the King of Travancore. Muhammad Yusuf with a part of the army marched immediately against this place, which the Travancores abandoned without resistance, and, being followed by him, retired behind their walls in the passes of the mountains at the foot of the promontory. At the same time the appearance of other detachments drove away the guards which Mahfuz Khan had placed in

Yusuf Khan's successes.

Papankuḷam, Aḷvārkurichi, and Bermadats (Brahmadēśam), and those stationed by the Poligar of Vadagherry (Vadagarai) in Tirancourchy (Tārankurichi). All these places lie to the north-west of Tinnevelly about Nellitangaville, and parties of sepoys were left to maintain them. Before this time no farther expectation remained of Mudali's abilities to manage the revenues; and he was called to Madras, in order to exhibit and explain the details of his administration; but remained sick and settling his accounts in the woods of Tondiman.

"Captain Calliaud's personal representations convinced the Madras Government that the disturbances would never cease, nor any revenue be collected adequate to the military expenses, whilst Mahfuz Khan maintained his force, pretensions and alliances in these countries. It was therefore proposed to the Nawab, who still continued at Madras, that Mahfuz Khan should be assured of receiving an annual income sufficient for his decent maintenance out of the revenues, provided he would quit the country with his cavalry, and disband his other troops. By this plan, if nothing should be got, nothing would be lost; and the French, frustrated of all connexions, would find it impracticable to get footing in these provinces. The Nawab approved the proposal and sent an agent to treat with Mahfuz Khan.

Proposals about Mahfuz Khan.

"The agent sent by the Nawab to Mahfuz Khan arrived at Nellitangaville on the 28th of February, and found him there encamped in paltry tents with 50 horse, ostentatious of his poverty, pretending much discontent against his allies, and much attachment to the Nawab; but when terms of reconciliation were proposed, nothing less would satisfy him than the government of the whole country as an appanage in fee; indeed he was never master of his own opinion, and at present not of his will, for the western Poligars, elated by the rising superiority of the French in the Carnatic, took the field, and obliged him, who depended upon them for his subsistence, to lend his name, and to appear with them in person as the pretension of their hostilities. The army was composed of the troops of the Pūli Dēvar, of Vaḍagarai of the three minor Poligars, Cotaltava,* Naḍuvakurichi, and Soranḍai; and from the eastern side of Eṭṭaiyāpuram, the dependent of Kaṭṭaboma Nāyaka, who himself continued firm to his new connexion with the English. The confederates had likewise persuaded the Poligar of Shatore (Sēttūr) under the hills, whose fort is only fifteen miles to the south of Srīvilliputtūr to enter so far into their views as to admit a body of the Pūli Dēvar's colleries into his fort, with whom and his own he made depredations into the adjacent country, whilst Muhammad Yusuf, apprehensive of the arrival of Haidar Ali and the French, kept his force collected in Madura. As soon as the news of Haidar Ali's departure was confirmed, Muhammad Yusuf took the field and marched againt Sēttūr. The Poligar on his appearance made submissions, turned out the Pūli Dēvar's men, and paid a fine in money; but as soon as the English troops returned to Srīvilliputtūr he renewed his depredations, on which Muhammad Yusuf attacked the fort again, which the Poligar, after a slight resistance abandoned; and one of his relations was appointed in his stead. In the mean time the confederates had in various attacks from Nellitangaville taken all the posts between this place and Tinnevelly, and many of the men placed to guard them were put to the sword; at Tārankurichi, which was taken by assault in the night, 27 horsemen and a greater number of sepoys were killed. The confederates, elated with these successes, threatened all who did not join them, and attacked the Poligar of Ootamalee (Ūttumalai) because he had refused. They likewise prepared to take possession of Tinnevelly, and boasted that they would reduce the fort of Palamcotta. But the approach of Muhammad Yusuf from Srīvilliputtūr stopped their progress, nor had

Confederacy against Yusuf.

Successes of the confederates.

* A sub-division of Maravas are called Kottāli Dēvas.

CHAPTER V.

they courage to give him battle; but having strengthened the posts they had taken, retreated to Nellitangaville, sending, however, detachments to harass and interrupt his operations, but without success; for all their parties which ventured to meet or could not avoid the encounter of the sepoys were beaten, and by the end of April all the posts which had been taken were recovered. Muhammad Yusuf then resolved to carry the war into the enemy's country, and to begin with the Poligar of Vadagarai, although the most distant, because the most powerful of the alliance. His villages in the plain were in flames, and the troops had begun to penetrate into the wood which encloses his fort, when Yusuf received advices and instructions from the Presidency at Madras and from Captain Calliaud at Trichinopoly, which called him and the troops under his command to services of much greater necessity and importance. This service was to help the operations of the English in Madras and the neighbourhood, whilst the siege of Madras was carried on by the French. In May the following year (1759) intelligence was received that the garrison of sepoys at Palamcotta in the country of Tinnevelly had ventured to stand an engagement in the field against Mahfuz Khan and the Pūli Dēvar joined by most of the other Poligars, and although the enemy quitted the field, so many of the sepoys were killed and wounded that the garrison could no longer appear out of the fort. It had before been resolved to send Muhammad Yusuf into the southern countries as soon as the army in the field could be diminished without risk."

Yusuf's reprisals.

Yusuf called to help the English.

Palamcotta besieged.

Yusuf Khan's Return.

"Yusuf Khan arrived at Madura on the 4th of May, and had been absent ten months. The force he left in the country, when called away, was fourteen companies of sepoys, six in the fort of Madura, five in Palamcotta, and three at Tinnevelly. Nothing more could be expected from either of these bodies than to defend the ground in sight of the walls they garrisoned. Accordingly all the districts of both provinces from the forest of Nattam to the gates of Travancore lay subject to their contributions or exposed to their ravages. The declension of the English affairs, which began with the surrender of Fort St. David (on which Muhammad Yusuf was recalled) and continued until the French were obliged to raise the siege of Madras, kept Mahfuz Khan in continual hopes that he should be joined by a body of French troops, and established with their assistance in the government of those countries; and the administration of Pondicherry by their letters and emissaries encouraged him to think so. Waiting this fortune, he remained with the Pūli Dēvar styling himself and styled a sovereign, but without any other means of subsistence than what the Pūli Dēvar chose to supply, who, never regulating his money by words, scarcely furnished him with common necessaries. The return of Yusuf Khan bettered his condition; as the Pūli Dēvar was afraid he might at length listen to a reconciliation with the Nawab, and Mahfuz Khan, always governed by the love of ease, felt no resentment at the humility to which he had been reduced. He presided at least

Mahfuz Khan's expectations.

Confederacy of the eastern Poligars.

in appearance in the councils of the eastern Poligars, who resolved to meet Yusuf with their united force, and invited the western to the common defence; who, having joined them against Palamcotta in the late distresses of the English affairs, expected no pardon and took the field. The western league consisted of six Poligars; Kaṭṭaboma Nāyaka, their former leader, was lately dead and had been succeeded by a relation, who took as usual the same name, and bore, instead of the indifference of his predecessor, an aversion to the English; Eṭṭaiyāpuram was always the next to him in importance and now in activity.

"The force which accompanied Muhammad Yusuf from Conjeeveram consisted only of six companies of sepoys and sixty horse, but he had on his march requested troops from Toṇḍiman and the two Maravars, with whom he had always continued on good terms; and 3,000 men, horse, colleries, and sepoys from the three Poligars joined him on his arrival at Madura, where he nevertheless immediately began to make farther levies, and by shifting and garbling out of all that were with him, composed a body of 300 horse and 700 sepoys who had seen service, which he sent forward to ravage the districts of Eṭṭaiyāpuram, where they were to be joined by three of the companies of sepoys from the garrison of Palamcotta, which had restored its losses by new levies. This body of troops were to maintain their ground until the last extremity, in order to prevent the junction of the western with the troops of the eastern Poligars until Muhammad Yusuf himself could follow with the main body from Madura, where he was under the necessity of remaining a while longer.

Yusuf's expedition against the Poligars.

"His first march was to Kollamkoṇḍān. He had taken this fort in 1756; but after his departure for the Carnaṭic the Pūli Dēvar and Vaḍakarai had extended their acquisitions thus far and placed their guard in Kollamkoṇḍān. It was a mud fort without cannon, and after a slight resistance submitted to him. From hence he proceeded to take up the large detachment he had sent forward against Eṭṭaiyāpuram, who, by continually ravaging the districts of this Poligar, kept his troops on their own ground and deterred both him and Kaṭṭaboma Nāyaka from marching across the country to join the Pūli Dēvar. Having sufficiently constrained these chiefs, the detachment proceeded against Kollārpaṭṭi, which stands nearly midway in the straightest road between Madura and Tinnevelly, about fifty miles from each. This fort had likewise been stormed in June 1756 by Muhammad Yusuf and carried with considerable loss. The Poligar was then taken prisoner; whether restored or succeeded by another we do not find; but the place was at this time in the hands of one who defended it as well; for 100 of the sepoys were killed and wounded in the attack which lasted three days, and then the Poligar made his escape by night. The fort was immediately razed to the ground, after which the detachment joined the main body with Muhammad Yusuf, and the whole proceeding by the way of Gangādaram (Gangai koṇḍān) arrived at Tinnevelly in the middle of July. They were scarcely arrived when Mahfuz Khan, whose mind always wavered

Capture of Kollārpaṭṭi fort.

CHAPTER V.

with every change of circumstances, wrote a letter to Muhammad Yusuf offering to quit his allies and proceed to the Carnaṭic, provided he was allowed a suitable jaghire for his maintenance. He even asked a safe guard to come to Tinnevelly. Muhammad Yusuf, without authority, assured him that his requests should be complied with, and recommended them to the Presidency, by whom they were referred to the Nawab.

The Poligar of Ūttumalai.

"The midland country, for thirty miles to the north of the town of Tinnevelly, is open and of great cultivation, and, lying between the eastern and western Poligars, had been the favourite field of their depredations. The principal station from which the western made their inroads into these districts was the fort and wood of Ūttumalai, situated thirty-five miles north-west of Tinnevelly. The Poligar, grown rich by easy plunder, had many colleries, who were well armed; and Muhammad Yusuf, soon after his arrival at Tinnevelly, marched against him with the greatest part of his force, and in a few days reduced his fort, in which he placed some troops, and stationed a guard of fifty horse and some peons and colleries in a place called Shorandah (Soraṇḍai) as an intermediate post. He was no sooner returned to Tinnevelly than a multitude of colleries belonging to the Pūli Dēvar and Vaḍagarai surprised the guard at Soraṇḍai, and either killed or took all their horses with their riders, on which Muhammad Yusuf detached seven companies of sepoys, who recovered the post and remained in it, in order to protect the adjacent country. Equal confusion prevailed in the districts to the south of Tinnevelly. The troops of the Maliaver, or King of Travancore, were making incursions from their wall to seize the harvests at the foot of the hills from Kaḷakāḍu to Cape Comorin. The variety of distractions which existed on every side could not be all opposed at the same time, unless a greater army were embodied than all the revenues of the two provinces could defray. But the king was the least inveterate enemy to the English, because the Poligar of Vaḍagarai had provoked his resentment by continually employing his colleries to make depredations in his country on the other side of the mountains, through the pass of Shencottah, which lies fifteen miles to the south of Vaḍagarai. On this ground of common enmity Muhammad Yusuf opened a negotiation with the king, who consented to a conference at the gates of his country near the promontory. They met in the end of August, and the interview passed with much politeness and seeming cordiality. The king at least publicly demanded nothing and agreed to desist from his inroads into the districts of Tinnevelly and to act with a considerable force in conjunction with Muhammad Yusuf against Vaḍagarai and the Pūli Dēvar. On the 3rd of September Muhammad Yusuf, still remaining at the gates of Travancore, was joined by 1,000 of the king's sepoys armed with heavy muskets made in his own country, and disciplined, although awkwardly, in the European manner; but they were well supplied with stores and ammunition. He then returned to Tinnevelly, and marching from thence with his whole force, in deference to the king proceeded directly against Vaḍagarai,

Travancore troops.

Alliance of the King of Travancore and Yusuf.

although twenty miles beyond Nellitangaville, the residence of the Pūli Dēvar. When arrived near Shencottah he was joined by an army full as large as his own, consisting of 10,000 more of the king's troops of various kinds of infantry, who had marched through the pass. This was perhaps the greatest force that had been assembled for some centuries in this country. Vaḍagarai defended his woods for a day, in which about 100 men were killed and wounded on both sides; but in the night abandoned his fort, and escaped away to the Pūli Dēvar at Nellitangaville.

Vaḍagarai's flight at Pūli Dēvar's fears.

"The arrival of such a guest, who, for the first time, had been reduced to such distress, frightened the Pūli Dēvar, and set his cunning to work to divert the storm from himself. The repulse of the English troops at the attack of the pettah at Vandiwash on the 30th of September was known in the country, and was believed, as the French had represented it, a signal defeat. Mahfuz Khan had received letters from Bassaulet Jung and the Government of Pondicherry, which encouraged him to think that they should very soon overpower the English in the Carnaṭic, when he might expect to be substituted for his brother Muhammad Ali, who was to be deposed from the Nawabship. This correspondence and these expectations the Pūli Dēvar communicated to the King of Travancore, and offered, if he would quit the English and join Mahfuz Khan against them, to give him whatsoever districts in the Tinnevelly country might lie convenient to his own. The king immediately exposed these documents to Muhammad Yusuf, and standing on his importance, demanded the cession of Kaḷakāḍu and the adjacent districts, for which he had so long contended against the Nawab's Government. He said, that more territory than he claimed had already been recovered with his assistance; that what might be refused by one would be readily given to him by another; and that, if he should join the Poligars, the Nawab's authority would never be established in the Tinnevelly country. Muhammad Yusuf, whilst perplexed with this dilemma, was informed that the two eighteen-pounders with 500 muskets, which had been sent, according to his request, from Madras, were lost at sea; and that the two six-pounders, although landed, were stopped by the Dutch agents at Tuticorin. This mischance gave greater weight to the king's arguments, and greater value to his assistance; for the force of Muhammad Yusuf alone was not sufficient to reduce the Pūli Dēvar, whom all the best colleries in the country were flocking to defend. He therefore surrendered the districts which the king demanded, and the Presidency approved the cession; but the Nawab suspected that it had been promised by Yusuf at his first interview with the king in order to secure his future assistance to his own ambitious views.

Travancore's proposals.

Attack on a subsidiary fort.

"As soon as this agreement was settled the Travancores moved again in conjunction with his troops. On the 16th of November they invested the wood and fort of Easaltaver (probably Īśvara Dēvar), which was one of the dependencies of the Pūli Dēvar. The colleries defended the wood three days and then abandoned both, and retired to Nellitangaville. After this success the want of ammunition obliged Mu-

CHAPTER V.

hammad Yusuf to remain until he received supplies from Madura, Palamcotta, and Anjengo. The army of Travancore, to prevent disgusts from disparity of customs, encamped separately, but in sight of Muhammad Yusuf's; and on the 20th of November a body of 5 or 6,000 colleries attacked the camp of the Travancores in open day. Muhammad Yusuf, on the first alarm, sent his horse and followed with his sepoys and other foot; but the colleries retreated before they came up, and their nimbleness, with the ruggedness of the country, rendered the pursuit of little avail. They had killed and wounded 100 of the Travancores before they went off. A day or two after this skirmish Muhammad Yusuf received three howitzers, with some stores, and a supply of ammunition from Anjengo; and the two six-pounders with their shot likewise came up from Tuticorin; he then moved with his allies, and on the 4th of December set down before Washinelore (Vāsudēvanallūr) another fort dependent on the Pūli Dēvar, much stronger than any he had, excepting Nellitangaville, from which it is situated twenty miles to the north-west and twelve in the same direction from Ūttumalai.

Yusuf receives supplies.

" Vāsudēvanallūr stood within three miles from the great range of mountains, at the foot of which ran a thick wood, extending two miles into the plain, and within 1,300 yards of the west and south sides of the fort; but turned to a much greater distance on the north, and to the east the plain was open, and everywhere covered with profuse cultivation. A very extensive pettah, the residence of some thousand inhabitants, commenced within forty yards, and extended 1,200 to the north-east of the walls: a thick thorn hedge, with barriers, surrounded both the pettah and the fort. The extent of the fort was 650 by 300 yards; it was of mud, but almost as hard as brick; it had four large square towers, one at each angle, and several smaller, which were round, between. Every tower was a separate redoubt, enclosed by a parapet, to command within as well as without the fort. The access to the tower was a steep ramp, only two feet broad, the entrance a narrow wicket in the parapet; the curtain between the towers had no parapet, and was only a rampart sloping on both sides from a base of 15 feet to 3 at top; but the slope from within was much less sharp than from without, so that, if assaulted, the defenders might easily run up to the top. The parapets of the towers have circular holes for the use of small arms, but no openings prepared for cannon, of which there was not a single piece in the fort. [See the account of the capture of this fort in 1767 by Colonel Donald Campbell.] This description only suits Vāsudēvanallūr, for the other forts in the Madura and Tinnevelly countries have parapets with loop-holes to their ramparts, as well as to their towers; but all are of earth excepting Madura and Palamcotta. The importance of Vāsudēvanallūr, and the great force which was come against it, brought some thousands of colleries to its relief; but all, excepting 8 or 900 chosen men allotted to defend the walls, kept in the woods. From whence every day and night parties sallied, and alarmed or attacked one or other, and sometimes both the camps; and greater bodies on three different days made general

Description of Vāsudēvanallūr fort.

Attack on the fort.

attacks on the batteries, of which these continued interruptions retarded the construction, insomuch that they were not finished until the 26th, twenty days after the arrival of the armies; but the howitzers had commenced before. The only efficacious gun was the eighteen-pounder which Muhammad Yusuf had brought from Madura, for the rest were only six-pounders and lower; but from excessive firing the eighteen-pounder burst the day after it was mounted; and by this time all the ammunition as well of the batteries as troops, excepting the quantity which prudence required to be reserved for defence, was expended. However, part of the parapet of the tower fired upon was beaten down, and Muhammad Yusuf resolved to storm the next day. Many troops of both armies waited on the assault, and as soon as it began, the Pūli Dēvar, with 3,000 chosen colleries, who had marched in the night from Nellitangaville, issued from the wood and fell upon the camp of Muhammad Yusuf, drove away the troops that guarded it, and began to commit every kind of destruction. Muhammad Yusuf sent back a large body to repulse them, and continued the assault; but the garrison within received double animation from the Pūli Dēvar's success, which was announced to them by the usual war cry and the sounding of their conchs. All the other colleries collected in the woods appeared likewise, as if on the same notice, and in different bands attacked the troops at the batteries and at the foot of the breach; and, although continually repulsed, continually rallied, and with the resolution of the garrison saved the fort until the evening, and then waited in the woods to interrupt the renewal of the assault in the night; but so much of the reserved ammunition had been expended in the day that Muhammad Yusuf deemed it dangerous to remain any longer before the fort, and drew off his artillery. Two hundred of his troops and of the Travancores were killed, but more of the enemy. The next day he moved to a distance, and dismissed the Travancores, who proceeded through the pass of Shencottah to their own country, and Muhammad Yusuf returned with his own troops and those lent him by Tondiman and the Maravars to the town of Tinnevelly.

Successful defence.

Yusuf's return.

"No events of great importance had happened during the course of this year (1760) in the country of Tinnevelly. The Commandant, Muhammad Yusuf, after the repulse before Vāsudēvanallūr in the end of the preceding year, was, from the want of battering cannon, no longer in a condition to attack the stronger holds of the Poligars; and contented himself, until supplied, with posting the greatest part of his army in stations to check the Pūli Dēvar and the western Poligars; but remained himself with the rest at Tinnevelly, watching Kaṭṭaboma Nāyaka and the eastern. The departure of Mahfuz Khan from Nellitangaville in the month of January left the Pūli Dēvar and his allies no longer the pretext of opposing the authority of the Nawab in support of the rights of his elder brother; and they debated whether they should treat with Muhammad Yusuf or wait the event of Mahfuz Khan's journey, who they supposed would return to them, if not received on his own terms by the Nawab. In this uncertainty they formed no vigorous designs,

His enforced inactivity.

Depredations of the Poligars.

CHAPTER V.

and employed their colleries in night robberies wherever they could elude the stations of Muhammad Yusuf; but attempted nothing in the open field or day. Nevertheless these depredations were so ruinous to the cultivation that Muhammad Yusuf thought it worth the expense to draw off some of their dependents and entertain them in the Company's service as best able to retaliate the same mischief on those by whom they had been employed; and towards the end of April several of these petty leaders with their followers, amounting in the whole to 2,000 colleries, joined him at Tinnevelly and faithfully entered on the duties for which they had engaged. Nothing, however, like regular fighting happened until the end of May, when Kaṭṭaboma Nāyaka appeared at the head of two or three thousand men, near Eṭṭaiyāpuram and stood the attack of seven companies of sepoys, drawn from the limits towards Nellitangaville, by whom they were dispersed, but with little loss. In May Muhammad Yusuf received intelligence of the hostilities commenced by the Mysoreans from Dindigul and the orders of the Presidency to oppose them; in consequence of which he sent the detachment we have mentioned, of 1,500 sepoys, 300 horse, and 3,000 peons."

Hostilities of the Mysoreans.

DUTCH INVASION.

A Dutch force arrives from Colombo.

"They were scarcely gone, when a new and unexpected alarm arose in the Tinnevelly country. The Dutch Government at the Island of Ceylon had received a large reinforcement of European troops from Batavia, which assembled at the port of Colombo, opposite to Cape Comorin, from whence a part of them arrived in the beginning of June at Tuticorin, a Dutch fort on the continent 40 miles east of Tinnevelly. Two hundred Europeans with equipments, tents, and field pieces immediately encamped, giving out that they should shortly be reinforced by more than their own number, and that 400 other Europeans had left Batavia at the same time with themselves, and were gone to Cochin on the Malabar Coast, in order to join the King of Travancore. The natives were frightened and pretended to have discovered that the force they saw was intended to assist the Poligars in driving the English out of the country of Tinnevelly, and to begin by attacking the town. Muhammad Yusuf immediately sent to the Dutch chief at Tuticorin to demand an explanation; who answered that he should give none. A few days after the troops advanced inland and halted at Alvar Tinnevelly (Āḷvār Tirunagari), a town in a very fertile district situated 20 miles south-east of Tinnevelly and the same distance south-west of Tuticorin, and at the same time another body of 200 Europeans landed from Colombo at Maṇapār, 20 miles to the south-east of Aḷvār Tinnevelly. Muhammad Yusuf had previously drawn troops from the eastern stations, and marching with 4,000 sepoys, and some horse, appeared in sight of the Dutch troops at Alvar Tinnevelly in the evening of the 18th of June, who, in the ensuing night, decamped in strict silence and marched back to Tuticorin. Those at Manapār went away thither likewise in the same embarkations which brought them; and no more was heard of this alarm."

Yusuf's preparations.

Retreat of the Dutch.

YUSUF KHAN'S OPERATIONS RENEWED.

Yusuf and the Pūli Dēvar.

"The depredations of the Poligars continued; but, deprived of Mahfuz Khan, and hearing how closely Pondicherry was invested, they ventured nothing more. The Pūli Dēvar's colleries were as usual the most active in the robberies; and to repress them Muhammad Yusuf again stationed the greatest part of his force towards Nellitangaville, which in December encamped at the foot of the hills within three miles of this place and Muhammad Yusuf joined them from Tinnevelly on the 12th; he had purchased several eighteen-pounders at Tuticorin, and had the two mortars sent to him the year before from Anjengo, but no shot or shells for either, and was moreover in want of gun-powder and flints, all which he expected from Trichinopoly, and whilst waiting for them made such preparations as the country afforded to attack Nellitangaville in form. On the 20th of the month, the colleries with the Pūli Dēvar at their head, attacked his camp, sallying as usual on all quarters at once and persisted until 100 of them fell; but they killed ten of Muhammad Yusuf's men, and wounded seventy, and some horses."

Unfortunately Orme's narrative here breaks off. From this time I have to depend for information on the results of my own examination of the Government records, preserved in the Government Office and Office of the Board of Revenue, Madras, and in the Treasury in Tinnevelly.

REVENUE ADMINISTRATION IN TINNEVELLY BY THE NAWAB.

Lushington's letter.

It has already been seen that the rule of the Nawab of the Carnaṭic commenced in Tinnevelly, as in the other districts in the Carnaṭic, in 1744, when Anwar-u-din Khan was appointed Nawab by the Nizam. The various districts in the south were held by officers appointed by Anwar-u-din. Anwar Khan was appointed Fauzdar and Amil of Tinnevelly, with whose appointment the accounts of the revenue administration of Tinnevelly commence. I quote here from a letter of Mr. Lushington, Collector of Tinnevelly, to the Board of Revenue, dated, in the year after the transfer of the Carnaṭic to the Company, 28th May 1802. It gives the names of the administrators of the revenue in Tinnevelly from 1744 to 1783.

Succession of administrators.

Anwar Khan was succeeded, he says, by Mir Ghulam Hussein Khan and Hussein Mahomed Khan, their joint management comprising a period of six years from 1744 to 1749. He mentions the amount of the jamabandi for each year in chakrams, but this I omit. When Anwar-u-din Khan was slain in battle an Amil (a native revenue officer) named Alam Khan was deputed by Chanda Saheb to take charge of Tinnevelly, who managed the district in his master's behalf in 1750 and 1751. To him succeeded for a short time Tīttārappa Mudali and Mundi Miya (Moodemiah),

CHAPTER V.

the agent of Chanda Saheb. The latter was slain near Tinnevelly. Upon Moodemiah's death the authority of Mahfuz Khan (the elder brother and for a time the representative of the Nawab Mahomed Ali) was established in the country. This was for 1754 and 1755. He formed the design of becoming independent of the Nawab, but Issoof (Yusuf) Khan, by the vigour of his mind, frustrated this ambitious design, and, re-establishing the power of Mahomed Ali Khan, delivered the management of the province for a year, 1756, to Alagappa Mudali. The distracted state of the country, owing to the depredations of the Poligars, requiring greater energy for their reduction than Alagappa Mudali possessed, Yusuf Khan was appointed to the sole administration from 1757 to 1763. He ruled the country for six years.

Yusuf's administration.

"During the three first years of Yusuf Khan's management he was engaged in constant struggles with the Poligars, with very various success; the necessities of the Company during this anxious period in the Carnaṭic demanded the employment of his force, and of his extraordinary military talents in more central parts of it. Tinnevelly was therefore left in his absence a prey to the depredations of the Poligars and the perfidious machinations of Mahfuz Khan, aided by the adherents of Travancore; the latter indeed wholly assumed during this period the most fertile taluk of the province, Kaḷakāḍu, but when Yusuf Khan could be spared from the siege of Madras to return to Tinnevelly, he had the address not only to detach the Rājā of Travancore from the league, but to acquire his assistance in punishing the Poligars. Notwithstanding the disadvantages (under which he laboured) of an usurped authority, he accomplished, by the vigour of his mind and military talents, the complete subjugation of the province. In his time the tribute of the Poligars was regularly collected; private property was in no danger from their depredations; and the revenue of the Circar lands was very largely increased. The effect of the subordination he established may be seen in his jamabaṇḍies from the year 1761 to 1764."

Fluctuations in revenue.

Dalavay Alagappa Mudali's management was in 1764; Rājā Hukumat Ram's from 1765 to 1769; Sheik Mahomed Ali's in 1770. The administration of Syed Mahomed Khan commenced in 1771 and lasted till 1775.

Two incidents worthy of note happened at this time. In 1771 the cutcherry of Tinnevelly, with all the records, was burnt to the ground, and in 1774 there was a famine of unusual severity. In 1780 the Poligars, again tempted by the war which raged in the Carnaṭic, threw off their allegiance and nearly overran the province, in consequence of which the revenue was reduced to a minimum for several years, viz., from an annual average of eight lakhs of chakrams to an average of half a lakh. In 1783 commenced Mr. Irwin's or the Company's administration, when the collections rose again to eight lakhs. Thus far Mr. Lushington's statements. I now return to Yusuf Khan and his fortunes. CHAPTER V.

MUHAMMAD YUSUF KHAN'S REBELLION.

Yusuf's offer to rent the province.

In 1761 Yusuf Khan informs the Government that the "Circar flag," that is, the flag of the Nawab of the Carnaṭic, had been hoisted by him on the forts of Madura and Palamcotta. He also offers to rent the Tinnevelly and Madura provinces for four years at seven lakhs of rupees per annum. The Nawab was unwilling to give his consent, Tīttārappa Mudali, the old renter, offering a larger sum, but the Madras Government was in favour of Yusuf Khan's offer, on account of his position and military fame and his ability to fulfil the engagements he entered into. They warned Yusuf, however, that his letters to the Nawab were not sufficiently respectful. They asked him for information with regard to the pearl fishery and the extension of their trade in cloths, &c. It is evident that up to the close of 1761 the Government had no suspicion of his intentions being disloyal.

The following remarks of Nelson relate to this period:—

Yusuf's position.

"The taking of Pondicherry by the English in January 1761 served to awe the rebellious Poligars into something like submission; whilst the departure of Mahfuz Khan from the Tinnevelly country and his apparent reconciliation with his brother had deprived them of all pretext for disobedience. The country, therefore, became more quiet than it had been for many years; and there seemed to be some grounds for the belief that it would so continue. Without counting troops employed in garrison duty, Muhammad Yusuf was certainly in command of a large force, for at the very time when he sent the expedition to Madura to act against the Mysoreans he was able to put himself at the head of 4,000 sepoys and some cavalry and march against a Dutch expedition. And his troops were well disciplined and well chosen. And certainly no Poligar and no combination of Poligars at that time was in possession of so considerable resources. Muhammad Yusuf continued to govern the Madura country for some time longer, and appears to have made himself exceedingly powerful."

Dissatisfaction of Government.

Notwithstanding the favour with which Yusuf Khan had been regarded by Government, it became evident in 1762 that his loyalty was doubtful. The Government wrote to him repeatedly ordering him to come to Madras at once and promising him a cowle of protection, but he only sent trifling excuses in reply. Not only so, but he had the audacity to make war on the King of Travancore without their knowledge or consent. In August he wrote to the effect that he was sorry for his past behaviour, promising obedience for the future, and repeating his offer to rent Madura and Tinnevelly himself for four years at a rent of seven lahks of rupees per annum. The Government regarded this letter and proposal as

CHAPTER V.

merely a device to gain time. They replied that they could not consent to allow him to retain the management of those provinces any longer, and that the only means he had for securing his life and effects was to surrender himself unconditionally.

Government suspicions of his designs.

The first time I find Government expressing their suspicions was in October. Some European troops were to march from Anjengo to Madras by land, but they were ordered to remain at Anjengo till further orders, lest they should be intercepted by Yusuf Khan, "as," said they, "we are very uncertain at present with regard to the intentions of Yusuf Khan, who, we fear, hath some thought of departing from his allegiance to the Nawab." In December it was clearly ascertained that he was enlisting troops in Tanjore and the Toṇḍiman's country, whereupon letters were written to the various Rājās and others warning them not to render him any assistance.

Yusuf's reasons for rebelling.

No statement of Muhammad Yusuf Khan's reasons for throwing off his allegiance appears in record. It can only be conjectured that he was irritated against the Nawab, and consequently against the Nawab's upholders, the English, by the refusal of his offer to rent Tinnevelly and Madura. Probably, however, his chief reason was that he had come to consider himself strong enough to thrust both of his masters aside and set up for himself, as had been done before him by every successful lieutenant. The latest examples of this had been Chanda Saheb and Hyder Ali. Doubtless he would have succeeded in his purpose if he had had to deal only with a feeble Nawab of Arcot or a still feebler Rājā of Mysore, but it was with the English that he had to deal, and notwithstanding his long service under them he quite miscalculated their power.

On the 11th April 1763, General Lawrence wrote to the Government recommending that a strong force should be sent immediately against Yusuf Khan. He stated that Yusuf Khan had at last declared himself independent. He had provided the forts of Palamcotta and Madura with stores and heavy artillery, and put many other forts of less consequence in a state of defence. His forces were estimated at 27,530 men, including 15,000 colleries badly armed. The rest were well armed, and he had succeeded in enlisting 200 European foot soldiers, mostly Frenchmen, and 30 French troopers, all under the command of a Frenchman called Marchand. His force was equipped with twelve or fourteen light pieces of field artillery and two howitzers, most of which had belonged to the Company. He had made Madura his head-quarters. He was daily receiving reinforcements from the French and from Hyder Ali's army, and General Lawrence considered him a man of such enterprising genius and ambition that it was necessary to proceed against him at once, lest, "like another

Yusuf's forces.

Chanda Saheb," he should entail on the Company another ten years' war. He did not think it prudent or practicable to proceed against so dangerous a rebel through narrow passes and intricate woods with a small force. The force he asked for was as follows:— European cavalry 163; artillery for 10 guns, 2 howitzers, 100; European military, rank and file 600; Coffres or Topasses (the latter Eurasian soldiers) 100; Company's sepoys 50 companies, including officers, 5,000; Nawab's sepoys 2,000; "Black horse" 2,000. The entire force he applied for amounted to 9,963 men. He did not obtain the force he asked for, and the force granted him proved insufficient. In particular it was not strong enough in cannon. Battering cannon had to be sent for from Trichinopoly, but even after its arrival the operations carried on were not successful. Colonel Monson, who was in command of the troops, had to retire for the rainy season of 1763 to a place where the troops could pass the monsoon with greater safety and comfort. Swartz, the celebrated missionary, visited the camp for two months during the siege to give spiritual comfort to the sick and wounded.

CHAPTER V.

General Lawrence's force.

Whilst the siege was going on Yusuf Khan endeavoured to obtain the help of the French. Peace had been declared between France and England, so that the Pondicherry Government could not send him help in men and munitions, but they called upon the English Government to countermand their expedition against him, on the ground that he was their ally, and that to wage war against their ally was virtually to wage war against them. The English Government appear to have made no reply to this ingenious representation. The siege continued with various fortunes till the 14th October 1764, when another assault was made. The assault failed, but Marchand, the Commander of the French contingent, came to the conclusion that it was now his best policy to capitulate, and in order to secure the most favourable terms for himself and his followers he traitorously seized his commander, Yusuf Khan, and delivered him up to Major Donald Campbell, the English officer in command.

Yusuf's negotiations with the French.

Treachery of the French commander.

I have not been able to discover any written record of the manner in which Yusuf Khan was disposed of. Nelson states on native authority that "the gallant soldier who had served in so many campaigns, always with marked distinction, was seized by a confidential servant and given over to his enemies, who, in May 1763 (error, see above), with a want of mercy which at this time seems all but inexcusable, hung him like a dog." This termination of his career would be in accordance with the instructions issued by Government in the previous year at the commencement of the siege to General Lawrence. They say that if Yusuf Khan were taken alive it was their wish that he should be sent to Madras, "not from any willingness to show him favour, but that they

Yusuf Khan's death.

CHAPTER V. might in their cooler hours dispose of him in such a manner as might appear proper." "We confess to you," they say, "that we think he will be a dangerous man to be entrusted in the hands of the Nawab, if his intentions are to make him a state prisoner; but if it be agreeable to you to order the Commanding officer to execute him upon the first tree in sight of the army, it will be quite satisfactory to us." Though there is no documentary evidence to be found I regard it as certain that the latter recommendation was carried into effect. It seems hard that such a man should have come to such an ignominious end. This must, however, have been one of the alternatives present to his mind from the commencement of his rebellion. He must have expected, if successful, to reign as a prince; if he failed, to be hanged as a traitor. Khan Saheb was hanged near the camp about two miles to the west of Madura. He was buried on the spot where he was hanged and a small mosque was erected over his tomb. An inscription describes it as "the Mosque of Khan Saheb." An intelligent old Muhammadan inhabitant of Madura, the uncle of the Cazi, who accompanied me to the spot, was full of the particulars of his death, as handed down to him by his ancestors. He was seized whilst at prayers by "Mussoo Mursan" (Monsieur Marchand) and his Hindu Dewan, Sinavasa Row, and was hanged, he said, by the orders of the Nawab. The old man professed to be 85 years of age, and proved to me the retentiveness of his memory by correctly repeating to me the names of the principal rebel Poligars hanged in the Madura and Tinnevelly countries in 1801. He confirmed the tradition that Khan Saheb was originally a Hindu. As there is no account of Khan Saheb's death on record, we may perhaps venture to conclude that the order for his execution, as the old man stated, proceeded not from the English, but from the Nawab himself. We may give the English Commander the benefit of the doubt.

On the capture of Madura and of Yusuf Khan the rebellion collapsed, but the country having lost one of the most vigorous rulers it had ever had, its financial prosperity rapidly declined.

Results of Yusuf's death.

"To Yusuf Khan," says Mr. Lushington, "succeeded one of the family of the Mudali's; his management, however, continued but for eight months when he was displaced by a Hindu named Rajah Hukumat Ram. The jamabandy of his management fell considerably short of those of Yusuf Khan, and his immediate successor, Shaik Muhammed Ali, who was in charge of the country for nine months, reduced it still more. Tempted by the imbecility of their superintendence, the Poligars returned to their former licentiousness and continued in the indulgence of their inveterate habits of encroachment and violence with little intermission from that period until their transfer to the Company's authority in 1792; nor did even this arrangement produce that improvement in the conduct and condition of these feudatories which had been hoped from it; the fluctuating

Yusuf's successors.

administration of the Nawab had given such confidence and success to their rebellious character, and the weak policy and corruption of his Amils had encouraged and confirmed in the Poligars so strong an influence over the minds of His Highness' subjects, that, under the weakness of a divided authority, a solid reform was impracticable. The vigour of Yusuf Khan's measures was indeed felt for some time after he suffered the death of a rebel, but the Poligars soon forgot the terror of his name and relapsed into former habits."

With regard to Madura Nelson states that after Yusuf Khan's death it was placed under the administration of Abiral Khan. He adds "the state of things in Madura during this period of Muhammadan domination may be imagined from the following facts, which were communicated to me by the grandson of one of these officers, and the truth of which I see no occasion to doubt. About the year 1772 there were only two substantial brick and stone buildings in the whole town, namely, the old palace and the residence of the Muhammadan manager; the only other dwellings were mud hovels thatched or tiled." Thus far Mr. Nelson. This state of things was not peculiar to Madura. I have sought but have been unable to find any trace of the existence of any private house in Tinnevelly, whether in the towns or in the rural districts, built of stone or burnt brick by any private native prior to the assignment of the Nawab's revenues to the Company's government in 1781. This fact furnishes us with a most telling illustration of the difference between the anarchy that had prevailed before, and the order and security that began to be introduced by the strong, peaceful government of the English.

State of Madura after Yusuf Khan's death.

CHAPTER VI.

TINNEVELLY ANNALS FROM 1764 TO 1799.

PART I.

FROM THE DEATH OF YUSUF KHAN TO THE ASSIGNMENT OF REVENUE IN 1781.

EVENTS FOLLOWING THE DEATH OF YUSUF KHAN.

CHAPTER VI.

Protection of Palamcotta.

COLONEL DONALD CAMPBELL, the officer in command in Madura and the south, was anxious to march into Tinnevelly, after the capture of Madura and Yusuf Khan about the end of 1764, to secure it against the inroads of the king of Travancore. Government did not apprehend that the king of Travancore would commence hostilities, at least till he knew their determination regarding the Kaḷakāḍu districts. They judged it necessary, however, that Palamcotta and any other post in that neighbourhood should be reinforced so as to protect the Kaḷakāḍu country from surprise.

1765. Accommodation is ordered to be provided at Palamcotta for troops. The king of Travancore endeavours to recover the Kaḷakāḍu district. The Nawab's sepoys are detained to defend Palamcotta. Captain Harper sets out with a detachment to the relief of Kaḷakāḍu. It is reported on the 25th May that Kaḷakāḍu is held by 2,000 armed Travancorians. During the absence of the Company's troops three or four hundred Collaries plunder the town of Tinnevelly. The Nawab's people are helpless. Paṇagudi and Tirukurungudi had been abandoned to the Travancore army, the detachments which held those places being very small. Those who capitulated had to promise to retire to Palamcotta. Shencotta also had been abandoned to the Travancorians by the

Retirement of the Travancore troops.

Nawab's troops. On the 12th of June the Travancorians retired from Kaḷakāḍu. They made a stand at Tirukurungudi, and Colonel Campbell was preparing to march against them, when they retired within the Aramboly lines. A complaint being made that the officers' quarters in Palamcotta are incommodious, Government order improvements to be made at the Nawab's expense; they also order the erection of a new magazine.

1766. Captain Frischman was at this time Commandant of Palamcotta, and as such the Company's representative in Tinnevelly. The good effects produced by Yusuf Khan's rigorous administration were now at an end, and to add to the difficulty always felt in keeping the Poligars in check and getting them to pay their tribute, most of the troops that had been brought down the previous year to act against Travancore had been withdrawn, on account of the necessity of counteracting the designs of Hyder Ali further north. All this was laid before Government by Captain Frischman in a letter dated 4th October, from which it appears that within fifteen or twenty miles of Palamcotta it was estimated that there were 20,000 armed Collaries roaming about and ransacking every village they came to. Captain Frischman had fitted out an expedition of the Nawab's troops under "the Buxy" (the Nawab's Commander—Bakhshi, a Muhammadan Commander-in-Chief) for the purpose of reducing a fort to the north-aest, doubtless Pānjālamkurichi. It was a strong force with artillery and a body of 1,000 horse, but Captain Frischman complained that it did nothing but merely waited outside the fort. He complained that half of the Nawab's troops were "mere coolies" and that their arms were bad and incapable of repair. There were 4,000 of them, but half the number would suffice if they were paid and disciplined by the Company. Such was the state of the country that the tappal had ceased and he found it very difficult to communicate with his out-stations. Ensign Foulsum of the Nawab's service, who commanded at Vadagarai, had attempted to relieve Vassa Nellore (Vāsudēva-nallūr) which was besieged by Poligars, but before his arrival the garrison had surrendered through want of water, and had leave to return with their arms to Tinnevelly. Foulsum had a skirmish with a body of 12,000 Poligars and then retired to his fort. The Government order on this letter is to the effect that they are much concerned to find that whenever their troops are withdrawn every petty Poligar takes the opportunity of plundering. They have often represented to the Nawab that it would be much better for him and for the country if he would consent to place the discipline and pay of his troops in their hands, and though he had never yet consented they would represent to him again the necessity of this arrangement.

Armed followers of the Poligars near Palamcotta.

Complaints of Government against the Nawab.

The year 1766 closed with the failure of an attempt on the part of Major Flint to reduce some of the more turbulent Poligars to obedience. On the 23rd of December he marched from Srīvilliputtūr for the purpose of attacking the fort of Calacunda (Kollamkoṇḍān). On the 27th an escort he sent back to Srīvilliputtūr for grain was attacked by the Poligars. A strong force was sent out to the support of the escort, but even this combined force was attacked and the attack was continued to within three miles of the camp. On the 29th, after a breach had been effected in the wall of the fort, an assault was made, but the place was defended by

Major Flint attempts to reduce Poligar fort.

CHAPTER VI.

such numbers and with such resolution that the assaulting party, after holding its ground for half an hour, had to return with considerable loss. Captain Painter and five Europeans were killed and several Europeans were wounded. The Poligar to whom the fort belonged had not got above 200 men of his own, but he was reinforced by parties sent to his help by all the other Poligars. On his retreat Major Flint had to fight his way through the enemy. Captain Harper was in command of his rear guard.

Flint's unsuccessful campaign.

1767. This year opens with another unsuccessful campaign against the Poligars. Major Flint retired first to Rājā Pāḷaiyam, then to Sitheath (Sittūttu ?), then to Parambūr, where he joined the camp of "the Buxy." Subsequently he got a supply of heavier artillery from Captain Frischman at Palamcotta and set out to attack the fort of Pānjālamkurichi. There were two other forts in the Eṭṭaiyāpuram country that he intended to attack first, but he altered his intention and commenced with Pānjālamkurichi, as being the most important place. Government were very anxious for his success, as they foresaw that the Poligars would be greatly encouraged by the failure of his recent attempt to take Kollamkoṇḍān, but as he was now well supplied with heavy guns and ammunition they hoped his future attacks on the forts of the Poligars would be successful.

Pānjālamkurichi.

Meaning of the name Pānjalamkurichi.

The importance of Pānjālamkurichi in the annals of Tinnevelly requires that a few words should be said about it here. The name has come up already in Orme's History, Colonel Heron having led an expedition against it in 1755. That expedition, however, was recalled, and it does not appear that Pānjālamkurichi was then really attacked. The first of the long series of sieges it sustained from the English was from Major Flint in 1767. Pānjālamkurichi was a large mud fort, situated near the present taluk town of Ōṭṭapiḍāram. Being the headquarters of a Poligar, the whole pāḷaiyam was called by this name. Pānchāla means anything pertaining to Panchāla,—now the Doab—the country of Draupadi, the wife of the five Pāṇḍava brothers. The name must have been given to the place by some person interested in the stories of the Mahābhārata. The second portion of the name is one of the many Tamil words denoting a village. It especially denotes a village in a forest or amongst the hills. There is no trace of a forest now in the neighbourhood, but up to the time of the last Poligar war nearly the whole black cotton soil country in the north of Tinnevelly was covered with thick woods. The conqueror that has cleared away those woods is cotton. But cotton would never have been able to prevail against the woods, if the rule of the Poligars had not come to an end. The Poligar of Pānjālamkurichi was a Nāyakan. We now return to 1767 and Major Flint.

CHAPTER VI.

SUCCEEDING EVENTS OF THE YEAR.

Assault on Pānjālamkurichi a failure.

On the 15th of February, Major Flint's preparations being completed, he endeavoured to take Pānjālamkurichi by assault. A battery was opened against it in the morning, the fire of which was kept up all day. In the afternoon the assault was made, but it had no better success than the assault on Kollamkoṇḍān a short time before. The killed and wounded amounted to 92, including 8 Europeans killed and 18 wounded. Major Flint resolved to turn the siege into a blockade, but during the night—as happened so often in after years—the defenders of the fort made their escape from it. Some took refuge in Tuticorin, some in Vypaur. Eṭṭaiyāpuram was also to have been attacked, but it was found to have been abandoned. The enemy also forsook Vypaur (Vaippāṟu).

It is singular that the remembrance of this siege has entirely passed away. No tradition of it, or any trace of a tradition, survives. The last of the many sieges of Pānjālamkurichi was immortalised by a native poet, but the previous sieges, beginning with Major Flint's, were not so fortunate. As Horace says, "they had no poet and they died."

Determination of Government.

Immediately on the receipt of this intelligence Government determined to despatch a sufficient force to Madura and Tinnevelly for the purpose of repressing the irrepressible Poligars. They found it more difficult to reduce them to obedience than had been anticipated, and it will be seen that this difficulty never ceased till the demoralising influence of a double government came to an end, and the country was wholly transferred from the Nawab to the East India Company. An officer was chosen for this command who was already acquainted with the disturbed districts. This was Colonel Donald Campbell, who had been in command at the capture of Madura and of Yusuf Khan in 1764, and had led a force into Tinnevelly in 1765.

Colonel Campbell's campaign.

On the 26th of April 1767 Colonel Campbell, who had marched from Rājāpālaiyam on the 25th, appeared with his force before Kollamkoṇḍān, where Major Flint four months before had sustained a repulse. His main object was to prevent the defenders of the fort from escaping, but notwithstanding all the precautions he took, on his opening fire on the morning of the 1st May the fort was found to be abandoned. This was a great disappointment to Colonel Campbell, for, as he observed, "unless the ringleaders of the rebels could be laid hold of, the only effect of taking and destroying their forts would be to oblige them to rebuild, which they could do at a far less expense than we could level."

CHAPTER VI.

Abandonment of Sēttūr.

From Kollamkoṇḍān the Colonel marched on the 3rd to Shattoor (that is, Sēttūr, a place not to be confounded with Sāttūr), where he met with more resistance. A considerable force of the enemy had taken up a position outside the fort from which they galled a portion of his camp. They were dislodged with some difficulty and driven into the pettah, but in this service two officers and 46 sepoys were wounded and three sepoys killed. Above 80 of the enemy were killed and more than 100 wounded. Colonel Campbell placed batteries and posted guards all round the fort, but before the works were completed the enemy, fearing that they were about to be hemmed in, made their escape in the night. As soon as he had notice of their elopement he sent after them Captain Harper's battalion and the Nawab's horse, but, he says, "they were far too nimble for the former, and as for the latter he found them generally more detrimental than useful. They consumed a great deal of provisions and did no kind of good." Colonel Campbell found Sēttūr a stronger place than he had supposed. The fort seemed to him almost as large as Palamcotta, and the pettah was encircled with a strong thorn hedge. He found in the fort about 1,000 bullock-loads of grain. He demolished the fort before leaving it.

Abandonment of Sivagiri.

The Colonel's next object of attack and his next disappointment was Sivagiri. On his arrival there on the 10th from Sēttūr he found the fort already abandoned. Its defenders on hearing of his approach fled from it to the hills, where, however, he pitied the deplorable condition they must have found themselves in, and concluded that they must have become truly penitent for their resistance to authority and convinced of its folly. He considered that much of the disloyalty that prevailed was owing to the misgovernment and oppression to which the Poligars as well as the rest of the people were subjected by the Nawab. In Sivagiri, which must have been inhabited, he thought, by 20,000 people, neither man, woman, nor child could be found. He found the fort of Sivagiri larger and stronger than that at Sēttūr. If the defences had been completely finished before they arrived, the taking of it would have been attended with some loss. He spent five or six days in levelling the fort. Colonel Campbell greatly admired the fertility of the neighbourhood, as appears from the conclusion of his letter to Government:—

"I heartily wish the Nawab would fall upon some method to preserve this delightful country from absolute devastation. It is really melancholy to reflect that unless a speedy and an effectual remedy is applied these fertile fields, the most beautiful I have ever seen, will next year be a barren waste."

Attack on Vasudēva-nallūr.

His next letter was from Washinellore (Vāsudēva-nallūr) on the 28th May. He arrived there on the 13th, leaving Major Flint to finish the demolition of the Sivagiri fort. He was joined on the 17th by Major Flint, and on the night of the 18th the garrison attempted to get away by Captain Harper's post, but were beaten back. On the 19th he commenced a cannonade of the fort in the hope of effecting a practicable breach, but the wall being constructed of sunbaked bricks cemented with clay, upwards of 500 shot were poured into one place without effect. Heavy rain now commenced which continued without intermission till the 25th—(the south-west monsoon had evidently commenced that year some weeks earlier than usual)—taking advantage of which the garrison forced their way out at three different places about 4 o'clock on the morning of the 20th and made their escape to the adjacent hills. The first fire of the besiegers did execution, but the second charge, owing to the rain, would not go off. Vāsudēva-nallūr being, he said, "a fort of long standing and commanding as fine a grain country as he had met with, he resolved not to demolish it, but to garrison it with all the Nawab's troops he had, under one Mr. Peter Davidson, who had the appointment of captain under the Nawab and had the reputation of being a person of energy." This he considered the strongest fort he had seen during his campaign—(see the description of this fort in the account of its siege by Yusuf Khan)—and he was astonished at the contempt of death the Collaries evinced during the cannonade. As fast as a breach was made, in the midst of shot and shell they went on quietly repairing it with palmyras and straw. He concluded as before by recommending more reasonable treatment of the people by the Nawab. All that could be done by a European force Government might depend on being done by the troops under his command, but he was anxious that some accommodation should be come to with the people, for which he had received no authority. There were three small forts to the southward of him, and by the time he had reduced them he hoped to receive the Government's commands. He considered that the Nawab had no time to lose, for without some agreement the people would never be persuaded to return and cultivate their fields. The Government were glad to hear of the reduction of Vāsudēva-nallūr, but did not approve of the Nawab's troops being left in so important a place, and ordered Colonel Campbell to garrison it with the Company's troops.

Colonel Campbell's care for the people.

Pending the arrival of authority from the Nawab to treat with the Poligars, Colonel Campbell appointed Captain Harper to establish a cantonment in Sankaranaiyanārkōvil. On the 13th June he wrote him an excellent letter of instructions as to the behaviour of his men, whether Europeans or sepoys, pointing out the necessity of their acting towards the people with justice and tenderness. Shortly after this the Nawab's letters authorising an accommodation with the Poligars arrived, whereupon Colonel

Cantonment at Sankaranaiyanar-kōvil.

CHAPTER VI.

Cessation of hostilities.

Campbell announced a cessation of hostilities and sent for the vakils of the various Poligars, with whom he entered into arrangements for the settlement of their dues and the punctual payment of their tribute in future. The Government recommended the Nawab to leave Colonel Campbell perfectly free to act as he should think best.

Arrangements made by the Nawab's manager.

Colonel Campbell's pacification of the country was very short-lived. Within two months Captain Frischman, Commandant at Palamcotta, informed the Government that on Colonel Campbell leaving the country with his troops the various Poligars began to refuse, as they had always done before, to pay the tribute they had agreed to. In this contumacious conduct the Poligar of Sivagiri was the leader. Captain Frischman succeeded in inducing them all to come to some terms again, which was brought about mainly through the exertions of Rājā "Hookoometron" (Hukumat Ram), the Nawab's manager or financial administrator in Tinnevelly at that time. He was also materially aided by the Poligar of Verdigarry (Vaḍagarai), who had been deprived of the whole of his *pollam* some time before, but had now nine villages restored to him in order to engage him to the Nawab's interest. This was in August 1767. Among other arrangements made during this time the Nawab's manager banished the Poligars of Sivagiri and Pānjālamkurichi from Tinnevelly and appointed others in their places. On the 2nd of September Government were informed by the Commandant that Hyder Ali had written to all the Poligars, calling upon them to join him against the Nawab and the British, and assuring them that if they joined him not only would all their ancient possessions be restored to them, but he would give each of them several additional villages.

Hyder Ali's communication with the Poligars.

In the course of 1767 95 English recruits who had landed at Anjengo were ordered to stay at Palamcotta till further orders.

1768. In February Lieutenant-Colonel Frischman is ordered to join the army in the field against Hyder Ali, and Captain Browne is appointed Commandant of Palamcotta in his room. Colonel Frischman is to supply Captain Browne with all the information in his power relative to the several Poligars, and Captain Browne is to afford the Nawab's manager all the assistance in his power to keep them in proper order.

On the 10th June Captain Browne reports that he had sent three companies of sepoys with a serjeant to destroy a fort which a Poligar was rebuilding. The name of the fort is not given, but the name of the Poligar is said to have been "Cambo-Naig," that is probably Kāmaiyā-Nāyaka. In August he is ordered to send troops and guns to reinforce Colonel Wood in command at Trichinopoly, but is unable to comply with the requisition on account of the troubles he apprehends from the large bodies of Collaries, some eight or

Assemblage of Collaries.

nine thousand in number, that were assembling under the pretence of settling some disputes among themselves, but really for the purpose of plundering the Sircar districts.

On the 24th October he reports that the emissaries of the dispossessed Poligars of Sivagiri and Pāṇjālamkurichi were raising disturbances in those districts. Both these Poligars were at that time living in the Rājā of Rāmnād's country, and it was supposed that they were receiving encouragement in their plots from him. Government accordingly wrote a letter to the Rājā of Rāmnād warning him against this line of action.

Behaviour of the Poligars towards Hyder Ali.

1769. Captain Browne engages the Poligars to act against Hyder Ali. They appear to act loyally at first, but afterwards join the enemy. He complains that the Nawab's troops behaved shamefully.

1770. Nothing transpires worth recording.

1771. Captain Browne is ordered with his battalion to Madras, and Captain Cooke is appointed in his place. Mr. Cumming is Paymaster and Storekeeper.

Burning of Tinnevelly cutcherry.

The Tinnevelly cutcherry was burnt down this year with all the records it contained.

Postal Communication between Madras and Bombay in the latter half of the Eighteenth Century.

Letters to Bombay how sent.

In 1771 I find it mentioned that a packet of letters from Madras to Bombay was sent by Government to the Commanding Officer at Palamcotta for transmission by him to Anjengo, a small town in the coast of Travancore between Trevandrum and Quilon, then belonging to the East India Company, from which it was to be sent on by sea by the earliest opportunity to the Bombay Government. Packets of letters were sent from Bombay to Madras in the same manner. This round-about mode of communication lasted right into the beginning of the nineteenth century, in consequence of the normal condition of the districts intermediate between Madras and Bombay being one of insecurity, through the wars and commotions caused by Hyder Ali, Tippu Sultan, and the Mahrattas. Though inland communication was at that time so imperfect, the beginnings of an overland communication had already been developed. Duplicates of urgent letters to the Court of Directors from the Madras Government were repeatedly sent home *viâ* Bassorah in the Persian Gulf, and duplicates of letters from home arrived by the same route.

Overland communications.

Orme, the historian, is said to have been born at Anjengo.

The first reference to Palamcotta in the journals of Swartz, the eminent Missionary, is in 1771.

CHAPTER VI.

1772. An expedition was planned for the reduction of the Poligars in Madura and Tinnevelly, especially the Poligar of Nālukōttai, that is, Sivagangai. It was entrusted to the command of Major Braithwaite, but was not carried into effect in consequence of troops being more urgently required further north.

1773. Nothing happens in Tinnevelly worthy of record.

1774. In this year there was a severe famine.

Earliest date on Palamcotta church-yard.

1775. The only incident of the year is that Captain Cooke is ordered with his battalion to Madras and succeeded by Captain Hopkins from Vellore. The earliest date I have found in the English church-yard at Palamcotta is in 1775.

1776. Captain Hopkins writes on the 7th January that the Poligar Kaṭṭaboma Nāyaka, who had been driven from Pānjālamkurichi by the Nawab's manager Rājā Hukumat Ram in 1767, had returned and put to death the Poligar who had been appointed in his room by Syed Mahomed Khan in 1771, and that he was again in possession. The Nawab's people, in Syed Mahomed Khan's absence, had collected a considerable force of horse and foot, who were emcamped near Pānjālamkurichi and were ordered to take the place. Nothing more seems to have been heard that year of that attempt to take Pānjālamkurichi.

1777. On the 16th February Captain Hopkins reports that two of the Nawab's battalions with a brigade of guns, under the command of Captain Pickard of the Nawab's service, marched from Tinnevelly against the Poligars. The force was sent out to collect the Nawab's revenues from the Poligars, who as usual had refused to pay. The expedition was especially directed against Sivagiri,

Expedition against Sivagiri.

where a large number of Collaries had collected. Strange to say the Nawab's force was joined by the Poligar of Pānjālamkurichi with 4,000 men. This was in consequence of his having made his peace with the Nawab's manager.

This force invested Sivagiri and attempted to reduce it. It is not stated what the result was—probably as usual a failure and a compromise.

Captain Eidington succeeds Captain Browne and soon after is ordered to resign his command.

1778. Captain Barrington is appointed to the command of Palamcotta in supersession of Captain Eidington.

On the 6th April Captain Barrington is ordered to send five companies of his battalion to assist the Nawab's manager in collecting the peshcush due from the Poligars. In the event of their resistance he was not to use force without express orders from Government.

Insults offered to Hindus.

1779. Colonel Braithwaite whilst passing through Tinnevelly reports to Government the violence shown to the Hindūs by the Nawab's people at the Moharram. They had broken an image to pieces and killed several Brahmans. This had led to the abandonment of all cultivation and manufactures on the part of the Hindūs, who insisted on justice and revenge. He feared that the Tinnevelly Poligars, who were a resolute people, possessed of many strongholds, might take the opportunity of breaking into rebellion. He reports also that the country was distracted by the animosities of the Nawab's late Fauzdar, the present one, and Dalavāy Mudali, the Hindū renter. Colonel Braithwaite was then on his way with a considerable force to Anjengo, where his troops were to embark for Tellicherry to take part in the fruitless operations of the army on the Malabar Coast. Captain Barrington writes from Palamcotta that he found it very difficult to obtain supplies for Colonel Braithwaite's force, on account of the disturbed state of the country consequent upon the insult offered by the Muhammadans to the Hindūs. Towards the end of the year Captain Eidington is reappointed to the command of Palamcotta.

1780. Captain Eidington reports that there had been an engagement between the Nawab's troops and the Poligar of Sivagiri. All the Poligars now openly or virtually threw off their allegiance, so that there was a great diminution in the revenue. Captain Eidington discovered that some of the Poligars were in correspondence with Hyder Ali. At this time the Paymaster at Palamcotta was Mr. William Light, by whom the cultivation of spices was first introduced into Tinnevelly. He had brought two young cinnamon trees from Colombo. The state of the Tinnevelly country was now so unsettled and unsatisfactory that the President of the Madras Council was requested to have a personal interview with the Nawab on the subject. Fortunately a more satisfactory arrangement was at hand and was introduced at the close of the following year.

Spices in Palamcotta.

The Tinnevelly Mission Register, or Register of the Native Christians resident in Palamcotta, begins in this year, 1780.

1781. Captain Eidington informs Government that the Sivagiri Poligar had invited Hyder Ali to send troops into the Tinnevelly country. He also states that he was convinced that the renter (Rājā Hukumat Ram) was secretly on Hyder Ali's side, being a near relative of the "Colt Rājā," who had been appointed by Hyder Rājā of Madura and Tinnevelly. He reports that he could get very little assistance from the Rājā of Travancore towards protecting the country from Hyder. The Dutch of Tuticorin promised the assistance of their Government of Colombo against Hyder Ali, whom they described as the common enemy of all Europeans. It will be seen that a little later on they took a different line.

Dutch estimate of Hyder Ali.

In February Captain Eidington despatches Lieutenant Halcott with three companies to get possession of the fort at Srīvilliputtūr,

CHAPTER VI. both in order to keep the restless Poligar of Sivagiri in check and also to secure possession of a place which he considered the key of Tinnevelly. He mentions that the real chief of Sivagiri was at that time in Palamcotta in prison. Lieutenant Halcott was attacked near Madura by 3,000 Collaries and three or four hundred horse, whom he beat off with loss to them and some to himself. Captain Eidington also mentions that as Hyder Ali had sent messengers to the Poligars to stir them up against the Nawab and the British, he had entered into negotiations with several of the principal Poligars, and found that they were willing to enter into an engagement, provided their relations who were in prison were released. He asks for 2,000 stand of arms in place of those taken by the Collaries in the Rāmnād country. Later in the year the Dutch were strengthening Tuticorin and apparently preparing for a war with the English. They were rendering great assistance to Kaṭṭaboma Nāyaka of Pānjālamkurichi, who had actually hoisted Dutch colours. This Poligar had been beaten off from the fort of Comrah (Kamudi), in the Rāmnād country, with the loss of a hundred men. In October on account of complaints made against him Captain Eidington is superseded by Captain Bilcliffe.

Dutch alliance with Poligars.

MEDITATED CESSION OF TINNEVELLY TO THE DUTCH.

In 1781 Mr. Hastings, then Governor-General, endeavoured to enter into a treaty with the Dutch, the effect of which, if it had proved successful, would have been to convert Tinnevelly into a Dutch province. The object of that measure was to obtain, through the Governors of Colombo and Cochin, a military force to assist in the expulsion of Hyder from the Carnatic. But as these Governors acted under the authority of the Government of Batavia, for whose sanction there was no leisure to wait, a tempting advantage was represented as necessary to prevail upon them to incur so unusual a responsibility. The negotiation was carried on through the medium of the Director of the Dutch Settlements in Bengal; and it was stipulated that for 1,000 European infantry, 200 European artillery, and 1,000 Malays, who should be paid and maintained by the Company during the period of their service, the province of Tinnevelly should be ceded to the Dutch, together with the liberty of making conquests in the neighbourhood of Cochin, and the exclusive right to the pearl fishery on the whole of the coast south from Rāmēśvavaram. In name and appearance the sovereignty of the Nawab, Muhammad Ali, was not to be infringed, and the treaty, framed and concluded for him, was to be ratified by his signature. The small value of the cession and the extreme danger of the Carnatic were urged as the motives to induce compliance on the part both of the Nawab and of the Government of

Madras. The ideas, however, of the Nawab and of the Government of Madras differed very widely from those of the Governor-General respecting the value both of what was to be given and what was to be received. They not only set a high estimate on Tinnevelly, but treated the offer of a body of troops, when they were much less in want of troops, than of money to pay and maintain those which they had, as a matter of doubtful utility. In consequence they declined to forward the treaty, transmitting their reasons to the Court of Directors. And the accession of the Dutch to the side of the enemies of England, of which Lord Macartney carried out the intelligence, superseded on that ground all further proceedings. See Mill, Vol. IV, Book 5.

PART II.

FROM THE ASSIGNMENT OF REVENUE IN 1781 TO THE COMMENCEMENT OF THE BANNERMAN-POLIGAR WAR.

THE ASSIGNMENT.

Committee of Assigned Revenue.

TOWARDS the close of the year 1781 a treaty was concluded between the Nawab of the Carnatic and the East India Company, in virtue of which Tinnevelly, with the other districts in the Carnatic, enjoyed for a few years the benefits of the Company's civil administration. This treaty was entered into and all the arrangements necessary for carrying it into effect were made in October 1781, but the treaty itself was not signed till the 2nd of December. The Board of Revenue was not then in existence (it was instituted in 1786), but a committee was appointed by Government on the 16th October, called the Committee of Assigned Revenue, consisting of six gentlemen, including Mr. George Proctor (the first civil officer appointed to Tinnevelly) and Mr. Eyles Irwin (his more eminent successor), for the purpose of receiving and administering the revenues of the Nawab. The object of the treaty is thus expressed by Government in their first letter to the Committee:—"His Highness the Nawab has assigned over the revenues of the Carnatic to the Company to be entirely under their management and control during the present war,[1] on the condition of allowing him one-sixth part of the revenue to defray the expenses of himself and family." At the same time a copy of the instructions of Government was furnished to the Committee for

[1] The war with Hyder Ali, subsequently continued and intensified under Tippu Sultan.

CHAPTER VI.

Superintendents of Assigned Revenue.

its guidance. The Governor of Madras at this time was Lord Macartney. In virtue of this arrangement functionaries styled at first Receivers of Assigned Revenue, then Superintendents of Assigned Revenue, were appointed in various places. A shorter title by which they were generally known was Civil Superintendents or simply Superintendents. These were the first civil officers appointed for the administration of affairs in the interior. Up to that time, as we have seen, the only civil administration with which the English Government had anything to do, that is, the enforcement of the payment of the Nawab's revenue, was carried on by the military officers in command of the troops in the various districts.

Intentions of Government.

The Government hoped that this new arrangement would contribute in various ways to the prosperity of the country. In the instructions issued to the Committee they conclude by saying, "By attending to these points the Company may arrive at much useful knowledge. They may be gradually able to free the country from oppression, to recover the lands and manufactures from their present most deplorable state, greatly to improve the revenue, and finally to establish wealth, credit, and prosperity throughout the country." This view of the objects of Government was, I need hardly say, widely different from that entertained by the Government of the Nawab.

First Collector of Tinnevelly.

The first "Receiver of Assigned Revenue" appointed to Tinnevelly—virtually the first Tinnevelly Collector—was Mr. George Proctor. He had been Auditor of Accounts in Madras, and then member of the newly-appointed Committee of Assigned Revenue. Lord Macartney's letter appointing him Receiver in Tinnevelly was dated 8th December 1781. Another letter a few days later gave him similar authority in Madura; another respecting the Ramnad peshoush. The Nawab gave orders to his Fauzdars and Amildars in Tinnevelly to obey the new functionary, whilst the Madras Government ordered Captain Eidington and Lieutenant-Colonel Nixon to render him any military assistance that he might require. He was accompanied by Mr. Orpen as his assistant.

1782. A Poligar named Sivarāma Talaivan had erected a fort Tirukurungudi near Tirukurungudi and was plundering the neighbourhood. The commandant sent a detachment, which took the fort and destroyed it. "Sivarāma Talaivan" is the hereditary name of the head of a powerful Marava family in that place.

Capture of Tuticorin.

War having broken out between the Dutch and the English, Captain Bilcliffe, Commandant at Palamcotta, sends a party under Lieutenant Wheeler to take possession of Tuticorin. The small Dutch garrison were made prisoners. Seventeen guns taken. There were 200 men in the garrison belonging to Pānjālamkurichi, who fled on seeing the approach of the Company's troops. It must have

CHAPTER VI.

been because they did not care to fight for the Dutch, for their behaviour at their own fort whenever it was attacked was very different. The Dutch factories at Punnaikāyal and Maṇapāḍu were demolished. The outworks erected by the Dutch at Tuticorin were also destroyed, and it was ordered that if a Dutch force landed the fort of Tuticorin was to be blown up and destroyed. The native inhabitants of Tuticorin, especially the Paravas, represented to Mr. Proctor, and Mr. Proctor represented to Government, the injustice done by the party under Mr. Wheeler in seizing on their property, with that of the Dutch, and requiring them to pay "gratifications" for the privilege of returning to the town and living under English protection. Government considered such conduct most culpable and ordered the commanding officer to confine himself to his duties in the fort.

Complaints of the Paravas.

In April 1782 Mr. Proctor wrote to the Committee complaining of the conduct of the renter, who at that time was Trimolipa (Tirumalaiyappa) Mudali, to the effect that he was unduly raising the price of the Government grain, listening to the advice of Captain Gibbings instead of his own, and playing into the hands of the Poligars. He proposed that a new renter should be appointed, and that the Receiver of Revenue (that is himself) should have absolute authority over him. He first proposed that Tīttārappa Mudali, the nephew of the present renter, should be appointed, and then Ranga Row, a stranger, then an Amil in Madura. The then renter (Tirumalaiyappa Mudali) at the same time complained to the Committee of Mr. Proctor's conduct; a complaint was also made by "the Company's Sherishtadar," and there was a serious misunderstanding between Mr. Proctor and the commanding officer. Captain Gibbings and the rest of their servants in Tinnevelly were ordered by the Committee to refrain from all interference in matters of revenue, but in other particulars the Committee were not disposed to adopt Mr. Proctor's recommendations. On the contrary they found fault with him for interfering in the rate of exchange, and for having failed to send them any account of his receipts from the time of his arrival. He was ordered to send them his accounts monthly in future.

Dispute between the renter and the Collector.

The Committee's dissatisfaction with Mr. Proctor's management appears from the conclusion at which they arrived, that "some further regulations were necessary to fulfil all the objects of the Assignment." They, therefore, resolved to recur to the directions at first given them by Government and proposed that from time to time as should appear necessary deputations should proceed, composed of members of the Committee, through the several assigned countries. The superintendence proposed being only temporary would not, they thought, prove prejudicial. The language they used bore heavily not only on Mr. Proctor, but on

Dissatisfaction with Mr. Proctor.

Conduct of European functionaries.

CHAPTER VI. the other European functionaries hitherto employed in the interior. They say this temporary superintendence would not "allow any temptation for interfering in the money transactions or intrigues of the country, nor would it be liable to the objections that the Committee are of opinion lie against all the European superintendence that has yet been established under the Company's government." The gentleman sent to Tinnevelly as a deputation from the Committee was Mr. Eyles Irwin, but his appointment falls amongst the incidents of 1783.

In December 1782 a letter was written during Mr. Proctor's absence in Madras by Mr. Orpen, his Assistant, Mr. Light, the Paymaster, and Captain Bilcliffe, the Commandant, asking permission to use strong measures against the renter.

1783. On the 27th January the Committee replied to the letter of the previous month from Palamcotta, to the effect that they were to wait till the arrival of Mr. Irwin, as they intended to entrust to him the management of all their affairs in Tinnevelly.

On the 28th January a Commission was issued by Lord Macartney to Mr. Irwin to proceed to Tinnevelly with full authority from the Committee of Assigned Revenue. The Commission begins thus:—

Commission to Mr. Irwin.

"The state of the Tinnevelly province, as represented by the Committee of Assigned Revenue, has determined us to send a person in whom we can confide to enquire into and remove, as far as may be practicable, the misunderstandings and dissensions which have arisen there to the prejudice of the revenue, and we have appointed you for the service, not only from the trust we repose in your zeal and capacity, but in compliance also with an early recommendation preferred to us by the Committee for employing its members occasionally in making circuits throughout the different districts of the Carnatic, agreeably to the original institution of the Committee."

Instructions to Mr. Irwin.

The Government were unable to determine which of the complaints and recriminations that had come before them from Tinnevelly were most worthy of investigation, but they recommended Mr. Irwin on his arrival to proceed to investigate such of the complaints as appeared to him to have any probable foundation, "particularly the insinuation thrown out by the late renter against Mr. Proctor concerning undue advantages made by the measurement of grain and exchange of money." Mr. Irwin is recommended to arrange that a fixed tribute, bearing a reasonable proportion to their possessions and not liable to alteration, should be paid by the Poligars; also that the complaints of the renters against the ryots and of the ryots against the renters should be inquired into and equitably settled. He is directed to endeavour to acquire as much knowledge as possible of the condition of things in general in Tinnevelly, in order that the welfare and improvement of the country may be promoted. He is to inquire whether any of the natural productions of the country are capable of being improved, and especially whether the cultivation of spices can be developed. He is to endeavour to throw light on the prospects of the pearl fishery, as also on the commerce of Tuticorin and the settlements in the Gulf of Manaar. All orders relating to revenue affairs sent previously to other persons are to be transferred to him, including the orders sent to Mr. Light for the inspection of the repairs of tanks, as Government do not wish any other gentleman in Tinnevelly to have the least pretence for interfering in the affairs of the country. He is directed to exercise a general oversight in Madura, as well as in Tinnevelly, there being no other person in charge there, and all military officers are ordered to obey his requisitions. They are to furnish him with a suitable escort in his tours through the country. The Government add that they wished him to correspond with Mr. John Sulivan, Tanjore, whose judgment and experience could not fail to be of value. Mr. Sulivan was at that time "Resident of Tanjore and Superintendent of Assigned Revenues of Trichinopoly and Marawar." The latter term meant Ramnad and Sivagangai. Finally, they say they allow him seven pagodas per diem for his expenses, the sum that was allowed to Mr. Proctor, "Receiver of the Revenues in the Tinnevelly country," and Captain's pay and batta to his Assistant.

Tuticorin complaints.

In another letter he was instructed to inquire into the complaints of the Parava inhabitants of Tuticorin. He was also instructed to present an honorary dress to the head of the Paravas (the Jātitalaivar) in the name of the Madras Government.

Mr. Irwin landed at Anjengo from the Company's ships going on to Bombay, whence he proceeded to Palamcotta, where he arrived on the 4th of March. Immediately on his arrival at Palamcotta he set out for Trivandrum, to wait on the king and present him with a letter with which he was charged from the Madras Government, requesting his assistance in the operations against Hyder Ali.

Mr. Irwin enters on his duties.

Mr. Irwin requested that another Assistant should be appointed instead of Mr. Orpen, who had been removed. Mr. Torin (afterwards Collector) was appointed his Assistant, then Mr. Kindersley.

Soon after his arrival in Tinnevelly he presided in a court of inquiry held by the authority of Government to inquire into Mr. Proctor's proceedings. The court considered Mr. Proctor's accounts unsatisfactory. It was found that he had entered in his accounts many items of expenditure of a personal nature without the authority of Government. It was found also that balances of receipts of revenue still remained in his hands. In consequence of this decision of the court he was relieved from his duties in the district and ordered to proceed to the Presidency. Government

Mr. Proctor ordered to leave.

CHAPTER VI.

required him to refund what he had improperly received, and on his delaying to do this ordered a suit to be instituted against him in the Mayor's Court, Madras.

In April Mr. Irwin in a letter to Government states the obstacles he finds standing in the way of every plan for the improvement of the country. First and foremost amongst those obstacles he places the refractory disposition of the Poligars. "Their licentiousness," he says, "not having been curbed or checked for these five years past, they are now become so hardened in their contumacy as to render it impracticable to reduce them to a proper sense of their interest and duty but by force of arms." It was evident that things were getting ripe for Colonel Fullarton's expedition. The operations to which he refers as having taken place five years before were those of Captain Pickard in 1777 and of Captain Barrington in 1778.

Mr. Irwin invites Colonel Fullarton.

In August the Government give Mr. Irwin full powers to rent the revenues of Tinnevelly to the best of his judgment. He repeatedly writes to Colonel Fullarton proposing that a portion of the southern army should be employed under his command in settling the Tinnevelly country. These letters, with the sanction of Government, led to Colonel Fullarton's expedition. Of this expedition Colonel Fullarton himself gives a graphic account. His able report to the Madras Government entitled "A View of the English Interests in India," republished in Madras in 1867, will amply repay perusal.

Colonel Fullarton's Expedition as related by himself.

"The districts of Madura, Mēlūr, and Pallemery (Paḷḷimaḍai) were so harassed with Colleries, Poligars, and the enemy, that your troops and subjects were often attacked within range of forts, and the sentries fired at on the works. All the Poligars of Tinnevelly were in rebellion, and closely connected with the Dutch Government at Colombo, from whence attempts were meditated, in conjunction with them and with Māpiḷḷai Dēvar, to reduce those countries and the Marava dominions. Nearly one hundred thousand Poligars and Colleries were in arms throughout the southern provinces, and being considered hostile to Government, looked to public confusion as their safeguard against punishment. Your southern force was inadequate to repress these outrages and to retrieve your affairs. The treasury was drained, the country depopulated, the revenues exacted by the enemy, the troops undisciplined, ill-paid, poorly fed and unsuccessfully commanded. During the course of these proceedings, your southern provinces remained in their former confusion. The Poligars, Colleries, and other tributaries, ever since the commencement of the war had thrown off all appearance of allegiance. No civil arrangement could be attempted without a military force, and nothing less than the whole army seemed adequate to their reduction. While such a considerable

Strength of the Poligars.

CHAPTER VI.

portion of the southern provinces remained in defiance of the Company's Government, it was vain to think of supporting the current charges of the establishment, far less could we hope to reduce the arrears, and to prepare for important operations, in the probable event of a recommencement of hostilities. It became indispensable, therefore, to restore the tranquillity of those provinces by vigorous military measures as the only means to render them productive of revenue."

Difficulties of the situation.

After having reduced the Poligars of Mēlūr and Sivagangei to obedience, Colonel Fullarton marched southwards. "There next remained a more important undertaking. The numerous Poligars of Tinnevelly, who had rebelled on the commencement of the war, committed daily ravages from Madura to Cape Comorin. They subdued forts and occupied districts belonging to the Circar, or held by a tenure different from their own. I had been repeatedly urged by Mr. Irwin, Superintendent of Madura and Tinnevelly, to proceed against the Poligars, in order to restore tranquillity and recover the revenues. It was now, for the first time, in my power to direct my operations towards that quarter, at a moment when the most powerful of the Poligars in confederacy against your Government, and in alliance with the Dutch, had assembled twelve or fourteen thousand men, and were actually besieging the fort of Chocumpatty (Chokkampaṭṭi), a Poligar place of some strength, below the hills that form the north-west boundary of the province.

Invitation to reduce the Poligars.

"When it was determined that we should march towards Tinnevelly, during the interval requisite for Colonels Stuart and Elphinstone's detachments to reach Dindigul, my object was to strike an unexpected blow, and to intimidate the Poligars into submission. Of all the Tinnevelly chiefs, the principal in power and delinquency, excepting Sivagiri, was Kaṭṭaboma Nāyaka. He was personally engaged at the siege of Chocumpatty, from whence his fort of Pānjālamkurichi, on the south-east quarter of Tinnevelly, is distant more than seventy miles. The usual route to Tinnevelly passes by Madura; and the Poligars, hearing of our movement towards Sivagangei, looked for us in that direction. To favour this opinion, I ordered provisions for the army to be prepared at Madura, kept my real intention perfectly concealed, and moved off with the force from Sivagangei, on the evening of 8th August, to Tropichetty (Tiru Pachetti), a place twenty miles distant on the southern border of the Mēlūr country. I there joined the remainder of the army, and leaving the 7th battalion and some irregulars to restrain the Colleries at Mēlūr, we proceeded next morning by Pallemery (Paḷḷimaḍai), Pandalgoody, and Naiglapore (Nāgalāpuram), and reached the fort of Pānjālamkurichi on the fourth day, being one hundred miles from Sivagangei.[1] As soon as the line

March into Tinnevelly.

Attack on Pānjālamkurichi.

[1] Fahrenheit's thermometer was frequently above 110 degrees during these marches.

CHAPTER VI. approached the fort, a flag was sent desiring the headmen to open their gates and hold a conference : they refused. The 18-pounders were, therefore, halted in the rear of an embankment, facing the north-east angle of the works ; a hasty battery was constructed, and in three hours we were ready to open on the bastion. The works were manned with several thousand people, and every circumstance denoted an intention of resistance. It was material to storm without delay, in order to strike terror by despatch and also lest Kaṭṭaboma Nāyaka, with his confederate chiefs, might hasten to obstruct our operations. We opened on the bastion, but finding ourselves retarded by its thickness, we resolved to breach the adjoining curtain, and to render the defences of the bastion untenable by the besieged. They kept up a constant and well-directed fire, and notwithstanding our utmost efforts, it was dark before a practicable breach was effected ; the attack was therefore deferred until the moon should rise. The storming party consisted of two companies of Europeans, supported by the 13th and 24th Carnatic Battalions, and continued in the rear of the battery. The cavalry, the 1st, and light infantry battalions, were posted at right angles with the other three salient angles of the fort, with detachments fronting each gateway, in order to prevent the besieged from receiving supplies or making their escape, while the other troops remained to defend the camp, which was within random shot.

Abandonment of the fort.

" Our next object was to remove a strong hedge fronting the breach and surrounding the whole fort, as is the practice in the Poligar system of defence. This dangerous service was effected with unusual skill by Ensign Cunningham, commanding the Pioneers, and about 10 at night, with the advantage of bright moonshine, the storm commenced. Our troops after they gained the summit of the breach found no sufficient space to lodge themselves, and the interior wall having no slope or talus, they could not push forward from the summit as they advanced. The defenders were numerous and opposed us so vigorously with pikes and musketry that we were obliged at last to retire, and reached the battery with considerable slaughter on both sides. Immediate measures were taken to renew the charge, but the Poligars, disheartened with their loss, abandoned the place, and sallied forth at the eastern gate. The corps posted round the works were so exhausted by the preceding marches that the fugitives effected their escape; the rest were taken prisoners. The breach was covered with dead bodies, and the place contained a large assortment of guns, powder, shot, arms, and other military stores, which were of course applied to the public service. 40,000 star pagodas were also found, and immediately distributed to the troops. Your Board was pleased to confirm this distribution on the footing of prize-money, than which no measure could more effectually tend to animate the army in our after operations. Some other facts respecting these transactions, and the treaty between the Dutch Government of Colombo and Kaṭṭaboma Nāyaka (of which the original was taken in his fort), were referred to in my letters of the 13th August addressed to your Lordship and the Board.

Attack on Sivagiri.

"Having left Captain Jacobs with five companies of the 25th Battalion to garrison the place I proceeded to Palamcotta, in order to inspect the state of that fort, and from thence by Sankaranāinār-kōil to Sivagiri. It was hoped that the reduction of that stronghold belonging to the most powerful of all the Poligars, in addition to the fall of Pānjālamkurichi, would intimidate the less considerable offenders, and convince the whole confederacy that their treatment would be proportioned to their misconduct. Besides, the outrages committed by the Sivagiri chief were atrocious, and could not be forgiven without a total surrender of your authority. He had barbarously murdered Captain Graham Campbell and cut off a detachment under the command of that officer. On former occasions he had beat off considerable detachments, and avowedly protected your enemies, who thought themselves secure in the fort of Shevigherry. He had collected magazines sufficient to supply the Dutch force that was expected from Colombo, as well as to resist the most tedious blockade, for he did not conceive his fort could be stormed, and every circumstance in his conduct marked that he held himself beyond the reach of military power. On our arrival before the town of Sivagiri he retired to the thickets, near four miles deep, in front of his comby[1] which it covers and defends. He manned the whole extent of a strong embankment that separates the wood and open country. He was joined by Kaṭṭaboma Nāyaka, with other associated Poligars and mustered eight thousand or nine thousand men in arms. In the present instance lenity would have been accounted imbecility, but the approach of Colonels Stuart and Elphinstone to Dindigul, and Tippu Sultan's refusal of the proposed accommodation, rendered me extremely anxious to finish this Poligar warfare, in order to proceed towards the enemies' frontiers. The Sivagiri chief and his associates were therefore informed that I meant immediately to attack the place, unless they would constrain the head Poligars of Tinnevelly, amounting to thirty-two chiefs, to liquidate all arrears and refund the amount of depredations committed since the commencement of the war, agreeably to authenticated vouchers in the different districts. It was further intimated that if they, on the part of the confederacy, would engage to pay £120,000 in lieu of all demands, I would forward their proposal to the Superintendent of Revenue (Mr. Irwin), and on his accept-

Abandonment of the fort.

Terms offered to the Poligars.

[1] Tamil, kōmbai; the dictionary calls it "a stronghold in the mountains;" rather a stockade in a forest.

CHAPTER VI.

ance that the troops would be withdrawn, and that they would be recommended to forgiveness. They wished to confer with me, but refused to visit me in camp. As their distrust arose from various outrages committed against them by former commanders, instead of increasing their apprehensions by any appearance of distrust or resentment, I proposed to meet them alone and unattended at their own barrier, adding that if any accident befel me, it would not pass unresented. The Sivagiri Chief, Kaṭṭaboma Nāyaka, and the deposed Poligar of Chocumpatty, with a large retinue, met me in front of their embankment; before they finished their explanations it was dark, and a musket inadvertently fired in the rear alarmed our advanced picket, who thought it was aimed at me. To prevent the ill-consequences of that mistake, I took leave of the Poligars expressing my wish to hear of their acceding to the terms proposed. We refrained from hostility next day, but finding that they trifled with proposals, the line was ordered under arms on the morning following, and we made the distribution of attack. It proved as desperate as any contest in that species of Indian warfare, not only from the numbers and obstinacy of the Poligars, but from the peculiar circumstances which had acquired for this place the reputation of impregnability. The attack commenced by the Europeans and four battalions of sepoys moving against the embankment which covers the wood. The Poligars, in full force, opposed us, but our troops remained with their firelocks shouldered, under a heavy fire, until they approached the embankment; there they gave a general discharge and rushed upon the enemy. By the vigour of this advance we got possession of the summit, the Poligars took post on the verge of the adjoining wood, and disputed every step with great loss on both sides.

Terms declined.

Attack on the stronghold.

Capture of the stronghold.

"After reconnoitring we found that the comby could not be approached in front. We proceeded, therefore, to cut a road through the impenetrable thickets for three miles to the base of the hill that bounds the comby on the west. The Pioneers, under Ensign Cunningham, laboured with indefatigable industry; Captain Gardiner of the 102nd supported them with the Europeans, and Captain Blacker with the 3rd and 24th Carnatic Battalions advanced their field pieces as fast as the road was cleared. These were strengthened by troops in their rear forming a communication with those in front. For this purpose two other battalions were posted within the wood, and as soon as we gained the embankment the camp moved near it and concentrated our force. We continued to cut our way under an unabating fire from eight thousand Poligars, who constantly pressed upon our advanced party, rushed upon the line of attack, piked the bullocks that were dragging the guns and killed many of our people. But those attempts were repulsed by perseverance, and before sunset we had opened a passage entirely to the mountain. It is extremely high, rocky, and in many places almost perpendicular. Having resolved to attack from this unexpected quarter, the troops undertook the service, and attained the summit. The Poligar parties posted to guard that eminence being routed after much firing on all hands we descended on the other side and flanked the comby. The enemy seeing us masters of the mountain retreated under cover of the night by paths inaccessible to regular troops, and we took possession of this wonderful recess. The particulars respecting ordnance, stores, and provisions found in the place are stated in my letter of the 3rd September. We left the 3rd and 9th Battalions to secure the magazines and moved the army to Srīvilliputtūr within four marches of Madura in order to awe the Northern Poligars of Tinnevelly.

Success of the expedition.

"It was little more than a month since we had left Trichinopoly. Your authority was re-established throughout the whole track that we had traversed, extending more than three hundred miles; and besides the arrangement with the Sivagangei Rājā, we were masters of the two strongest places belonging to the Poligars. We remained some time in expectation of their proposing a general accommodation, but they knew that Tippu still invested Mangalore, and that I must quickly join the force at Dindigul. This intelligence corroborated their spirit of procrastination. I therefore convened the Vakeels[1] whom the chief Poligars had sent to treat with me in camp, and directed them to inform their respective principals that I should leave the province on the 21st September. I added that if they did not return to their allegiance, I should make a vow to Siven, the Gentoo god, whose attribute is vengeance, to march back and spread destruction throughout every possession of the defaulting Poligars: this declaration alarmed the whole assembly. I wrote to Mr. Irwin expressing my regret on leaving the province before any settlement was concluded with the Poligars. He forwarded to me the terms on which he thought it expedient to restore their forts to Kaṭṭaboma Nāyaka and Sivagiri. Vakeels from these chiefs waited on me at Trimungulam[2] (Tirumangalam) and stipulated in the name of their masters that they would pay thirty thousand chuckrums each, in lieu of all preceding claims. They likewise gave their bonds for fifteen thousand pagodas, or £6,000 each, in consideration of the restitution of their forts. I farther exacted obligations that the defences of Pānjālamkurichi should be demolished, the guns, stores, and ammunition removed to Palamcotta, and that the road which we cleared to the comby of Sivagiri should continue open; that the means of defence should be removed

The Colonel's threat.

[1] Vakeels are deputies, agents, or ambassadors.

[2] Trimungulam (Tirumangalam) is twelve miles south-west of Madura.

CHAPTER VI.

Conditions of peace imposed.

from the place, and that the southern commanders and the Company's troops should at all times be admitted within their forts and barriers. I concluded with injunctions to observe a more submissive conduct if they valued their lives, property, or posterity. As soon as the restitution of the forts and prisoners[1] could possibly take place, the 3rd and 9th Battalions, under Captain Mackinnon, were directed to march from Sivagiri and to join me at Dindigul, whither I proceeded by the route of Madura."

In the beginning of the following year Colonel Fullarton visited Tinnevelly again, but only for the purpose of expediting the collection of money and means of transport for the force with which he was preparing to cope with Tippu Sultan.

Satisfaction of Government.

On the 26th October Mr. Irwin mentions that Kaṭṭaboma Nāyaka and the Sivagiri Poligar had submitted. It will be seen from a general order of Government, reviewing the position of things in 1875, that they were highly gratified both with the military results of Colonel Fullarton's expedition and with the financial settlement he had made.

Kaṭṭaboma's treaty with the Dutch.

Mr. Irwin transmits the originals and translations of Kaṭṭaboma Nāyaka's correspondence with the Dutch and their treaty with him, found in his fort on its capture, as mentioned by Colonel Fullarton in his narrative, which he observes will fully justify the severity with which he was treated. He recommends also that if the Dutch should return to Tuticorin, peace having been concluded, as was expected, measures should be taken to prevent them from giving their support and encouragement to Kaṭṭaboma Nāyaka as before.

Pearl fishery.

1784. The first pearl fishery carried on by the East India Company was in 1784, under Mr. Irwin's superintendence, but the result, as has so often been the case since, was unsatisfactory.

Mr. Irwin's policy.

In a letter to the Committee in May Mr. Irwin represents the advantages that have accrued to the province from the combination of severity and clemency in Colonel Fullarton's dealings with the Poligars. In carrying out this policy himself he states that he had released most of the Poligar prisoners held in detention in Palamcotta jail, in the belief that this unexpected act of clemency would confirm them in their allegiance to the Company. The Poligar of Kollarpaṭṭi had been imprisoned for more than twenty years. His son, who was an infant when his father was committed to prison, had succeeded to the pollam and had been in possession ever since. Notwithstanding this he applied for his father's release and in Mr. Irwin's presence he voluntarily resigned to his father

[1] Among the prisoners there was the daughter of Kaṭṭaboma Nāyaka, who, as well as all the others, amounting to many hundreds, were treated with the utmost attention.

the authority he had so long held. Mr. Irwin was much struck with this instance of filial duty. Hindu readers will be reminded of Bharata's behaviour to his brother Rāma.

Instance of filial duty.

In October he repeats that the Pāñjālamkurichi and Sivagiri Poligars, who had been singled out for punishment by Colonel Fullarton, were still very punctual in their payments, and he hopes that the rest of the Poligars will learn to be equally punctual.

Swartz's visit.

1785. Swartz visited Palamcotta in 1785, when he dedicated the church that had been erected there.

Tuticorin given up.

Captain Bilcliffe, Commandant of Palamcotta, is directed to make over Tuticorin, with the stations dependent on it, to Mr. Meckern, the Dutch Governor, in behalf of the Dutch. The treaty, in virtue of which this cession was at length made, had been entered into two years before, viz., in 1783. Towards the end of the year Mr. Torin acted as Paymaster for Mr. Oakes. The appointment of Paymaster was then always held by civilians.

Surrender of the Assignment.

The surrender of the Assignment reluctantly agreed to by Government.

The principal event of this year, and one which was productive of much mischief to every district in the country, Tinnevelly included, was the surrender to the Nawab of the assignment of his revenues, in virtue of which the civil administration of the Company, with all its advantages, ceased for seven years. The surrender took place, after many ineffectual protests on the part of the Madras Government, on the 28th of June, whereupon the proceedings of the Committee of Assigned Revenue came to an end, and the Committee itself was soon after dissolved. They were to cease receiving their special allowances from the 5th of July, but were to continue to meet as a committee till all the balances were settled. They were thanked by the Supreme Government for their zealous services. On the 24th June Mr. Irwin wrote a letter to Government earnestly deprecating the surrender of the assignment, as a retrograde measure fraught with the worst consequences. In the event of the surrender appearing to be inevitable he pleaded that a stipulation should be inserted, exempting Tinnevelly and Madura from its operation till October. He argued that those two districts having been remodelled by himself were in an exceptional position. Reforms and pacificatory measures had been introduced, but there had not been time to carry them far. His wish could not be acceded to. Before his letter reached Madras the surrender had been formally made. In virtue of this conclusion, on the 10th July, Mr. Irwin reports that he had delivered over the district to the Amildars on that date, with the balance due from the 28th of June. In doing so he again expressed his apprehension of the evils that were likely to ensue. In September Mr. Irwin on his way

CHAPTER VI. from Tinnevelly to Madras, at Mēlūr in Madura, writes to Government a letter in which he highly lauds the conduct of Mr. Torin, his Revenue Assistant in the Madura District, who was afterwards the first Collector of Tinnevelly under the Assumption in 1790 and the Treaty of 1792. After his arrival in Madras, in October he submitted to Government in an able letter his views respecting the condition of the southern districts from Trichinopoly to Tinnevelly that had been under his charge, reiterating his conviction that all the old evils would revive and gather strength through the withdrawal of the Company's authority, both on the side of the Nawab's agents, who would now be able to misgovern with impunity, and on that of the Poligars, whose habits of insurrection and plunder would now go on unchecked.

Irwin's foreboding.

The Committee of Assigned Revenue, in resigning their functions, submitted to Government, on the 31st of December, a general statement of their proceedings, in which they enlarged on the circumstances of the Tinnevelly Poligars, the impolicy of the dealings with them of the Nawab's agents, and the principles on which their own method of dealing with them had been grounded. They describe the Poligars as thirty-two in number, with an array of followers armed with pikes and matchlocks, estimated at 30,000 men, and possessed of strongholds which the Nawab's troops had often found it difficult to reduce and from which, even if they were taken, it was easy to escape into the woods. When the Nawab was strong he levied as much tribute from the Poligars as fear induced them to yield; when, on the other hand, he was weak he had to content himself with their gratuitous offerings and wait for a more favourable opportunity for enforcing his demands.

The Nawab's relations with the Poligars.

Mr. Irwin calculated in 1783 that, during the eighteen years previous, of the average tribute of more than one lakh of chakrams per annum due by the Poligars only an average of about 40,000 chakrams per annum reached the treasury, in consequence of which, if they balanced against this small gain what was lost by depredations and expended on military expeditions, it would appear that the Nawab must have been a loser of several lakhs of pagodas in his transactions with the Poligars during that time. "But this," they say, "was not the only inconvenience attending the system. A state of frequent warfare and perpetual distrust took place of that mutual confidence which ought to have made the Poligars good subjects in time of peace and useful auxiliaries in time of war. The consequence was naturally that when Hyder Ali invaded the Carnatic in 1780 they availed themselves of that opportunity to withhold the payment of their tribute, to plunder the country, and commit other acts of violence and hostility which obliged the Company to send a large force against them in the midst of the war. The army under the command of Colonel

His losses.

Fullarton by a well-timed expedition against two of the principal Poligars brought the whole to a sense of obedience, and the equity of the subsequent settlement improved that obedience into a real confidence in the Company's government."

The Nawab's administration.

In another paragraph they expressed their regret at having learnt that, though so short a time had elapsed since the Assignment had been surrendered into the Nawab's hands, he had already commenced, as in former times, to "anticipate the revenue by borrowing money and requiring advances from the different renters as the price of their confirmation." This practice they deprecated not only because of the interest that would have to be paid on the sums borrowed, but still more on account of the power it placed in the hands of the renter to reimburse himself at the expense of the country.

They proceeded also to compare the expensiveness of the Nawab's government with the inexpensiveness of theirs during the Assignment. When uncontrolled authority came into their hands they reduced the Nawab's separate disbursements upon the peace establishment from thirteen and a half lakhs of pagodas per annum to little more than two lakhs; and during the time they had the collection of the revenue, even in time of war, the charges did not exceed 11 per cent. upon the gross *jumma* of the assignment.

I append to this statement the following description by Mr. Lushington of the state of disorder into which Tinnevelly relapsed, after the *Assignment* was surrendered and Mr. Irwin left the district in 1785, till the commencement of the period of the Assumption and Mr. Torin's management in 1790:—

Effects of the Nawab's rule.

"With the knowledge of these facts it will appear very natural that the inhabitants should look back to the Company's management as an era of comparative happiness, and contrast it in a very feeling manner with three succeeding years of extortion under Iktibar Khan, when the system of mortgage and gadayom (sale) prevailed in its worst rigours. From these intolerable oppressions the inhabitants fled in numbers to Travancore, and the ruin of the country was fast approaching; but the fears of the Nawab were at length raised to the calamities of the country by the remonstrances of the Right Honourable Lord Hobart. The accuracy with which the evils of this system were developed, the determination subsequently shown by the Company's Government to put an end to them, and especially the establishment of the Commercial Investment about this period may be said with the strictest truth to have arrested the destruction of Tinnevelly, for the alarm excited at His Highness' Durbar and in the breasts of all those who participated in these enormities materially changed the nature of His Highness' management. The system of usurious mortgage grew from that period into disuse, for those pernicious transactions which had before covered the province were of a very different character from the inferior advantages that a few adventurers subsequently derived from a partial and fearful monopoly of grain."

Improvements introduced by Government.

CHAPTER VI.

Iktibar Khan, commonly styled "the Cawn," was the Nawab's manager in Tinnevelly during most of this period.

Board of Revenue.

1786. On the 1st May 1786 the Board of Revenue was constituted at Madras.

The Commandant of Palamcotta places five companies of Captain Blacker's battalion at Sankaranaiyanārkōvil at the "request" of Iktibar Khan, the Nawab's manager.

1787. Mr. Oakes resumes his post of Paymaster in Palamcotta. A dispute takes place between Major McLeod, an officer at the head of a detachment, and the Paymaster, respecting the loss his troops had sustained by the rate of exchange the Paymaster had fixed.

Colonel Bridges is Commandant of Palamcotta, and reports in February that the Nawab's Fauzdar had assembled a considerable force at Tenkānji, (properly Tenkāsi, the Southern Benares, commonly Tenkānji, the southern Conjeveram), for the purpose of operating against the Poligar of Chokkampaṭṭi, who had built a fort and was furnishing it with arms and provisions. Colonel Bridges had recommended that the Fauzdar should not commence hostilities without the consent of the Madras Government.

Fears of Tippu Sultan.

1788. A Dutch detachment marches from Tuticorin to Cochin, both of which places then belonged to the Dutch. The Madras Government advises that they be warned that in passing through the territories of Travancore and Cochin they should take great care not to be intercepted by Tippu Sultan. Tippu's assault on the northern Travancore lines was in the following year.

Cultivation of spices.

1789. In January Mr. Oakes resigns and Mr. Torin, who had previously acted for him, is appointed Paymaster and Storekeeper in his room. Mr. Torin requests the grant of a piece of land in Palamcotta for the cultivation of cinnamon on a larger scale. The piece of ground he asked for was near the Nawab's garden and the Company's garden. It was close also to the Paymaster's house. According to tradition this cinnamon garden was identical with a piece of land now cultivated with paddy to the north-east of the Judge's house. The commencement of this cultivation was by Mr. Light, a previous Paymaster. (See 1780). The experiment, so far as it had gone, was a promising one. It was from the two trees brought from Ceylon by Mr. Light that he had been going on propagating more. It would be easy to make cinnamon trees grow in the alluvial soil near the river at Palamcotta, but in so hot and dry a climate the cultivation would not be found to pay. It was from Mr. Torin's trees that cinnamon was introduced into the "Spice Gardens" at Courtallum. See 1791.

A proposition of Mr. Torin's to rebuild the Paymaster's house (his own) at a cost of 1,000 pagodas is sanctioned.

1790. All the Paymasters south of the Coleroon, including Palamcotta, are ordered to be ready to comply with all the requisitions of Colonel Musgrove, the Commander-in-Chief, who was then preparing to meet an expected invasion by Tippu Sultan. Provincial battalions were being formed in each division.

CHAPTER VI.

The Period of the Assumption.

Difference between the Assignment and the Assumption.

On the 7th August 1790 a new period in the relations subsisting between the Madras Government and the Nawab of the Carnatic commenced. The Government, finding it impossible to induce the Nawab to consent to the reintroduction of the Assignment, or any similar arrangement placing the general administration of affairs in English hands, took possession of the management of the country, without treaty, by proclamation. The expression they use is, that they have "assumed the management of the Nawab's country," and the period came to be styled "the period of the Assumption," lasting from 1790 to 1792, in contradistinction to "the period of the Assignment," lasting from 1781 to 1790. From 1792 commenced the period of a new treaty. A Board was at the same time instituted called at first, as before, the Board of Assigned Revenue; but this name was erroneous; it implied the Nawab's consent to the arrangement; and accordingly on the 28th September the Government write to the Board: "The management of the countries of the Nawab and the Rājā (of Tanjore) having been assumed, not assigned, the name of your Board must henceforward be changed accordingly." After this order it was called the Board of Assumed Revenue. This Board was not independent of the Board of Revenue, but was simply a department of its work.

Mr. Torin Collector under the Assumption.

Before the proclamation was issued various necessary arrangements are made. On the 23rd of July Collectors are appointed for the management of the various districts, who are to report their proceedings to the Board. Mr. Benjamin Torin, previously Paymaster of Palamcotta, is appointed Collector of Tinnevelly and the dependent Poligars. Mr. Macleod is at the same time appointed Collector of Madura, Mēlūr, and the Marawars. On the 7th August orders are issued to the Commandant of Palamcotta "to support the Collector upon his written requisition with such military aid as he may from time to time require, in support of the trust with which he is invested."

Mr. Marten is appointed Paymaster *vice* Mr. Torin. Mr. Torin, now Collector of Tinnevelly, under the Assumption, proposes to Government that the Nawab's troops in Tinnevelly, now left without pay or discipline, be entertained by Government and put under the command of Captains Dighton and Everett, hitherto officers in the Nawab's service. The proposition is approved.

Mr. Meckern, Dutch Governor of Tuticorin, obtains permission to march 400 men, Europeans and Malays, coming from Cochin through Tinnevelly to Tuticorin, there to be embarked for Ceylon.

CHAPTER VI.

1791. Specimens of the cinnamon grown at Palamcotta are sent to Madras and approved. Mr. Torin proceeds to cultivate mulberries. Cinnamon cultivation is extended by Mr. Torin to Tenkāsi. Probably Courtallum is meant, though it is also said that the cultivation of spices was introduced into Courtallum in 1800 by Mr. Casamajor.

On the 11th October Mr. Torin sends to Government, for the information of the Governor-General, Lord Cornwallis, an account of the conduct of the Tinnevelly Poligars. He states that the lenity shown to two of them—the Poligars of Sivagiri and Pānjālamkurichi—by Colonel Fullarton had only encouraged them in their rebellious spirit, and recommends that more decided measures should be adopted, especially with regard to Pānjālamkurichi. He mentions that a military guard had been sent to occupy the fort of Pūli Dēvar, but that the Dēvar's men had taken up the men of the guard bodily, weapons and all, carried them out and set them down outside the fort. He mentions this incident as showing both their dread of our power and their resolution not to submit.

Pūli Dēvar again.

Torin's opinion of the results of Fullarton's lenity.

Mr. Torin's opinion of the result of Colonel Fullarton's policy differed widely, we see, from Mr. Irwin's. His representations led to Colonel Maxwell's expedition. But the result showed—as the result of every similar expedition, whether before or after showed—that no permanent pacification would be brought about, whether by "lenity" or by more "decided measures," so long as the double government of the Nawab and the Company subsisted. Having two masters the Poligars always succeeded in defying both. The Government are so much gratified with Mr. Torin's zeal and diligence that his pay and allowances are doubled. He is constantly endeavouring without success to induce the late renter, Tīttārappa Mudali, to refund the taxes received by him.

THE TREATY OF 1792.

Conditions of the new treaty.

1792. This year occupies a still more important place in the history of the period than 1781 or 1790, for the treaty entered into this year between the Nawab and the East India Company remained in force for nine years—a long time for any such arrangement to last—and came to an end only on the formal and final transfer of the country from the Nawab to the English Government in 1801. The treaty was signed on the 12th July, but virtually it dated from the beginning of the year. By this treaty the Madras Government undertook to collect the whole of the Poligar peshcush or tribute at their own expense and risk. The Nawab was not to be responsible either for any deficiency that might arise in the Poligars' payments, or for the expense incurred by any coercive measures which it might become necessary to adopt to enforce payment from them. With the exception of a few districts the rest of the country was to be restored to the management of the Nawab on certain conditions. Amongst the excepted districts were the districts south of Trichinopoly, including Tinnevelly and Madura. These were to remain in the Company's hands till the revenue, after deducting the charges of collection, equalled the amount of the kist that had fallen into arrears. One of the conditions of the treaty was that in time of war the entire management of the country was to be in the Company's hands.

New appointments.

A new commission, in virtue of the treaty, was issued to Mr. Torin on the same date as the treaty itself, the 12th July. He was hereby appointed "Collector of the Zemindar and Poligar peshcush in the Tinnevelly, Madura, Trichinopoly, Ramnadpuram, and Shevigunga Districts." This was in advance of the special instructions he was shortly to receive from "the Board of Assumed Revenue." Those instructions related especially to his co-operation with Lieutenant-Colonel Maxwell in the expedition on which he was about to enter.

Colonel Maxwell's expedition.

In accordance with Mr. Torin's representations Government had determined to send a detachment, under Colonel Maxwell, into Tinnevelly. The special object of the expedition was "to punish the Poligar of Sivagiri, who in contempt of all authority, and of every principle of justice and humanity, had made a violent attack with his peons on the Poligar of Sēttūr and put him and his family to death." He was instructed to endeavour to apprehend the Poligar of Sivagiri, and not to operate against the other Poligars except in the event of his finding them confederates with him. The existence of this confederacy was ere long clearly proved. Colonel Maxwell set out on his expedition in July and proceeded from Madura to Srīvilliputtūr. From thence he marched on Sivagiri. He attacked and reduced the "kōmbai" (the hill stockade) of the Sivagiri Poligar, in which service Captains Steward and Torrens greatly distinguished themselves. See the account of the capture of this stronghold by Colonel Fullarton in 1783.

Colonel Maxwell's settlement.

Colonel Maxwell now proceeded, in conjunction with Mr. Torin, to make a settlement with the various Tinnevelly Poligars, but they did not agree in some particulars as to the course that ought to be taken. Orders were issued by Colonel Maxwell, in accordance with the instructions of the Board, respecting the arrears due by the Poligars. No remission was to be made to Sivagiri. The Chokkampaṭṭi Poligar refused to accept Colonel Maxwell's offer and was deposed. Chennalgudi Pollam was temporarily resumed. One element in the settlement made by Colonel Maxwell was that a certain Sankaralingam Pillai should be prohibited from receiving any employment or encouragement from any of the Poligars. This Sankaralingam Pillai was one of the persons who subse-

CHAPTER VI. quently instigated the son of the Poligar of Sivagiri to rebel against his father. Mr. Torin disapproved Colonel Maxwell's policy towards this man, and Colonel Maxwell complained to Government of Mr. Torin's interference with his authority. He also represented Mr. Torin's *dubash*, or confidential interpreter, in whose faithfulness his master placed implicit reliance, as secretly in league with the Poligars. On a reference being made to Government Mr. Torin was ordered to dismiss his dubash and Colonel Maxwell's authority over the affairs of the Poligars was made absolute. Hereupon Mr. Torin resigned, and his dubash was sent to Madras under a guard. Mr. Torin's Assistant at this time was Mr. Thomas Scott Jackson. His resignation was accepted, and Mr. James Landon was appointed his successor. He gave over charge to Mr. Landon on the 12th November 1792. Mr. Landon was to receive 250 pagodas per mensem and 1⅓ per cent. commission at the expiration of the year. Mr. Torin's name is chiefly remembered in Tinnevelly in connection with the rebuilding of the Marudūr anicut. An inscription on the anicut records his name and the year 1792. Colonel Maxwell's Secretary or Assistant throughout these expeditions was Captain Bannerman, afterwards in command of a similar but more important expedition in 1799.

Mr. Landon, Collector.

Marudūr anicut.

1793. Mr. Balmain is Assistant to Mr. Landon, and at Mr. Landon's request receives an addition to his salary of 50 pagodas per mensem.

Mr. Landon states that the Poligar of Woodoocaud (probably Ōrkādu) had murdered a Tahsildar employed in his district by the Nawab's manager.

Troubles at Sēttūr.

The Sēttūr Poligar being a minor his pollam is placed under a manager by Mr. Landon, but the manager is dispossessed and imprisoned by a usurper. Government, sensible that such lawless acts, if allowed to pass entirely unnoticed, would lead to greater mischief, now directed Captain Dighton to proceed with his detachment against Sēttūr in order to capture the usurping manager. He appeared before the fort in July 1793, but the gates were closed againt him, and the troops of the Ootoomaly (Ūttumalai) and Ovidiapuram (Āvuḍaiyārpuram) Zemindars, who were within the walls, threatened to open fire on him if he did not withdraw. He withdrew, but the Collector ordered Major Stevenson to proceed with his troops to Captain Dighton's assistance and to apprehend the two Poligars. Government, however, despatched orders to Major Stevenson forbidding him to attack the rebels, and desiring him to content himself with warnings for the present. Government also interdicted Mr. Landon from interfering in the police and internal management of the pollams, and told him that he was to confine himself to the duty of collecting the peshcush. They held that no further right but that of collection was con-

CHAPTER VI.

ferred on the Company by the treaty of 1792 with the Nawab. The Government felt obliged to temporise from want of troops, but this policy would necessarily have reduced the country ere long to anarchy. These counter orders of Government were sufficient to embolden even the most inconsiderable Poligars, and accordingly Major Stevenson, a few days subsequently, warned Government against a general rising, at the same time announcing that Kaṭṭaboma Nāyaka was plundering the eastern parts of the province and murdering the people, and that Pūli Dēvar had thrown himself across the path of Lieutenant St. Leger in his pursuit of the manager of Sēttūr and closed the gates of his fort against him. In the settlement made by Colonel Maxwell shortly before the boundaries of the several pollams were rearranged, and part of this new arrangement was that two villages should be transferred from Pānjālamkurichi to Eṭṭaiyāpuram. Kaṭṭaboma Nāyaka, however, positively refused to surrender those villages, and the Collector was unable to enforce obedience. Captain Dighton commanding Streevalapatore (Srīvilliputtūr) also informed Government that danger was approaching, as the Poligars had bodies of armed peons marching about daily, but the Government had no troops to spare. The Poligars regarded the inactivity of Government as a sign of weakness, and so (in 1798) Kaṭṭaboma Nāyaka's people attacked and plundered the important towns of Āḻvār-Tinnevelly (Āḻvār-Tirunagari) and Streeviguntam (Srīvaikuṇṭham) and carried off the principal inhabitants of each town.

The Government obliged to temporise.

Disorders increasing.

Proposed disarming of the Poligars.

Notwithstanding the weakness that had been shown by Government and their inability to enforce obedience, they requested Mr. Landon, in conjunction with Major Stevenson, to determine how an object involving the greatest possible difficulty should be accomplished, that is, how the Poligars should be disarmed, whether gradually by peaceable means or all at once by force. This subject of the disarming of the Poligars occupied from this time onward the attention of successive Governments, but nothing was actually done beyond the writing of paragraphs—no measures were adopted for carrying their wishes into effect—till the close of Major Bannerman's campaign in 1799. Government also request Mr. Landon to inquire into and report upon the claim set up by the Poligars to *disai-kāval* (or district watch) fees. This question assumed larger proportions as time went on, but it was not finally settled till the country was ceded to the Company in Mr. Lushington's collectorate in 1801.

1794. Colonel Campbell is Commandant of Palamcotta. The Board of Revenue, alarmed at the progress of rebellion, recommend Government to order detachments of troops to be stationed in various parts of Tinnevelly for the purpose of keeping the Poligars in check. This recommendation does not seem to have been acted on.

CHAPTER VI.

Mr. Powney Collector.

Mr. Landon died this year on the 22nd June. Mr. Balmain, his Assistant, took temporary charge. Mr. Landon's successor was Mr. George Powney, who had been Resident at Trevandram from 1788. He was the first Resident there. At this time, as in Mr. Torin's, the Collector of Poligar peshcush had authority over all the Poligars from Trichinopoly to Tinnevelly, including the Manapara Poligars, the Rājā of Ramnad, and the Poligar of Sivagangai.

Mr. Powney is directed by Government to proceed with the inquiries commenced by Mr. Landon into the claim of the Tinnevelly Poligars to *disai-kāval.*

1795. The Commandant of Srīvilliputtūr complains of the robberies committed by the dependents of the Sivagiri Poligar, and Mr. Powney expresses his regret that detachments of troops, according to Colonel Maxwell's plan and the Collector's recommendation, had not been located in various places to keep the Poligars in awe. Mr. Powney receives and publishes an order of Government respecting the Poligar districts, in which the Poligars are prohibited from obeying any orders of the Nawab, except such as are communicated to them through the channel of the Company's Government. Tuticorin is taken this year from the Dutch.

Orders of Court of Directors.

The Court of Directors send out positive orders "for disarming the Poligars, for punishing the refractory, for adjusting their disputed claims, and for the introduction of such a system of internal arrangement as shall have a tendency to restore these distressed provinces from their present state of anarchy and misery to a state of subordination and prosperity." Extracts from another letter from the Court of Directors dated the same year to a similar effect will be found further on in the sketch of the political position between 1781 and 1801.

The Board of Revenue request the Collector of Tinnevelly to report on the best mode of carrying these orders of the Court of Directors into effect. It seems scarcely necessary to repeat here what has been so often shown, that neither recommendations, expostulations, nor "positive orders" could produce the slightest improvement so long as the double Government lasted. It would be only like issuing orders for oil and water to combine.

1796. Measures are adopted by Mr. Powney to obtain the voluntary surrender of the fort of Chokkampaṭṭi to the Company.

1797. The Nawab complains of the refractory, disrespectful behaviour and predatory habits of the Tinnevelly Poligars. Government order the Collector to inquire strictly into these complaints.

A Poligar shot by another Poligar.

Mr. Powney reports to the Board of Revenue that the Poligar of Ōrkādu had been shot during a hunting expedition by the Poligar of Singampaṭṭi, whom he describes as a drunkard and a man of violence, but laments that there was no power competent to administer criminal justice in the pollams, so that it seemed impossible to bring the offender to trial.

Rebellious conduct of the Sivagiri Poligar's son.

In another paragraph he states that the son of the Poligar of Sivagiri, instigated by Mauply Vanien (Mapiḷḷai Vanniyan) and Sankaralingam Pillai, had conspired against his father's government and taken measures to wrest the management of the pollams from his hands. It will subsequently be seen that this rebellious son was in league with the rebellious Pānjālamkurichi Poligar. Before Mr. Powney left the district he reported that the rebels collected by the Sivagiri Poligar's son had been dispersed, but that the son himself had escaped to the hills. Sankaralingam Pillai, however, was caught and sent to the Presidency to be transported to Bencoolen in Sumatra—the Andaman Islands of that period.

The following paragraphs in a letter from the Board of Revenue to the Governor of Madras in 1797 throw some additional light on this transaction. They also seem to indicate the complicity of the Ūttumalai Poligar:—

Ūttumalai Poligar.

"Should the operations of the detachment prove successful in securing the person of Mauply Vanien and Sankaralingam Pillai, we recommended that Mr. Powney should be authorized to send them under a guard to the Presidency. Your Lordship in reply entirely approved of this suggestion, as well as of the conduct of the Collector under the circumstances represented. By subsequent information from Mr. Powney we were advised that Captain Dighton, having received intelligence that Sankaralingam Pillai had taken refuge in the Ūttumalai Pollam, despatched a guard of sepoys with some of the Sivagiri peons in search of him, who seized him and were conducting him to the Collector's cutcherry when Ūttumalai's peons assembled to the number of about 300 and rescued him. It was, however, satisfactory to us to find from a further report that the Ūttumalai Poligar had not so far lost all sense of his duty to the Company as to hesitate in delivering up the person of Sankaralingam Pillai upon his requisition. But as the attack of his people upon the Company's sepoys, if done either by his order or with his connivance, must be considered a very flagrant breach of his allegiance, we have informed Mr. Powney that it behoves him to trace by every possible means with whom it originated. We have, therefore, directed him to summon the Poligar and all the parties concerned in this affair immediately to his cutcherry, and, after making such examinations as to his judgment may appear necessary, to transmit the whole with his opinion of the punishment that should be inflicted for our consideration."

Mr. Jackson Collector.

At the close of this year Mr. Powney is succeeded as Collector by Mr. Jackson. The principal events of his time will take their place in the account of the Bannerman-Poligar war, which will be found in the next part.

1798. Kaittār discontinued as a station for troops, and Captain Bannerman ordered to join his corps.

CHAPTER VI.

Major Bannerman.

1799. In the beginning of this year Captain (now Major) Bannerman was not permitted to accompany his battalion to the field in the final campaign against Tippu Sultan, but was charged with negotiations with the Rājā of Travancore and the collection of cattle and other supplies for the Bombay army. He was temporarily appointed Resident of Travancore with a salary of 250 pagodas a month. His campaign against the Poligars in Tinnevelly commenced, as will be seen, later on in the year, shortly after Tippu Sultan's fall.

Mr. Lushington Collector.

Mr. Lushington succeeds Mr. Jackson as Collector of Tinnevelly on the 12th January 1799. The events of his period will be found in the next chapter.

CHAPTER VII.

THE BANNERMAN-POLIGAR WAR.

SKETCH OF THE POLITICAL POSITION BETWEEN 1781 AND 1801.

CHAPTER VII.

IN order to have a clear idea of the causes that led to the various Poligar wars, and eventually to the cession of the country to the Company, it seems necessary that I should endeavour to furnish the reader with a succinct explanation of the political position, that is, of the relation subsisting between the Nawab of Arcot and the Government of the East India Company between 1781 and 1801. In doing so I may have to repeat some particulars already more or less fully mentioned under the head of the years in which the events occurred. Though the connection of the English Government with Tinnevelly commenced in 1781, up to Mr. Lushington's Collectorate in 1799, the disorders prevalent in the country had not been removed, and had scarcely even been mitigated. One cause of this inaction consisted in the necessity for massing troops north of Trichinopoly and in the neighbourhood of Mysore, so long as the safety of the State was threatened by such formidable foes as Hyder Ali and Tippu Sultan. This difficulty came to an end by the capture of Seringapatam and the death of Tippu on the 4th May 1799.

The Assignment of 1781.

The principal reason why more thorough measures for the subjection of the Poligars of Tinnevelly were so long deferred is to be found in the unsatisfactory nature of the relations which subsisted during the whole of that period between the English Government and the Nawab. On the 2nd December 1781 an agreement was made between the two parties to the effect that the Revenues of the Carnatic, including of course those of Tinnevelly, should be assigned by the Nawab to the English Government during the continuance of the war, one-sixth of the revenue being paid to the Nawab for his private expenses. In virtue of this arrangement we have seen that a Committee of Assigned Revenue was constituted at Madras, and that functionaries styled Superintendents of Assigned Revenue were appointed in various important centres by the English Government, one of them in Tinnevelly. Though this assignment of revenue was intended to last during the continuance of the war, the Nawab almost immediately endeavoured to get it set aside. Accordingly in June 1785 the assignment was relinquished

CHAPTER VII.

by the Company and an annual payment by the Nawab out of the revenue for the payment of his debts was promised instead, with territorial security for punctuality. Another treaty was made on the 24th February 1787, differing but little from the preceding one in regard to the amount of the annual payment that was to be made, but containing an important proviso, binding the Company to supply the Nawab with troops for "the security and collection of his revenue, the support of his authority, or the good order and Government of his dominions, whenever he represented to Government the necessity of such a force and the objects to be obtained thereby." This, as we shall see, was naturally disapproved by the Madras Government as establishing a divided authority and impeding their attempts to establish order.

Treaty of 1787.

Assumption in 1790.

Negotiations with the Nawab for the assumption of the revenues of the Carnatic and the control of their expenditure having failed, the Madras Government took the management of the country into their own hands, without treaty, by a proclamation on the 7th of August 1790. A Board of Assumed Revenue, virtually only a department of the Board of Revenue, was constituted in Madras. The preceding period from 1781 to 1790 was called the Period of the Assignment; the period from 1790 to 1792, the Period of the Assumption.

Treaty of 1792.

On the 12th of July 1792, a new treaty was concluded with the Nawab which provided that the whole country should be garrisoned by British troops, for the expenses of which the Nawab should make an adequate contribution. In the event of war the Company was to take the entire management of the affairs of the country into its own hands, but in time of peace all that it was to be permitted to do for the good government of the country was to collect the peshcush or tribute of the Poligars in the Nawab's name and give him credit for it in his contribution. See further details under the head of 1792. By this arrangement the Poligars were brought more directly than before under the control of the English Government. It seemed even to give the Government a distinct and definite right to reduce the Poligars to submission, but this right, as we shall see, was in a great measure neutralised by the circumstance that the sovereignty over the Poligars was still allowed to remain in the Nawab's hands, so that the measures adopted by the English Government to establish order were more or less thwarted. The civil officers appointed under the treaty of 1792 to represent the Government were commonly styled "Collectors of Poligar Peshcush."[1] The subsidy due by the Nawab was regularly paid, but

[1] This functionary's titles seem to have been very various and indefinite. Mr. Torin, the first Collector of the series, was generally styled "Collector of Assigned Poligar Peshcush south of the Coleroon," "Collector of Poligar Peshcush south of the Coleroon," or sometimes simply "Collector south of the Coleroon." In the

to enable him to meet his liabilities he contracted heavy loans and to liquidate those loans he assigned to his creditors the revenue of various districts of the country. It is true that in 1781 an assignment of revenue had been made to the Company; but the assignment of the revenues of the country to irresponsible private individuals was a very different proceeding, and one which led to much oppression and misery.

CHAPTER VII.

The Nawab's debts.

The arrangements introduced by the treaty of 1792 not having been found to work well, several attempts were made to remedy their defects, one of which was a special arrangement made for the regulation of the collection of disai-kāval and talam-kāval fees in Tinnevelly. In 1795 the Madras Government endeavoured to effect a more satisfactory arrangement with the Nawab with respect to the southern Poligars, especially those of Tinnevelly and Madura. The right of levying, receiving, and appropriating the Poligar Peshcush possessed by the Company by treaty was found to contribute little to good government, so long as the right of sovereignty remained with the Nawab. The then Governor of Madras, Lord Hobart, on the failure of his endeavours to obtain the concurrence of the Nawab to the arrangement he proposed, intimated his intention to resume the district of Tinnevelly for the liquidation of the debt termed "The Cavalry Loan." To this, however, the Supreme Government refused its assent. For additional particulars respecting each of these arrangements see the notices of the events of each year.

Lord Hobart's proposal.

At length after the discovery, on the capture of Seringapatam, that a treasonable correspondence had been carried on by the two late Nawabs, Mahomed Ali and his son, with Tippu Sultan, the British Government determined to assume the entire possession and government of the Carnatic, making a provision for the family of the Nawab. This was carried into effect by a treaty entered into with the grandson of Mahomed Ali on the 31st July 1801. On that happy day results were achieved by a single stroke of a

Final determination of the Government.

letter of Government conferring on him his appointment he is appointed "Collector of Zemindar and Poligar Peshcush in the Tinnevelly, Madura, Trichinopoly, Ramnadpuram, and Shevigunga Districts." I find a long list of titles given to Mr. Lushington in official documents. He is styled Collector of Poligar Peshcush and Ramnad, Collector of Ramnad and Poligar Peshcush, Collector of the Assigned Peshcush, Collector of Southern Peshcush, Collector in (not yet of) Tinnevelly, and sometimes simply Collector for short. On his appointment by the authority of the Governor of Fort St. George in Council on the 31st July 1801, on the final cession of the Carnatic by the Nawab, he is addressed as "Collector of Southern Poligar Peshcush," but the designation in the body of the document of the appointment then conferred upon him is that of "Collector of the Province of Tinnevelly." From this there was but a step to the later title still in use, "Collector of Tinnevelly." In 1781 the title of "Collector" belonged to a class of native subordinates resembling Tahsildars, and the European civilian was called "Receiver." The subordinate "collected," the chief "received."

CHAPTER VII.

pen which fifty-seven years of war and twenty years of negotiation had failed to effect. See Aitchison's Treaties and Engagements.

VIEW OF THE POLITICAL POSITION OF TINNEVELLY AND THE POLIGAR COUNTRY GENERALLY TAKEN BY THE COURT OF DIRECTORS PRIOR TO THE COMMENCEMENT OF THE LAST POLIGAR WARS.

"Extract of a general letter from the Honourable the Court of Directors, in the Public Department, dated 10th June 1795.

"55. The disastrous consequences of the hostile conduct of the Rājā of Ramnad against the Cheroker[1] or Minister of Shivagangai, as mentioned in your advices and proceedings, but more particularly in the latter, have given us very great concern; and we observe what is stated in your subsequent despatch of the 29th of September last that it is impossible to apply any effectual remedy to the general evil, so long as a divided authority over the Poligar countries shall be permitted to exist.

Evils of divided authority.

"61. But what in reality was the nature and extent of the authority exercised by the Nawab over these Poligars both previous and subsequent to this treaty?

Small amount of the Nawab's collections.

"It was scarcely felt among them, and with all the exertions he could make, it is a fact recorded and incontrovertible, that the sum he was able to collect from them on account of their stipulated peshcush, in the course of seven years, did not exceed the amount collected by the Company under the Assignment in less than two years.

Transfer of tribute.

"62. Under this shadow of authority possessed by the Nawab over the Poligars, receiving a small and precarious revenue collected at a heavy expense, the Nawab by the 5th article of the treaty of the 12th of July, 1792, most advantageously for himself, assigned over to the Company, the tribute or peshcush payable by certain Poligars, which was taken at their full amount, as part of his subsidy, and which peshcush or tribute was to be collected by the Company at their own expense and risk, without charging the Nawab either the expenses attending the collection, or with any deficiencies that might arise thereon. The Nawab's sovereignty over the said Poligars is recognised by the 6th article, and the Company engage to the utmost of their power, and consistently with the realisation of the tribute or peshcush from them, to enforce the allegiance and submission of the said Poligars, to the said Nawab in all customary ceremonies, and in furnishing the Poligar peons according to established custom for the collection of revenue, &c., and all acts of authority are to be exercised in the Nawab's name.

The Company's obligations.

"It is difficult, however, to conceive for what purpose the words 'and in furnishing the Poligar peons, according to established custom, for the collection of the revenues,' were introduced into the treaty, since

[1] This title will be explained further on.

the collection of the revenue is by the preceding article entirely assigned to the Company.

"63. Divested of the sword, and relinquishing the power of collecting a revenue, it is not easy to define what rights of sovereignty, contended for by the Nawab with so much zeal and jealousy, remain behind. They cannot perhaps be more aptly described than in the words of the treaty, customary ceremonies. The nominal sovereignty of the Nawab over the Poligars we do not attempt to deny, at the same time, we are only bound to preserve it so far as may be consistent with the realization of the tribute, which he has thus assigned over to us; and of the many circumstances which have a tendency materially to affect that object in the districts under the Poligars, may be mentioned the following. Their keeping up a military force, by which they are enabled to make war or commit depredations, as their local interests or their passions may lead them, upon each other. Their adoption of means, whether of finance or internal regulation which have a natural tendency to impoverish their treasuries and prevent the regular payments of the peshcush made over to the Company. Their committing acts of cruelty, and oppression on the inhabitants. These must ever have a tendency to depopulate a country, and of course to affect the revenue; and if we have not the power of applying a remedy in these and similar cases, it is evident that we shall ultimately lose that revenue which we have acquired the right of collecting. And thus the treaty will become not only nugatory, as far as it respects the proportion of the Nawab's subsidy to be received from the Poligars, but considerable annual loss will likewise accrue to the Company so long as the beforementioned abuses are suffered to exist.

Poligar misgovernment.

Anticipated loss to the Company.

"64. We shall here collect into one point of view such parts of your records as have principally led to the present discussion, and which have convinced us of the necessity, so forcibly urged by the Bengal Government and by yourselves, of adopting some decisive measures for the better government of the districts under the several Poligars.

"66. Upon the whole therefore, after having given to this important subject every degree of deliberation which it merits, as well with respect to the power vested in us under express stipulations, as with respect to the degree of authority reserved to the Nawab over the Poligars; and reflecting also, that by our determination, we neither wrest from His Highness one single prerogative, which it was in his power to exercise, or which he did actually exercise over these people, in virtue of his nominal sovereignty, either previous or subsequent to the late treaty; nor add one inch of territory to our possessions, or a single pagoda to our treasury. We have resolved to empower you upon the sole authority of the Company to take such measures from time to time, with the approbation of the Governor-General and Council, as shall be deemed expedient, and consistent with the situation of affairs on the receipt of this despatch, for disarming the Poligars, for punishing the refractory, for adjusting their disputed claims, and for the introduction of such a system of internal arrangement as shall have a tendency to restore those distressed provinces, from their pre-

A better system to be introduced.

CHAPTER VII.

sent state of anarchy and misery, to a state of subordination and prosperity.

The Nawab's refusal anticipated.

"It were to be wished, that upon your representation of the absolute necessity we are under of prescribing this line of conduct for the Poligar tributaries, His Highness's acquiescence could be obtained herein; but from the tenor of some of his late letters upon record, this acquiescence is more to be desired than expected. We can only, therefore, in case of his refusal, direct you to take the most effectual means to counteract his endeavours to thwart the execution of these orders; which cannot but be considered, as disinterested on our part, as highly essential to the happiness of thousands, as contributing to the peace and prosperity of the country, and therefore as ultimately beneficial to the real and permanent interests of the Nawab."

Conclusion arrived at.

It is evident from the above that though the course of events in Tinnevelly was likely to vary a little from time to time as decisive or temporising counsels predominated, yet that it was unreasonable to expect that any thorough or permanent reform could be effected, that the oppression and misrule of the Poligars and renters could be brought to an end, that peace could be firmly established, or that any solid foundation could be laid for future prosperity, till the entire undivided sovereignty over all classes in the country should come to be vested in the English Government, and the Nawab be allowed to retire from the business of government on a pension.

Kaṭṭaboma Nāyaka.

Succession of the Poligars of Panjālamkurichi.

The Poligar of Pānjālamkurichi was a Nāyaka of the Kambaḷa division of the caste. The name by which he was known, Kaṭṭaboma Nāyaka, was not his personal name, but a title appropriated to the head of the family, though a personal name at the outset. The first of the line mentioned in the genealogical list prepared by Mr. Jackson, the Collector, succeeded to the pālaiyam in 1709. I find four persons of this name mentioned in the annals of the time. The first was the Kaṭṭaboma Nāyaka against whom Colonel Heron sent an expedition in 1755. The second succeeded in 1760, the third in 1791, the fourth in 1799. Both the third and the fourth were hanged. Boma is a common Telugu name, to which in the Tamil country descriptive Tamil adjectives are prefixed as Chinna Boma, Little Boma, or Kaṭṭa (properly Kaṭṭai) Boma, Short Boma. The English mode of writing the name was Cataboma Naig, which was shortened into "the Cat," the name by which he was ordinarily called by the English soldiers. The last Kaṭṭaboma Nāyaka was called Karuttaiyā, properly Vīra Pāṇḍya Kaṭṭaboma. He had a dumb brother, a celebrated character, of whom some account will be given in the sequel, and whose name appears as "Kumāraswāmi Nāyaka, the dumb-boy," in the list of prisoners sent to Colonel Agnew at the close of the war. Another brother, younger than "the dumb-boy," and perhaps the real head of the party during the two last rebellions, was Suppā Nāyaka, commonly called Sivattaiyā, whose name we shall find amongst the last list of prisoners. Karuttaiyā and Sivattaiyā mean respectively dark-complexioned and fair-complexioned—literally black and red.

CHAPTER VII.

The Poligar's brothers.

The Pānjālamkurichi Poligar's great rival was the Poligar of Eṭṭaiyāpuram, whose pāḷaiyam was situated a little to the north. Eṭṭaiyāpuram is said to take its name from one Eṭṭappa Nāyaka, the traditional founder of the family. The place is said by the Native historian of the family to have been founded in 1565 during the reign of Kumāra Krishnappa Nāyaka, ruler of Madura. Eṭṭ'appa and Eṭṭ'aiyā are equivalent forms.

Eṭṭaiyā-puram.

Events preceding Major Bannerman's Expedition.

What Pūli Dēva was in Tinnevelly in the middle of the last century, that Kaṭṭaboma Nāyaka was towards its close—the centre of all disloyalty and misrule. From his fort of Pānjālamkurichi the Poligar used to sally forth at the head of his armed followers, and making incursions into Circar villages, as well as into the villages of other Poligars, sack and plunder all that came in his way, often times carrying off some of the principal inhabitants. In 1797 rebellion broke out in the Ramnad country, and many of the Tinnevelly Poligars joined the insurrection, almost all of them, with Kaṭṭaboma Nāyaka at their head, refusing to pay their kists to Government. Some alarm was created at Madras by the state of things in the south, and the Collector was ordered to repair to Ramnad and to ascertain from the Poligars the nature and extent of their demands. See Kearns's Introduction to his Account of the last Poligar War.

Conduct of Kaṭṭaboma.

Orders of Government.

The Collector here referred to was Mr. Jackson, who was Collector of Southern Peshcush and Ramnad at the time, and whose head-quarters were at Ramnad. The commencement of the final struggle with Kaṭṭaboma Nāyaka was through an order issued to him by Mr. Jackson in 1798, commanding him to appear before him at Ramnad and give an account of his conduct. After many excuses and delays leading to many repetitions of the command, he made his appearance at Ramnad on the 9th September 1798. At an audience with the Collector on the evening of the same day, whilst the correspondence that had taken place between him and the Collector was being read to him, he pretended to get alarmed and rushed away from the Collector's presence and out of the fort, accompanied by his armed retainers. At the gate he had an encounter with the guards, headed by Lieutenant and Adjutant Clarke whom he stabbed, it was said, with his own hand. Having thus broken away he returned to his fort at Pānjālamkurichi,

Commencement of final struggle.

CHAPTER VII.

Kaṭṭaboma breaks away.

plundering all the Government villages that lay on his way. The Madras Government hereupon censured Mr. Jackson for mismanagement, and issued a proclamation calling upon Kaṭṭaboma Nāyaka to deliver himself up to Mr. Jackson's successor in the Poligar administration, Major-General Floyd, or to the Collector. Of this order the Poligar took no notice but continued to make raids into the neighbouring country, especially into the territories of the Poligar of Eṭṭaiyāpuram as before.

The following extracts from letters from the Board of Revenue to the Governor of Madras will throw light on the disapproval with which Mr. Jackson's proceedings were regarded by the Government:—

"201. The nature of Mr. Jackson's remarks in relating the circumstances which preceded this unhappy event, compelled us to enter upon a very full explanation of our motives in recommending to your Lordship, under date the 31st July, that a last effort should be made to save this young man from ruin, to show that his late atrocious act did not originate in any mistaken lenity towards him.

Mr. Jackson's proceedings disapproved.

"202. This explanation was submitted to your Lordship on the 27th ultimo, as well as the manner in which the Collector proceeded to execute our orders for ascertaining whether the Poligar had received and understood all the letters he had written him, which he seemed to have considered the first object of his attention. How far his conduct was judicious in executing this order under the circumstances of the case was for your Lordship to decide. Instead of the mode observed by him, we thought it would have been less liable to any misconstruction had he required the Poligar to produce the letters he had received from the Collector, and Mr. Jackson would then have seen whether all had been delivered without any alteration. This would have guarded against any mistake as to the intentions of the Collector, for there appears too much reason to believe, ignorant as he is reported to be, that the Poligar might have construed the severe passages in the Collector's letter of the 23rd May to be the sentence of deprivation of his pollam, which immediately awakening fears for his personal safety, seemed to have impelled him to the atrocious act that ensued.

Kaṭṭaboma defended.

"203. As we could not conceive what motive could have governed, or what object could be gained by, a premeditated plan on the part of the Poligar to appear at the Collector's cutcherry, within the fort of Ramnad, and then fly from it with the precipitation of a criminal, we could not accede to the Collector's conclusion, certain as he must have been of the ruinous consequences to himself. The appearance of 4,000 armed men the moment the Poligar had quitted the fort was an extraordinary circumstance; but we apprehend that the numbers must have been greatly overrated in the accounts obtained by the Collector, and it was not probable that such a body of men could have accompanied the Poligar, who followed the Collector the whole of the way to Ramnad, and have contrived to conceal themselves in different places so as to be ready to act in this supposed meditated plan the day succeeding the Poligar's arrival there. But upon this circumstance we intimated our intention of requiring a more particular explanation, and we suggested the propriety of calling upon the commanding officer to explain by what means so large a body of men could approach unobserved so near to the fort and conceal themselves under the very walls of it, for such must have been their situation if they appeared at the moment when the Poligar escaped.

CHAPTER VII.

Kaṭṭaboma condemned.

"204. Whatever might have influenced the conduct of this Poligar, the enormity of the crime of which he had been guilty appeared to call for exemplary punishment. With regard to the force to be employed against him and the Collector's proposal of offering a reward of 5,000 Rupees for his apprehension, we submitted these points to your Lordship's consideration; but so strongly were we impressed with the necessity of a severe example being made on this occasion, that we further recommended the pollam shall be declared sequestered for ever, that it may become the interest of the families of Poligars to guard them against crimes and rebellion to the authority of Government, a principle which the Court of Directors have approved.

"205. The circumstances stated by the Collector in regard to the family of the late Lieutenant Clarke we begged leave to submit to your favourable consideration and to recommend that whatever pension you might be pleased to fix should be declared payable out of the revenue of the Pollam of Pāñjālamkurichi.

Subsequent letter of the Board of Revenue to the Madras Government.

EXTRACTS.

Hopes of Government.

"165. We noticed in our last general report the unfortunate affray that had taken place in the fort of Ramnad, and the consequent flight of the Pandalamcourchy Poligar. Under date the 3rd October your Lordship informed us that you had thought it advisable to take immediate measures for assembling a detachment of troops of sufficient strength to assert the authority of the Company's Government and to enforce the submission of this Poligar, but having reason to hope from advices since received that Cattaboma Naigue might be induced to submit himself without the necessity of coercive means, you desired that no time must be lost in publishing the proclamation which accompanied, and in providing that it might be conveyed to the knowledge of the Poligar, for which purpose we immediately transmitted it in duplicate to Mr. Jackson.

Collector superseded.

"166. Your Lordship afterwards apprised us of your still entertaining the hope of the Poligar's submission, but that as he had evinced a total want of confidence in Mr. Jackson you had superseded the Collector's authority and directed Major-General Floyd to open a negotiation with him, and to prevent the collision of authority, you desired that this resolution might, without delay, be made known to the Collector, which was done on the same day.

CHAPTER VII.

An inquiry to be instituted.

" 167. Upon a consideration of the impressions under which it was impossible for the Pandalamcourchy Poligar to have acted, we were further informed your Lordship had judged it advisable to institute a full inquiry into the circumstances which produced and which attended the late unpleasant affair at Ramnad, and for this purpose you had been pleased to appoint a committee consisting of Lieutenant-Colonel Brown, Lieutenant-Colonel Oram, and Mr. John Casamayer. You directed that the committee might have free access to the records of the Collector, and that they might have the assistance of the cutcherry in conducting their business, and that all persons in the Revenue Department whose attendance might be required should be ordered to comply with the summons of the committee, and we were at the same time apprised that as the communication which Major-General Floyd had been desired to open with the Poligar of Pandalamcourchy would then be more naturally conducted by Lieutenant-Colonel Brown, as being both at the head of the committee and of the eventual expedition, General Floyd had been authorized to transfer it to that officer. A copy of these resolutions was transmitted to Mr. Jackson, and the correspondence that passed regarding the Pandalamcourchy Poligar in the interest of the Collector's authority over him being suspended, is noted in the margin under date 2nd March. The proceedings of this committee, together with the resolutions of Government thereon, were forwarded to this Board, and agreebly to the orders we received they were transmitted to the present Collector for his information and guidance and with particular directions for having them well explained to the Poligar.

Fresh orders from Government.

Recapitulation.

" 168. In their resolutions Government observed that after having taken into consideration all the circumstances, it appeared in consequence of representations and complaints of the Collector against the contumacious conduct of Cattaboma Naigue that he was ordered by the Board of Revenue to summon that Poligar to make his appearance at Ramnad; that on this order being communicated to the Poligar, there was no unnecessary delay on his part in preparing to proceed to Ramnadapooram, but on the contrary that he showed an earnest desire to take the first opportunity of evincing his submission to the directions of Government by personally attending upon the Collector, but that the conduct of Mr. Jackson to him upon that occasion was unnecessarily harsh and severe, and that the manner in which he compelled the Poligar to follow him for twenty-three days was subjecting him to a mortifying degradation in the eyes of the inferior Poligars through whose pollams he was passing and unauthorized by the orders from the Board of Revenue.

Disapproval of Jackson's severity.

" 169. That the treatment of the Poligar after his arrival at Ramnad in the cutcherry by the Collector, and those acting under his authority was attended with circumstances of unusual rigour and humiliation, and that such treatment could not fail to intimidate him and alarm him for his personal security; that his attempt to escape was a natural consequence, and that the affray which happened at the gate did not proceed from any premeditated intention in the Poligar of proceeding to the extremities of forcing guard and resisting the authority of Government.

Acquittal of the murder of Lieutenant Clarke.

"170. That from the whole of the evidence produced before the committee it was doubtful by whose hands Lieutenant Clarke fell, but that as the committee, who had the fullest means of investigation and the advantages of local knowledge, had declared it to be their unanimous opinion that he was stabbed by a pikeman in the Poligar's train, and not by the Poligar himself, it was resolved that Cattaboma Naigue should be formally acquitted of the murder of Lieutenant Clarke; that as the Poligar, however, must be held responsible for the act of his followers, and as Lieutenant Clarke fell in the discharge of his duty, and acting under the orders of the Collector, it was determined to require the Poligar to make a provision equal to the pay and allowances of the deceased Mr. Clarke, for the maintenance and support of the widow and children of that deserving officer.

A new arrangement to be made.

"171. In communicating these resolutions to Mr. Lushington, Government were pleased to direct that he should be instructed to acquaint the Poligar that he was accordingly acquitted of the charge of the murder of Mr. Clarke, to settle with him an arrangement for the payment of the provision intended for the widow and children of that officer, to point out the great security which he enjoyed under the protection of Government, which, by an impartial and dispassionate investigation of his case under circumstances apparently most unfavourable to him, had brought it to this conclusion, to admonish him of the necessity and advantage of paying implicit obedience to the orders of the Company, and finally to restore him to the full and complete possession of his pollam."

Conclusion arrived at.

The Government could not but acquit the Poligar, in accordance with the finding of so respectable a committee appointed by itself; and if his subsequent conduct had been fairly loyal and dutiful it might have been taken for granted that Mr. Jackson had erred and that the finding of the committee was right; but the rebellious spirit he showed to Mr. Lushington, Mr. Jackson's successor, notwithstanding his friendly advances, tended to vindicate the propriety of Mr. Jackson's opinions and policy. The native author of the history of the Eṭṭaiyāpuram Zamindari adopts Mr. Jackson's view of the affair and represents Lieutenant Clarke to have been killed by Kaṭṭaboma Nāyaka himself. He attributes the decision of the committee of inquiry to the Poligar's clever falsehoods. It is to be remembered, however, that the Eṭṭaiyāpuram family were the chief opponents of Pānjālamkurichi and the chief gainers by Kaṭṭaboma's fall.

Mr. Jackson's character.

Mr. Jackson appears to have had too hasty a temper. He was subsequently taken to task by the Board of Revenue for various matters and was dismissed by Government from employ on account of the insubordinate spirit he displayed. He was accused also of peculation, but was acquitted of this charge.

CHAPTER VII.

Mr. Lushington's dealings with Kaṭṭaboma.

On the 12th January 1799 Mr. Lushington succeeded Mr. Jackson, and on the 16th March he wrote to Kaṭṭaboma Nāyaka an exceedingly polite letter, informing him that he had been honourably exculpated from the charge of murdering Lieutenant Clarke, and restoring him to the full possession of his pollam; at the same time desiring him to attend him (Mr. Lushington) at Ramnad and bring with him his arrears of kist. Kaṭṭaboma Nāyaka's letter in reply overflowed, as might have been expected, with expressions of gratitude and dutiful obedience, but it contained also reasons why it was quite impossible for him to pay his kist just then or proceed to Ramnad, till he had received everything he considered due to him from Government. In short his tone had changed, but his conduct remained the same.

All Mr. Lushington's endeavours to induce Kaṭṭaboma Nāyaka to submit to his authority, appear before him in person without an armed force, or pay his arrears of kist having proved in vain, he at length referred the matter to Government. The following is the principal paragraph in his letter :—

He refers to Government.

"In bringing before you the flagrant conduct of the Poligars alluded to in this letter, I mean not to recommend that any immediate measures should be taken to punish those who have been most culpable. I am clearly of opinion that no coercion should be attempted until a proper detachment can be formed under an officer who has had experience of these countries, whose integrity is incorruptible, and until some general system for the future government of the Poligars has been determined upon. A small force would endanger combinations and troublesome resistance, whilst the expense of a large detachment is of too weighty consideration to be sacrificed to the sequestration of two or more of their pollams. The radical reduction of their barbarous power cannot however be too early undertaken, and until it be effected, the inhabitants of these countries will not be secure in their property or lives, nor will the Poligars be otherwise than insolent and disobedient."

An expedition recommended.

Government, on receiving this communication, resolved to temporise no longer, as it was evident that a rebellious spirit was spreading amongst the rest of the Poligars. The example of the Poligar of Pānjālamkurichi, who had never consented to obey a Collector, and who, as was generally believed, had slain a European officer with his own hand with impunity, was sure to prove infectious.

Different sides taken by different Poligars.

The principal Poligars who took Kaṭṭaboma Nāyaka's side against Government and gave him assistance were the Poligars of Nāgalāpuram, Kollārpaṭṭi (called also Kōlavārpaṭṭi and Kollapaṭṭi), and Eḷāyirampaṇṇai. On the same side were the Poligars of Kāḍalguḍi and Kuḷattūr. He was joined also by the Pūli Dēva of that day, the Poligar of Āvuḍaiyārpuram, whose fort was at Orme's "Nellatangaville," viz., Nelkaṭṭansevval. Before all was over, however, the latter Poligar went over to the side of Government. The principal focus of rebellion amongst the western Poligars was in Sivagiri. The old Poligar himself was loyal, but his son had been endeavouring to set him aside, with the help of an armed force sent by Kaṭṭaboma Nāyaka, and the less open assistance the rest of the disaffected Poligars. The son was afterwards pardoned by Major Bannerman, in behalf of Government, and allowed to succeed his father in the Poligarship. The principal leader of rebellion, however, in Sivagiri was not the old Poligar's son, but a member of his family, called Māppiḷḷai Vanniyan described as a daring, popular leader, possessed of great local influence. [The Sivagiri family are the only Zemindar family, I believe, in Tinnevelly who belong to the caste of Vanniyas.] Further north Kaṭṭaboma Nāyaka was aided by the sympathy and counsel of the Marudu, the chief of Sivagangai. The strongest supporter of Government in the struggle was the Poligar of Eṭṭaiyāpuram. The same side was also taken by the Poligars of Ūttumalai, Chokkampaṭṭi, and Talaivankōṭṭai in the west, and in the east by the Poligars of Maṇiātchi and Mēlmāndai. The only real help, however, the Government received was from the Poligar of Eṭṭaiyāpuram.

Mr. Lushington, the then Collector, had the confidence of Government (subsequently he became Governor himself), so that he found it comparatively easy to convince the Government of that time of the necessity of fully and finally vindicating their authority in Tinnevelly and quelling the rebellious spirit that was beginning to spread. They temporised, however, a little till Seringapatam was taken; shortly after which event, their chief anxieties being at an end and their troops free to move, they came to the conclusion that the time for carrying into effect the intention they had for some time formed had arrived.

Troops set free by the taking of Seringapatam.

MAJOR BANNERMAN'S EXPEDITION.

A force was equipped for the purpose of enforcing obedience in Tinnevelly and placed under the command of Major Bannerman, an officer of great ability, whose reports and memoranda, preserved in the records and collected and published by Mr. Kearns, furnish a complete account of everything that occurred. Major Bannerman's instructions were dated on the 19th August 1799, and by the 21st of October, in the short space of two months, he had succeeded in accomplishing the task committed to him.

I shall here give the originals of the most important documents relating to Major Bannerman's expedition. The originals themselves will be found more interesting than any narrative compiled from them could be :—

CHAPTER VII.

Letter of Government to the Board of Revenue.

Reasons of Government.

"We are concerned to observe from the late requisition of the Collector of Poligar Peshcush, that no sense of the indulgence of the Company's Government, nor of their own allegiance, has restrained the Poligars, during the late temporary absence of the troops from resorting to their refractory habits, under the administration of the Nawab. We were sanguine that the spirit of forbearance, conciliation, and justice, which was manifested in the late inquiry and decision on the conduct of Kaṭṭaboma Nāyaka would have inspired the Poligars in general, and himself in particular, with a better sense of the mildness and equity of the British administration ; but his refusal to attend the Collector without his armed followers, his delay in the discharge of his peshcush, and his present actual levying of war against the Sivagiri Poligar deprive us of all hope of beneficial consequences from the farther pursuit of conciliatory measures. We have, therefore, judged it expedient to assemble a sufficient body of troops in the Southern Provinces to assert the authority of the Company's Government, and to punish this wanton provocation of their resentment. The command of this detachment, we have judged it expedient to intrust to Major John Bannerman ; and in order that the Collector may be fully apprised of our intentions, we enclose for your information on a copy of our instructions to that officer.

"In communicating to the Collector these instructions, we desire that you will direct him to comply with any applications which he may receive from Major Bannerman for the furtherance of the present service ; and as we deem it indispensable to the success of the expedition that arrangements and orders of that officer should be carried into effect with the greatest degree of promptness, we have no doubt that Mr. Lushington's knowledge of that necessity, as well as his zeal for the public service, will induce him to give the most effectual support to the powers with which Major Bannerman has been invested."

This letter was signed by Lord Clive, then Governor of Madras, son of the celebrated Clive.

"*Proclamation by the Collector.*

"To all Poligars, Landholders, and Inhabitants of every description within the countries commonly called the Tinnevelly Pollams.

"Whereas repeated admonitions were given by me to several of the Tinnevelly Poligars during the late hostilities against the deceased Tippu Sultan, that by persisting to withhold the peshcush, and to be otherwise disobedient, they would draw upon themselves the severest displeasure of Government; yet, notwithstanding such admonitions, and unmindful of the punishment inflicted upon those Poligars who had been refractory during former wars, certain of them had the temerity to continue in their contumacy, and to set the Company's power at defiance by committing depredations, disturbing the tranquillity of the country, and wantonly murdering the peaceable inhabitants. Now be it known that these admonitions, and the total disregard of them, having been made known to the Right Honourable the Governor-

General in Council, His Lordship has observed with extreme concern that no sense of the indulgence of the Company's Government nor of their own allegiance was of effect to restrain the Poligars, during the late temporary absence of the troops, from resorting to their refractory habits.

"The Right Honourable the Governor-General was sanguine that the spirit of forbearance, conciliation, and justice, which was manifested in the late enquiry and decision on the conduct of Kaṭṭaboma Nāyaka, would have inspired him in particular, and the Poligars in general, with a better sense of the mildness and equity of the British administration; but his refusal to attend the Collector without his armed followers, his delay in the discharge of his peshcush, and his present actual levying of war against the Sivagiri Poligar, in conjunction with other contumacious persons, deprive the Right Honourable the Governor-General in Council of all hopes of beneficial consequence from the further pursuit of conciliatory measures towards him or them. His Lordship has therefore judged it expedient to assemble a sufficient body of troops in the southern provinces to assert the supremacy of the Company's Government, and to punish the wanton provocation of their displeasure. The command of this detachment has been intrusted to Major John Bannerman, and, in order to render his authority more efficient, the Right Honourable the Governor-General in Council has thought it expedient to vest him with powers to use miliary execution.

"All persons are therefore solemnly warned to forbear from acts of disobedience and rebellion, as the power of inflicting death will be used with the utmost rigour.

"It is hereby declared that all Poligars are held responsible for the good conduct of all descriptions of people belonging to their respective pollams, and that they do not act in any respect against the Company's authority, or in any manner disturb the peace of the country, after the publication of this proclamation.

"Be it further known to all Poligars, Sherogars, Landholders, and Inhabitants in the Pollams of Tinnevelly that Major Bannerman has authority to communicate with and issue such orders to them as he may judge necessary; these orders must be obeyed with the utmost promptitude, and the Collector will refuse all intercourse with such Poligars as have already proved, or may hereafter prove, refractory, until Major Bannerman shall have reported to the Collector their return to a state of order and obedience."

Attempt to take Pañjālamkurichi.

On the 5th September Major Bannerman arrived at Pāñjālamkurichi, and attempted to take the fort the same day by storm, without waiting for the arrival of the European portion of his force. His reason for not waiting for the arrival of the Europeans was that he was afraid the Poligar would endeavour to make his escape during the night, and get away across the country to Sivagiri. This apprehension was not a groundless one, for this was the course that was taken by the father of this very Poligar when his

CHAPTER VII. fort was suddenly taken by Colonel Fullarton in 1783. The assault was unsuccessful. I give the account in Major Bannerman's own words:—

"*To the Secretary to Government.*

"In conformity with my letter of yesterday's date, I left Palamcottah and arrived this morning at Pānjālamkurichi, where I was joined by the troops stationed at Coilpatti and Kaittār. The detail of Europeans and the two 12-pounders not being sufficiently advanced, were ordered to Kaittār. The sudden approach of the troops was not looked for. Lieutenant Dallas, without a moment's delay, and with much judgment, surrounded the fort with his cavalry, and his parties were supported with every possible expedition by infantry. Soon after this a considerable body of Poligar peons endeavoured to force themselves into the garrison, but were repulsed with loss by Lieutenant Dallas. I lost no time in ordering the Poligar to surrender at discretion to the Company. If I would grant a written cowl, he said, he would come to me; but not without. I left no consistent means untried to induce him to give himself up; however, at half past nine o'clock I gave him half an hour more to determine his line of conduct.

Call to the Poligar to surrender.

The Poligar's escape anticipated.

"Having attentively and deliberately reconnoitered the fort, it appeared in my judgment that the south gate and to the left of it could be stormed with almost a certainty of success; and that the place might be carried with a trifling loss on our part. I consequently determined on the measure: I was not only guided by this motive, but by the importance of getting possession of the person of the Poligar, and the impossibility with safety of keeping the fort surrounded during the night, so as to prevent the Poligar from escaping, which I was confident he would attempt. I then carried with me Captains O'Reilly and Bruce, the senior officers, who were to command the storming troops, and communicated my orders to them. Their opinions with regard to the success of the assault corresponded with mine.

Failure of the attack.

"At ten o'clock the Poligar sent me a message that in four hours he would attend me, if I would send him a regular cowl. The troops were then posted for the storm. The flank companies of the 1st Battalion of the 3rd Regiment and the four flank companies of the 13th Regiment of Native Infantry were allotted for the assault, with a 6-pounder to blow open the south gate; this party was covered by three field pieces and the battalion companies of the 1st Battalion of the 3rd Regiment of Native Infantry and three companies of the 1st Battalion of the 13th Regiment. At the same time an attack on the north face of the fort was made by two companies of sepoys regulated by Lieutenant Dallas. The troops, in the first instance, advanced to the attack with order and resolution; but from a panic could not be prevailed on to ascend the breach, or to enter by the gate which had been blown completely open by the 6-pounder. The attempt was persevered in so long as there was a shadow of success, and never was European energy more gallantly displayed than by the officers on this unfortunate occasion. Our loss, you will observe by the accompanying return, is very severe; but I cannot apply to myself any share of censure. However, I cannot but experience great anxiety until I find my conduct held free from it by His Lordship in Council. I have ordered the detail of the 19th Regiment of Foot and two 12-pounders to join me immediately, and I have sent to Palamcottah for a 24-pounder. I have little doubt in my mind but the place could be carried so soon as the Europeans arrive without waiting for cannon to make a breach; but any further check might be attended with serious consequences.' I shall therefore proceed with every consistent caution. The moment my time will allow of it, I shall state to the Commander-in-Chief my sentiments relative to the conduct of the native officers and troops. The circumstance of one native officer being only wounded, contrasted with four European Officers killed and two wounded, will sufficiently mark the want of energy on the part of the natives."

Dissatisfaction with Native troops.

The fort abandoned.

The Poligar did not wait for the recommencement of the attack on his fort. Two days afterwards, late in the evening, the European portion of the force arrived, and preparations were made by Major Bannerman for another assault the following day. In the course of the night, however, the fort was completely evacuated by the Poligar and all his followers; soon after the Eṭṭaiyāpuram Poligar started in pursuit and came up with Kaṭṭaboma Nāyaka at Kollārpaṭṭi, where some fighting ensued with loss on both sides. Kaṭṭaboma effected his escape and fled for refuge first to Sivagangai and then to the Tondiman Rājā. Thirty-four of his principal adherents were secured at Kollārpaṭṭi, amongst whom his principal manager, Subrahmaṇya Pillai, who was taken to Major Bannerman, who had now proceeded to Nāgalāpuram, where he was hanged and his head sent to Pānjālamkurichi. At the same time Saundara Pāṇḍya Nāyaka, the brother of the Poligar of Nāgalāpuram, who had headed his brother's plundering and murdering expeditions into the Ramnad country, was hanged at Gōpālpuram. Kaṭṭaboma Nāyaka himself was speedily captured by the Tondiman Rājā, and sent with some of his relations to Major Bannerman, by whom he was tried and executed on the 16th October in a conspicuous place near the old fort of Kaittār, in the presence of all the Poligars of Tinnevelly, who witnessed the unwonted sight with wonder and silent awe. The details of these events will now be given in Major Bannerman's own words.

The Poligar's end.

"*Major Bannerman to the Secretary to Government.*

Particulars of Major Bannerman's expedition.

"For the information of the Right Honourable the Governor-General in Council, I have the honour to acquaint you that the detail of His Majesty's 19th Regiment and the two 12-pounders reached this place yesterday afternoon, about six o'clock, which was too late an hour, added to the men being much fatigued, to take any immediate measures for recommencing an attack on the fort; and in the course

CHAPTER VII. of the night it was evacuated by the Poligar and all his followers. It is some satisfaction to me—though but a small one—to report for the information of the Right Honourable the Governor-General in Council that upon a minute examination of the points of attack I had chosen it now appears I had selected the most eligible places, and such indeed as to leave so little reflection on my own judgment on the occasion that they must have been carried, and the place got complete possession of in a few minutes, had the native troops behaved with the energy and spirit which I have often witnessed them exert on less trying occasions."

EVENTS WHICH FOLLOWED THE POLIGAR'S ESCAPE.

The following letters describe the pursuit and capture of Kaṭṭaboma Nāyaka and his principal adherents:—

"Soon after the dispatch of my letter of the 6th instant, having obtained intelligence, on which I could depend, of the direction in which Kaṭṭaboma Nāyaka had moved, I lost no time in addressing letters to the several Poligars, particularly to those who I knew were his enemies, informing them of his flight, and calling upon them to use every exertion in their power to secure his person. On the letters for the Poligars being ready for dispatch I put the detachment in motion in a northerly direction, after having placed the wounded men in Pānjālamkurichi, where every means had been taken for their comfortable accommodation, and where a sufficient party was left for their protection.

Assistance of Eṭṭaiyāpuram.

"On my march I threw off parties to my left, the first consisting of the two troops of cavalry under Lieutenant Dallas, and the other four hundred grenadiers under Captain O'Reilly, in order that they might be in readiness to act, as I should see occasion, in co-operation with the Poligars, to the westward of the tract in which I had determined to move with the main body. I had not proceeded far, when I received an answer from the Eṭṭaiāpuram Poligar, promising faithfully that no exertion on his part should be wanting to carry into effect the orders of Government, which he had received through me, and informing me that he had assembled a party of his people, with which he would himself immediately proceed in pursuit of Kaṭṭaboma Nāyaka, and requesting I would afford him the assistance of some sepoys, and recommending that they should be sent after him without delay.

Capture of important prisoners.

"Instructions were accordingly sent to Lieutenant Dallas, with a guide to conduct him in the track of the Eṭṭaiāpuram man, and to Captain O'Reilly to follow in support of the cavalry as fast as possible. The party with Eṭṭaiāpuram came up with Kaṭṭaboma Nāyaka at the fort of Kollārpatti before it was possible for it to be joined by the cavalry. Some skirmishing ensued, in which both parties sustained considerable loss. Kaṭṭaboma Nāyaka's followers were, however, dispersed; but he effected his escape, attended by only six persons, who with himself were mounted on horses; thirty-four of Kaṭṭaboma Nāyaka's principal dependents were secured; among whom are Subrahmaṇya Pillai, his principal manager, and Subrahmaṇya's brother. I conceive the seizure of these two men, particularly the

CHAPTER VII.

former, of more importance to the future success of my operations, and the consequent re-establishment of order and tranquillity in these countries, than if Kaṭṭaboma Nāyaka was my prisoner ; for they are men of good ability, and of the most intriguing dispositions ; and the former has acquired considerable wealth, which I have every reason to believe he would willingly expend in making resistance to the authority of Government. There can be no doubt but this Subrahmaṇya had acquired such influence over Kaṭṭaboma Nāyaka as entirely to regulate every public act in which he engaged ; and that the latter's conduct, in resisting the Company's authority, and in the exercise of independent power, contrary to his allegiance, was the effect of Subrahmaṇya's advice."

* * * *

Subrahmaṇya Pillai's guilt and sentence.

"Subrahmaṇya Pillai is this instant brought a prisoner to my tent. I have given directions that the Eṭṭaiāpuram man's party, which came in charge of him, may be handsomely rewarded, and that Subrahmaṇya Pillai shall be hanged in the most conspicuous part of the village of Nāgalāpuram, and his head afterwards carried and fixed on a pike at Pānjālamkurichi. His brother and the other prisoners will be kept in confinement, in order to their being disposed of as circumstances may hereafter require. By having, in this instance, determined to make a severe and melancholy example of a man who has been the author of the late disturbances and enormities which have provoked the resentment of Government, I trust I shall not be deemed by the Right Honourable the Governor-General in Council to have exceeded the bounds of that authority with which it was thought necessary to vest me ; or, in exercising it, to have lost sight of that caution and forbearance which have been recommended to me in my instructions, which shall in all cases be the guides of my conduct."

* * * *

"While the parties under Captain O'Reilly and Lieutenant Dallas were advancing in support of the Eṭṭaiāpuram Poligar, I moved on and took possession of this place (Nāgalāpuram) on the 9th instant. Soon after my arrival the Poligar came and surrendered himself to the Company's authority. As the conduct of this man has been of a nature the most flagitious, and marked by acts, in the Ramnad country, of murder and destruction, which shock humanity, I shall detain him for the present in close confinement, and am not without hopes of getting hold of the person of his brother, who commanded his parties in the execution of his barbarous orders during his irruption into the Ramnad country. The Eṭṭiāpuram Poligar is still in pursuit of Kaṭṭaboma Nāyaka : the parties, however, which I had sent in support of him I deemed it necessary to recall after I received intelligence of the dispersion of Kaṭṭaboma Nāyaka's followers, and they joined me in camp during the night of the 9th."

* * * *

Two principal offenders executed.

"I succeeded in securing Saundara Pāṇḍya Nāyaka, brother to the Nāgalāpuram Poligar, on the afternoon of the 12th instant, and kept him prisoner in the fort of Nāgalāpuram till yesterday morning, when I assembled all the Vakeels of the different Poligars, who attended me, and after calling their attention to the proclamation by the Revenue

CHAPTER VII. Board, which had been issued through the Collector, Mr. Lushington, I explained to them the nature and the extent of the powers with which I had been vested, and the urgent reasons which Government had for ordering a strict enquiry to be made into the cause of the disturbances, which had so lately existed in this country, and during which such scenes of murder and devastation had occurred, which called for the most exemplary punishment. I acquainted them that in consequence of the information I had obtained, I should, in the first place, be under the painful necessity of punishing with death such of those individuals as had been most actively employed in these disturbances which had provoked the Company's resentment; and should then take such other measures as I thought necessary for securing future obedience to all the Company's orders which might be conveyed through the Collector to their masters, and for preventing a repetition of these scenes of rapine and murder which had desolated the country and destroyed the inhabitants. I farther informed the Vakeels that the result of my enquiries had pointed out Subrahmaṇya Pillai, the head manager of Kaṭṭaboma Nāyaka, and Saundara Pāṇḍya Nāyaka, brother to the Nāgalāpuram Poligar, as the most active agents in the atrocious scenes of which Government complained; and that I had in consequence determined that they should suffer death. That the former should be hanged in the most conspicuous part of the Nāgalāpuram village, and his head sent to be fixed on a pike at Pānjālamkurichi, and the latter I should send to be hanged at the village of Gopalpuram, in the taluk of Palamurrah (Paḷḷimaḍai) in the Ramnad country, which village a party under his command had destroyed, after inhumanly murdering its inhabitants. After both these men had been carried off to execution, I delivered copies of my proclamation to the different Vakeels, and desired that they would transmit them to their masters. I enjoined them to write also a faithful account of what had passed at our meeting that morning; and to add that they had it farther in command from me to say that the severe but necessary examples which had been made ought not to create any alarm amongst those who were innocent of similar crimes; but on the contrary should serve to convince the inhabitants that the Company had, on this occasion, been forced to adopt measures of severity, only because their former lenient and merciful conduct towards the refractory Poligars had failed to produce the wished-for reform. The Vakeels were now dismissed, and I have reason to believe a proper impression was made on their minds by what had passed at this interview."

* * * *

"I have learned from Mr. Lushington that he has received a letter from the Tondiman informing him that he had succeeded in his exertions to seize the person of Kaṭṭaboma Nāyaka, and desiring to be furnished with orders respecting the disposal of that rebellious Poligar. Mr. Lushington has, at my request, been so obliging as to write to the Tondiman desiring that Kaṭṭaboma Nāyaka might be immediately sent prisoner to Madura, and delivered over to the commanding officer at that station, if no orders to the contrary had been

CHAPTER VII.

received from Government. I shall order a party from this detachment to escort Kaṭṭaboma Nāyaka from Madura to camp, in order that he may be proceeded against agreeably to the spirit of my original instructions, which authorise me to use 'military execution against such of the rebellious Poligars and their followers as shall be found in open rebellion and in arms against the authority of Government.' "

Kaṭṭaboma taken.

* * * *

Assembly to witness the execution of Kaṭṭaboma.

"The party which I had sent to Madura to receive and conduct the rebellious Poligar Kaṭṭaboma Nāyaka to camp returned with the prisoner on the forenoon of the 5th instant. There were also brought prisoners with the Poligar six of his nearest relations, including Kumāra Swāmi Nāyaka, his dumb brother. With a view that the orders of Government respecting Kaṭṭaboma Nāyaka might be made public and carried into execution in as solemn and impressive a manner as circumstances would permit, I summoned all the head Poligars to attend me yesterday forenoon at 10 o'clock. On their being assembled, I informed them that I had called for their attendance upon that occasion that they might be present while I communicated to Kaṭṭaboma Nāyaka the awful sentence pronounced upon him by Government in vindication of their authority so grossly injured by the late contumacious conduct of that Poligar, which had occasioned the many evils to the country which they had all witnessed, and by his subsequent daring rebellion in resisting by force of arms the Company's troops, which had been sent under my orders to recall him to obedience and a proper sense of his duty.

"I then directed Kaṭṭaboma Nāyaka to be brought in before the assembly, and proceeded to take the examination and the confession of the Poligar, which you will find detailed in the inclosed paper marked 'A,' bearing my signature, and those of Major Robert Turing and of Mr. George Hughes, the Tamil Translator, whom I had directed to attend me on the occasion.

"From this paper the Right Honourable the Governor-General in Council will observe that the rebellious Poligar Kaṭṭaboma Nāyaka confessed or could not deny that he had withheld his kists; that he did refuse to wait upon the Collector Mr. Lushington on his summons, unless permitted to be attended by a party of armed peons; that he did receive a summons to attend me at Palamcottah on the 4th of September last for the purpose of having explained to him the orders which I had received from Government respecting him, which he refused to obey upon the idle pretence of its being an unlucky day.

Sentence on Kaṭṭaboma.

"From the paper above alluded to it will likewise appear clearly proved by the evidences, independent of his own confession, 'that Kaṭṭaboma Nāyaka, in contempt of the Company's authority, did send an armed force, of between 700 and 1,000 Peons, under the command of one of his own relations, in the months of July and August last, to join the Sivagiri Poligar's son and Mappillai Vanniyan, who were in open rebellion against that Poligar; that while in his fort of Pānjālamkurichi, on the morning of the 5th September last, he did receive a summons to wait upon me at a small distance from his fort, which

CHAPTER VII.

he refused to obey; and that he did remain in his fort during that day, and was present while his people fired upon and killed many of the Company's troops, who were ordered to compel his submission to the authority of Government. After what passed, as detailed in the paper marked 'A,' I proceeded to communicate to the Poligar, Kaṭṭaboma Nāyaka, the awful resolution of Government, which sentenced him to suffer the punishment of death in vindication of the injured authority of the Company. He was then carried off to execution and hanged on a conspicuous spot near to the old fort of Kaittār.

Address to the assembled Poligars.

"When Kaṭṭaboma Nāyaka was led off to execution, I addressed myself to the Poligars, who had witnessed all that had passed in silent awe and with astonishment, and caused to be clearly explained to them that the Poligar, Kaṭṭaboma Nāyaka, had compelled Government to inflict upon him such rigorous punishment by repeatedly acting in contempt of the Company's authority, and by being guilty at last of open rebellion, notwithstanding he had frequently, and on so late an occasion, experienced the most signal lenity and justice from the Government, of which none of the Poligars present could be ignorant. I then dismissed them after having expressed an earnest hope that the examples which had lately been made, and the measures which had been adopted, would convince them and their posterity that no rank or condition of life amongst them would in future screen from punishment such as should dare to act in disobedience of the Company's orders, or in contempt of the authority of Government, which they must ever consider it their duty to respect.

Execution of Kaṭṭaboma.

"It may not be amiss here to observe that the manner and behaviour of the Poligar during the whole time of his being before those who were assembled yesterday at the examination which took place was undaunted and supercilious. He frequently eyed the Ettiapuram Poligar, who had been so active in attempting to secure his person, and the Poligar of Sivagiri with an appearance of indignant scorn; and when he went out to be executed he walked with a firm and daring air, and cast looks of sullen contempt on the Poligars to his right and left as he passed. It was reported to me that on his way to the place of execution he expressed some anxiety for his dumb brother alone; and said, when he reached the foot of the tree on which he was hanged that he then regretted having left his fort, in the defence of which it would have been better for him to have died."

The following proclamation by Major Bannerman dispossessing five of the Poligars who had combined with Kaṭṭaboma Nāyaka against the Government, together with that Poligar himself, was published nearly a month before, but it will come in most appropriately at this juncture :—

Camp at Kaittār, 17th October 1799.

Disloyal Poligars dispossessed.

"Be it known to all the Tinnevelly Poligars, and all the inhabitants of the pollams, that Major John Bannerman, commissioned by the Honourable Company to make enquiry into the misconduct of the Tinnevelly Poligars in communication with the Collector, and to punish

CHAPTER VII.

such as may be found deserving thereof; and having, on a full enquiry into the conduct of the several Poligars of Ēḷayirampaṇṇai, Nāgalāpuram, Kollārpaṭṭi, Kāḍalguḍi, and Kuḷattur, discovered that they were leagued with Pānjālam kurichi in the late levying of war against the Poligar of Sivagiri, who is under the Company's protection; and that the conduct of all these Poligars has been alike disobedient and rebellious to the Government of the Company, in disregarding the authority of the Collector, refusing to pay Company's kists, committing depredations, disturbing the peace of the country, and oppressing and murdering its inhabitants, he has deemed it expedient, by virtue of his instructions, and the powers with which he is invested from the Company, to mark in the strongest manner their displeasure against such criminal proceedings; and therefore proclaims that the Poligars of Pānjālamkurichi, Nāgālapuram, Ēḷāyirampaṇṇai, Kollarpatti, Kāḍalguḍi, and Kulattūr are dispossessed of their pollams. And be it known to all the inhabitants thereof that they are assumed by the Company, who have accordingly taken possession of them.

"Be it further known that all the forts in the aforesaid palaiyams being deemed useless and unnecessary by the Company, are hereby ordered to be destroyed. And, further, as the carrying of arms by the peons and people thereof has been attended with much mischief, and violence to the whole country, it is strictly enjoined that no peon, sherogar, cowalgar, inhabitant or any other person of any description whatever shall hereafter use or keep either firelock, matchlock, pike, or spear, under pain of being put to death; and any person whatever found concealing or possessing them will be also subject to the same punishment; and it is therefore strictly commanded that every peon or inhabitant of the aforesaid pollams possessing arms shall immediately deliver them up to such persons as Major Bannerman may appoint to receive them, and every head inhabitant will be held subject to severe punishment who makes not the fullest enquiry, and gives not the most speedy information of all arms concealed in his village; and, in order more effectually to preserve the tranquillity of the assumed pollams and that the peaceful inhabitants may pursue their cultivation in safety, all head inhabitants of villages are hereby solemnly warned that in whatever village resistance may be made to the Company's servants, and if it shall be discovered that any firelock, matchlock, pike, or spear has been used in such affray, the head inhabitant of such village will be liable to suffer death, unless he shall, in three days after such affray has happened, report the names of those inhabitants who were engaged in such resistance, and prove that he has done every thing in his power to seize the offenders. And be it also most fully known to all the rest of the Poligars that while the assumption of the abovementioned six pollams has been the severe and necessary consequence of very criminal proceedings, that provided all the rest conduct themselves hereafter with the most respectful and submissive obedience to the Company's Government, neither more of the lives of their people will be taken, nor more of their countries assumed; and being duly impressed therewith they will act accordingly. Under these assurances let therefore the inhabitants of every description, and

Disarmament ordered.

Penalties for disobedience.

CHAPTER VII. particularly those sherogars and peons who have been accustomed to carry arms, cheerfully lay aside all offensive weapons; and, betaking themselves to the cultivation of the land, increase their own happiness and merit the favour of the Company, who will protect them from every danger."

I add Major Bannerman's account of his interview with all the Tinnevelly Poligars at Kaittār on the 27th September, when he read and explained to them his proclamation respecting the demolition of their forts and the delivering up of their arms, and induced each Poligar to volunteer to carry this work of demolition into effect himself:—

"I met all the Poligars who had, in obedience to my summons, arrived at Kaittar. I first endeavoured to make the Poligars sensible of the justness of the punishment which had already been inflicted. I then cautioned them against believing that because no farther examples had yet been made I was ignorant of the many acts of disobedience of which they had been guilty, of the refractory disposition of the Poligars in general, and of the innumerable evils which such causes had produced.

Explanation of reasons.

"I then told the Poligars that there were two modes of carrying into effect the orders of Government as signified by the proclamation. The one was that they should give their own orders to destroy the forts and collect the arms and deliver the latter to officers whom I should send with small parties to receive them and see that the forts were properly demolished. The other mode was that I should march with the whole of my detachment through their pollams and see the orders of Government carried into execution. I acquainted them that I was prepared for either, but left the choice with them. That in the event of the detachments marching all the Head Poligars must attend me in the camp. If the other mode were to be adopted, the Poligars should remain with me at Kaittâr and send their managers with small parties, which I should direct to proceed, and superintend the execution of the Company's orders.

Forts to be demolished.

"I assured them that as soon as I had received reports that the arms had been surrendered and the forts demolished, each man should be permitted to return in peace to his own pollam. Before my interview was over I believe I may venture to assert that I obtained from the Poligars their fullest consent to the demolition of their forts and the surrender of their arms. They seemed convinced by my arguments that it would be more creditable for them to destroy their own forts than to have the business done by our pioneers; and they did not appear insensible of the mischief that would be prevented by keeping so large a detachment out of their pollams, their apprehension of which I did not fail to raise as much as possible.

"I have much pleasure in being able to report to you that the last of the parties which I found it necessary to detach to superintend the demolition of the forts and the collection of the arms left Kaittar this morning; and that the Poligars have sent their managers and positive orders, with the different parties, to see that the orders of Government on this subject be strictly complied with.

"The Head Poligars themselves have agreed to remain with me at Kaittar till I shall be satisfied that the orders which they have sent by their managers are obeyed. I cannot omit reporting in this place that I had created in the Poligars, before we parted, so anxious a desire to appear forward in complying with the orders of Government, that some of them even requested that I would obtain for them the assistance of coolies from the Circar villages in their neighbourhood to assist in demolishing their forts; and that I have in consequence applied for the necessary orders from the Nawab's Kutchary, which shall be immediately forwarded to the villages most contiguous to the pollams in which such assistance has been required. The coolies are to be paid at the expense of such Poligar whose fort they assist to demolish. I have much reason at present to believe that by the plan in which I have got the Poligars to acquiesce every fort in the pollams, amounting to forty-two, will be effectually destroyed before the end of this month. With respect to the arms, I am not so sanguine in my hopes of their being all surrendered so readily. The prejudices and long habits of the Poligars oppose the measure; but the carrying into execution the threats held forth in the proclamation, in a very few instances at first, will soon overcome their partiality to the custom of carrying arms, and convert the armed Poligar into a tame and peaceable cultivator of the soil."

Poligars ask for help to demolish their forts.

The Madras Government approved of the disarming of the Poligars, but, in order to facilitate, as they supposed, the carrying of the measure into effect, ordered, in opposition to Major Bannerman's judgment, that the arms should not be seized, but that a reward, or price, should be paid to each person for each description of arms delivered up.

Approval of Government.

Within a month Major Bannerman had reason to believe that all the Poligar forts in Tinnevelly had been demolished. On the 21st October he writes:—

"I enclose the returns which I received from the different Poligars showing the number of forts each had in his pollam, of the guns and wall-pieces of each fort, and the number of peons retained in each Poligar's service, specifying the number and description of arms which they used. As also a general report of the forts which have been destroyed, and of the arms already collected, made out from those reports which I have received from the officers in charge of the different parties which I had detached to superintend the demolition of the forts, and the surrender of the arms in those pollams which have not been sequestered. I likewise inclose a copy of a letter which accompanied the reports from Captain Bruce, the officer placed in the general command of the parties dispersed in the western pollams, from which it is satisfactory to observe how attentive all the managers employed by the Poligars have been in obeying the orders they had received respecting the demolition of their forts, &c. You will also find a copy of the report I received from Lieutenant Bagshaw, who was employed, with the pioneers under his command, in demolishing the fort of Pānjālamkurichi, and a return of the arms collected in the six sequestered pollams.

Results.

CHAPTER VII.

"As the purpose for which the Poligars were detained at Kaittar has already been pretty completely answered, I summoned all of them to attend me this morning in order to give them permission to return to their respective pollams; and as I thought it of consequence fully to impress upon their minds before their departure that Government would hereafter act toward them in a strict conformity with the measures which I had on this occasion been instructed to adopt, I had prepared a proclamation, a copy of which was delivered to each Poligar; and they were informed that other copies inscribed on brass should be prepared, and one sent to each of them as soon as possible, in order that it might be fixed up and kept in a conspicuous place in the principal village of each pollam for the general information of the inhabitants;[1] and that each Poligar would be held responsible that this order was strictly complied with."

Proclamations inscribed on brass.

The Poligars of Ēḷāyirampaṇṇai and Nāgalāpuram were banished to Madras, where they died. A letter of Major Bannerman's will explain his views regarding these Poligars and some of their principal associates:—

"In conformity with the spirit of my instructions, I had determined to send all the Head Poligars of the sequestered pollams prisoners to the Presidency. The Nāgalāpuram and Ēḷāyirampaṇṇai Poligars have been placed under Lieutenant Turner's charge. Kaṭṭaboma Nāyaka and the Head Poligar of Kāḍalguḍi have been proscribed by my proclamation of the 18th instant. But as the Poligar of Kollārpaṭṭi is a poor, weak, blind youth, and the Poligar of Kuḷattūr is a weak, infirm man of between 60 and 70 years of age, their infirmities seem to point them out as objects who should be treated with as much lenity as due attention to the public good will admit of, and as there is no danger to be apprehended from their intrigues, I have delivered them over to Mr. Lushington, that he may send them for the present to Ramnad, and they can be hereafter disposed of as Government shall be pleased to direct. As Satagopah Pillai, the manager of the Nāgalāpuram Poligar, was a principal adviser of his master, and possesses much influence in the pollam, I have judged it indispensably necessary that he should accompany the Poligar into banishment. Saunderalinga Nāyaka was declared by his blind brother-in-law, the Poligar of Kollārpaṭṭi, to have been his adviser on all occasions, and confessed himself to have been the manager of all the public concerns of the pollam. Chinna Vettoo Nāyaka, son of the Kuḷattūr Poligar, is also notorious for having been the wicked adviser of his father; and he and Armogam Pillai were the sole managers of his public concerns; and Paradampermal Pillai possesses much influence, as having been the adviser and manager of the Ēḷāyirampaṇṇai Poligar. I could not therefore hesitate in removing individuals of such description from this country.

Leniency to certain Poligars.

Banishment of dangerous persons.

"The public records leave no doubt of Sivagiri Māppillai Vanniyan being the person whose influence over the Sivagiri Poligar's son instigated him to acts of rebellion against his father, and produced

[1] These brass plates are said to be still in existence, but are kept in the houses of the Zemindars.

those horrid scenes and disturbances in the Sivagiri pollam by which not only that country but the neighbouring pollams have suffered so much, and to quell which the Company have been repeatedly obliged to fit out an armed force. This man possesses talents which qualify him in a very superior degree for being a public incendiary, and is distinguished among the Poligars for being a daring, brave, and active fellow, which makes him a favourite leader, whom they are desirous to follow upon all occasions. Government will, I think, see the propriety of taking particular care that such a character is not permitted to return again to this neighbourhood."

Māpillai Vanniyan.

Most of Major Bannerman's prisoners were sent to Palamcotta and kept in confinement in the jail there, with the prisoners that had surrendered themselves to Captain Davison, the officer in command at Tuticorin. The most important of the prisoners sent by Major Bannerman to Palamcotta were the two brothers of the recently executed Poligar of Pānjālamkurichi. It was found after a time that the fort of Pānjālamkurichi, which was supposed to have been utterly demolished, was ready to rise again from the ground, as strong as ever, the moment it was required. Government were very much disconcerted when this discovery was made, but after the strictest inquiry it was ascertained that the demolition both of Pānjālamkurichi and of the other forts had really taken place—that of Pānjālamkurichi before Major Bannerman left the district—but that mud forts, however completely demolished, could speedily be re-erected, so that where a thousand or two enthusiastic labourers worked day and night there was nothing incredible in the circumstance that such a fort as Pānjālamkurichi should rise from the ground again in a day or two, as if by the wave of magician's wand. Whatever might take place afterwards there is no doubt that Major Bannerman's work, so far as it went, was very completely done; the voluntary demolition by the Poligars themselves of their forty-two forts was an unparalleled triumph to the cause of order, and it was achieved as much by tact and policy as by the force of arms. Having thus repressed all opposition to Government, and restored peace to the district, Major Bannerman left for Europe on furlough, accompanied by the cordial thanks and congratulations of all the authorities. The peace he established lasted for more than two years, an unusually long time for peace and order to last in those troublous days, but this state of things was destined to be rudely disturbed at last by another Poligar war—the most formidable of all, but fortunately the last.

Reappearance of the demolished forts.

Major Bannerman's success.

CHAPTER VIII.

THE LAST POLIGAR WAR.

Events preceding the Outbreak.

Chap. VIII.

General Welsh's account.

In addition to the information respecting the last Poligar war supplied by the reports and documents contained in the Tinnevelly records, we have the advantage of possessing two independent accounts of the war, written by persons who were engaged in it from its commencement to its termination. The first of these is contained in the "Military Reminiscences" of General Welsh, a very interesting book published in London in 1830. General (then Captain) Welsh was staff officer to the officer in command throughout the campaign. The other account is entitled a "Narrative of the

Mr. Hughes's account.

last Outbreak and final Subjugation of the Southern Poligars, by Mr. George A. Hughes, of Tatchanallúr, Translator to the force." This was published in 1844, nine years after Mr. Hughes's death.[1]

---

[1] Mr. Hughes's name is so well known in Tinnevelly that people would probably like to know some particulars about him. The following notice is prefixed to Mr. Hughes's Narrative by the Editor of the *Madras Journal of Literature and Science* in which the narrative appeared:—

"Mr. Hughes, an Indo-British gentleman, well known for his commercial enterprise and successful speculations in the southern districts, was the son of Mr. Hughes, of the Madras Civil Service, formerly Paymaster of Madura. He was sent to England at an early age and received an excellent education under the charge of his uncle, Dr. Hughes, Principal of Jesus College, Cambridge. On his return to India, after serving as a clerk under the Resident of Travancore, and in the office of Mr. S. R. Lushington, Collector of the Southern Poligar Peishcush, he was appointed by Colonel Bannerman, the officer entrusted with the charge of quelling the Poligar insurrection of 1799, to be Malabar and Gentoo Interpreter with the force on the pay and allowances of a Captain, which was confirmed by Government on the 26th September 1799. He continued in the same situation under Colonel Agnew in 1801, and afterwards in 1808 he accompanied the force under General St. Leger during the Travancore war and received the thanks of Government for his services on the 27th February 1809. In the interim he had engaged in commercial pursuits and entered into partnership with Mr. Charles Wallace Young, who, between 1805 and 1808, obtained a lease of a large extent of waste land for the cultivation of coffee, indigo, and cotton, in Tinnevelly, at an annual rent of 2,000 rupees, to continue to the close of the Company's Charter.

"On the death of Mr. Young, in the latter part of 1809, Mr. Hughes succeeded to the lease, as assignee of that gentleman; and on the expiration of the Charter, the grant was renewed in 1814, on the same terms, for the period of the next Charter. Mr. Hughes likewise purchased the Kuḷattûr and Kāḍalguḍi Miṭṭahs, and continued engaged in various speculations with fluctuating success until his death, which took place on the 26th February 1835."

I may add that Mr. Hughes was never married, though he had several children, whom he brought up as Hindus.

CHAP. VIII.

The two Pānjālamkurichi brothers.

The Poligar of Pānjālamkurichi, who was executed at Kaittār in September 1799, left two brothers, as has been mentioned, both of whom were kept in confinement in the Palamcotta Jail. One of these brothers, the elder, was described as a feeble person, but would have been heir to the pāḷaiyam if it had not been confiscated, and was regarded by his sympathising adherents and the natives generally as the true heir all the same, and called accordingly by the family title Kaṭṭaboma Nāyaka. The other, the younger, though dumb and a mere boy, was a person of great energy and full of resources, and was regarded by the natives almost as a divinity. In addition to the two brothers there were some other persons confined with them in the Palamcotta Jail who had been implicated in the outbreak of 1799. The most intriguing and dangerous member of the deposed family, Sivattaiyā, a near relation, who had escaped the vigilance of the authorities and was still at large, was the leader of a party of sympathisers who were waiting for an opportunity to effect the escape of the prisoners and help them to commence the struggle afresh.

Escape of the Prisoners from the Palamcotta Jail and subsequent Events.

Position of things prior to the outbreak.

Mr. Hughes thus describes the position of things in Tinnevelly prior to the escape of the prisoners and the recommencement of hostilities :—"Major Bannerman left the detachment to embark for Europe early in 1800, under high and well-earned encomiums from the Government. The command devolved on Major Robert Turing, who, having preferred a high situation on the general staff, left us about February. He was succeeded by Major Colin Macaulay, who with the command of the district, held also the appointment of Resident at Travancore. The state of affairs soon admitted of the separation of the detachment, and the Governor-General requiring his services for a time at the Travancore Durbar, the 3rd Regiment N.I. was cantoned at Shenker ninaur Covil (Sankaranainārkōvil) (now under the command of Major Sheppard), a few companies of another corps were left at Kaittār, and Palamcotta was garrisoned by Lieutenant Knowle's provincial corps and some other details. The main body of the force returned to Trichinopoly and other stations, and at the close of the year there was to all appearance the most prosperous settlement of all the objects of the Government, combined with the most perfect tranquillity in the country."

The following is General Welsh's account of the escape of the prisoners :—

Escape of the prisoners.

"On the 2nd of February 1801, while our force was cantoned at Sankaranainārkōvil, about thirty miles to the eastward (north-west), and the whole of the remaining community, about twenty ladies and

CHAP. VIII.

gentlemen, were dining at Major Macaulay's garden-house at Palamcotta, a number of Poligar prisoners confined in the fort made their escape by overpowering their own guard and the one at the fort, whom they disarmed. As men of consequence and State prisoners, they had been hitherto kept in irons and very strictly guarded; but the small-pox having recently broken out amongst them, their chains had been removed a few days before. This evening a number of their adherents in disguise, and with concealed weapons, had entered the fort, and, at a preconcerted signal, forced the prison-gate, whilst the prisoners attacked the two sentries in front. A few of the guard were wounded, and the whole instantly disarmed; when the prisoners, seizing the musquets of their *ci-devant* gaolers, headed their adherents, and rushing on the gate-guard, succeeded in overpowering them, when passing through the gates, they made such good use of their heels that, before morning, they had arrived at Pānjālamkurichi, a distance of thirty miles; having surprised and disarmed nearly one hundred men at different stages on the road, and at one place an entire company under a native officer. In their haste to secure a safe retreat, they however let slip the fairest opportunity they ever could have enjoyed of crippling our force, for the party assembled at our commandant's included the civilians of the station, all the staff officers, and several others of the force; the house was protected by a Naigue's guard only, and not above a mile out of their route; and there we must all have perished, unprepared and unresisting, since they were several hundred strong, even before they left the place. Unaware of the extent of the mischief, small parties were sent out, as soon as they could be collected, to overtake the fugitives, and lucky it was for them that they returned unsuccessful. Indeed all the sepoys then in Palamcotta would have been inadequate for that purpose."

Unavailing pursuit.

Measures adopted by the authorities.

Major Macaulay, the Commanding Officer in the Tinnevelly District, concerted measures at once for the recapture of the fugitives, and moved off with all despatch to Kaittār the disposable part of the garrison of Palamcotta and a few of the Nawab's horsemen drawn from his establishment of Sīvalapērai. The troops under Major Sheppard at Sankaranainārkōvil were ordered to march to Kaittār, and all the Palamcotta officers joined at that place on the 6th. The Nawab's troopers were mounted on horses belonging to the English gentlemen lent for the purpose.

Attack on the camp by the Poligars.

"A body of European cavalry had originally formed a part of the southern field force, and with some infantry corps had been only lately removed, under an appearance of perfect tranquillity being established in this hitherto turbulent district. Our force was therefore consequently now reduced to nine hundred firelocks, and all native, excepting a detachment of Bengal artillery, with two 2 and two 4 pounders. On the morning of 8th February, having marched half way the day before, the detachment reached the village Kulayanallūr, nineteen miles from Kaittār. The camp was formed in a small square, and all hands were preparing to enjoy a hearty meal, when a body of Poligars to the number of a thousand or twelve hundred, armed with musquets, pikes, and swords, made their appearance on a rising ground in front of the line, and inclining to the right and left, made a simultaneous attack on three faces. The small village, situated about a mile in the rear, had been previously taken possession of by our picquets; and while we were employed in front by the first assailants, a body of the enemy, advancing under cover of a deep ravine, immediately attacked it. Although many of our men, being new drafts and recruits, had never seen a shot fired, yet the whole behaved well, except the Nawab's cavalry, who would not charge even a small party of the enemy, and we began to wish we had our horses back again. In about an hour, however, the Poligars withdrew, leaving forty dead upon the field, and carrying off their wounded; they were not pursued very far, and all was quiet again in our little camp by noon. Our loss was not more than six men, a proof of the bad firing of the enemy. The post in the village was strengthened, being a kind of key to our position, and all remained perfectly quiet till about nine o'clock at night, when a peal of musquetry in the direction of the village again roused us; an attempt being made to surprise that post, which was, however, completely foiled before a reinforcement could arrive to its relief. After a sleepless night, we marched the next morning, and reached a plain close to Pānjālamkurichi by nine o'clock, when, to our utter astonishment, we discovered that the walls, which had been entirely levelled, were now rebuilt, and fully manned by about fifteen hundred Poligars."

Arrival of troops at Pānjālamkurichi.

Mr. Hughes says they found the Poligar force not only securely entrenched, but armed far beyond expectation, and, to crown all, displaying an exulting front, in consequence of the success which had hitherto attended their enterprise. An entrenchment and breastwork had been run up with incredible celerity. All the concealed arms, he adds, had been quickly restored to light, it having been the policy of the time (imposed as we have seen by the Madras Government on Major Bannerman) to invite the surrender of arms by the payment of a liberal price for them, rather than to adopt a vigorous scrutiny for their seizure. The population of the sequestered pollams seemed to be delighted with the opportunity afforded them of trying their strength with the English once more, being thoroughly discontented, no doubt, with the peaceful life now required of them.

Condition of the fort.

Retreat from Pānjālamkurichi.

I return to General Welsh's narrative:—

"Without a single battering gun, and, I may add, without even a few Europeans to lead the storming party, to have attempted to take the place in open day would have been next to madness; a spot of ground was therefore selected near the village of Ōṭṭapiḍāram, about a mile from the fort, and there we formed our camp, in a square, with high grain to the northward; the bund, or bank, of a tank to the southward; the village near the eastern face, and Pānjālamkurichi opposite to the west. After taking some little rest and refreshment,

Preparations for resistance.

CHAP. VIII. it was proposed to form the detachment into two storming parties, and to escalade the works at two different points, as soon as darkness should conceal our approach from the enemy. A short time after, some of our scouts came in, with the agreeable intelligence that the Poligars, now amounting to five thousand, were prepared to assault our camp at nightfall. Here then was an unlooked for occurrence: in the first place, we were opposed by a strong fort, raised, as it were, by magic, in six days; and in the second, its defenders, increased beyond all possible calculation, were likely to become the assailants. It was decided, therefore, *nem con* that we had no business to remain there; and as both men and officers were already nearly exhausted by two grilling marches and a sleepless night, it was doubtful whether they could keep awake another, to receive with due alacrity such a nocturnal visit as was in contemplation. The troops were therefore warned, and at two o'clock P.M. being formed in oblong square, the baggage in the centre and field pieces distributed in front and rear, we drew out, as if preparing to assault the fort. In an instant every part of the works was manned, and we could plainly discern a body of fifteen hundred or two thousand men outside of the boundary hedge, their long spears glittering in the sun.

"As soon as the formation was completed, we commenced our march, not for the fort, but for Palamcotta, and had actually accomplished a third of our journey, when we were overtaken in the dark by a body of the enemy, who rushed on us with shouts and screams, almost to the bayonet. The rear face of our column, for it was now no longer a square, was luckily composed of the grenadiers of the 1st Battalion of the 3rd Regiment, with the two 6-pounders under Captain Vesey. He allowed them to approach without molestation, the more fully to effect his purpose, when giving the word himself, a couple of vollies, poured in with grape and musquetry, levelled one hundred and ten of our assailants; the astonished remainder made a very precipitate escape, and we were no more molested during a long and severe march, which lasted all night, than by imagination, which placed an enemy behind every bush on the road. Our loss on this occasion was only two men and a woman, and we safely reached Palamcotta at nine o'clock A.M. on the 10th."

Mr. Hughes says that the question for consideration was whether the attack on the fort should be made forthwith on the arrival of the troops from Palamcotta, and thus in the event of a check being received run the hazard of much more extensive commotions, or whether it were more advisable that the detachment should withdraw for a time and await reinforcement from Trichinopoly. He adds:—

Hughes' opinion.

"Happily, the latter alternative, painful as it seemed, was agreed on with perfect concurrence by Majors Macaulay and Sheppard. The steady and firm conduct of the 3rd Regiment N.I. carried the detachment through the perils of the night.

Failure of attack in Kaḍalguḍi.

"In the meantime various affairs took place, most of which were to the advantage of the rebels. On the 27th February an attack was made by a detachment on the fort of Kāḍalguḍi, supposed to be weak, and ill defended. Our opponents, however, got intelligence of the march in sufficient time to send a body of two thousand men to assist the defenders, and our men were consequently so well received, that, after every exertion that bravery and discipline could oppose to numbers, they were compelled to retreat, leaving three men killed and eighteen wounded on the ground; the loss of the enemy was never ascertained.

CHAP. VIII.

Defence of Srivaikuṇṭham.

" In this way several of the smaller forts belonging to Government fell into the hands of the Poligars, by which means they gained possession of about a thousand muskets with their ammunition. One solitary pagoda, Srivaikuṇṭham, slightly fortified, on the bank of the river, about fifteen miles below Palamcotta, held out beyond example or expectation. To relieve this brave handful, Major Sheppard marched at the head of the 1st Battalion of the 3rd Regiment, with two 6-pounders. Arriving at Palamcotta, on the 13th of March, the heavy baggage was thrown in there, and on the morning of the 16th they came in sight of the Pagoda of Srivaikuṇṭham, on the opposite side of the river, and were immediately attacked by swarms of the enemy; through whom they forced their way to their comrades on the opposite shore. All the troops behaved well, particularly the grenadiers, who charged a large body of the enemy and put them to flight. The Poligars, intent on capturing the place, had beset it on every side, and raised a large mound of earth to overlook the pagoda. They were also busy in making scaling ladders for an escalade, when our corps relieved them. The garrison was withdrawn, and on the march back to Palamcotta the enemy annoyed them the whole way, though repeatedly charged by our soldiers. Our loss was not so heavy as might have been expected, and the corps remained resting at Palamcotta till the stores necessary for a siege could be collected."

Whilst the country was in this disturbed condition, the Native Christians of that time, though few in number, had to share in the troubles of their Christian rulers. We learn this from a report of the Christian Knowledge Society for 1802 :—

The Native Christians.

" The congregations in the south suffered severely from the turbulent Poligars, who resisted the British rule and seem to have identified the Native Christians with the English. In their incursions into the Company's territories they plundered, confined, and tortured the Christians, destroyed some of their chapels, and burned the books they found in them. As there appeared to be little prospect of the termination of these troubles, the people were obliged to leave their homes and flee to the woods for refuge."

General Welsh gives here a brief account of the Poligars in general and of the Poligar of Pāñjālamkurichi in particular. In doing so he fell into the error of confounding together two different persons. He says :—

Welsh's error.

"Their chief, called Kaṭṭaboma Nāyaka, having successfully defended the fort against a force under Colonel Bannerman two years

CHAP. VIII.

before, had at length been taken prisoner, with the rest of his family, and kept in close confinement."

We have seen from the preceding narrative that the Kaṭṭaboma Nāyaka who defended his fort against Major Bannerman had been hanged, and that the Kaṭṭaboma Nāyaka who was imprisoned was his surviving brother.

RETURN TO PĀNJĀLAMKURICHI.

When the expected reinforcements were on the advance from Trichinopoly, Major Macaulay moved the detachment forward to Kaittār and took up ground in such a position as to allow the reinforcements to join. Having no opponents out of our camp, the enemy made good use of their time and seized on Tuticorin. This incident has been described already in the account of Tuticorin under the Dutch. General Welsh gives the details of the force assembled at Kaittār for the reduction of Pānjālamkurichi. It amounted in all to nearly 3,000 men, with nine guns :—

March to Pānjālamkurichi.

"Our first march was to Otrampatti, only eight miles; the second to Pasuvandalai, eight miles also, on the road to which we first encountered the enemy; a body of five or six hundred of whom appeared shortly after we left our ground, and boldly advanced to meet us, on which the Major ordered the cavalry to charge them. The two troops, having rear and flank guards out, did not amount to more than ninety men, if so many; but they were led by James Grant, one of the finest and bravest fellows I ever knew. They had two small galloper guns with them, which were fired as the enemy approached, and this, first appeared to induce them to retire, which they did leisurely, keeping up a running fight, though it was evident that the men who had firearms were most anxious to escape. When our cavalry had got within a few hundred yards, Lieutenant Grant gave the words 'Saint George, and charge :' the enemy at the same time halting, faced about, and presented an abatis of pikes to the horses' breasts; but so great was the impetus, that in an instant this formidable phalanx was borne down, and our men were afterwards engaged in single combat with these brave but unskilful pedestrians, until a thick wood luckily intervened, through which they made their escape. The ground being, what is called in India 'black cotton,' with the shrub actually growing on it, was very unfavourable for our men, and so determined was the resistance that Lieutenant Grant fell, wounded with a pike through the lungs, and his Subadar, Sheik Ebraum, and four troopers were killed. Lieutenant Lyne lost his Naigue, and eleven troopers were wounded; and two horses were killed, and twelve wounded. Of the enemy, ninety-six dead bodies were counted on the field; what number of wounded they carried off of course could not be ascertained. Grant killed four with his own hand, the last after he had received his desperate wound; and his Subadar also killed four or five before he fell. The next day, the 31st of March, we came within site of the Gibraltar of these insurgents.

Skirmish on the way.

First Assault and Failure.

Chap. VIII.

Description of fort.

We found the fort an irregular parallelogram, two sides of which were about 500 feet and the other two about 300 feet only, built entirely of mud of a very solid and adhesive quality :—

"The wall was, generally, about twelve feet high, with small square bastions, and very short curtains. A few old guns were mounted in these bastions, and the whole was surrounded by a thick hedge of thorns, but no ditch. Arriving before it at eight o'clock A.M., preparations were instantly made for breaching the north-western bastion, with the two iron 12 and one 8 pounder, from a bank about nine hundred yards distance ; and at half past eight we opened fire, though, by no means so destructive as was anticipated. At noon, therefore, the guns were moved on to another bank, about four hundred yards from the wall, and continued playing till half past three, when the breach appearing practicable, the storm was ordered."

It was found afterwards, however, when it was too late, that the breach, considered to be so by the artillery officer, was no breach at all :—

The assault on the fort.

"The party for assault advanced with alacrity under the heaviest fire imaginable from the curtains and five or six bastions, the defences of which we had not been able to demolish. Our men fell rapidly, but nothing impeded their approach ; even the hedge was speedily passed, and repeated attempts were made to surmount the breach, but all in vain," so daring and determined was the garrison and so difficult of access the point of attack. "Every man who succeeded in reaching the summit was instantly thrown back, pierced with wounds, from both pikes and musquetry, and no footing could be gained. At length a retreat was ordered, and a truly dismal scene of horror succeeded ; all our killed, and many of the wounded, being left at the foot of the breach, over which the enemy immediately sprung, and pursued the rear, while others pierced the bodies both of the dying and the dead. The immediate defence of the breach was with pikes from eighteen to twenty feet long, beyond which a body of men from an elevated spot kept up a constant fire, while others in the bastions took the assailants in flank. In the confusion of the moment a howitzer was left near the breach, which was afterwards rescued by six officers, and about fifty sepoys, under a fire, which killed one of the officers and several of the men and wounded two other officers and five or six men. Of the enemy's loss we had no account. No sooner had we gained a safe distance from the fort, than the line was formed, and encamping ground marked, the nearest part being at a distance of 1,500 yards from the walls. We had a high ridge in the centre of the line running parallel to the fort, and our ammunition and stores were placed in the rear, out of sight of the enemy. Our pickquets were posted on the bank from whence we first attempted to breach, and it was completely dark before we could get under cover. As all had alike partaken in the dangers and discomfiture of the day, a dead silence reigned throughout our line, the only tribute we could then pay to the memory of our departed brethren ;

The defence.

CHAP. VIII.

and the enemy so far respected our grief, as to allow us its unmolested indulgence.

"Our total failure this day was perfectly inexplicable, and how the breach was defended appeared almost miraculous; for none of the actual defenders ever showed themselves above the broken parapet, and certainly that was entirely destroyed, and a practicable passage apparently made to the terreplein of the bastion long previous to our attack. Yet here a grove of pikes alone presented itself to our view; and the enemy appearing in every other part of the works, exposing themselves without the smallest reservation, were constantly shot by our men, who were covering the storm, and as constantly replaced by others; whilst they kept up a most unnatural yell the whole time, from upwards of five thousand voices, which only ceased with our retreat. Of one hundred and twenty Europeans on the storming party, only forty-six escaped unhurt; and including officers and artillery, one hundred and six were killed and wounded of the whole force. I should mention that a body of one thousand Ettiapuram Poligars, heriditary enemies of the Pānjālamkurichi race, had joined us on the march, having a company of sepoys, and Captain Charles Trotter attached to them. These brave and faithful allies made some unsuccessful attempts at an escalade on the other side of the fort, whilst we were on the west face, but were repulsed with considerable loss, though we had no official returns of their casualties."

Bravery of the enemy.

Aid of Ettaiyāpuram.

It was evident that Major Macaulay's means were quite inadequate to his object, the guns were quite useless as battering pieces, and a repetition of the attack was not to be thought of.

More extensive preparations.

"The Government was now awakened to the whole severity of the service. A great native force was ordered from different stations of the Carnatic, an European corps, H.M. 77th, was called round from the Malabar Coast, a corps of cavalry was put in motion, and a powerful train of artillery despatched from Trichinopoly, the command of the service being transferred to an officer of higher rank. This was Colonel Peter Agnew, a person of great military experience, and well known as the Adjutant-General of the Army for many years."

Help obtained from Ceylon.

The Collector of Tinnevelly at this time applied to, and obtained from, the Government of Ceylon a detachment of troops to help forward the operations against Pānjālamkurichi. This he did without authority, and his action in the matter called forth a decided expression of disapproval from the Madras Government.

"It was the best part of two months," Hughes says, "before this new formation of the force could assemble at the scene of action, and in the interval little more was in the power of Macaulay than to restrict as much as practicable the range of the enemy, for which purpose he kept his station on a small ridge, a mile or two to the westward of the fort. Their night annoyances on our position and skirmishes with our foraging parties in the day were very frequent, and they seemed to have taken up the notion that the muskets of our sepoys were of little security against their spears during the fall of rain."

I quote here from Welsh an account of the incident to which Hughes briefly refers. Chap. VIII.

Sortie from the fort in a storm.

"On the 22nd a heavy thunder storm, accompanied by wind and rain, suddenly assailed us; and as such a time was the most favourable in which to oppose pikes to firearms, we began to fall in; when in a twinkling the thunder was succeeded by the flash and sound of our 6-pounder on the most distant outpost, and a strong party dashed towards it immediately. This consisted of a company of sepoys, with a party of artillery, and one gun on the bund of a large tank, five or six hundred yards to the southward of the fort, and one thousand two hundred from our nearest post. Lieutenant H. Dey (noon being the time of removing all our outposts) observing an unusual collection of clouds, and sagaciously auguring therefrom the probability of a storm, being senior officer, had very sensibly taken upon himself to detain the other company. The squall approached, beating in their faces, and was immediately followed by one thousand pikemen. Our poor fellows, assailed by two such enemies at once, strove to give a fire, but hardly a musquet would go off; and the gun, after being discharged once only, was in the enemy's possession. The Poligars, more intent on seizing the ordnance than on injuring its defenders, wounded only eight men of the party, and were pushing off with their prize, as fast as the wet cotton ground would permit, when our reinforcements appearing, Lieutenants Dey and Clason rushed back, accompanied by many of their men, and we succeeded in rescuing our cannon from the hands of the Philistines, although many hundreds more rushed out of the fort to their assistance; and, as the rain ceased, they poured out multitudes with firearms, who being confronted as readily by similar parties from our camp, a general action ensued, which, I may well say, ended in smoke; both parties making much noise, and neither doing much execution. After about an hour's fighting, as if with one accord, the firing ceased; both parties retired to count their casualties, of which the most serious tally must have been ball cartridges."

The Final Assault.

The expected corps all came up by the middle of May and Colonel Agnew assumed the command on the 21st.

"From his arrival to the 24th there was the greatest activity in making a breach, and it was so thoroughly effected by that day that to all appearance it admitted of running up with the utmost facility. The enemy, however, had thrown a very wide abatis of new felled thorn trees all along the approaches on every side, and this occasioned some short interruption. On the morning of the 23rd of May, at sunrise, we opened two batteries at once on the south-western bastion of the fort, while the grand battery favoured them with salvos, which soon demolished the southern faces and salient angle of the bastion. By noon the storming party was ready to advance, but our old commandant took Colonel Agnew aside, and, backed by another old friend,

CHAP. VIII.

A breach made by the battery.

persuaded him to delay the assault until the next day, much against, what appeared to him, his better judgment. The firing was therefore kept up all night to prevent the enemy from repairing the breach. The next morning the guns were all turned to demolish the defences and cut off the breached bastion, which being completely effected, at one o'clock P.M., having run the tower guns half way down to the fort, the storming party was ordered to advance.

Successful assault.

"Notwithstanding the strength of the storming party, with the whole force ready to back them, the defenders shrunk not from their duty, but received our brave fellows with renewed vigour, and the breach was so stoutly defended, that although the hedge was passed in a few minutes, it was nearly half an hour before a man of ours could stand upon the summit, while bodies of the enemy, not only fired on our storming party from the broken bastions on both flanks, but others sallied round and attacked them in the space within the hedge. At length, after a struggle of fifteen minutes in this position, the whole of the enemy in the breach being killed by hand grenades, and heavy shot thrown over among them, our grenadiers succeeded in mounting the breach, and the resistance afterwards was of no avail, although one body of pikemen charged our grenadiers in the body of the place and killed three of them."

Mr. Hughes says :—

"Arrived at the top of the breach, it was by no means easy to descend. Here the garrison had excavated the bastion or ground all around so deeply as not to be easily grappled with, and, it is said, had carried the excavation so cleverly under the brink of the breach as to be able to strike with their spears, in comparative safety, those who leant forward to fire on the defenders below. These were a good deal checked, it was imagined, by hand grenades, but I believe the place was at last carried by entrance at the flanks, which, however, had been strongly palisaded, and moist earth was in constant supply to repair the damage to the walls on each side of the breach.

The enemy abandon the fort.

"A general panic now seized the enemy, and they fled from their assailants as fast as possible; but no sooner had they got clear of the fort, than they formed into two solid columns, and thus retreated, beset but not dismayed ; but our cavalry attacked them in flank and rear, and succeeded in cutting off six hundred. The remainder, however, made good their retreat, and a column of about two thousand ultimately escaped. Four hundred and fifty dead bodies of the enemy were also found in the fort, those killed on former occasions having been disposed of outside to the eastward."

Mr. Hughes says :—

"The whole of the surviving Poligar body retired from the fort with the most imposing regularity, unarmed persons and the women repairing to the centre, and the armed men closely ranging on each side. The cavalry, however, made dreadful havoc on this body, which was soon broken and dispersed. Our loss on this day was Lieutenant

Killed and wounded.

Gilchrist of the 74th, Lieutenants Spalding and Campbell of the 77th, and Lieutenant Fraser of the 4th, killed ; Lieutenants M'Clean, Scotch

Brigade, Captain Whitley of the Malays, Lieutenant Valentine Blacker of the 1st Cavalry, Lieutenant Campbell of the 74th, and Lieutenant Birch of the 4th, wounded. Lieutenant Blacker was piked in two or three places; but emulating James Grant, who was always the foremost in danger, he would not desist, until our trumpets had sounded the recall. Europeans killed nineteen, and wounded seventy-six; natives killed twenty-four and wounded ninety-six, making a total, including officers, of two hundred and twenty-three.

The interior of the fort.

"To us, who had suffered so severely in our unsuccessful assault a sight of the interior of this abominable place was most acceptable, the more so, as this was the first time it had ever been taken by storm, though frequently attempted. Nothing could equal the surprise and disgust which filled our minds at beholding the wretched holes under ground in which a body of three thousand men, and for some time their families also, had so long contrived to exist. No language can paint the horrors of the picture. To shelter themselves from shot and shells they had dug these holes in every part of the fort, and though some might occasionally be out to the eastward, yet the place must always have been excessively crowded. The north-west bastion, our old breach, attracted our particular attention; and a description of it will therefore serve for every other in this fort. It was about fifteen feet high on the outside, and nearly square: the face we breached was thirty feet long, and a parapet of about three feet thick at the summit gradually increased sloping down into the centre, which was barely sufficient to contain about forty men, the passage in the gorge, being only wide enough to admit two at a time. The depth in the centre, being originally on a level with the interior, was increased as the top mouldered down, so as to leave the defenders entirely sheltered from everything but the shells and shot, which we had latterly used, more by accident than design. These were of course thrown over from the outside, and nothing else could have secured us the victory, since every man in the last breach was killed, and the passage blocked up before our grenadiers obtained a footing above. Their long pikes, used in such a sheltered spot, must be most powerfully effective. No wonder, then, that every man who got to the top was instantly pierced and thrown down again. He could never get at his enemy, and, indeed, could scarcely tell from whence the blow was inflicted. The system of defence adopted by these savages would have done credit to any Engineer. Nothing could surpass it but their unwearied perseverance. Had the bastions been solid, or their defensive weapons only musquets and bayonets, we should not have had the mortification to be before it for two months; and had our cavalry been more efficient, we should not have had a continuance of this warfare for six months longer. The fugitive phalanx, making good its retreat to Sherewele, was there joined by twenty thousand men of the Murdoos."

Description of the enemy's defences.

Where Sherewele was and who the Murdoos were will appear in the sequel.

Destruction of the fort.

"The three companies of the 9th, under Captain Hazard, being left with the Pioneers to destroy the fort, a work by no means to be envied, on the 25th of May, a company of the 16th under Captain

CHAP. VIII.

M'Donnell, was sent ten miles off to garrison Tuticorin, which the enemy had abandoned."

Reminiscences of the Dumb Brother.

"I have already," says General Welsh, "made mention, but I cannot close this account of horrors, without a few words, in memory of one of the most extraordinary mortals I ever knew; a near relation of Kaṭṭaboma Nāyaka, who was both deaf and dumb, was well known by the English under the appellation of dumby or the dumb brother; by the Mussulmans, as Mookah, and by the Hindus as Ūmai—all having the like signification. He was a tall, slender lad, of a very sickly appearance, yet possessing that energy of mind, which, in troubled times, always gains pre-eminence; whilst in his case, the very defect which would have impeded another proved a powerful auxiliary in the minds of ignorant and superstitious idolaters. The Ūmai was adored; his slightest sign was an oracle, and every man flew to execute whatever he commanded. No council assembled at which he did not preside; no daring adventure was undertaken which he did not lead. His method of representing the English was extremely simple; he collected a few little pieces of straw, arranged them on the palm of his left hand to represent the English force; then with other signs, for the time, &c., he drew the other hand across and swept them off, with a whizzing sound from his mouth, which was the signal for attack; and he was generally the foremost in executing those plans for our annihilation. Whatever undisciplined valour could effect was sure to be achieved wherever he appeared; though poor Ūmai was at last doomed to grace a gallows. He had escaped, as it were, by miracle, in every previous engagement.

Veneration in which the dumb brother was held.

"On the 24th of May when the fort was wrenched from them, and the whole were retreating, pursued by our cavalry, poor Ūmai fell, covered with wounds, near a small village, about three miles from Pānjālamkurichi. As soon as our troops had returned from the pursuit, Colonel Agnew instantly ordered the Ettiapureans to follow them till night, offering rewards for any men of consequence, dead or alive. Our allies, consequently, set out with great glee, somewhat late in the evening; and in the meantime an appearance of quiet induced some women of the village to proceed to the field of carnage, in the hope of finding some of the sufferers capable of receiving succour. Amongst the heaps of slain they discovered the son of one of the party still breathing, and after weeping over him they began to raise him up, when exerting his little remaining strength, he exclaimed, 'O! mother, let me die, but try to save the life of Swamy, who lies wounded near me.' The word he used fully justifies my assertion of their adoration, as its literal meaning is a deity. The woman, animated by the same feelings, immediately obeyed her dying son, and speedily found Ūmai weltering in his blood, but still alive; and these extraordinary matrons immediately lifted and carried him to the mother's house, where they were busily employed stanching his wounds, when they were alarmed by a sudden shout from the Ettiapureans in pursuit.

He is discovered amongst the wounded.

There is nothing like the ingenuity of women at such a crisis. They conceived a plan in an instant, which not only proved successful but most probably saved the lives of several others. They covered the body over with a cloth, and set up a shriek of lamentation peculiar to the circumstances. The Ettiapureans, on their arrival, demanded the cause, and, being informed that a poor lad had just expired of the small-pox, fled out of the village, without even turning to look behind them. How he was afterwards preserved I could never learn; but certainly he was present, and as active as usual on the 7th and 10th of June; and was taken alive at the conclusion of the campaign and hanged along with his gallant and ill-fated relation on the tower we had erected in the plain before Pānjālamkurichi, now the only monument of that once dreaded fortress, if we except the burying-ground of six or seven hundred of our slaughtered comrades, in its vicinity." CHAP. VIII. His concealment.

The following are the records on the tomb stones of the officers who fell in the various assaults on Pānjālamkurichi :—

At Ōṭṭapiḍāram one mile from Pānjālamkurichi.

"In memory of Lieutenants Douglas, Dormieux, Collins, and Blake, and Gunner Finny, who fell in the attack of Pānjālamkurichi, 5th September 1799."

In the Cemetery at Pānjālamkurichi.

"Sacred to the memory of Captain John Campbell, Lieutenants A. Campbell, D. Gilchrist, and P. Shank, of H.M. 74th Regiment. Lieutenants J. Spalding and A. Campbell, H.M. 77th Regiment. Lieutenant M. Egan, 1st Battalion 3rd Regiment N.I. Lieutenants W. Fraser and K. Mangnall, 1st Battalion 4th Regiment N.I., and Lieutenant C. Torriano, 1st Battalion 9th Regiment N.I., who bravely fell or died of wounds received in the assaults on the fort of Pānjālamkurichi, the 31st March and 24th May 1801."

Also

"Here lie the remains of Dougald W. Gilchrist, Lieutenant of His Majesty's 74th Regiment. This gallant youth, who had not attained his one and twentieth year, was killed on the 24th May 1801, in the breach of the fort of Pānjālamkurichi in the moment of victory. By his death His Majesty's Service lost an officer of great enterprise and valour, and society a beloved and valued member."

THE PĀNJĀLAMKURICHI EPIC.

The events of the last siege form the subject of a native poem, called, from the style of versification employed, the Pānjālamkurichi Sindhu. The author was one Namasivāyam. I have already mentioned that I consider Indian poetical compositions the least trustworthy of all the sources of historical information respecting India in our possession. The poem referred to forms a striking illustration of the accuracy of this estimate. It relates events that took place within the memory of the writer, and it is still sung and occasionally acted in the presence of people, every one of whom has from tradition a tolerably correct general idea of the facts, especially the great fact of the final capture and demolition of Pānjālamkurichi, yet we find every event falsified in the most unblushing manner. Mr. Kearns gives the substance of each *Sindhu* or canto of the poem. It will be sufficient to quote here the substance of the last :—

VICTORY CANTO.

One Veḷḷai Marudu, a Maravan, now arrived to assist the chief. Things were very bad. The chief was in great fear, he saw no way out of his fort or his difficulties. This Veḷḷai Marudu, however, volunteered to attack the British army, as it then was in position, and this he insisted upon doing *alone*. Accordingly (contrary to fact and even beyond fiction) he sallied out, attacked the British, cut up the cavalry, routed the infantry, and captured the battery of 100,000 guns. The disordered remnant of the British fled to Palamcotta and the Poligar was left to reign ever after in happiness and splendour !

CHAPTER IX.

CONCLUSION OF THE POLIGAR WAR. CESSION OF THE CARNATIC TO THE ENGLISH GOVERNMENT.

TRANSFER OF THE WAR TO SIVAGANGAI.

CHAPTER IX.

Armed retainers of the Poligars still at large.

WE now reach the closing scenes of the Poligar war and the termination of Kaṭṭaboma Nāyaka's career, as well as of the history of Pānjālamkurichi. The fort which had so long defied all the efforts of the Government troops had at length been taken and the Poligar and his surviving adherents had fled; but so long as such formidable foes were at large there was no prospect of peace being restored. Mr. Lushington estimated the number of armed men still openly or secretly maintained by the various Poligars at 22,000, all ready at a moment's notice to follow their masters on any expedition. General Welsh's opinion was that an organized force of 20,000 Pānjālamkurichi men would have been irresistible, and we have seen that a considerable body of those very men, including the Poligar himself and his dumb brother, had escaped on the capture of the fort and fled northwards to Sivagangai. They were received by the usurping Poligar of Sivagangai with open arms. The incidents that follow belong, it might be said, rather to the history of Madura than to that of Tinnevelly, but it would be impossible to do justice to this portion of the history of Tinnevelly without following the war into the Sivagangai country. Besides which, both Sivagangai and Rāmnād at that time were included with Tinnevelly in Mr. Lushington's jurisdiction, as Collector of Southern Poligar Peshcush.

Welsh's estimate of the Poligars.

Fort of Kamudi.

On May 28th, five days after the capture of Pānjālamkurichi, the whole force encamped at Nāgalāpuram, from whence a detachment was sent to relieve Comeri (Kamuri, properly Kamudi; in the Ordnance Map Kaumoory), a small but well built stone fort belonging to Rāmnād, which the rebels were besieging. This being accomplished, a force was left there to keep the rebels in check in that neighbourhood.

Rāmnad.

On the 2nd June the force arrived at Tirupūvaṇam, a town in the Sivagangai country, where the enemy first made his appearance, from which time till the 14th July, whilst the troops were marching towards Rāmnād, they were continually exposed to attacks. The country was then very jungly and difficult to

CHAPTER IX.

traverse. On the way there were two places where it was with much difficulty that they succeeded in forcing their way through the enemy, and where they suffered considerable loss, including many Europeans. At Rāmnād Colonel Agnew had the benefit of much communication with Colonel Martinz (said to have been a European Portuguese), who had in his earlier days seen much Poligar service. It was here found that Caliar covil (Kāḷaiyārkōvil), a fortified pagoda to which it was expected that the Murdoos would retire, was naturally so strong and had been placed in such a state of defence that it appeared likely that there would be a renewal of the scenes of Pānjālamkurichi. It was found also that the eastern approaches to this place were of so much greater extent and so much more difficult of access than the western that it was necessary to abandon the idea of endeavouring to take the place from the east. Accordingly the forces marched to the north-west, to Tirukaḍaiyūr near Tirupattūr, where they were joined by another force from Dindigul under Colonel James Innes (whom Mr. Hughes calls Colonel James), which had recently been employed in putting down the Virūpākshi Poligar and his adherents. After this junction the whole force, now at least 7,000 strong, moved forward to the attack of " Sherewele" which lay to the east.

Colonel Martinz.

Junction with Colonel Innes's force.

THE " MURDOOS" AND " SHEREWELE."

Sivagangai was originally a portion of the great Rāmnād pāḷaiyam or zamindari. The ruling race being Maravas, and the Marava caste being predominant, Rāmnād was commonly called by the early Europeans the Marawa country, and when a division took place between Rāmnād and Sivagangai, and Sivagangai became independent, the two districts used to be called by Europeans the two Marawas, and severally the Greater Marawa and the Little Marawa. The word was often also written Marawar. The separation appears to have been effected in the early part of last century, a sāsana being in existence, dated in 1733, in which Sēshavarṇa Dēva, the founder of the separate dynasty of Sivagangai, then living, was represented as an independent sovereign. The partition was a peaceable one, two-fifths of the territory being made over to Sivagangai, whilst three-fifths remained with Rāmnād. Dēva is the caste title of the Maravas, but the chief of Rāmnād preferred to be called by his special hereditary title of Sētupati, Lord of Rāma's Bridge. The family title of the Sivagangai Poligar was Uḍaiya Dēva, but he was often also called Nālukoṭṭai Dēva, not in consequence of there being four forts in his dominions, but because his ancestral village was called by this singular name Nālukōṭṭai, the four forts. This is the title which Orme writes as Nellicotah, a name which might easily be confounded with Nilakoṭṭai, the name of a totally different pāḷaiyam in the Madura

The two Marava States.

Orme's Nellicotah.

District. The following extracts from Colonel Fullarton's paper will show how ready Sivagangai had always been under all its masters to resist the authority of the English Government:—

Description of Sivagangai.

"The territory of Shevigunga (Sivagangai) or the Little Marawar, stretches from the sea-coast on the east to the Districts of Mellore (Mēlūr) and Madura on the west, and from the country of Tondiman and the Nattam Collieries upon the north, to the territories of the Great Marawar on the south, containing about fifty miles in length and forty miles in breadth. The soil, in general, is unfriendly to the growth of corn, though not quite destitute of running streams or artificial reservoirs, but the country is overgrown with thorns and bushes. The woods of Calicoil (Kāḷaiyārkōvil), nearly forty miles in circumference, are secured with barriers and other defences around the fort of Kāḷaiyārkōvil, which is situated in the centre of the thickets, and considered as a refuge from exaction or invasion. These woods and the surrounding country abound with sheep and cattle; the inhabitants are numerous, and can bring twelve thousand fighting men into the field, armed with swords, pikes, spears, and fire-locks.

The people of Sivagangai.

Though less barbarous than the Collieries, their neighbours, yet arts and industry have made little progress among them. The country is capable of great improvement, but at present hardly yields more than five lakhs of rupees to the Rājāh, who pays 1,75,000 rupees to the Nawab of Arcot. The Rājāh is of the Taver (Dēvar) family, and a descendant of the sovereigns of the Great Marawar, from which Sivagangai was separated at no very distant period. At the reduction of this territory, in 1773, by General Joseph Smith, the Rājāh having been killed, his widow, then with child, and some of the leading people of the country, escaped to the Mysore dominions, and there lived under the protection of Hyder Ali, until the commencement of the late war. During that period the country was managed by a renter, and in quiet times the people acknowledged themselves to be tributaries of the Nawab Muhammed Ali; but while their woods and barriers are suffered to remain, their disaffection may be dreaded on the first prospect of their profiting by disturbance."

Usurpation in Sivagangai.

It may here be added that Rāmnād was reduced by General Joseph Smith in the same year (1773), from which time till the final cession of the whole country to the English Rāmnād was occupied by the troops of the Nawab. In 1783, when Colonel Fullarton marched against Sivagangai, the government of the country had passed from the hands of the ancient family into the hands of usurpers. On the death of the chief in 1773 his ministers fled to Hyder Ali for protection, and afterwards, on his invasion of the Carnatic, returned with him, governing the country under his authority, and ravaging the territories of the Company and the Nawab. They had been more than once in arms against the Nawab, and had as often successfully bought their pardon.

Conditions offered to the rulers of Sivagangai.

Colonel Fullarton says:—

"With the remaining troops we marched on the 4th August to Sivagangai, about twenty miles east; from thence the two Murdeens

CHAPTER IX.

(Murdoos), who rule the Little Marawar, fled precipitately with their young Rājāh to the woods of Kāḷaiyārkōvil, and collected there a force to the amount of 10,000 men, nor could they be prevailed on to return to their habitations and trust to any assurances. Besides the immediate discharge of their arrears of tribute, I demanded from their deputies 90,000 rupees in compensation to the Company for the ravages they had committed, and concluded with declaring that if these conditions were not fulfilled, I should attack their woods, storm their fort, and drive them from the country. Notwithstanding the procrastinating spirit of Gentoos (Hindus), they paid nearly 40,000 rupees, and gave security for their remaining debt. I felt a cordial satisfaction in contrasting the lenity and despatch of this transaction (for it was concluded in four days) with the circumstances of the expedition in 1773 against this very place. On that occasion the Rājāh, trusting to the woods and barriers that surrounded the fort of Calicoil, and expecting to conclude the business by negotiation, conceived himself in security, when the place was surprised, and he was killed in the attack. I rejoiced to mitigate the vigorous treatment which the delinquency of the successor, or rather of his ministers, merited, in consideration of the severities which the predecessor had experienced."

Death of the chief.

Colonel Stewart's expedition.

The Murdoo's submissiveness did not last long, for again in 1789 it was found necessary to send an expedition against him to reduce him to some degree of submission to the Nawab's Government. This expedition was commanded by Colonel Stewart, who took Kāḷaiyārkōvil, the Murdoo's citadel, after a resolute resistance. He met most resistance, it appears, on the western side, whereas it was on the southern side that the force of 1801 met with most difficulty.

THE MURDOOS.

The "Murdoos," the rulers of Sivagangai at that time, were two brothers, Veḷḷai Marudu, commonly called Periya Marudu, and Chinna Marudu. They belonged neither to the family of the ancient Poligars nor to their division of the caste, but were retainers of the family. Parivāras is the Tamil term for such—belonging to a lower division of the caste. The title peculiar to this class is Sērvaikāra, and they are bound to do service to their Poligar masters. Hence in all English letters and narratives pertaining to that time they are called "Sherogars," that is, Sērvaikāras, never Dēvas or Poligars.

Origin of the title Marudu.

Marudu, or Murdoo as it was written by the English, was their family title, not a personal name. Marudu is the name of a tree, the *Terminalia alata*. How then did the name of a tree become a family title? At the temple of Naināṛkōvil, in the Rāmnād Zamindari, Siva is supposed to have appeared in the shape of a lingam at the foot of a Marudu tree. Hence, as worshipped in that place, he is called Marud'appa or Marudēśvara. This being the family divinity of the Siruvayal people, each of them, in honour of their divinity, took the title of Marudu. Servaikāran was the caste title, Marudu the family name. Both the chiefs were called Marudu, with this distinction only, that one was Periya, the older, and the other Chinna, the younger. Periya Marudu was the nominal ruler of the country. It is he that is meant when *the* Sherogar or *the* Marudu is mentioned, but the real ruler was Chinna Marudu. The elder brother devoted himself wholly to field sports and left the administration of affairs in his younger brother's hands. I cannot refrain from availing myself here of General Welsh's warm description of the two brothers. It will be seen that though he knew and appreciated their kindness, he knew nothing of their family history :—

The two brothers.

"Of the two brothers, so frequently mentioned in this narrative, the elder brother was called Wella or Velli Murdoo, but he had nothing to do with the management of the country. He was a great sportsman, and gave up his whole time to hunting and shooting. Being a man of uncommon stature and strength, his chief delight was to encounter the monsters of the woods ; and it was even said, that he could bend a common Arcot rupee with his fingers. Unencumbered with the cares or trappings of government, he led a sort of wandering life ; and occasionally visited his European neighbours at Tanjore, Trichinopoly, and Madura, by whom he was much esteemed. If any one wanted game, a message sent to Velli Murdoo was sure to procure it ; or if he wished to partake in the sports of the field, Velli Murdoo was the man to conduct him to the spot, and to insure his success, as well as to watch over his safety. Did a royal tiger appear, while his guest was surrounded by hardy and powerful pikemen, Velli Murdoo was the first to meet the monster and despatch him. The minor game was, however, politely decoyed, or driven in front of his European friend, who might thus, with less danger, kill hogs, elks, deer, peafowl, &c., in abundance. From this Oriental Nimrod I had received many marks of attention and kindness when stationed at Madura in the year 1795, and then one of the youngest subalterns in the place, a pretty certain proof of his disinterestedness.

Veḷḷai Marudu.

"The Cheena (Chinna) Murdoo was ostensible sovereign of an extensive and fertile country, and his general residence was at Sherewēle (Siruvayal). Though of a dark complexiòn, he was a portly, handsome, and affable man, of the kindest manners, and most easy access ; and though ruling over a people to whom his very nod was a law, he lived in an open palace, without a single guard ; indeed, when I visited him in February 1795, every man who chose to come in had free ingress and egress, while every voice called down the blessing of the Almighty upon the father of his people. From a merely casual visit, when passing through his country, he became my friend, and during my continuance at Madura, never failed to send me presents of fine rice and fruit ; particularly a large rough-skinned orange, remarkably

Chinna Marudu.

CHAPTER IX.

sweet, which I have never met with in such perfection in any other part of India. It was he, also, who first taught me to throw the spear and hurl the Collery stick, a weapon scarcely known elsewhere, but in a skilful hand capable of being thrown to a certainty to any distance within one hundred yards. Yet this very man I was afterwards destined by the fortune of war to chase like a wild beast; to see badly wounded, and captured by common peons; then lingering with a fractured thigh in prison; and lastly, to behold him, with his gallant brother, and no less gallant son, surrounded by their principal adherents, hanging in chains upon a common gibbet!"

End of the Marudus.

The village of the Marudus.

The village to which the Marudus originally belonged was not Sivagangai, but a smaller place called Siruvayal (little field). This is the place which General Welsh calls "Sherewele" and Mr. Hughes "Sherevail." After the Marudus' elevation to power they attempted to turn the name of Siruvayal (little field) into Śrī-vēli, the sacred enclosure. This may perhaps account for the spelling Sherewele adopted by General Welsh. General Welsh describes it as a handsome, well built village. The collateral heirs of the family continued to reside there after the war and are there still. They are called the Marudappa Sērvaikāras. The Marudus showed their determination and spirit at the outset of the final struggle of 1801 by setting their handsome village on fire, to prevent its being made use of by the English force.

Reasons for Kaṭṭaboma's taking refuge in Sivagangai.

It might be asked why the Poligar of Pānjālamkurichi, on the capture of his fort, fled to Sivagangai. It was the only considerable pāḷaiyam to which he could flee. The Tondiman Rājāh had always been a fast friend of the English, and had surrendered his elder brother to them two years before. The Rāmnād Sētupati was also on the English side. Had it not been indeed for the English his territories would have been swallowed up ere then by the Marudus. He had also a rival amongst his own relations, one Mūlappan, whose plots were only kept in check by the energy and vigilance of the English. In addition to this, Rāmnād had long been the head-quarters of the Collector of the South, and even after the cession of the country it continued to be under the Collector, Mr. Lushington, whose Head Assistant administered its affairs. What, however, especially rendered it impossible for the Pānjālamkurichi Poligar to expect any help or sympathy from Rāmnād was the circumstance that he and his fellow conspirator, the Poligar of Nāgalāpuram, had long been in the habit of sending plundering expeditions into the Rāmnād territory. Only two years before the brother of the Nāgalāpuram Poligar had been hanged for the atrocities he had committed in those expeditions. It was out of the question, therefore, that Kaṭṭaboma Nāyaka and his adherents should betake themselves to Rāmnād. It was natural, on the other hand, that Kaṭṭaboma Nāyaka should betake himself in his emergency to the Marudus, because it was mainly

Mr. Lushington's policy.

through the counsel of the Marudus that he had been instigated to rebel. Mr. Lushington, as we learn from the records, had become acquainted with the correspondence that had taken place between Sivagangai and Pānjālamkurichi, but he was obliged to refrain from taking any notice of it in his communications with the Marudu till Pānjālamkurichi had been taken. He wisely concluded that it was sufficient to have one Poligar war on his hands at a time. Neither General Welsh nor Mr. Hughes was aware of this circumstance; neither were they aware of the special reason why the Marudu was so hostile to the English Government and so ready to share the fortunes of its enemies.

Explanation of the hostility of the Marudus.

On Mr. Lushington's taking charge of the Southern Poligar administration he sent for the Marudu and called upon him to produce the documents which proved him to be descended from Sēshavarṇa, the founder of the family, and to be entitled to hold the estate. The Marudu promised to produce the documents, well knowing that it was impossible for him to do so, seeing that no such documents existed, as he did not belong to the family at all, nor even to the same caste, but was an outsider and a mere usurper. This demand of Mr. Lushington was sufficient to convince him that danger was in store for him. He would probably also conclude that no amount of submissiveness on his part would suffice to avert the danger, and that, therefore, his best policy would be to set his back to the wall and fight it out. This accounts for the eagerness with which he espoused the cause of the defeated Poligar of Pānjālamkurichi and the resolute courage with which he fought to the end. Amongst other devices he wrote a letter to the Madras Government against Mr. Lushington, denouncing him as the stirrer-up of all disturbances, and asking for his removal and the appointment of a better Collector in his room.

Smaller forts attacked.

After the English force left Rāmnād, with the intention of marching on the Marudu's capital and citadel, he took the opportunity of sending a force into the Rāmnād country, which seized possession of the northern Rāmnād taluks and beset and threatened Rāmnād itself. Mr. Lushington thought it best to leave those taluks unrelieved till the termination of the campaign. The fort of Kamudi, garrisoned by an English force, was hardly pressed, but held out beyond expectation. The fort of Tirupattūr, which was occupied by a party from Colonel Martinz' Rāmnād Corps, was seized in great triumph by the Marudus.

Small naval war.

Whilst these affairs were going on, a naval war, on an exceedingly small scale, was being carried on in the Bay of Tondy, or Palk Strait. Though the Zamindari of Sivagangai was altogether inland, it had been agreed by the Sētupati, when the territory was partitioned, that a town on the sea-coast should be given to Sivagangai, so that it might have an outlet for its commerce.

CHAPTER IX.

This was the sea-port town of Tondy (pronounced Toṇḍi, but properly Tuṇḍi)[1] of which the Poligar of Sivagangai was appointed lord. The Marudu commissioned a number of *dhoneys*, or small coasting country vessels, at Tondi to seize all dhoneys found sailing in the bay with cargoes of rice. The rice thus seized was sent into the interior, to the Sivagangai country, to help to victual the forts that were, or were likely to be, beleagured. Thereupon the Master Attendant at Paumban, by Mr. Lushington's orders, equipped a superior kind of country vessel as a cutter, armed her, and cruised along the coast to suppress this new sort of piracy. He soon succeeded in his object, capturing some of the Marudu's vessels and burning others. Another object in view was to prevent the escape of any of the rebels by sea.

Success of Master Attendant of Paumben.

THE CAPTURE OF KĀḶAIYĀRKŌVIL.

I now return to the operations of Colonel Agnew's force against the Marudu. The first place attacked was Sherewele, that is Siruvayal, the Marudu's capital, called in the Ordnance Map Serravail, situated almost due north of Kāḷaiyārkōvil :—

Nature of the enemy's resistance.

"This town had become of some note since the rise of the Marudu's fortunes. He made it his constant residence, and it was conjectured that he might here make some vigorous stand. The march, not more than 8 or 9 miles, occupied us all the day, though the main road was a very good one; it lay through a strip of country of the general breadth of 1,200 or 1,500 yards, shut in on each side by high and strong jungle, whilst the intermediate space was everywhere crossed or flanked by the banks of tanks, close palmyra topes, or occasional patches of thin and common jungle, all that the Poligar could covet for his desultory warfare. The enemy was abundantly armed, and he possessed a great number of the small guns of his own particular description. The firing on his part was incessant all the day through, and a distant hearer might have concluded that we were in desperate conflict, but happily it was all noise and random firing, and did no serious harm; our own field-pieces rarely opened but when the Poligars were in great crowds in front and on the flanks. Whenever our parties closed in upon them, they retreated to other points. The country to the left, north of our main body, seemed that in which the enemy harboured with most confidence, and on this side was stationed Major Shephard with his corps as a flanking column. Our equipments and baggage were an enormous mass, and would have afforded much temptation to a more enterprising enemy. At sunset we reached our ground, and found the large town of Sherevail in general conflagration."

Burning of Siruvayal.

The people had set fire to their houses with their own hands and fled into the jungles. The flames, accelerated by a high wind,

---

[1] There is a sea-port town also on the Western Coast called Tuṇḍi or Kaḍal-tuṇḍi, the Tyndis of the Greeks.

spread with great fury, so that the fine extensive village, with its broad and regular streets, and the Marudu's palace fell into the hands of the troops without opposition. This was on the 30th of July. On the following day the army commenced to cut its way through the jungle to Kāḷaiyārkōvil, one of the thickest and most impenetrable jungles in the Carnatic.

A road to be cut through the jungle.

"Colonel Agnew entertained a sanguine belief that the opening for the force of an entire new road to Kāḷaiyārkōvil would be a far more eligible operation than assaulting strong and numerous barriers that were known to be constructed with all the care and ingenuity the Poligars show in such defences, and which at that moment would certainly have cost us very dear. The work of opening this road commenced with considerable alacrity, though it indeed proved throughout a most laborious undertaking. The line that was to be opened was estimated at not less than 5 or 6 miles from the skirts of the jungle opposite the encampment to the pagoda of Kāḷaiyārkōvil, and by far the larger part of this was accomplished when sickness spread over our camp and much yet remained to be done. The enemy too had now for some time learnt to carry on, under secure cover, a very harassing resistance to our parties, as they moved up each successive morning, exposed in the open space or avenue they had made for themselves, to pursue the work of approach to Kāḷaiyārkōvil."

General Welsh wrote a journal of each day's proceedings. The following extracts describing the work done for four days in succession in cutting a road through the jungle under fire will give a clear idea of the nature and difficulty of the undertaking.

Attack on a post.

"*August 6th.*—The detachment accompanying our working party was commanded by Major Graham, who found a high bank, at the end of the road cut the day before, had been scooped out and formed into a cover for a large body of the enemy, where they had thrown across three separate hedges, and got four guns to bear from it upon the road. This post they defended with great resolution, and killed and wounded many of our men, whose determined bravery, however, nothing could repel, and their opponents were at length put to flight. Their constant habit of dragging away their dead and wounded upon all occasions where they were not too closely pursued led us to suppose their loss to have been considerable, as their blood could be traced in every direction through the surrounding jungle. Our loss was also very great; but after the bank was stormed and taken the work proceeded without opposition, and by the evening we had cut two hundred and thirty-seven yards.

Another post taken.

"*August 7th.*—A foraging party under Lieutenant-Colonel Dalrymple obtained a large quantity of straw without opposition. The working party under Major M'Leod being heard firing for upwards of an hour, Lieutenant Little was sent out with a detachment to bring away the wounded. He returned with the pleasing intelligence, that not a man had been seriously hurt, though the bank was again defended and again stormed. It was at length taken in flank, but the enemy succeeded in carrying off their guns and all their killed

CHAPTER IX. and wounded. The jungle was so impenetrable that only one party under Lieutenant King gained their flank in time; another, despatched in the opposite direction, under Major M'Pherson, did not arrive till some time afterwards, or they would have secured the enemy's guns. No further opposition was offered, and the party returned, after having cut about three hundred and fifty yards.

A post taken.

"On the 8th the foraging party under Major Sheppard again brought in a considerable quantity of straw; and by the covering party under the command of Lieutenant-Colonel Dalrymple, the bank was found again raised, hedged, and defended, and was again gallantly taken in flank. The right party alone, however, under Lieutenant Fletcher, put the enemy to flight; since the left division did not arrive in time, on account of the thickness of the jungle. The Poligars, on finding themselves likely to be out-flanked, fired a volley down the road, which did no damage, and absconded. Considering the strength of their position, our loss was very small. The pagoda of Kāḷaiyār-kōvil, to which we were working, was this day distinctly seen by the covering party, who returned after cutting five hundred yards.

A redoubt erected.

"On the 9th our working party was commanded by Major Sheppard, who changed his mode of attack, by opening all the guns, and throwing a few shells into the work, by which plan he took possession without the loss of a man. In consequence of the very powerful and repeated impediments to our speedy advance, which this bank had already thrown out, we were to-day ordered to fortify it as a post; and by the evening therefore a tolerable field redoubt for three hundred men and three guns was completed and occupied before we came away, by a fresh party from the camp under Colonel Innes. It was a square of thirty yards, the south face being on the bank towards Kālaiyārkōvil with an enormous tamarind tree of such dimensions that we could not cut it down, close to it; from whence both Sherewele (Siruvayal) and Kālaiyārkōvil were clearly visible.

"This turned out a very irksome and dispiriting warfare, as the hand that dealt the blow was rarely seen, and to return it on our part with any effect was next to impossible. Our supplies too, from the extreme closeness of the country and the crowds of peons about, became very precarious, and at last they could be brought up only by the movement of whole corps at a time for their protection."

An entire month was spent in this arduous endeavour to reach Kāḷaiyārkōvil by cutting a way to it through the jungle. Accordingly General Welsh says:—

The attempt to cut through the jungle abandoned.

"To-day, August 30, it was resolved to quit this place, without further prosecuting our attempt to reach Kāḷaiyārkōvil from the Sherewele side; and the rejoicing was unanimous, at the prospect of leaving a place which had been the grave of so many of our brave comrades. Even the honour which we lost, in abandoning the lābours of a whole month, was forgotten, in viewing the comparative facility which the opposite direction held out. Our camp had become sickly, and many were suffering from diarrhœa and dysentery; indeed, both officers and men had died of this vile scourge; while even those who continued to enjoy good health, were heartily sick of a standing camp, in a spot where the only green that met the eye was the impenetrable forest in which we had been foiled by cowards, of such a persevering nature, however, that although beating them every hour, they had succeeded so completely to surround us, that we could neither send a letter, nor receive one, even from Palamcotta, for a whole month. Many attempts had been made to elude their vigilance, but I believe every one failed. I had myself given a friendly Poligar, who, knowing the people and every inch of the country, had volunteered the adventure, an advance of five pagodas, with one small letter; and he was on delivery to have received a similar sum, equal in the whole to four pounds sterling; I afterwards learned, that though he set out in a dark night, he was discovered and put to death within a few miles from our camp.

Attempts to convey letters.

"On the 1st of September, a working party was sent out, with the usual escort, to destroy all our thirty-two days' handiwork in the jungle which they fully accomplished, by demolishing the redoubts and burning all the brushwood in their neighbourhood; and returned with the out-guards to camp without opposition."

The force moves off.

The force now moved off to make a detour by the western and northern approaches, which were ascertained to be more open to attack.

This period was marked by a proceeding that had a most beneficial influence on our affairs.

"The Collector of the Poligar Peshcush had with great judgment sought out the heir to the pollam, and under the authority of the Government, this personage now received in camp an investiture of his country with great ceremony and publicity. He had in his childhood been adopted by the last representative of the proper family of the pollam, but had been compelled to forego his expectations, to fly for his life and remain in deep obscurity, the Marudu in his early days being much too powerful a chief to allow him to entertain any hope of restoration. His adherents now, however, pressed his claims with much zeal, and the Government with very seasonable justice and consideration determined on their entire recognition of them, and his elevation was hailed by the population in general with the highest satisfaction."

The true heir proclaimed.

The person thus elevated was described by Mr. Lushington as collateral heir on the failure of direct heirs. He did not rest his claim on his having been adopted in his childhood by the last Poligar. There was a still nearer collateral heir, who was rejected by Mr. Lushington on account of his having married a daughter of Vellai Marudu and being attached to his cause. The new Zamindar was called Permattoor Odeya Tavar (properly Paura-Vallaba-Uḍaiya-Dēva of Padamattūr). On his appointment he was made Zamindar, not Poligar, and in this case, as has been shown elsewhere, the difference in name denoted a real difference. General Welsh gives an animated account of Uḍaiya Dēva's institution. The effect his appointment produced in drawing

CHAPTER IX.

Success of the measure.

away at once from the Marudus many of their followers vindicated the wisdom of Mr. Lushington's policy. It was a measure, however, which sooner or later he would have carried into effect all the same, for he did not wish so high a hereditary dignity as that of Zamindar of Sivagangai to remain in the hands of a usurper.

Capture of a fortified pagoda.

" Colonel Agnew about this time made a night movement with the cavalry and some native details to attack Peramally, which was surprised and taken possession of without any material occurrence. It was judiciously chosen, and it had been reported that the garrison was collecting stores for some ulterior object, and its situation also allowed of parties from it much disturbing our communication with Trichinopoly, which led to this visit. The post itself consisted of a handsome pagoda situated on the brow of a hill, from whence ran a wall enclosing a small village below. The garrison seeing our movements to turn their rear, escaped by a close passage in that direction leading to jungles on the opposite side of the hill. The resistance it offered was very feeble."

Meaning of Kāḷaiyārkōvil.

By Peramally (Prawmullay in the Ordnance Map) we are to understand Pirāmalai, properly Pirān-malai, a shrine sacred to (Pirān) Vishnu. I may mention here that Kāḷaiyārkōvil is a Saiva shrine of considerable celebrity. Kāḷai is the Tamil word for a bull, and stands here for Siva's Vrishabha or sacred bull. Siva is worshipped there as Kālai-īśvara.

Attack on the place in three divisions.

On the 1st of October the whole force advanced upon Kāḷaiyārkōvil in three divisions, converging on the place from three directions. One of these divisions marched the previous night so as to endeavour to reach Kāḷaiyārkōvil under cover of the darkness by the road cut through the jungle. The other divisions met with considerable opposition, but at length succeeded in forcing their way to the citadel. The fortunes of the division which started the previous night shall be told by Mr. Hughes himself :—

Success of the advance through the forest.

" During the critical period he (Mr. Hughes) had watchfully fixed his attention on the state of the road that had been opened by the force from Sherevail. All his intelligence went to corroborate the account that this point was now left entirely unguarded, the enemy seeming to view it as far too remote from our main body to need any precaution. The distance indeed was something to be considered by ourselves, but it was certain that the enemy would be sharply employed everywhere, and Colonel Agnew therefore approved of the movement of a small column in that direction. It was arranged that it should proceed in such deep secrecy overnight that even our own camp should not be apprized of its movement, since we had now many of the inhabitants about us who might play us false, and it was urged, as equally desirable, that in its passage forward it should carefully avoid every hamlet that no alarm might be given. It met not with the smallest impediment, and from the end of the excellent road that had been abandoned a month before as altogether unavailable, paths were found which had been traversed by the enemy whilst opposing our working parties, quite open to the very walls of Kāḷaiyārkōvil. The surprise and panic by our sudden appearance in this most unlooked-for quarter, caused an instantaneous abandonment of the place, and as rapid an escape of every soul to the contiguous jungle; Colonel Agnew was kept at a stand for a short time from the numerous obstacles thrown in the way of his attack—there was of course the usual incessant firing and much general uproar—but the first barrier being penetrated at the flank, the flight of the enemy became general through the numerous narrow paths about, and they had been apprized, it is palpable, of the fall of their stronghold, which must have much enfeebled their resistance. Every point of defence from the interior one to Kāḷaiyārkōvil was found deserted, and on discovering the pagoda, our Commandant had the high satisfaction of perceiving our sentinels on the walls. The meeting indeed was alike happy to every one, since here was an end to this irksome service."

CHAPTER IX.

Meeting of the attacking forces.

"The pagoda of Kāḷaiyārkōvil," says General Welsh, "is a very large and handsome building, surrounded by a strong stone wall about eighteen feet in height and forming one angle of the fort, which was nearly dismantled. The enemy seemed quite disheartened and bewildered by our different attacks at the same moment, and hardly a soul appeared during the remainder of the day. We found here twenty-one guns, mostly mounted, and a great quantity of stores; there were also many articles of European furniture, and amongst them two clocks and several pier-glasses. The fort had been well built and was extensive, but the town, covered by a thick hedge only, formed one face of it and contained many excellent houses. It had indeed, never been a place of very great strength, but our local information was never such as could be relied upon, and no European in the camp knew anything about the state of the country. I had, myself, to my shame be it mentioned, actually passed through it a few months before, and been entertained by Vellai Marudu in his palace at Sherewēle; but had not then the slightest idea of ever again entering it, much less as a foe."

Description of Kāḷaiyār-kōvil.

Events that followed the Capture of Kāḷaiyārkōvil.

Kāḷaiyārkōvil was taken on the 1st of October (1801), and from that day all resistance in the field was abandoned by the rebels as hopeless. General Welsh gives the details of the hunt after the refugees.

"On the 3rd a division under Major Sheppard marched from camp at sunrise, with orders to proceed, *vid* Kāḷaiyārkōvil, to Mangalam, where it was understood we were to meet a large body of the enemy. We arrived there, however, without opposition, at half past 2 P.M., and formed our camp with the rear to the village and an immense tank in our front, on the bund or bank of which our quarter-guards were

Advance to Mangalam.

CHAPTER IX.

posted. The villagers, on seeing a white flag at our approach, came out to meet us, saying, that Marudu with two thousand men had been lately there, but had retreated into the jungle; and in the evening the headmen from nine villages came in to take cowle from Major Sheppard. The road from Kāḷaiyārkōvil to this place was entirely through jungle, in some parts very thick, and though hardly wide enough for carriages, was in other respects very good when we had removed the thorns and milk-hedges which were occasionally thrown across it. There was only one barrier on the skirt of the jungle, about six furlongs from Mangalam, intended to defend the approach from Ramnad, and this our Pioneers demolished in about two hours, and then returned under an escort to Kāḷaiyārkōvil. Colonel Agnew having returned to Madras on the 4th of October, we were again put under the orders of Major Colin Macaulay, and remained inactive, waiting to hear from him. The headmen of fifty villages came in to-day to take cowle, and brought intelligence that the Marudus had disbanded their forces; and, with only two hundred followers, had secreted themselves in the Shangrapoy jungle. This we considered as very good news, for we were not a little weary of such a tedious and unprofitable warfare. What followed afterwards was, indeed, of little importance, the enemy nowhere making head against us; parties were sent to hunt them down in the different jungles.

The rebels disbanded.

Execution of the principal rebels.

In a few days both the Marudus, with their families, Kaṭṭaboma Nāyaka, Daḷavāy Pillai, and the Dumb Brother, were all taken, and the men all hanged, excepting Dora Swamy, the youngest son of Chinna Marudu, and Daḷavāy Pillai, who, being of less consequence, were transported for life to Prince of Wales' Island, with seventy of their devoted followers; and thus ended this most harassing warfare, in which the expenditure of life had been profuse and the result any thing but honourable to the survivors."

Results of the victory.

When General Welsh speaks of the result of the campaign as dishonourable, he speaks from the point of view of a military critic. He meant that the English force gained no honour by the loss of time, life, and treasure it incurred in putting down so uncivilized a foe. From the point of view of Government, of the civil community, and of posterity, the results of the war were highly satisfactory. This Poligar war achieved the distinction of being the last of its kind.

The Marudus were hanged on the highest bastion of the fort of Tirupattūr, a town and fort in their own territory already referred to. Kaṭṭaboma Nāyaka and his dumb brother, the persons chiefly responsible for all this loss of life, were brought back to Pānjālamkurichi, and there hanged on the mound near the fort which had been erected for the use of the breaching battery. The mound is still visible. Colonel Agnew, leaving a corps in Sivagangai, returned to Palamcotta, and Captain Welsh was detached to command Tuticorin, where he superintended the transportation of seventy of the convicted rebels, including Chinna Marudu's younger

Minor rebels sent to Tuticorin.

son, a youth whom he treated with the greatest kindness consistent with his duty to the State. Strange to say, eighteen years afterwards he met his former prisoner in Penang. Not only was the fort of Pānjālamkurichi pulled down and levelled to the ground, but, to make assurance doubly sure and to produce an impression on the popular mind, the site was ploughed over and cultivated. It was ordered also that the name of Pānjālamkurichi should be removed from all maps and accounts. Notwithstanding this it found a place afterwards in the Ordnance Map, where it appears as "Pānjālamkurichi in ruins." Nothing now remains to mark the spot but a few traces of the mound erected as a breaching battery, on which the Poligar and his dumb brother were hanged, and the enclosure in the neighbourhood containing the tombs of the officers and men who fell in the last two assaults. The remains of those who fell in the first assault are just outside Ōṭṭapiḍāram.

Fate of Panjalamkurichi.

During Colonel Agnew's absence and up to the end of the year the Collector, Mr. Lushington, had been strenuously exerting himself in hunting down those rebels that were still at large, apprehending their friends and sympathisers, and restoring to Sivagangai and Rāmnād, as well as to Tinnevelly, a feeling of protection and security.

Capture of Sivattaiya.

The principal rebel then captured was Sivattaiyā Nāyaka, who was regarded by many as the real author of the rebellion, though he had always managed to escape conviction. An amnesty was proclaimed, on the Government passing from the Nawab to the East India Company, from which, however, two persons were excepted. One of these exceptions was Sivattaiyā Nāyaka, who was captured near Srīvilliputtūr and brought by a strong military escort to the fort of Palamcotta. Another person excepted from the amnesty, also captured, was the Mūppan of Kulasēkharapaṭṭaṇam. Another was one Daḷavāy Pillai, who led the authorities a long chase, but was at last caught. The Maravas of Nānguṇēri gave him an asylum, and got up a little rebellion on his account, as well as on their own, so that it was found necessary to send a force of 100 sepoys, under a European officer, to reduce them to submission. Some of these petty rebels were sent off to be imprisoned in the fort of Kamudi, in the Rāmnād country. The most formidable of their ringleaders were sent to Madras.

The Maravas of Nanguneri.

I quote the following from Mr. Lushington's letter to the Madras Government already cited.

Lushington's dealings with the Kavalgars.

"Upon the transfer of Tinnevelly in July last, the condition of the Kavalgars, the nominal protectors of the villages, urgently demanded my consideration. During the rebellion of Panjalamkurichi they fomented and aided the disturbance in every quarter; and after the

CHAPTER IX.

reduction of the place many of them continued to wander about the country in armed bodies plundering the villages, robbing the people, and intimidating the Mahajens (Brahmins) and principal inhabitants to obtain their pardon from the Circar. As the peace and prosperity of the country demanded immediate measures to arrange these disorders, and as I apprehended no ill-consequence from the return of the Kavalgars to their villages, they were invited to come in peace to their habitations with the exception, however, of those whose conduct had been particularly atrocious. Their long connection with the Poligars and occasional sufferings from a faithless administration created at first in their minds a distrust of my intentions; but when I succeeded in convincing them of the sincerity of the pardon offered to the obedient, they returned, and have remained from that period regardless of the endeavours made by Dalavoy Pillai to seduce them from the strict performance of all their duties. The regular enjoyment of their russoom (fees) and privileges seems to have converted them from plunderers to the submissive servants of the Circar, and there appears to me to be nothing wanting to destroy the influence of the Poligars over them, and to fix their attachment to the Company upon the solid ground of self-interest, but formally to relinquish all claims upon them to kaunikai or peshcush, which they were always compelled to pay to the Poligars, nominally from their russooms, but really from their depredations. The amount in the whole Province is as shown in No. 16, and I have given them hopes of a remission of these sums, which I trust you will find it just and politic to confirm. The use which they made of the Poligar's name, whilst they remained at his devotion, rendered the acquirement of this amount a matter of perfect facility to them at that period, but now that every effort is made to keep them rigorously to the performance of their watching duties the whole of their privileges are no more than sufficient for their subsistence.

Remuneration of Kavalgars.

Exception of the Nānguneri Maravars.

"From the satisfaction given by the Kavalgars in general, you are aware, that I have to except the Marava Kavalgars of Nangancherry (Nānguneri). The notorious profligacy and savageness of their character always checked any sanguine expectation of retaining them, but no effort was omitted to accomplish their reform by convincing them of the justice of the Company's Government. But their obstinate concealment and protection of rebels proscribed by Lieutenant-Colonel Agnew and their refusal to tender any surety of their submission and allegiance compelled the exercise of that coercion which was explained in my correspondence of October last. Upon mature investigation Lieutenant-Colonel Agnew conceived their conduct to have been of so heinous a tendency and of such dangerous example as to make them fit objects of transportation and banishment from the country. The eight principal Kavalgars of Nangancheri were accordingly sent as convicts from Tuticorin, and the duties have been since very satisfactorily performed by the original possessors of the kaval of the village, the Shanar inhabitants."

Whilst the disloyal Poligars suffered the punishment due to them for their rebellion, Government did not forget to reward those Poligars that remained loyal, especially those that were near neighbours to Pānjālamkurichi and who might have been expected to take the rebel chief's side. The Poligar of Maṇiyāṭchi, whose refusal to join in the rebellion brought down upon him a great deal of local odium, fled for refuge at the beginning of the war to Palamcotta, where he remained, with the permission of the Collector, till its close. The Poligar of Mēlamāndai also refused to join in the rebellion and fled to Rāmnād. The Board of Revenue warmly eulogised his conduct. They observed that, "though of the same caste with the family of Pānjālamkurichi, he resisted every artifice and threat that was made use of to force him into the league." Both these Poligars were liberally rewarded for the service they rendered to the State by keeping out of the rebellion. At the close of the war the two southern "Māgānams" of Pānjālamkurichi were conferred on the Maṇiyāṭchi Poligar, whilst the Poligar of Mēlamāndai was rewarded by a present of a portion of the lands of the deposed Poligars of Kāḍalgudi and Kuḷattūr. The Ettiāpuram Poligar had already been liberally rewarded by a gift of four out of the six Māgānams into which the forfeited estate had been divided. The Government were anxious to avoid even the appearance of wishing to derive any pecuniary advantage from the punishment inflicted on the rebellious Poligars, and therefore in every instance of the forfeiture of a pālaiyam for rebellion, instead of appropriating the pālaiyam, or any part of it, to itself, the only use it made of the forfeited lands was to divide them as rewards amongst its loyal adherents. It will be seen from the proclamation issued by Government at the close of the rebellion that this was its fixed line of policy in such cases.

CHAPTER IX.

Loyal Poligars rewarded.

Cession of the Country to the English Government.

Tinnevelly, together with the rest of the Carnatic, had now been peaceably ceded by treaty to the East India Company, a cession which brought with it not merely a change of rulers, but a change of principles, a change in the objects and methods of government, a change out of which an infinite number of beneficial changes were sure to be developed as time went on. The act of cession was dated on the 31st July 1801, and on the same day an order was issued by the Nawab to his principal Amildar in Tinnevelly to transfer all his accounts to the Company's representative and by the Madras Government to Mr. Lushington, appointing him their Collector, to be responsible to them alone in future for all matters of administration. One of the first works that occupied Mr. Lushington's attention after the close of the war was the "settlement" of Sivagangai.

Results of the cession.

CHAPTER IX.

I here give the principal portions of the important proclamation of the Madras Government issued at the close of the last Poligar war:—

Fort St. George, 1st *December* 1801.

PROCLAMATION.

Consequences of the rebellion.

1. By a Proclamation bearing date the 9th day of December 1799, the Right Honorable Edward Lord Clive, Governor in Council of Fort St. George and all its dependencies, proclaims to all the Poligars of the Province of Tinnevelly, the consequences of the rebellion of Kaṭṭaboma Nāyaka of Pānjālamcourchy which has terminated in the ignominious death of that chieftain and of two of his confidential ministers.

Future condition of Poligars.

2. By the same Proclamation, the Governor in Council further proclaims a definition of the future condition of Poligars, and of the system of government which it was the intention of the Governor in Council to introduce for the administration of the affairs of the Poligar countries.

Kaṭṭaboma's offence.

3. Before the Governor in Council could proceed to carry into execution the current system of measures described in that proclamation, the brother of Kaṭṭaboma Nāyaka, instigated by the evil advice of Veḷḷai Marudu and Chinna Marudu, Sērvaikāras of Sivagangai, was induced to disregard the awful example which had recently been exhibited to the Poligars of the Southern Provinces and to place the happiness and security of himself and of his adherents, not on the protection of the Honorable Company, but on the desperate hazard of defying in arms the power of the British Government.

Suppression of the rebellion.

4. The consequences of those infatuated councils were anticipated, and proclaimed to the Poligars and inhabitants of the Southern Provinces, at the time when the Right Honorable the Governor in Council assembled the British troops for the purpose of suppressing the rebellion excited, and maintained in arms, by the Poligars of Pānjālamcourchy and of Virāpākshi, and by the Sērvaikāras of Sivagangai.

5. At the same time that the Right Honorable the Governor in Council regrets that the desperate resistance opposed to the British troops should have been attended with so great a loss of life to the deluded inhabitants, His Lordship feels it to be his duty to impress on the minds of the Poligars, Sērvaikāras and inhabitants of the Southern Provinces, the danger of provoking the just indignation of the British Government, and the fruitless attempt of opposing the united strength of the Poligars, to the steadiness, valour and discipline of the British troops. The people of the Southern Provinces have now witnessed, that the difficulty of resisting the force of the Company's Government in open arms is not greater, than that of evading the perseverance, vigilance and activity of the Company's troops, in the native woods of the Poligars.

Proofs of British Government's strength.

Punishment of rebellion necessary.

6. From the centre of those woods, the authors of the late rebellion have been brought before the tribunals, erected by the Government in Council, for the trial of that hateful and desperate offence; and the infatuated obstinance of those chieftains, in neglecting the warning voice with which the Governor in Council had announced to them the danger of rebellion, has rendered indispensably necessary the signal punishments of their crimes: and the Governor in Council encourages a well-founded expectation, that the ignominious manner in which those misguided chieftains have terminated their ambitious and criminal career, will indelibly fix on the minds of their surviving families, and of the inhabitants of Tinnevelly, the danger of defying the British Government to arms.

Loyalty rewarded.

7. At the same time that the Right Honorable the Governor in Council directs the attention of the Sherogars, Poligars and people of the Southern Provinces to the just punishment of unprovoked rebellion, His Lordship contemplates with just pride and satisfaction the examples of steady attachment and honorable fidelity which the British Government has experienced from many of its dependants in the course of this unnatural and unavoidable warfare. As in the former case, the

Governor in Council has been reluctantly compelled to exhibit a memorable example of the crime of sedition, so in the latter instance, His Lordship in Council has had the pleasure of augmenting the security, wealth and happiness of those whose zeal and loyalty have entitled them to the distinguished favor and protection of the British Government.

Estates of rebels not appropriated by Government.

8. It will not escape the observation of the Poligars, Sherogars and inhabitants of the Southern Provinces, that the decisive success which has attended the progress of the British troops has created no deviation from the principles stated in the Proclamation bearing date the 9th December 1799. They will have observed that although the necessity of preserving tranquillity and regular government has compelled the Governor in Council to punish the authors of rebellion, His Lordship has abstained from appropriating to the Company the lands forfeited by that dangerous crime; they will have had the satisfaction of noticing the confidence reposed by the British Government in its subjects, by applying those forfeited lands to the means of augmenting the Pollams of the faithful Poligars, and from these examples they may derive the certain means of appreciating the principles of the British Government.

Hopes for the future.

9. On the foundation described in this Proclamation, the Right Honorable the Governor in Council encourages a reasonable hope that the causes of future commotion in the Southern Provinces have been suppressed, and the Poligars, Sērvaikāras and inhabitants will rely on the protection of the British Government in the assurance of enjoying their civil rights and the religious institution of their ancestors.

All weapons prohibited.

10. Wherefore the Right Honorable Edward Lord Clive, Governor in Council of Fort St. George, with the view of preventing the occurrence of the fatal evils which have attended the possession of arms by the Poligars and Sērvaikāras of the Southern Provinces, and with the view of inforcing the conditions of the Proclamation published by Major Bannerman on the 2nd day of October 1799, formally announces to the Poligars, Sērvaikāras and inhabitants of the Southern Provinces, the positive determination of His Lordship in Council to suppress the use and exercise of all weapons of offence, with the exception of such as shall be authorized by the British Government.

Arms no longer necessary.

11. The military service heretofore rendered by the Poligars having been suppressed, and the Company having in consequence charged itself with the protection and defence of the Poligar countries, the possession of fire-arms and weapons of offence is manifestly become unnecessary to the safety of the people; the Right Honorable the Governor in Council therefore orders and directs all persons, whether Poligars, Colleries or other inhabitants possessed of arms in the Provinces of Dindigul, Tinnevelly, Rāmnādpuram, Sivagangai and Madura, to deliver the said arms, consisting of Muskets, Matchlocks, Pikes, Gingauls and Sarabogoi to Lieutenant-Colonel Agnew, the Officer now commanding the forces in those Provinces, or such persons as he may appoint to receive them.

Evil custom to be relinquished.

12. The Right Honorable the Governor in Council, in the determination of carrying this resolution into effect, is governed by no other motives than those connected with the sacred duty of providing for the permanent tranquillity of those countries. His Lordship disclaims every wish for subjecting the chiefs and hereditary landlords to any humiliation, but the discountenance of the general use of arms, according to the prevailing habits of those countries, being indispensably necessary to the preservation of peace and to the restoration of prosperity, the Governor in Council expects that the chieftains will with cheerfulness sacrifice a custom, now become useless, to the attainment of those important objects.

Amnesty to all but a few.

16. The Right Honorable Edward Lord Clive, Governor in Council of Fort St. George and its dependencies, having now laid the foundation of a future permanent tranquillity in the Southern Provinces, by the entire suppression of the late united, extensive, and flagrant rebellion, and being further enabled to corroborate those foundations by the establishment of the undivided authority of the Company's Government in those Provinces, His Lordship in Council is desirous of relieving the minds of the Poligars, Sērvaikāras and people of the Southern Provinces from further solicitude or apprehension of the punishment provoked by the late rebel-

CHAPTER IX.

lion, wherefore the Right Honorable Edward Lord Clive, Governor in Council aforesaid, proclaims to the said Poligars, Sērvaikāras and inhabitants that, with the exception of Vīrapāṇḍya Nāyaka and Mookat Nāyaka of Pānjālamkurichi, Mūlapen of Rāmnad, and the persons now under restraint, whom it is the intention of His Lordship in Council to punish by banishment beyond the seas, the British Government now extends to all other persons who may have been induced to follow the desperate fortunes of the principal rebels, a free and full pardon of the offences which they have committed against the Company. The Governor in Council, therefore, assures such persons as may have been implicated in the crime of the late rebellion, that His Lordship in Council has relinquished every intention of prosecuting the punishment of that rebellion, deeming the examples already exhibited to their observation to convey a sufficient impression of the power of the British Government.

A permanent assessment promised to the Poligars.

17. In the confident expectation of redeeming the people of the Southern Provinces from the habits of predatory warfare, and in the hope of inducing them to resume the arts of peace and agriculture, the Right Honorable Edward Lord Clive, Governor in Council of Fort St. George aforesaid, announces to the Poligars and to all the inhabitants of their Pollams, that it is the intention of the British Government to establish a permanent assessment of Revenue on the Lords of the Pollam upon the principles of Zemindary tenures, which assessment, being once fixed, shall be liable to no change in any time to come, that the Poligars, becoming by these means Zemindars of their hereditary estates, will be exempted from all military service, and that the possession of their ancestors will be secured to them under the operation of limited and defined laws, to be printed and published, as well for the purpose of restoring its own officers to the regulations and ordinances of the Government, as of securing to the people their property, their lives, and the religious usages of their respective castes.

(By the order of the Right Honorable Governor in Council.)

(Signed) P. A. AGNEW, Lieutenant-Colonel,
Commanding S. M. Districts.

CAMP PALAMCOTTAH,
26th December 1801.

This Proclamation forms as a very suitable termination of one period of the history of Tinnevelly and an equally suitable commencement of another.

CONCLUDING REMARKS.

A mixed government, partly carried on on English principles and partly controlled by the Nawab's prejudices, came thus to an end and was succeeded by a government purely English, at unity with itself, and as just as it was powerful. The results of this change have been most important and valuable. Professor Wilson in his "Historical Sketch of the Kingdom of Paṇḍya" places in a striking light the course things would have taken if the English Government had not been enabled to interpose with authority.

Professor Wilson's anticipations.

"It may be concluded," he says, "that had not a wise and powerful policy interfered to inforce the habits of social life, the fine districts to the south of the Kāvēri, most admirably fitted by nature to support an industrious population, would have reverted to the state in which tradition describes them long anterior to Christianity, and would once more have become a suitable domicile for the goblins of Rāvaṇa or the apes of Hanumān."

Chapter IX.

War the normal condition of the country.

The first reflection that arises in one's mind on reading the foregoing sketch of the history of this district is, that war seems to have been the normal condition of Tinnevelly, as of the rest of the old Pāṇḍya country, and doubtless also it may be said, as of the rest of Southern India from the beginning of man's abode in these regions till A.D. 1801. A district that never from the beginning knew peace for 80 months together—probably never even for 80 weeks—has now enjoyed profound, uninterrupted peace for 80 years! and in consequence of this all the arts of peace have had time to be developed and to approach something like perfection.

Condition of things getting steadily worse.

Another conclusion which we seem to be entitled to form is that prior to the cession of the district to the English, the administration of public affairs and the condition of the country and people, instead of improving as time went on, in virtue of the lessons taught by the accumulated experience of the past, were steadily getting worse and worse. Things were worse under the Nāyakas than under the Pāṇḍyas, worse still under the rule of the Nawab, and worst of all—as the night is at its darkest just before the dawn—during that deplorable period immediately before the interference of the English—when the Nawab's power had become merely nominal and the only real power that survived was that of fierce Poligars and avaricious "renters."

The Poligar has become a Zamindar.

Of the many beneficial changes that have taken place since then one of the most remarkable is that which we see in the Poligars themselves. The Poligar has become a Zamindar, and has changed his nature as well as his name. One can scarcely believe it possible that the peaceful Nāyaka and Marava Zamindars of the present day are the lineal descendants of those turbulent and apparently untameable chiefs, of whose deeds of violence and daring the history of the last century is so full. One asks also, can it be really true that the peaceful Nāyaka ryots of the present day are the lineal descendants of those fierce retainers of the Poligars, who were so ready, at the merest word of their chief, to shed either their own blood or that of their chief's enemies? The change wrought amongst the poorer class of the Maravas is not perhaps quite so complete, but many of them have merged their traditional occupation of watchmen in the safer and more reputable occupation of husbandmen, and it may fairly be said of the majority of the members of this caste that, though once the terror of the country, they are now as amenable to law and reason as any other class.

Improvements introduced.

The whole aspect of things in Tinnevelly has changed for the better in a wonderful degree since the assumption of the government of the district by the English, and beneficial changes of all kinds are still in progress. The thick impervious jungles which covered most of the plains and which had for generation after generation furnished the haunts and hiding-places of banditti have

CHAPTER IX.

disappeared (perhaps only too completely), and cotton and food grains cover those tracts instead. Good roads have been made wherever they were required, all the rivers and the principal nullahs have been bridged over, carts have to a large extent taken the place of pack-bullocks, and transit duties have been utterly abolished. The whole district has been twice surveyed and mapped. Courts and cutcherries for the settlement of civil disputes and the repression of crime have succeeded to the arbitrary awards of irresponsible Pandits and illiterate Poligars. Well-considered legal codes have been introduced. A police force has been organized. Hospitals and dispensaries—institutions unknown before even by name—have been established in populous places. The Government in the great recent famine of 1877 has not left the people to perish, as they would have been left, and could not but have been left, in former times, but has set itself at whatever cost to preserve them from dying of hunger. Education has made great progress, not only amongst the Brahmans and the class of officials, but even amongst the poorer classes. The benefits of postal communication have been widely extended, and in our own day we have seen introduced the wonders of the railway and the telegraph. A truly paternal government has not only helped the people in every emergency, but it has helped them to help themselves. It has not only governed them better than they were ever governed before, but has taught and encouraged them, as far as is possible at present, to govern themselves. It has endeavoured not to raise a few classes only, but to lift the whole community to a higher level. So quiet, peaceful, and contented has the district become that it is governed by the merest handful of Europeans. The population amounts (roughly) to seventeen lakhs (17,00,000), whilst the number of Europeans directly engaged in the government of the district, including the commanding officer of a single company of sepoys, themselves natives, does not exceed ten. We have thus the extraordinary spectacle of seventeen hundred thousand natives submitting to be governed by ten Englishmen! Nor would it be sufficient to say merely that they submit to be governed, they accept our government readily and willingly as the best government they have ever had and the best they are likely to have in this age of the world. This might almost be called a miracle, but it is at any rate a striking proof—and so I believe it is regarded by the natives themselves—that a strict administration of justice and unselfish efforts for the public good will ever ensure the loyal obedience of the best portion of the people and the approbation of the Supreme Ruler of the world. Race after race of rulers has risen up in this country, has been tried and found wanting, and has passed away. Can it then be expected that the rule of the English is to last for ever? perhaps not;

Good government. | Proportionate numbers of English and Natives. | Prospects for the future.

"for ever" is a strong expression; but this I think may safely be predicted, that their rule will be allowed to continue as long as they rule, as on the whole they have ruled, or at least endeavoured to rule, hitherto, not for their own selfish ends merely, or for the benefit of a particular class merely, but for the benefit of the whole people of the land.

NOTE ON THE SEPARATION OF RĀMNĀD FROM TINNEVELLY.

Rāmnād, together with Sivagangai, though never considered a portion of Tinnevelly, was always included with Tinnevelly for the purposes of government under the same head, from the first introduction of English control, in the person of a Superintendent of Assigned Revenue in 1781, to 1803. During Mr. Lushington's Collectorate, Mr. Parish, his Head Assistant, took special charge of Rāmnād affairs. On the introduction of the permanent settlement into Rāmnād that year and the establishment of a Zillah Court therein, Mr. Parish was appointed Collector of the Rāmnād Zillah, including the districts of Madura and Dindigul. Mr. Cochrane, who was appointed Collector of the now diminished "province" of Tinnevelly, took charge of the district on the 5th November 1803. Thus, whilst Mr. Parish was the first Collector of Rāmnād with Madura, &c., Mr. Cochrane was the first Collector of Tinnevelly alone. Even then his authority did not extend over the whole district, for the "Pollams" or Zamindaris in Tinnevelly remained for some years in connexion with Rāmnād as before.

Rāmnād occupied the place of honor in the new arrangement. The Board of Revenue say, "the Zillah of Rāmnād, which includes the Zamindari of Shevagungah and the Zemindaries of Tinnevelly, and the districts of Dindigul and Madura, with their dependent Pollams and those of Manapara, form one Collectorate under the charge of Mr. G. Parish." The shorter title generally used was "Zillah Rāmnād, Dindigul, and Madura," and sometimes "Zillah Rāmnād" alone. In 1808 the Zillah of Rāmnād was abolished, and the twenty-nine small Zamindaris, formerly denominated "the Tinnevelly Pollams," were incorporated with the district of Tinnevelly.

CHAPTER X.

MISSIONS IN TINNEVELLY PRIOR TO THE CESSION OF THE COUNTRY TO THE ENGLISH, 1801.

PART I.

ROMAN CATHOLIC MISSIONS.

CHAPTER X.

Portuguese expedition.

It has already been mentioned, in our account of the settlements of the Portuguese on the Tinnevelly coast, that the commencement of the Roman Catholic Mission in Tinnevelly dates from 1532, when certain Paravas, representatives of the Paravas or fishing caste, visited Cochin for the purpose of supplicating the aid of the Portuguese against their Muhammadan oppressors, and were baptized there by Michael Vaz, Vicar General of the Bishop (not yet Archbishop) of Goa. The same ecclesiastic, with other priests, accompanied the fleet which sailed for the purpose of chastising the Muhammadans, and as soon as that object was accomplished, set about baptizing the Paravas all along the coast, in accordance with the agreement into which their representatives had entered. The entire Parava caste adopted the religion of their Portuguese deliverers, and most of them received baptism. Some, however—probably in the villages on the Rāmnād coast—did not receive baptism from some cause till Xavier's time, ten years afterwards. The Paravas thus Christianized—called generally at that time the Comorin Christians—inhabited thirty villages, and numbered, according to the most credible account, twenty thousand souls. These villages extended all the way along the coast at irregular intervals from Cape Comorin to the island-promontory of Rāmēśvaram, if not beyond, and the coast itself, called at first the Comorin coast, came to be more commonly called, on account of the pearl fishery for which it was famed, the "Fishery Coast," or simply "the Fishery." It does not appear that any village in the interior joined in the movement; and even in the fishing villages on the coast Vaz's work seems to have been very superficial, for though he is described as a kind protector of the Paravas, they appear to have continued totally uninstructed till Xavier appeared on the scene.

Baptism of the Paravas on the Tinnevelly coast.

XAVIER.

Francis Xavier's arrival and work.

This celebrated Missionary, Francis Xavier, commenced his labours amongst the Paravas on the Tinnevelly coast towards the close of 1542, and laboured amongst them for about two years. He himself explains his own plan of procedure. Immediately after his arrival on the coast he had the Creed, the Lord's Prayer, the Ave Maria, and the Decalogue translated into the vernacular. He then committed the translations to memory. Four months were occupied in this work, during which he resided in one of the Christian villages. Thus furnished, and accompanied by young Native interpreters, trained at Goa and able to speak Portuguese as well as Tamil, their mother tongue, he commenced his labours in the villages. Going about bell in hand he collected in every village a large concourse of people, whom he proceeded to instruct.

Estimate of Xavier.

It seems a pity that a man of such mental powers and devotedness as Xavier should have expended his strength and nearly the whole of his brief Indian life in the very rudimentary work described in his letters, and especially amongst people so ignorant and so destitute of influence in the Hindu community as the fisher people—that is, the Paravas on the eastern coast and the equivalent caste of fisher people, the Mukkuvas on the western coast—must then have been. It is to be remembered, however, that though a man of pre-eminent ability and of pre-eminent devotedness, he was not also a learned man. Up to the last he seems never to have been able to speak Tamil, but was always obliged to use the services of interpreters. In this particular he was less fitted to labour successfully as a missionary amongst Hindus than some of his successors of the same Society in Southern India, such as Robert de Nobili and Beschi (Italians) in the Tamil country, and Stephens (an Englishman), Arnold (an Italian), and Hanxleden (a German), on the western coast. On the other hand a Christian cannot but remember that Christ himself represented it as an evidence of the truth of His religion, that "to the poor the Gospel was preached."

In one of Xavier's letters, written to the Jesuit Society at Rome, of which he was a member, he gives a detailed account of his proceedings which has often been quoted. I here quote, however, only the conclusion.

"How great is the multitude of those who are gathered into the fold of Christ you may learn from this, that it often happens to me that my hands fail through the fatigue of baptizing; for I have baptized a whole village in a single day: and often, by repeating so frequently the Creed and other things, my voice and strength have failed me."

Visits from village to village.

Xavier adds that when he had sufficiently accomplished his work in one village he removed to another, till all those thirty villages had been visited.

"All being thus surveyed, my labour comes over again in the same order. In each village I leave one copy of the Christian Instruction. I appoint all to assemble on festival days, and to chant the rudiments of the Christian faith; and in each of the villages I appoint a fit per-

CHAPTER X.

son to preside. For their wages the Viceroy, at my request, has assigned 4,000 gold fanams.[1]

The low moral condition of the Parava Christians at that time must have been a still greater trial to a man like Xavier than even their ignorance. The following extracts from a letter written in 1544 to his Assistant, Francis Mancias at Punnaikāyal, nearly two years after his labours amongst them commenced, will speak for themselves.

Xavier's administration.

"To proceed to other matters. As both reason and precedent teach us that it is often useful to employ force, in order to crush the obstinacy of the more rebellious among these people, who are subjects of His Portuguese Majesty, I send you an apparitor, whom I have obtained from the Viceroy. I have ordered him to inflict a fine of two silver pence, which is the amount of the coin they call a fanam, upon any woman who, in defiance of the public regulations, shall drench herself with the intoxicating drink they call arack; besides which, he shall imprison for three days all who are found guilty of such intemperance. You must see to the rigorous execution of this law in all the villages, and have it published in all the assemblies, so that no drunken woman when punished may plead ignorance.

"I cannot yet say when I shall be able to come to you; but, till then, you must enjoin the Patangats[2] to correct their wicked manners. Tell them, that if I find them still plunged in their old vices, I have made up my mind, in virtue of the power which I hold from the Viceroy, to have them apprehended, and carried in chains to Cochin; and they must not flatter themselves with the hope of being soon released with a slight punishment, for I am thoroughly resolved to employ every means in my power to prevent their ever returning to Punicael. It is quite evident that the fault and blame of all the crimes and villanies of which there are too many which disgrace this country rests with them alone.

"Take the greatest pains to discover the workshops where the idols are secretly made and carved."

Xavier's successor's death.

Notwithstanding the shortcomings of the Paravas nothing could exceed the devoted zeal with which Xavier laboured for their welfare. We had many illustrations of this in the account of the Portuguese Settlements contained in a preceding chapter, especially in connection with his efforts for the protection of his people from the Badages or Nāyakas. His mantle also seems to have fallen on some of his successors, for it is said that his immediate successor, Antonio Criminalis, when his people were attacked by the Badages, threw himself into their midst, covered his people's flight, and perished under the darts of the enemy. This event is said by some to have taken place at Maṇapār, by others at a place called

[1] Three and a half gold fanams were equivalent to a rupee.

[2] Paṭṭangkaṭṭi, the title of a headman amongst the Paravas and a few other castes.

Vēdālai near Paumben, but there is a much more distinct and credible tradition of its having taken place at Punnaikāyal, where, as we have seen, the Portuguese suffered a defeat in 1552, eight years after Xaxier left the coast. Criminalis is regarded by the Jesuits as the first martyr of their Society. A martyr to his people's welfare he certainly was, but hardly a martyr to the faith. He is said by some to have died in 1562.

The Period after Xavier.

There is much in the letters of the Jesuit Missionaries in the century subsequent to Xavier respecting the mission established in Madura in 1606 by the celebrated Robert de Nobili, his proceedings, and the discussions caused by his peculiar modes of work. Much light is also thrown by their letters on the political condition and history of the Madura country and Rāmnād, as may be seen in Nelson's Madura Manual; but unfortunately little has been found for almost an entire century respecting the progress of the mission in Tinnevelly, whether on the coast or in the interior. The principal exception is a notice of the condition of things in the missions on the coast contained in a book published in Spain in 1604; from which Dr. Burnell has been so kind as to furnish me with an extract.

Missions on the coast in 1600.

(Guerrero, Relacion Annal, Valladolid.) It states that there were then (in 1600) twenty members of the Society of Jesus in the mission, *viz.*, seventeen fathers and three brothers. The fathers were distributed over twenty-two parishes, sixteen of which were on the coast, six inland, including the residences at Madura, the court of the Nāyaka, the lord of those lands. Besides these there are others in the island of Manar. There are in all that coast more than 90,000 Christians (Barrello, Bishop of Cochin, puts down their number as above 60,000), and the fathers visit all the parishes and churches there, going from one to the other according to necessity, though the principal residences are in seven chief places.

Tuticorin.

The college of Tuticorin was the chief; in it resided three fathers and three lay-brothers. They did not attend to parochial work, as there was a Vicar with two Curates. The festivals were celebrated with much zeal, especially that of N. Senora de la Nieves. The church is still called by this name. The corresponding Tamil name is "Pani-maya-Mātā," "dew" (pani) replacing "snow." See Tuticorin under the Portuguese. "This year," 1600, "more than 700 communicated." Father Henrique Henriquez was buried in the church there and was commonly regarded as a saint. [It will be remembered that relief-houses were established by this missionary during a famine in 1570.]

He mentions the following statistics for 1600. Seventy-four

CHAPTER X. were baptized in the college last year, 300 in Manar, 100 in Vypar, 15 in Priaparan (Periapaṭṭaṇam in the Rāmnād country ?), 100 in Vembar, 4 in Madura, 45 inland. In all 547, with about 50 others in other places. More attention, he says, was given to instructing converts already made than to making new converts.

The next notice I find is of the establishment of a congregation at Kaittār in the interior in 1640. There were probably congregations in the interior before this, seeing that 45 persons in inland places were baptized in 1600, but this is the first inland congregation the name of which I find mentioned.

KĀMAIYĀNĀYAKANPAṬṬI.

The next record I find is of the establishment of a congregation at Kāmaiyānāyakanpaṭṭi in 1660. In the same year, it will be seen, that Tuticorin, which had lately passed from the hands of the Portuguese to those of the Dutch, was visited by Baldens, whose statements show that the Paravas up to that time continued firmly attached to the religion taught them by Xavier.

Kāmaiyānāyakanpaṭṭi is a village in the Eṭṭaiyāpuram Zemindari. The following inscription cut on a stone preserved in the church at this place forms an interesting memorial of the period :—

Inscription. "Year—year 865, the 19th day of the month Chitrā. We Jaga-vīra-Eṭṭappa Nāyakar Avargaḷ (make proclamation as follows): As in our father's days, twenty-five years ago, this church of God in our territory and the Maṭha of the ascetics of the city of Rome were preserved from harm, so also now we being resolved to do the same have visited this church and the priests and have given and set up this stone. Wherefore if any person should do any harm to this church of God or the priests, or their disciples, not only will he become a traitor to us, but let him also incur the guilt which would ensue from slaying a black cow and Brahmans on the banks of the Ganges. Thus we have ordained as long as sun and moon endure. Jaga-vīra-Eṭṭappa Nāyakar. May the Lord preserve (us)."

Date of inscription. The era according to which time was calculated then in Tinnevelly was the Malabar or Quilon era, of which the 865th year synchronized with A.D. 1689-1690. The year commences in August —September. Consequently the early part of the following year, including Chitrā (April—May) belonged to 1690. The year of the Malabar era was preceded in the inscription by the year of the cycle of 60, but unfortunately the name of the year has been obliterated, only the letter p remains. The year of the cycle of 60 corresponding to the Malabar year 865, and commencing with the month of Chitrā, was the fourth year of the cycle, Piramōtūtha (Brahmōdūta).

Zemindar's name. Jaga-vīra-Eṭṭappa Nāyaka is not a personal name, but a family title of the Poligars or Zemindars of Eṭṭaiyāpuram. The Poligar of this inscription, that is of 1690, according to the family historian was Jaga-vīra-Rāma Kechila Eṭṭappa Nāyaka. His father to whom he refers was Jaga-vīra-Rāma Eṭṭappa Nāyaka. The troubles referred to as having taken place about 1690 and those which took place twenty-five years before (about 1665) appear to have been owing to the violence of the common people of the neighbourhood. On both occasions the Poligar himself, who was the only ruler in his territory, gave his help and sympathy to the Mission priests.

Origin of the troubles.

The first troubles appear to have taken place soon after the establishment of the congregation. The Portuguese had lately been expelled from Tuticorin by the Dutch and the priests of the coast congregations had been obliged to take refuge in the interior. This may have incited some of the people in the Poligar's territory, which was not far from Tuticorin, to take advantage of the downfall of the European friends of the priests and endeavour to drive them away from their stations.

It will be seen that later on, in 1715, the celebrated Beschi, who then ordinarily resided at Kāmaiyānāyakanpaṭṭi, was exposed to serious danger from the hostility of some people in the same Poligar's territory at a place a little further to the west.

CONDUCT OF THE DUTCH.

In a letter written by Father Martin in 1700, from which I have already made a quotation, illustrative of the condition of the town of Tuticorin, I find some reflections on the hard treatment the Paravas received at that time from the Dutch.

"Though the Dutch are not masters of the coast, they yet have often behaved in such a manner as if it had been entirely subject to them. Some years since they dispossessed the poor Paravas of their churches, which they turned into magazines (warehouses), and lodged their factors in the houses of the missionaries. The fathers were then forced to withdraw into the woods and there build themselves huts, in order that they might not abandon their flocks at a time when their presence was so necessary."

Intolerance of the Dutch.

This statement, from the point of view of the toleration generally prevalent at the present period, seems so extraordinary that one would naturally wish to hear the other side of the story. The other side has been given us by Baldaeus, an able Dutch Minister and Missionary, who visited Tuticorin in 1660, two years after it had been taken from the Portuguese by the Dutch. Unfortunately this other side is confirmatory of Martin's statement! Baldaeus says he found the priests of the Paravas very numerous. They were principally natives of Goa, and so absolute was their influence over this untutored people that they were able to counteract all his efforts to gain their attention. The Dutch had

CHAPTER X. expelled the priests from the towns of Negapatam and Tuticorin, but they remained near enough to control the Paravas, who durst not enter the church when Baldaeus preached, though he preached in Portuguese. From another incident he mentions it appears that the Dutch had removed the images and other ornaments from the church and converted it to their own use, so that the Paravas would not enter it and preferred to say their prayers in the street. Later on we find that the Dutch had become more tolerant and erected churches for themselves. The date of the erection of their church in Tuticorin, now used by the English, is 1750.

BESCHI.

The Tinnevelly coast was the scene of the commencement of the missionary labours of Xavier. It was also, about 200 years afterwards, the scene of the termination of the labours, and also of the life, of Beschi, another celebrated missionary of the Society of Jesus. It now also appears that it was the scene of the commencement of his labours.

As a missionary Beschi belonged to the Roman Catholic Church. As a Tamil scholar and poet Protestants have always taken as much interest in his career as Roman Catholics, perhaps even more. A list of Beschi's numerous works, in verse and prose, in Tamil and Latin, will be found in the Madras Literary Journal for April 1840. The following estimate of his position in the Tamil world of letters is taken from the Introduction to my Comparative Grammar of the Dravidian Languages.

Beschi as a Tamil scholar.

"The post of honour, not only in the beginning of the eighteenth century, when they flourished, but throughout the entire modern period, is to be assigned to two contemporary poets, one a native, the other a foreigner. The second of these, whose poems occupy a still higher place in literature, was the celebrated Beschi, not a Tamilian, like every other Tamil poet, but an Italian, a missionary priest of the Jesuit Society, who acquired such a mastery over Tamil, especially over its classical dialect, as no other European seems ever to have acquired over that or any other Indian language. His prose style in the colloquial dialect, though good, is not of pre-eminent excellence; but his poems in the classical dialect, especially his great poem, the Tēmbāvaṇi, a long and highly wrought religious epic in the style of the Chintāmaṇi, are so excellent—from the point of view of Hindu ideas of excellence; that is, they are so elaborately correct, so highly ornamented, so invariably harmonious—that I have no doubt he may fairly claim to be placed by the votes of impartial native critics themselves in the very first rank of the Tamil poets of the second class; and when it is remembered that the first class comprises only three, or at the utmost four works—the Kuraḷ, the Chintāmaṇi, the Rāmāyaṇam, the Nāladiyār—it seems to me, the more I think of it, the more wonderful that a foreigner should have achieved so distinguished a position. Though the Tēmbāvaṇi possesses great poetical merit and exhibits an astonishing command of the resources of the language, unfortunately it is tinged with the fault of too close an adherence to the manner and style of 'the ancients'—that is, of the Tamil classics—and is still more seriously marred by the error of endeavouring to Hinduise the facts and narratives of Holy Scripture, and even the geography of Scripture, for the purpose of pleasing the Hindu taste. It is a remarkable illustration of the difference in the position occupied in India at present by poetry and prose respectively, that Beschi's poetry, however much admired, is now very little read, whilst his prose works, particularly his grammars and dictionaries of both the Tamil dialects, are in great demand."

Memoirs of Beschi.

It is surprising that, notwithstanding Beschi's great eminence, both as a missionary and as a Tamil scholar, no memoir of his life seems ever to have been written by any member of his own Society or by any European competent to do so. Many notices of his life are in print in English, but I have traced them all to one source, a Tamil memoir drawn up by a Roman Catholic native, who worked up all the traditions he found surviving amongst natives respecting Beschi seventy years after his death. He made some use of a meagre Tamil memoir published in Pondicherry in 1796 by one Sāmināṭha Pillai, but seems never to have consulted any European records. The native here referred to was A. Muttusāmi Pillai, "Manager of the College of Fort St. George," who in 1816-17 undertook a tour to the south, at the instance of Mr. Ellis, the celebrated Tamil scholar, for the purpose of procuring a collection of Beschi's works. In the course of this tour he states that he collected from the children of Beschi's disciples and others many particulars respecting his life. In 1822 at the request of Mr. Babington and Mr. Clarke, members of the College Board, he published in Tamil the life of Beschi to which I have referred, with a catalogue of his works and extracts from some of the principal; and at the request of Mr. (now Sir Walter) Elliot, a somewhat abbreviated translation of this Tamil memoir was made into English, by the author himself, helped by two English Roman Catholic Missionaries, and published in the number for April 1840 of the Journal of the Madras Literary Society. We have every reason to suppose that the author of this memoir was right in regard to the principal facts of Beschi's life, but it seems certain that he was in error in regard to the dates both of Beschi's arrival in India and of his death. This would very naturally happen in the case of a native, however intelligent, who had no access to records, or who did not think it necessary for his purpose to consult such as were to be had.

Errors in regard to date.

For the dates and other particulars which follow I am indebted to extracts from letters to the Society at Rome and other authentic records kindly supplied me, through the good offices of the Rev.

CHAPTER X. Paul Rottari, S.J., by the Rev. N. Pouget, S.J. They have never yet, so far as I am aware, appeared in English.

Constantius Beschi was born at Castiglione in Italy on the 8th November 1680. On the 21st October 1698, being eighteen years of age, he entered the Society of Jesus.

His native biographer states that he arrived in India in 1700, but Fr. Pouget shows that this was impossible. He must have passed two years in novitiate and then engaged in theological studies for four years. No member of the Society of Jesus is ordained priest before he is twenty-five years of age. He cannot, therefore, have sailed for India before 1706. The voyage at that time occupied at least six months; and after he reached Goa it would be considered necessary, according to the custom of the time, that he should remain there one or two years learning Tamil, the language of the district to which he was to be appointed. It seems probable, therefore, it is said, that he did not commence his missionary career in Tinnevelly before 1710. For my own part, accepting the data that have been mentioned 1708 seems the latest date that can be assigned for his arrival in Tinnevelly. His Tamil biographer says that he spent five years in learning Tamil. It might be said, doubtless, with still greater truth of so devoted a scholar that he was learning Tamil as long as he lived. In whatever year his career as a missionary actually commenced, it cannot now be doubted that it commenced in Tinnevelly, and it is equally certain that it was to Tinnevelly that he came to breathe his last.

Beschi's stations.

We pass out of the region of probabilities into that of certainties when we mention that Brandolini, who founded the congregation at Vaḍakankuḷam in Tinnevelly in 1714, states that in the years 1714, 1715, and 1716 Beschi was stationed at Kāmaiyānāyakanpaṭṭi in Tinnevelly, from which place he often visited Kaittār. Kaittār, then a more important place than it is now, is situated on the road from Palamcotta to Madura, 18 miles from Palamcotta. Kāmaiyānāyakanpaṭṭi lies to the north-east, in the Eṭṭiāpuram Zemindari. Beschi was imprisoned by the Brahmans at Gurukkaḷpaṭṭi, and they were about to put him to death, when he was rescued by the Christians of Kaittār. Gurukkaḷpaṭṭi is a village near Ālankuḷam in the Sangaranainārkōvil Taluk. Beschi himself relates this incident in a letter to the General Superior of the Society dated Kāmaiyānāyakanpaṭṭi, 12th January 1715. I felt doubtful at first whether it could be true that Brahmans could have really intended to put him to death, but I find that there is a distinct tradition to that effect surviving amongst the Native Christians in all these villages. The village of Gurukkaḷpaṭṭi belongs to Brahmans and is inhabited partly by Brahmans. They themselves admit that they have heard that their forefathers pulled down a maṭha erected by Beschi and drove him out of their

His life in danger.

CHAPTER X.

village, together with a Brahman convert he had made. They show the ruins of the maṭha he erected. Shortly after this event Beschi seems to have left for the north. In 1716 he was in Madura, but there is no record of his stay there; and in 1720 we find him, where we ever find him afterwards, near Trichinopoly. The place where he then was stationed was Vaḍugarpaṭṭi. The annual letters between 1720 and 1729 were unfortunately lost, but in 1729 we find him at Āvūr, near Trichinopoly, where he seems generally to have resided.

Beschi acquired his Tamil in Tinnevelly.

It has always been known from Muttuswāmi Pillai's memoirs that Beschi terminated his course in Tinnevelly, but it was never known till now that it was in Tinnevelly also that he commenced his career. We now know that Tinnevelly can claim him for the first five years, probably for the first seven, of his missionary life; and as it was necessarily during those years that he laid the foundation of his marvellous knowledge of Tamil and his still more marvellous skill in making use of the knowledge he acquired, Tinnevelly might almost seem to have the right of classing him amongst her literary celebrities. Unfortunately for this claim, however, it does not appear that any of his compositions, whether in prose or in verse, was written in Tinnevelly. His greatest work, the Tēmbāvaṇi, was published in 1726, to which the explanation of the same by himself was added in 1729. His Vēdiaroḻukkam, an excellent prose work for the use of catechists, was written in 1727.

According to the custom then, as now, prevailing amongst Jesuit Missionaries, Beschi adopted a native name. This was Dhairya-nātha Svāmi(yār), a translation of his own Christian name Constantius. After the publication of his Tēmbāvaṇi he received, we are told, from the poets of the Tamil country the title by which he is now universally known amongst natives. This was Vīra-mahā-muni (in Tamil Vīramāmunivar), the "Great Champion Devotee." This name is not by any means so well suited to one who was above all things a scholar as that of Tattvabōdhaka Swāmi, "the Philosophical Doctor," was to the metaphysical tastes of Robert de Nobili.

Dewan to Chanda Saheb.

During four of the later years of his life, from 1736 to 1740, Beschi seems to have been employed as Dewan to Chanda Saheb, whose treacherous seizure of Trichinopoly, and therewith of authority over the whole Madura country, has been mentioned in the political history as the event by which the Nāyaka dynasty was brought to an end. Chanda Saheb became by this stroke of state a Nawab and virtually a rival to the Nawab of the Carnatic. Beschi's native biographer states that in order to fit himself for an interview with Chanda Saheb, Beschi learned the Persian and Hindustani languages in the short space of three months, and that

CHAPTER X.

Chanda Saheb was so much struck with his attainments and ability that he presented him with the revenues of four villages and appointed him to be his Dewan or Prime Minister. I do not see any reason for doubting the substantial truth of this statement, which is confirmed by the circumstance that Beschi's visit to Chanda Saheb in 1736 is mentioned in a letter to Europe. In 1740 he paid a visit to Daust Ali Khān, the real Nawab of the Carnatic at that time, at Vellore, to whom he presented some European curiosities and a letter addressed to him, the Nawab, by the General Superior of the Jesuits, dated at Rome, 29th October 1739.

Chanda Saheb was besieged in Trichinopoly in 1740 by the Mahrattas under their two Generals Raghuji Bhonslai and Futta Sing. He surrendered the fortress to them in March 1741, and was by them sent prisoner to Sattara. Beschi's native biographer represents Beschi as escaping from Trichinopoly on his master's surrender, but letters written at the time to Europe state that before that event, as soon as the Mahrattas arrived in 1740, all the missionaries, Beschi apparently included, had to leave the districts which the Mahrattas occupied and flee to the south. On Chanda Saheb's surrender the Mahrattas appointed one of their Generals, Morari Row, Governor of Trichinopoly, and another, Appaji Row, Governor of Madura, and therefore of Tinnevelly. The whole country, except in so far as the Poligars, who cared little for any rulers, were concerned, was now in the hands of the Mahrattas, who were zealots for Hinduism, and enraged against Chanda Saheb, both as a Muhammadan and as a usurper. The missionaries were supposed to be on the side of Chanda Saheb, and the Mahrattas were not likely to show much consideration for Chanda Saheb's Dewan if he fell into their hands. Naturally, therefore, he would endeavour to make his escape at the earliest opportunity.

Flight of Beschi on the approach of the Mahrattas.

It is stated in the letters to Europe that Beschi fled first to the Marava country, that is, to Rāmnād, and then to the sea-coast. The place in the Marava country where he lived for a time is not known, but both his native biographer and the letters written at the time to Europe agree as to the place on the sea-coast where he took up his abode. This was Maṇapār (Maṇapāḍu) on the Tinnevelly coast (literally Maṇal-pāḍu, the sandy lagoon), then a Dutch possession, a small fishing and trading town, with a considerable Roman Catholic population, and far away from the reach of hostilities. It is certain from authentic records that Beschi was

Beschi's last days at Maṇapār.

"Rector" of Maṇapār in 1744 and that he died there in 1746. This was in the 66th year of his age and the 40th of his residence in India. It is very probable that Maṇapār was the first place in the Tamil country where Beschi resided after he left Goa, in consequence of which he might naturally wish to end his days there ; in addition to which it is to be remembered that the Dutch, to whom Maṇapār belonged, were always more or less inclined to range themselves on the side opposed to that espoused by the English, and therefore likely to be willing to take under their protection a friend of Chanda Saheb's, who had fled to them from the Mahrattas. The Dutch were Protestants, it is true, but they had learned by that time to be tolerant. It has been supposed by some that the Maṇapār where Beschi died was the Maṇapār, properly Maṇapārai, near Trichinopoly. For this idea however there is no foundation. The people of Maṇapārai themselves, including the Roman Catholic Missionary of the place, admit that Beschi died at Maṇapār in Tinnevelly.

His death.

Beschi did not long survive his arrival in Maṇapār. He resided there, his native biographer says, in the maṭha of the Society of Jesus, occupying his time in expounding his works and giving instruction in divine things. The exact date of his death is unknown, but it is certain it was in 1746. Thus peacefully ended the career of the most learned, if not the most renowned, of the great Jesuit missionaries of former times.

Beschi's grave.

He is said to have been buried in the chancel of the church at Maṇapār, but the oldest of the churches is now completely buried in the sand. There must be at least fifteen feet of sand over it, and the people say that no tomb-stone was erected to mark the place where Beschi's remains lay, and that in the same chancel other missionaries also were buried. Some again say that when the second church was erected two sets of bones were taken from the chancel of the older church and interred in the chancel of the later one, but without any record to show whose bones they were. One may safely say, I think, that Beschi was not much appreciated by the fishery people at Maṇapār. If he had cared to acquire the reputation of a worker of miracles, doubtless his tomb would have been carefully preserved.

Period after Beschi.

Some years after Beschi's death troubles began to gather round the Missions of the Jesuits all over the world. In 1755 the support of the missionaries from Europe ceased. In 1760 the Jesuits at Goa were deported to Lisbon by Pombal's orders. The Jesuits that remained in Tinnevelly at Vaḍakankuḷam, Tāḷai, Maṇapār, Vīrapāṇḍiyanpaṭṭanam, &c., died one by one, and their places were supplied by native priests from Goa. In 1773 the Society of Jesus was formally suppressed by the then Pope, Clement XIV. In 1814 the Society was restored by Pope Pius VII, and in 1838 two Jesuit Missionaries, Fathers Martin and Duranquet, arrived in Palamcotta to recommence their ancient mission in Tinnevelly.

CHAPTER X.

"Tinnevelly has always been attached to the Madura Mission, the history of which, associated with the names of Fathers Robert de Nobili, de Brito, Banchet, Arland, from 1616 to 1748 is of much interest. At the latter date it was estimated that there were 385,000 Christians in the eastern part of India; then, as above stated, there followed the suppression of the Jesuits, by which the Madura Mission was for the time destroyed. About the year 1831 the restoration and return of the Jesuits to Madura took place and the Mission recommenced afresh."—*Stuart's Tinnevelly Manual, page 62.*

PART II.

MISSIONS OF THE CHURCH OF ENGLAND.

SWARTZ.

A mission had been commenced in Tinnevelly before the close of the eighteenth century, but very little had occurred to warrant any expectation of the progress the mission was destined to make. At first the Tinnevelly Mission was merely an offshoot of that in Tanjore. The first reference to missionary work in Tinnevelly in connection with the Missions of the Church of England appears in

Swartz.

the memoirs of the celebrated Swartz, a man of apostolical simplicity, devotedness, and zeal. This was in 1771. Swartz notices Palamcotta in his journal of that year as "a fort and one of the chief towns in Tinnevelly, belonging to the Nawab, but having an English garrison." He mentions the fact that there were a few Christians there then. Swartz first visited Palamcotta in 1778, when the widow of a Brahman was baptized by him. Her name (Clorinda) appears at the head of the small list of 40 persons

Congregation and Church in Palamcotta.

constituting the Palamcotta congregation in 1780. Soon after she set herself to erect a small church in the fort, and this she succeeded in doing through the help of two English gentlemen. This was the first church connected with the Church of England ever erected south of Trichinopoly. It was dedicated to the worship of God by Swartz in 1785, when he found that the little congregation had increased, in consequence of which he sent from Tanjore an able catechist, Satyanāthan, to take care of it.

JAENICKE.

The congregation in Palamcotta continuing to increase and openings presenting themselves in the surrounding country Swartz became desirous of sending a European Missionary to take charge of the infant mission. This desire he was able to gratify in 1791, when Jaenicke, a German like himself, but like himself a missionary of an English Society, the Society for Promoting Christian Knowledge (the precursor in India of the Society for the Propagation of the Gospel), arrived in Palamcotta and commenced his labours. By that time the number of Native Christians in Palamcotta and the neighbourhood had increased to 403. Even at this early period education had not been neglected. From the time of Swartz's visit in 1784, as they have done ever since, the congregation and the school went hand-in-hand. Satyanāthan, the Palamcotta catechist, had now been ordained in Tanjore, and returned to Palamcotta a few months before Jaenicke's arrival. He was a man of ability, who left his mark in the district. He was the first Native Minister ever located in Tinnevelly, and it was through him, as will be seen, that a Christian movement amongst the Shanars commenced. Jaenicke, though not so distinguished a man as Xavier and Beschi, the two great Roman Catholic missionaries referred to in the previous pages, would have been quite able to hold his own with any of the rest of the Roman Catholic missionaries in Tinnevelly of that period. His journals show that he was a devout, zealous, and prudent man, well fitted in every way for laying the foundations of a mission, but unfortunately his stay in Tinnevelly was short. In the beginning of January 1792, only a few months after his arrival in Palamcotta, he went out on a tour in the neighbourhood of the hills, in company with Mr. Torin, the Collector, who was then making his first official visit as Collector of the Nawab's Revenue in the East India Company's behalf, in virtue of the Treaty of 1792. The party visited Kaḷakādu, Pāpanāsam, and other places along the range of the hills, besides penetrating into the hill country, as far as the falls of Bāṇatīrttam. On the 12th of February Jaenicke visited Courtallam, and on the 25th returned to Palamcotta. On the 1st of March jungle fever of a severe type set in. Many other members of the party were attacked by the same fever, of which several died. Apparently it was not then known to Europeans that it was unsafe to be much amongst the hills at that season of the year. Yet only a few years later (in 1800), General Welsh mentioned it as a well known fact that the hills were safe to Europeans only during the rains of the south-west monsoon. Jaenicke struggled on with the fever for many months, carrying on his work at the same time indefatigably and with considerable success. In the course of the year he visited Tuticorin and Maṇapār, both of which places then belonged to the Dutch, in each of which he found a Native congregation under the care of a Catechist. The congregation at Maṇapār, consisting chiefly of weavers, was at that time the largest in Tinnevelly. The Governor of Tuticorin at that time was a Mr. Meckern, who was very friendly to Jaenicke and desirous of helping him in all his plans. As the fever continued

Satyanāthan.

Fever caught in the hills.

and became aggravated, Jaenicke found it necessary in the end of 1792 to leave Tinnevelly and return to Tanjore for a time. He arrived in Tanjore after an absence of one year and two days.

From this time till his death in May 1800 Jaenicke generally resided at Rāmnād, where he erected a church, or at Tanjore, making occasional visits to Palamcotta as his strength allowed, but he kept up a regular correspondence with Satyanāthan, the Native Minister.

Commencement of the Christianization of the Shanars.

The most important event of the time was the commencement, in 1797, of that movement towards Protestant Christianity amongst the Shanars in Tinnevelly, which has, directly or indirectly, contributed so largely to the improvement of the district, and which has been the precursor of so many similar movements in different parts of the country.

First Shanar convert.

It had long been known that a certain Sundaram, *alias* David, had been the first Shanar catechist, but I have ascertained also that he was the first Shanar Protestant Christian, and that it was through him that Christianity was introduced amongst the Shanars in Tinnevelly. David's birth-place was Kālangudi, a small village near Sāttānkulam, but he wandered off in early youth as far as Tanjore, and there became a Christian and was baptized and instructed by Mr. Kohlhoff. In 1796, in consequence of Satyanāthan's application for an assistant, Swartz, knowing that David belonged to that neighbourhood, sent him to Palamcotta as a catechist. Jaenicke was in Palamcotta when David arrived and entered upon his work. After a short time David went to visit his relatives, who had long given him up as dead, and told them all the wonders he had seen and heard. On his return to Palamcotta he brought with him a young nephew, whom Jaenicke proceeded to instruct. Shortly after this David was sent out to Vijayarāmapuram, a village near his birth-place, to labour amongst his relations there and in the neighbourhood, and some Tanjore catechists also rendered their assistance from time to time. In March 1797 Satyanāthan visited the place himself, when four families of Shanars placed themselves formally under Christian instruction and under his pastoral care.

Establishment of Mudalūr.

In a subsequent visit some converts belonging to the same class were baptized at a place called Shaṇmukhapuram, near the place now called Kaḍātchapuram. These were the first Shanars baptized. The Vijayarāmapuram people were also baptized during the same year. Two years afterwards the first Christian village was founded in connection with the Tinnevelly Mission. The new Christians in Vijayarāmapuram found themselves exposed to many annoyances from their non-Christian neighbours. Their little prayer-house was twice pulled down, and they were obliged to assemble for worship under the shade of a tree. At length they determined to abandon the village where they had been so unkindly treated. A piece of land was purchased for them by David a few miles off, near the village of Aḍaiyal, where a well was dug and a little church erected, chiefly through the help obtained from a Captain Everett in Palamcotta. The land was purchased in August 1799 in Mr. Jaenicke's name. As this little settlement was the first place in Tinnevelly which could be called a Christian village, it received the name of Mudalūr, "first-town." The population of the village at the commencement of the century amounted to only twenty-eight souls. It now contains upwards of 1,200. These interesting facts about the commencement of the movement towards Christianity amongst the Shanars in Tinnevelly and the founding of Mudalūr had well nigh passed into oblivion. I discovered them in Tanjore in a bundle of Tamil letters that had been addressed by Satyanāthan and others to Jaenicke. He had been regularly informed by Satyanāthan of every thing that occurred, and the answers to his queries with which Satyanāthan's letters are filled show that, though absent in body, he was present in spirit. He was permitted to see this new field of labour from a distance only, nad though it was then but a day of small things, he must have rejoiced to see this confirmation of the opinion he was led to form on first commencing his labours in the south, that of all the districts with which he was acquainted, Tinnevelly was that in which Christianity was most likely to prevail.

Hough.

The revival of Jaenicke's Mission, after years of neglect, by the arrival of missionaries of the Society for the Propagation of the Gospel, and the establishment of the missions of the Church Missionary Society in Tinnevelly, were mainly owing to the representations and efforts of the Rev. J. Hough, Chaplain at Palamcotta from 1816 to 1820; but this portion of history falls far behind the date of the cession of the province to the English in 1801, the date at which these annals cease.

Additional information on this subject will be found in the author's "Records of the Early History of the Tinnevelly Mission."

APPENDICES.

APPENDICES.

APPENDIX I.

RELATIONS BETWEEN TRAVANCORE AND TINNEVELLY.

APPENDIX I.

Alternations of Government in the southern districts.

ADJACENT districts, like Tinnevelly and Travancore, must necessarily have stood at different times in different relations to one another. Generally, however, those relations seem to have been peaceable. During the early Pāṇḍya and Chōla period the southern Tamil-speaking district of Travancore, called Nānji-nāḍu, together with Purattāya-nāḍu, the district in which Cape Comorin is included, appear to have belonged to the Pāṇḍya kingdom. At a later period, during the decay of the Pāṇḍyas, this state of things was reversed and the southern portion of Tinnevelly seems to have been included in what is now called the kingdom of Travancore, but which was then generally called in Tinnevelly merely Kuḍa-nāḍu, the western kingdom, a synonym for Malayāḷam in general. Each of these changes rests on the evidence of inscriptions, but in neither case is there any trace or tradition of the change having been effected by force of arms. The weaker side for the time being seems to have quietly given place to the stronger.

I have mentioned already from time to time such particulars, illustrative of the relation subsisting between Tinnevelly and Travancore, as seemed to be necessary for the comprehension of Tinnevelly history, but I here subjoin the notices I find in P. Shangoonny Menon's *History of Travancore*, in which events are narrated from a more distinctively Travancorian point of view. In a few cases I may seem to go over the same ground, but it will be found that the Travancore accounts are fuller and more numerous.

Travancore Possessions in Tinnevelly in the 15th and 16th Centuries proved by Inscriptions.

"1. An inscription on the inner stone wall of the (Shermadevy) Chera Mahā-Devi Pagoda, dated Malayalam or Kollum year 614 (1439 A.D.), commemorating a grant by the Travancore king Chera Oodiah Marthanda Vurmah to the pagoda at that place while the grantor was residing in the Chera Mahā-Devi Palace.

"2. $\frac{\text{644 M.E.}}{\text{1469 A.D.}}$ On the large bell at Thrikanankudy (Tirukurunguḍi), denoting that the bell was presented by the Travancore king Adithiya Vurmah.

Inscriptions in Tinnevelly.

"3. $\frac{\text{685 M.E.}}{\text{1510 A.D.}}$ Commemorating a grant to the pagoda by king Marthanda Vurmah while residing in the Veera Pandyan Palace at Kalacaud.

APPENDIX I.

"4. $\frac{\text{688 M.E.}}{\text{1513 A.D.}}$ Commemorating a grant of land to the pagoda at Mannarkovil by the same king Marthanda Vurmah, and also making provisions for lighting a lamp in the palace where the king's uncle died.

"5. $\frac{\text{707 M.E.}}{\text{1532 A.D.}}$ Commemorating a grant of land to the pagoda of Chera-Chola Pandyēswaram in Thrikaloor near Alwar Tinnevelly, by Marthanda Vurmah, Rajah of Travancore."—Shangoonny Menon's *History of Travancore*, pp. 34, 35.

The Mannārkōvil mentioned in the fourth inscription is a village in the Ambāsamudram Taluk.

Shermadevy.

Shermadevy is properly Chēran-Mahā-dēvi, that is, (the temple of) the Mahā-dēvī, that is, Pārvati, worshipped by the Chēran, the king of the Western or Malayalam State. It is stated by the Travancore historian that the king of Chera occasionally resided there.

"In Chera-Maha-Devi, Thencasi, Kalacaud, Thrikanankudy, Valliyoor, &c., the Travancore Rajahs resided up to the seventeenth century, a fact clearly proved by documents and inscriptions."—p. 34.

Referring to the reign of Chēra Udaya Mārtāṇḍa Varmā, who reigned, it is said, for 62 years, from 1382 to 1444, the historian says :—

"During the reign of this sovereign all the south-eastern possessions of Travancore on the Tinnevelly side were regained, and the sovereign often resided at Valliyoor and Chēran-Mahā-Dēvī.

Gains and losses.

"In consequence of the mild and unwarlike disposition of this king, some of the subordinate chiefs in the east became refractory, and there was constant fighting, and latterly, while this sovereign was residing at Trevandrum, the chief of Rettiapuram invaded Valliyoor, and the king's nephew being defeated in battle, fearing disgrace, committed suicide.

"In these places, several grants of land made by this Kulasekhara Perumal remain, some of which we have already noticed. Chēra-Mahā-Dēvi was his favourite residence, and consequently, this sovereign was called Chera Udaya Marthanda Vurmah.

"Towards the close of his reign, suspecting unfair proceedings on the part of the chief men of the Pandyan State, the residence of the Royal family was removed to Elayadathunaud Hottarakaray ; and a Governor was appointed to rule Valliyoor and other possessions in the east.

"This sovereign died in 619 M.E. (1444 A.D.), at the ripe age of seventy-eight years."—p. 95.

Travancore annals when historical.

From the commencement of the 18th century the Travancore annals become historical. Prior to that time they are evidently more or less legendary.

The author admits that "from 1458 to 1680, a period of about two and a quarter centuries, no detailed accounts of the reigns of the sovereigns can be found, except a list of their names, the dates of their accession to the musnud, and the period of their reign."

Appeal for help to the Nāyakas of Madura, whose headquarters were at that time in Trichinopoly.

APPENDIX I.

"His Highness was a close observer of the difficulties and dangers to which his nephew was subjected by the Ettu Veetil Pillamar and Madempimar, and he was determined to punish them for their disloyalty and rebellious conduct.

Appeal to Trichinopoly for help.

"His Highness, in consultation with his intelligent nephew, proceeded in 901 M.E (1726 A.D.) to Trichinopoly with some of the officers of the State. He entered into a treaty with the Madura Government and secured its support by offering to renew the lapsed attachment to that crown, and to bind himself to pay a certain sum of money annually. At the same time, a suitable force was applied for to punish and bring to their senses the Madempimar and other refractory chiefs. After some discussion and preliminary enquiries, the sovereign was successful in obtaining a force consisting of one thousand cavalry, under the command of M. Vencatapathy Naiken, and two thousand Carnatic sepoys, headed by Thripathy Naiken, and others, in charge of fifty sirdars, including Raghava Iyen and Subba Iyen, &c.

"On the arrival of this force in Travancore, all the Madempimar and other refractory chiefs and insurgents fled, and consequently there was no work for the army, which was however retained for the purpose of overawing the insurgents."—History, p. 109.

"The late Rama Vurmah Rajah was compelled in 901 M.E. to proceed to the Pandyan (Nayaka) capital (Trichinopoly), and to enter into an agreement with the Pandyan Government, by which he promised to pay an annual tribute of about 3,000 rupees and obtained from the Governor a force of 1,000 horse and 2,000 foot, for the purpose of overawing the turbulent chiefs and nobles.

Trichinopoly Contingent.

"The pay of this contingent, as well as the annual tribute, was in arrears for a few months, when the Maha Rajah ascended the throne, and on the demand of the troops for their pay and the tribute, His Highness referred them to his Dalawah, Arumugam Pillay, who, on delaying payment, was seized and removed to Thrikanamkudy by the force, whereupon he borrowed money from the Kottar merchants and others, and adjusted most part of the pressing demands. The Dalawah was however still detained by the force at Thrikanamkudy.[1]

"In the meanwhile His Highness commissioned Cumaraswamy Pillay, the Commander-in-Chief, and Thanu Pillay, his assistant, to raise an army of Maravers and a few hundred horse, to raise up barriers in the shape of mud walls between Kadakaray and Mantharamputhur Aramboly, and Cape Comorin; to construct special gates for passages, and to guard them by companies of Maravers and troopers. These arrangements were effectually carried out in the course of a few months, and Travancore was secured against the attacks of foreign invaders.

Maravar troops.

"Cumaraswamy Pillay, with a force of Maravers, was then ordered by the Maha Rajah to proceed to Thrikanamkudy for the purpose of releasing the Dalawah, and that brave officer executed the command

[1] Tirukurungudi, a town in the south of Tinnevelly.

APPENDIX I. with promptness and vigour. The Maha Rajah was extremely pleased with him, as he had by this exploit extricated the Dalawah from a painfully embarrassing position, and removed the burden of care and anxiety that weighed upon his head.

"The Maha Rajah then thought that he could safely do away with the Trichinopoly force and ordered it to march back to that town. His Highness communicated his resolution to the Pandyan Government, and requested the Governor to release His Highness from the conditions entered into with the former by the late Maha Rajah.

A rival embassy to Trichinopoly.

"The feudatory chiefs and nobles, after the withdrawal of the Trichinopoly contingent force, began to rebel again, and as they had always been striving to get their independence, they combined and formed a confederacy as before, and were joined by the two sons of the late sovereign, known by the names of Kunju Thambies *alias* Papu Thamby and Ramen Thamby, who held high rank among the nobles during the lifetime of their father and were in affluent circumstances. But they were now reduced to the level of the ordinary nobles of the country and they felt their degradation keenly. The confederates sympathised with them, and considering them proper instruments for overthrowing the royal authority, they persuaded them to claim their father's throne; and one of them (Papu Thamby) being furnished with sufficient means, proceeded to Trichinopoly in 905 M.E. (1730 A.D.), and represented to the Pandyan Governor his imaginary grievances, saying that great injustice was done to him by the kingdom being forcibly usurped by Marthanda Vurmah. He entered into certain terms with that chief to put him in possession of the kingdom. The Governor, annoyed by the refusal of payment of the peishkush and the dismissal of the contingent forces by Marthanda Vurmah Maha Rajah, readily listened to Papu Thamby's false representations.

"The Governor ordered one of his agents Alagappa Moodelliar to proceed with a sufficient number of men and horses to Travancore, and institute enquiries into the claims of Papu Thamby, giving him authority to enforce the same if found valid.

"The Moodelliar set out from Trichinopoly, accompanied by Papu Thamby and arrived at Udayagherry, where he commenced to institute the enquiry into the claims of the Thamby. The Maha Rajah, on learning this, deputed the State Secretary Rama Iyen and his assistant Narayana Iyen to the Moodelliar, and they were furnished with valid documents to prove the absurdity and fictitious character of Papu Thamby's claims.

"While Papu Thamby was utterly unable to produce any documentary evidence in support of his pretended rights, Rama Iyen fully proved the claims of the Maha Rajah to his uncle's throne. The Moodelliar was very indignant with Papu Thamby, and his false complaint was at once rejected. He was told that he should be loyal and obedient to his king in accordance with the customs of the country.

"The Maha Rajah informed the Moodelliar of the renewed outbreak of a rebellious spirit among his chiefs, and asked him to place one half of his force at His Highness' disposal. The Moodelliar complied with this request and returned to Trichinopoly loaded with presents.

"Though the Maha Rajah was enraged with the conduct of the Kunju Thambies and the chiefs and nobles, yet His Highness pretended to be indifferent about the matter. As His Highness had the strong support of the Trichinopoly force, besides his own Maraver troops, he directed his attention to certain important affairs of government in which he was engaged before the peace of his kingdom was menaced by the plots of his enemies."—*History of Travancore*, pp. 115–118. APPENDIX I.

Help obtained from Tinnevelly Maravas.

Aid from Tinnevelly Poligars.

"Notwithstanding the death of the Rajah, the spirit of the Kayemkulam army was not thoroughly broken, for the fallen Rajah's younger brother succeeded, and he being more obstinate and courageous than his late brother, the war was continued with redoubled vigour. The Maha Rajah repaired to Quilon, accompanied by the heir apparent, who infused fresh courage into the Travancore army. A special body of recruits was raised for the war with Kayemkulam. Secretary Rama Iyen, finding that the army in the field could not successfully withstand the Kayemkulam force without sufficient reinforcement, proceeded to Tinnevelly, brought a regiment of Maravers under the command of Ponnam Pandya Deven, procured a thousand mounted sepoys from some of the Palayapattucar (Poligars), and marched the reinforcement by the hill roads through Kottarakaray. After holding a consultation among the officers, including the Dalaway and the Sthanapathy, Rama Iyen assumed the chief command of the army. In the battle the next day he distinguished himself with signal success, and the Kayemkulam force met with a defeat for the first time. But the war continued, and Rama Iyen's army began to gain ground slowly and to advance into the Kayemkulam territories day by day."

Annexations in Tinnevelly.

"In 909 M.E. (1734 A.D.) the Maha Rajah annexed Elayada Swaroopam, embracing Shencottah, Clangaud, Kerkudi, Valliyoor, on the Tinnevelly side, and Kottarakaray, Pathanapuram, &c., on the northern limits of Travancore. The Rajah Veera Kerala Vurmah, who was in charge of those territories, was a relative of Travancore and died leaving as his successor a princess. The administration of the State was conducted by a Sarvadhikariakar, a very unscrupulous person, and anarchy began to prevail in the province. The Maha Rajah called the minister to Trevandrum and pointed out to him various instances of mal-administration and banished him from the country in disgrace. A proper and fit man was appointed to the responsible post of Sarvadhikariakar to the State, and the Maha Rajah took the government of the principality into his own hands, advising the Ranee to come and reside at Trevandrum, or to remain at Kottarakaray in her own palace as she pleased. The Ranee preferred the latter course."—p. 129.

APPENDIX I.

Irruption of Chunda Sahib and Bada Sahib.

"About this time, a strong party of marauders, headed by Chunda Sahib and Bada Sahib, relatives of Dost Ali Khan, the Nabob of Arcot, who were permitted to wander about for the purpose of securing a principality for the Nabob's son, and also to plunder for themselves in the dominions of the native princes, entered the territories of Travancore by the Aramboly gate. They took possession of Nagercoil, Sucheendrum, and the rich town of Kottar: they plundered the shrine at Sucheendrum; burnt the great car; mutilated many of the images of the pagoda; and perpetrated many other deeds of atrocity and devastation, the favourite process generally adopted by the Mussulman chiefs.

Invasion of Chunda Sahib.

"Rama Iyen Dalawah was ordered to march an army and drive the marauders out of Travancore, but on meeting them he found them powerful in horse, and his own force no match for the Mussulmans. However, the Dalawah challenged them and commenced a battle, but his exertions were not attended with his usual success. But the Dalawah had reason to know that the object of the party was principally to secure pecuniary gain, and consequently they were made to retreat without offering resistance to his army."—p. 138.

The enemy bought off.

Collision with the Nawab.

"During the continuance of war in North Travancore, several changes took place in the government of the Pandyan provinces, including Madura, Trichinopoly, &c., and the sovereignty finally fell into the hands of the Nabob of the Carnatic. The Maha Rajah's attention having been directed, for a long time past, to the management of the internal affairs of his kingdom and the suppression of the rebellion in the north, he had neglected adopting measures for the protection and maintenance of his eastern possessions, including Valliyoor, Kalacaud, &c. The Nabob's Governor at Trichinopoly took advantage of this opportunity and annexed those tracts to the Madura province, and thus the Maha Rajah was deprived of those places for a long time.

Possessions in Tinnevelly lost.

"In 927 M.E. (1752 A.D.) Moodemiah, the Nabob's Viceroy at Trichinopoly, growing powerful, established himself as an independent chief, and being a very covetous man, disposed of villages and territories on receiving sufficient consideration for them. The Maha Rajah, understanding this disposition of Moodemiah, deputed Rama Iyen Dalawah to Tinnevelly, where Moodemiah had arrived on a visit. The Dalawah represented the Maha Rajah's ancient claims to the territories in the east. Possession of the country lying between Cape Comorin and Kalacaud, to the extent of about 30 miles, including Valliyoor, was obtained for a sufficiently large consideration. Rama Iyen Dalawah returned to Trevandrum after stationing about 2,000 of the Travancore Maha Rajah's force at Kalacaud, for the protection of the districts thus purchased by Travancore.

Negotiations.

"In 930 M.E. (1755 A.D.) Mahomed Ali, the Nabob of the Carnatic, wished to supplant Moodemiah, who had proved refractory and had

APPENDIX I.

proclaimed himself the sole ruler of the Pandyan empire. The Nabob appointed his General, Maphuz Khan, to supersede Moodemiah, and sent him with a small force requesting the Nabob's allies, the English at Madras, to send a detachment to assist the Khan, not only in assuming his office, but also in bringing the inhabitants into subjection. Colonel Heron, with 500 Europeans and 2,000 Natives, was ordered to Trichinopoly under the pretext of assisting Maphuz Khan, but probably the English too had an eye on the beautiful and highly productive Pandyan empire, comprising the rich countries of Madura, Trichinopoly and Tinnevelly. The allied forces arrived at Tinnevelly Kumbham 930 M.E. (March 1755 A.D.) after having reduced Madura on their way. When this intelligence reached Kalacaud the Travancore garrison, consisting of 2,000 sepoys stationed in that fort, was alarmed and finding that they were no match for the combined forces of the Nabob and the English, the Travancore commandant abandoned the fort and Kalacaud, and withdrew the garrison to Thovalay. In Meenam-madom (April) Maphuz Khan, after taking charge of the fort and establishing his authority there, went to Tinnevelly and Colonel Heron returned with the English force to Trichinopoly.

Travancorians retreat from Kaḷakāḍu.

"Moodemiah, who fled from Tinnevelly after his defeat, found an asylum under the protection of Pulithaver, a Poligar, and on the departure of the English troops from Tinnevelly to Trichinopoly, he applied to the Maha Rajah for assistance and urged on him to take back the lost territory of Kalacaud. Pulithaver also offered his resistance, as that Poligar was for a long time dependent on Travancore. A strong force, consisting of 2,000 infantry and an equal number of cavalry, was despatched from Travancore, accompanied by the prince and Moodemiah, and without much resistance Kalacaud was taken. The Maha Rajah, however, thinking that such a proceeding would offend the English Government, ordered the withdrawal of his troops for some time, and postponed all operations till he made himself sure that the retaking of his usurped territories would not offend the English. The Maha Rajah subsequently ordered back a sufficient force, under the command of Captain D'Lanoy assisted by the Poligar Pulithaver. Maphuz Khan's troops were defeated, the Kalacaud fort captured, and the 500 infantry and 200 cavalry, who defended it, were taken prisoners. Thus the Maha Rajah once more recovered Kalacaud and all the territories appertaining to it. The Travancore kingdom now extended from Periar in the north to Kalacaud in the south."—p. 162.

Kaḷakāḍu regained.

Treaty with the Nawab.

"It has been already said that during the reign of the former Rajahs, Travancore had made an agreement with the Governor of the Pandyan empire at Trichinopoly, promising to pay a nominal annual tribute for obtaining military aid, but subsequently, the Nabob of the Carnatic having taken the direct government of that empire, the Maha Rajah considered it wise and prudent to renew this treaty directly with the Nabob, which was accordingly done upon more

APPENDIX I.

Subsidy to the Nawab.

favourable terms and conditions. By this treaty the powerful aid of one of the greatest potentates of Southern India was secured to Travancore, which was bound to pay to the Nabob 6,000 rupees, and a tribute in the shape of an elephant annually, the Nabob promising to afford every protection to Travancore from foreign and local enemies. Thus Travancore became perfectly secure, having two powerful allies to guard and protect her, the Nabob in the east and the Dutch in the west, while the English merchants at Anjengo were also ready to assist her when needed."—p. 172.

Maphuz Khan and Yūsuf Khan.

"Maphuz Khan Sahib, the Governor of the Pandyan empire, under the Carnatic Nabob, who was stationed at Trichinopoly, rebelled against his master and made a descent on Kalacaud, the eastern possession of the Maha Rajah, at the western frontier of Tinnevelly. He attacked the Travancore garrison stationed there and drove them into the Aramboly lines, following them up with the Khan's forces. The Maha Rajah hearing this ordered one of his native commandants named Thamby Kumaren Chempaka Ramen Pillay, who was then stationed at Trevandrum, to march with his force to meet the invading army. He started at once and the battle which took place when this worthy warrior met the enemy was so severe and decisive, that the Mahomedan chief was obliged to beat a retreat from the Aramboly lines; but the Khan not only retained possession of Kalacaud, but assumed possession of the district of Shencottah and all the other eastern districts belonging to Travancore.

Battles with the Muhammadans.

"The Maha Rajah represented this matter to the Nabob, who was already so seriously displeased with the Khan, on account of his disobedient and refractory conduct, that he had it in contemplation to appoint a new Governor in the room of Maphuz Khan. A very able man named Yusuff Khan was appointed and sent as successor to the rebellious Maphuz Khan.

"Yusuff Khan on coming to Trichinopoly found it difficult to subdue the refractory Governor and sought the Maha Rajah's assistance. The Carnatic Nabob and the English East India Company at Madras requested His Highness at the same time to co-operate with Yusuff Khan in the subjection of the refractory Khan, and the Maha Rajah gladly acceded to their wishes.

Yusuf Khan's army.

"Five thousand men, under the command of Thamby Kumaren Chempaka Ramen, then stationed at Thovalay, were ordered to join Yusuff, and 10,000 men from Quilon were sent through the Ariencavu Pass to Shencottah. Yusuff was now at the head of a powerful army consisting of 20,000 men, which enabled him to drive away the Poligar of Wadakaray, and subsequently Maphuz Khan fled from the position he hitherto held and Yusuff established his power.

"As a grateful acknowledgment of the readiness with which the Maha Rajah lent his assistance, Yusuff Khan restored all His Highness' eastern possessions, and Kalacaud again became a part of His Highness' dominions.

APPENDIX I.

"The Maha Rajah, however, did not retain possession of Kalacaud for any lengthened period; for His Highness lost this portion of his territories under very peculiar circumstances. Yusuff Khan, the Nabob's Governor, in his turn became disobedient to his master and began to endeavour to shake off the Nabob's authority and establish himself as an independent chief; to accomplish this object Yusuff secured aid from the French in India. Yusuf Khan's rebellion.

"In 937 M.E. (1762 A.D.) a joint force of the Nabob and the English was sent against Yusuff, and the Travancore Maha Rajah was also requested to co-operate with his army, which was to take possession of Madura and Tinnevelly and capture Yusuff Khan. The Khan had already applied to the Maha Rajah for assistance, offering all the territories west of the town of Tinnevelly, including Palamcottah, which had once belonged to Travancore, in return for the help His Highness would give him towards the retention of the Pandyan provinces under Yusuff's independent possession; but the wise Maha Rajah declared that whatever may be the prospect of gain before him by aiding Yusuff, His Highness would not go against his old ally the Nabob, and would not take arms against the English.

"The Maha Rajah sent a strong force to Trichinopoly to co-operate with the combined force against Yusuff, and that rebel, finding that resistance would be of no avail, gave himself up and was hanged by the Nabob's order in 1762 A.D.

"Yusuff Khan's successor thought it proper to assume possession of all the countries lying on the eastern side of the ghauts, as belonging to the Pandyan empire, and accordingly not only Kalacaud, but also Shencottah and all the other eastern possessions of Travancore were annexed to the Nabob's dominions.

"The Maha Rajah despatched a special messenger, Manik Lalla by name, to Madras, and represented the injustice of the Nabob's officers in unlawfully annexing territories belonging to Travancore, but the Mussulman potentate, intoxicated with his recent victories and the punishment awarded to Yusuff, would not listen to the representations of the Maha Rajah's agent, and His Highness was therefore under the necessity of seeking the mediation of the Governor of Madras, who, though he once confirmed the claims of the Maha Rajah to the districts of Kalacaud and other eastern possessions, now wavered in his opinion. After a good deal of discussion, the Nabob agreed to restore some of the Travancore territories, including Shencottah, Cape Comorin, &c. The Nawab seizes possession.

"The Mahamedan chief did not appear to be satisfied with the unlawful annexation of the Kalacaud District, which was the legitimate possession of Travancore from time immemorial, and was recently acquired by purchase from Moodemiah. That purchase was confirmed by two of his successors, the Nabob himself, and by the Honourable East India Company. The Nabob now pressed a demand for the few previous years' revenue on the Kalacaud District. The claim to Kalakadu.

"A settlement was effected by the intercession of the Governor of Madras, Mr. Robert Palk, who, after arranging matters with the Nabob, wrote to His Highness in 1765 A.D. in reply to a communica-

APPENDIX I.

tion from the latter, to the effect that the English Company had taken some steps in restraining the victorious Nabob from further hostilities, in putting a check to his demands, and also in advising him to conclude the treaty. For such services Travancore was reminded of the debt it owed to the Honorable East India Company, and the Governor hoped that the Company would be amply rewarded for their assistance.

"The sagacious Maha Rajah saw the desirability of adopting the Governor's suggestion and the necessity of entering into a treaty with the Nabob, against whom resistance was at that critical period almost impossible.

The claim to Kaḷakāḍu renounced.

"The principal conditions of the treaty with the Nabob were, that Travancore should renounce all claims to the Kalacaud District; that His Highness should increase the tribute to 15,000 rupees; that he should pay two lakhs of rupees in liquidation of some pretended demands on the Maha Rajah in connexion with the Kalacaud District; that he should never assist any of the Poligars against the Nabob; that the Maha Rajah should assist the Nabob with an army in his war against Madura and Tinnevelly; and that the Nabob should assist Travancore against all her enemies, foreign as well as internal."—p. 197.

Travancore Contingent sent to assist the British Forces.

"Intimation of the unwarrantable proceedings of Hyder Ali Khan was given by the Maha Rajah to the Governor of Madras, as also to the Bombay and Bengal Government, and a general war against Hyder resulted.

"The Maha Rajah was asked by the Government of the Honourable East India Company to co-operate with the Company's army, and His Highness most willingly consented to do so, entailing thereby great loss of money and life.

Travancore aid against HyderAli.

"The war was continued by the East India Company and the Maha Rajah assisted them to the extent that lay in his power. Travancore regiments of infantry and cavalry placed at the disposal of divisional commanders of the Company were taken to distant places, such as Calicut, Palghaut, Tinnevelly, &c., &c., and they were 'universally allowed to have behaved remarkably well.'

"After strongly fortifying the northern and eastern frontiers of Travancore, the Maha Rajah sent a portion of his army under able officers to the north, to co-operate with the Bombay army, under Major Abington at Calicut. His Highness' troops were engaged in the war and were successful in their united actions. Another portion of the Travancore army which was despatched to co-operate with the British army in Tinnevelly against Hyder was stationed at that town for a period of two years."—p. 205.

Journey of the Mahā Rajāh through Tinnevelly, &c., to Rāmēsvaram.

"In the year 959 M.E. (1784 A.D.) His Highness the Maha Rajah, partly to perform a religious ceremony and partly to satisfy his curiosity to see some other parts of the country in the east and south of Travancore, proposed making a pilgrimage to Ramaswaram and seeing the districts of Tinnevelly and Madura on his way to and from that renowned resort of Hindu pilgrims.

" But before starting from Trevandrum on this pilgrimage, His Highness had to take the precaution of effecting some arrangements through the means of His Highness' allies, the English East India Company and the Nabob of the Carnatic. The districts through which His Highness had to travel to Ramaswaram, viz., Tinnevelly and Madura, though subject to the sovereignty of the Nabob, were divided and were in the possession of Palayapattacars (Poligars), the majority of whom were rude and lawless chieftains.

Dangers from Poligārs.

" His Highness obtained the assistance of a few companies of sepoys of the English East India Company and some responsible officers from the Nabob's Government to escort him to Ramaswaram. With these and a large portion of His Highness' own army and a number of followers, he set out with all the pomp and grandeur usually attending the movements of Indian sovereigns of the rank and celebrity of the Maha Rajah.

Examination of public works.

" His Highness took great care to inspect and examine all the important irrigation works, roads and bridges, sathrums or choultries built for the comfort and convenience of the public in Tinnevelly and Madura, this being the chief object for which he undertook the tour.

" His Highness reached Ramaswaram in good health and performed the ablutions and other ceremonies there : and after spending a large sum in ceremonies and charities, returned, taking care to visit every place of note, to his own capital (Trevandrum), quite delighted with all he saw during a very agreeable journey.

" His Highness lost no time in turning to account the knowledge of irrigation works, &c., he had acquired during the tour, and introduced improvements in several works of this description in the southern districts comprising Nanjenaud, &c."

Major Bannerman, the first Representative of the British Government in Travancore, in 1788 *and* 1789.

Tippu's proposals.

" The Maha Rajah, with his usual prudence and faithful attachment to his allies the English, resolved to see no messenger of the Sultan or receive any communication from him, except in the presence of a British officer. His Highness wrote to the Governor of Madras, Sir Archibald Campbell, to depute an officer of integrity and ability to the Maha Rajah's court, with whom His Highness might consult on some important points connected with the Sultan's mission. The Governor was quite delighted with the Maha Rajah's prudence and wisdom and ordered Major Bannerman, then stationed at Palamcottah, to proceed to the Maha Rajah's court with a small detachment under his command."— p. 214.

The first British Resident in Travancore.

" According to the agreement, two regiments commanded by Captain Knox were stationed near Aycottah in the northern frontier

APPENDIX I. of Travancore in the year 964 M.E. (1788 A.D.). At the same time, as a medium for communicating between the Maha Rajah and the Madras Government, Mr. George Powney, a civil officer under the English East India Company, was also stationed in Travancore. He may be reckoned as the first Political Resident and British representative in the Maha Rajah's Court."—p. 219.

Mr. Powney was Collector of Tinnevelly from 1794. The celebrated Colonel Macaulay was Resident of Travancore from 1800.

New treaty signed in 1805.

In 1805 a force was suddenly collected in Tinnevelly under General MacDowel for the purpose of compelling the Rajah to sign a new treaty with the British Government. The Rajah at length consented to sign the treaty and the force was countermanded.—*See* pp. 310–323.

INSURRECTION IN TRAVANCORE; ATTACK ON THE RESIDENT; TAKING OF THE TRAVANCORE LINES IN 1809.

The commotions in Travancore out of which the war arose commenced in 1808. The management of affairs in Travancore had been for some time in an unsatisfactory state, whereupon the British Resident interfered. The Dewan was irritated and dragged his master into hostility to the English. He intrigued with the Dewan of Cochin and with the French. A vessel with thirty-one privates and a surgeon belonging to the 12th Regiment put into Allippie. The men were decoyed on shore, tied in couples back to back, and with stones tied round their necks were thrown into the backwater. This massacre was perpetrated by the Dewan's brother. The Resident's house at Cochin was attacked and he escaped with difficulty. Sir G. Barlow was then Governor of Madras and took prompt measures to suppress the rebellion and restore the authority of the English Government. A considerable force was sent to enforce obedience, and the forces of the Travancore State were assembled for the purpose of preventing their entrance into the country. The rebellion was disowned by the Raja of Travancore of that time, Rāma Varmā, who attributed the whole blame to his ministers, but the forces of the State were set in motion in resistance to the authority of the English as completely as if the Raja himself had been the leader of the rebellion.

I here quote the information given us in Shungoony Menon's *History of Travancore*:—

Causes of the outbreak.

"Paliathu Menon deputed a private messenger to Quilon, with a secret despatch to Valu Thamby Dalawah and the leaders of the disaffected military, proposing to them the massacre of the British Resident and his small garrison in the fort at Cochin, and offering his co-operation in the affair.

"These officials were delighted at such a desirable proposal from the Cochin minister, and Valu Thamby, from his own vanity, thoughtlessness, and desire of revenge, agreed to the proposal, and a programme was arranged between the two ministers. A short account of this has been thus recorded by Lieutenant, now Colonel, Horsley: 'We are unable to trace the successive steps that led to the war, or more properly the insurrection, which took place in 1808; but it is perhaps to be attributed less to the people in general, who had everything to lose from any change which should extinguish British influence, than to the Rajah and to his principal native servants, provoked as they were at a control that threatened to moderate their excesses. The Cochin minister seems to have been implicated in those transactions. The character of this personage and the cautious manner in which he conducted these measures, countenance suspicion, that he was one of the most zealous and artful promoters of the troubles that ensued.'

The Dewan seeks allies.

"The Dewan now determined to resort to hostilities, though in a covert way. He issued secret orders for the recruiting of Nairs and people of other castes and the strengthening of fortifications and the storing of ammunition. He wrote to the Isle of France and the Zamorin of Calicut for aid, and warlike preparations were made by the Cochin minister Paliathu Menon.

"The Resident little knew of these internal arrangements. He continued, as usual, to press the Dewan and the Maha Rajah for the payment of arrears. The Madras Government continued their demand upon the Maha Rajah for immediate payment.

Plot to assassinate the Resident.

"The Dewan had by this time formed the resolution of assassinating the Resident. But he still feigned that he was using all his endeavours to cause the early payment of arrears, and on the Resident's demanding either the liquidation of the amount or a change in the ministry, the Dewan pretended that he was on the point of retiring, and wrote to Colonel Macaulay that he would start for Calicut and take up his residence there on a pension, and asked him for a party of British troops to escort him thither, his object being to draw the best part of the Resident's escort from Cochin to Alleppey, where the Dewan was then located.

"Valu Thamby issued orders to the garrison at Alleppey and Paravoor and sent a detachment from Quilon preparatory to making a sudden descent upon the fort at Cochin for the massacre of the Resident together with Cunju Krishna Menon, arranging at the same time for the attack on the British garrison at Quilon, which was stationed there under the command of Colonel Chalmers.

Failure of attack on the Resident.

"The detachment moved from Quilon and Alleppey in covered boats, accompanied by Vycome Padmanabha Pillay, an intimate friend of the Dewan, who acted as his chief secretary, and the troops collected in the northern districts under the command of Cunju Cuty Pillay Sarvadhikariakar, stationed at Alangaud, also moved in covered boats to Cochin, and both the forces effected a junction at Calvathi, at about midnight on the 28th December. They surrounded Colonel Macaulay's house and opened fire. The sudden report of musketry at an unusual hour surprised Colonel Macaulay, and with the assistance of a confidential Portuguese clerk he managed to conceal himself, and in the morning got on board a pattimar at first, and subsequently on board the British ship "Piedmontese," which had just reached the Cochin roads; Cunju Krishna Menon also effected his escape uninjured, and joined Colonel Macaulay on board the ship.

Appendix I.

"The Travancore sepoys overpowered the few British sepoys who formed the Resident's escort, killing many who resisted, and afterwards entered Colonel Macaulay's residence, ransacked the house, murdered the domestic servants and others whom they found in the house, and afterwards returned, considerably chagrined at not finding the Resident and Cunju Krishna Menon.

"The disappointment consequent on this attempt to murder Colonel Macaulay had cast a great gloom and dread among all the Travancore officials. Nevertheless, they prepared themselves for a defence against the attack which they expected every moment. They committed depredations in the town of Cochin, and returned to Travancore the next day. Valu Thamby foresaw the result and quitted Alleppey at once and proceeded to Quilon.

"During this interval, three European military officers, including Surgeon Hume, together with a lady in one party, and twelve European soldiers of His Majesty's 12th Regiment, and thirty-three sepoys forming another party, were proceeding from Quilon to Cochin, and on coming near Poracaud, they were taken up by the military who had been scattered over those parts in large bodies, and who now began to exhibit a declared enmity towards the Company's people. In consultation with the ministerial officials stationed at Alleppey, all these were confined, the first party in the Poracaud bankshall, and the second at Alleppey. Subsequently the matter was reported to Valu Thamby Dalawah, with an application for his sanction for the immediate execution of those unfortunate and innocent men. The hard-hearted minister, who was a perfect stranger to mercy, sanctioned the wholesale murder of the helpless party without the least hesitation, and the unfortunate and unoffending men were all cruelly murdered there.[1] The three officers were butchered in cold blood at the sea-beach at Poracaud, and the European soldiers and sepoys were consigned to the bottom of the Pallathurthee river, on the eastern side of Alleppey. The lady was allowed to proceed to Cochin unhurt, it being contrary to the laws of Travancore to kill women, and she was besides in bad health, and many of the local officials pitied her weak and helpless condition.

Massacre of English officers and sepoys.

"The Resident lost no time in despatching a report to the Madras Government on the subject, and the following is an abstract of the report with which we were kindly furnished, together with a copy of the proclamation, issued under date the 15th January 1809, by the Government, by Mr. Ballard, the late British Resident in Travancore :—

The Resident's report to Government.

"'For some days past, I had been engaged in negotiation with the Dewan at his own earnest solicitation, and had concluded everything to his own entire satisfaction, and was waiting only his arrival from Alleppey to carry into execution the measure upon which he had

[1] "This information was given to us by one Ramalingum, Major Sobudar of M.N.I. Regiment VI, who accompanied these three unfortunate gentlemen and the sickly lady, and was present when they were murdered. He was then a dressing boy under Colonel Chalmers."—p. 337.

Appendix I.

resolved on removing to Calicut, and had at his earnest request weakened the party with me to provide for his security, and had at his suggestion placed my boats and palanquins in convenient places to take him on with comfort and expedition. When a little past midnight, a party of Nayrs to the number of about one thousand, headed by the Dewan's confidential friend Pulpnabha Pillay and by the Minister of the Rajah of Cochin, surrounded my house to prevent all escape, and commenced a smart fire of musketry at every opening, first disarming the guard and killing a few who attempted resistance, and then broke into the place to destroy me; their design was providentially and somewhat miraculously defeated, and after having broken open every place and package, pillaging the house of the whole of my effects, they withdrew at break of day. The chief inconvenience at present attending this proceeds from the loss of books of record and official papers, but as the Dewan has now broken out into open rebellion, and will be likely to assemble his followers on every side in the hope of producing an impression on the subsidiary force, I have sent to Colonel Cuppage a request to embark without delay for Quilon all force that he can spare.' There had been a simultaneous attack on the subsidiary force at Quilon on the morning of the 29th December 1808. The Dewan arrived at Quilon, and encouraged the Travancore force concentrated thereabouts, and then proceeded to Kundaray, east of Quilon, whence he issued a proclamation."—p. 335. See this proclamation in *History of Travancore*, p. 339.

"By the Dalawah's strongly worded and powerful proclamation, the whole populace of Travancore was incensed and disaffected, and a revolt against the British force stationed at Quilon took place at once. The cantonment was attacked by large bodies of militia, assisted by the Travancore regular troops stationed about Quilon, but they were repulsed as often as they attacked by the able Commandant Colonel Chalmers. The failure of the attempt to murder Colonel Macaulay had not totally disheartened the Sarvadhikariakar of Alangaud, as he appears to have entertained hopes of success again. About 2,000 men, consisting of regular infantry and militia and the rabble, were kept up in the vicinity of Cochin, and the town was visited by them now and then. The Cochin minister, Paliathu Menon, had also collected a force of about 2,000 men and kept them also in the neighbourhood to attack the town. The Judges and other Company's officers closed their offices and many of the inhabitants and merchants left Cochin for Calicut, and the fear of a combined rebellion in Travancore and Cochin against the English East India Company now became general. But the arrival of Lieutenant-Colonel Cuppage on the northern frontier, and of Major Hewitt's detachment at Cochin, with whom the Travancoreans had fought and failed, discouraged the northern Travancore force entirely, and they retreated to the south, thus leaving Cochin safe and secure in the hands of the Company.

Quilon troops attacked.

Reinforcement.

"At Quilon the action under Colonel Chalmers was decisive, for on the 18th January the Dewan's force was completely defeated during a contest which lasted six hours."

APPENDIX I. *The inhabitants of Tinnevelly warned by the Madras Government not to take part in the Rebellion.*

"The Madras Government published the following proclamation in Tinnevelly and Malabar, which completely quieted the population of those districts :—

"'PROCLAMATION.

"'The Honourable the Governor in Council of Fort St. George having been informed that the Dewan of Travancore has been endeavouring by artful intrigues to excite the inhabitants of Tinnevelly to rise in arms against the British Government, the Governor in Council thinks it proper to caution the inhabitants of Tinnevelly against listening to the delusive insinuations which the Dewan of Travancore has endeavoured to disseminate. The Governor in Council has no doubt that the inhabitants of that province will be sensible of their own interests and will continue to enjoy in tranquillity the advantages which they possess under the protection of the British Government.

"'Dated in Fort St. George, the 15th day of January 1809.'"

—Page 345.

Proclamation of the Madras Government to the inhabitants of Travancore.

"The Government published the following proclamation on the 17th January 1809 for the information of the people of Travancore :—

"'PROCLAMATION.

"'It is known to the inhabitants of Travancore that during many years the closest alliance has subsisted between the British Government and the Government of the Travancore country; that the British troops have long been employed in defence o Travancore, and that it was by the exertion of the British armies that Travancore was saved from subjection to the power of Tippoo Sultan.

"'Under these circumstances, the Honorable the Governor in Council of Fort St. George has heard with extreme surprise, that military preparations of great extent have lately taken place in Travancore for purposes hostile to the interests of the British Government; that the person of the British Resident has been attacked by the Travancore troops; and that an assault has been made on the subsidiary force stationed at Quilon.

A force to be sent to restore order.

"'The Honorable the Governor in Council has reason to believe that these unprecedented outrages have proceeded from the desperate intrigues of the Dewan of Travancore, who has been also endeavouring by injurious insinuation to excite rebellion in the territories of the Honourable Company. In order that the daring plans of the Dewan may be defeated, the Honorable the Governor in Council has directed a large body of troops to move into Travancore, who will, in a short time, put an end to the power of the Dewan, and to restore order and peace in the country of Travancore. The Honorable the Governor in Council thinks it proper at the same time to make known to the inhabitants of Travancore that the approach of the British troops need occasion no alarm in the minds of those inhabitants who conduct themselves peaceably. The British Government has no other view in directing the movements of troops than to rescue the Rajah of Travancore from the influence of the Dewan, to put an end to the power of that dangerous minister, and to re-establish the connection of the two Governments on a secure and happy foundation.

"'The Honourable the Governor in Council calls on the inhabitants of Travancore to co-operate in accomplishing these objects, and such of the inhabitants as shall not oppose the advance of the British troops may be assured of the entire protection of their persons and property ; particular orders will also be given to give no disturbance to the Brahmins and religious establishments throughout the Travancore country.

" 'Dated in Fort St. George, the 17th day of January 1809.

" 'Published by order of the Honourable Governor in Council.

(Signed) C. BUCHAN,
Chief Secretary to Government.' "

—Page 346.

"The Travancore minister and his colleagues, as well as the military officials, had not to wait long for their fate, for a British force, under the command of the Honorable Colonel St. Leger, arrived at the southern frontier of Travancore and commenced an attack on the Aramboly lines and forced an entrance into the forts on the 10th February 1809.

"Valu Thamby Dalawah, who was at that time near the Aramboly garrison to support the operations, found it impossible to resist the British soldiers, and therefore had escaped to Trevandrum hastily." —Page 347.

TAKING OF THE TRAVANCORE LINES.

General Welsh.

Our information with regard to the principal event of the war, the taking of the Travancore Lines, is derived mainly from General Welsh's *Military Reminiscences*. General (then Major) Welsh was the officer by whom the lines were stormed, and it will be remembered that it is to the same soldier and author that we are indebted for the fullest account of the last Poligar war.

Description of the lines.

The force, assembled for the purpose of asserting the authority of the English Government, was under the command of the Honorable Colonel St. Leger. When Major Welsh joined the force on the 5th February 1809 it was encamped six miles from Aramboly (properly Ārāvāy-moḻi) on the Tinnevelly side of the pass. The lines by which the entrance into Travancore through the pass was defended were about two miles in length, stretching across the gap from one range of mountains to another. They included a rugged hill to the southward, strongly fortified, and a strong rock about half way called the northern redoubt. The works consisted of small well-built bastions for two and three guns, joined at intervals by strong curtains, the whole cannon-proof and protected by a thick hedge of thorn bushes, the approach to which was difficult from the wildness of the country. Major Welsh proposed, and the Commanding Officer reluctantly consented, that an attempt should be made to take the lines by escalade ; and on the 10th of February this daring feat was accomplished. The southern fortified hill was escaladed during the night, and though defended by fifty pieces of cannon and ten thousand men the whole lines were in the possession of the English force by eight o'clock A.M. The approach was so difficult that it took six hours scrambling to reach the foot of the walls, but the troops had escaladed the southern redoubt before their approach was suspected. As soon as it was seen that Major Welsh had secured a footing in that commanding position a detachment was sent to his aid, whereupon he stormed and carried

Successful assault.

APPENDIX I.

the main lines, including the fortified gate. The northern redoubt was then abandoned, and the Travancore troops fled in all possible directions, leaving the English in possession of the whole of the lines, the arsenal, and the stores. Before evening the English force was encamped two miles inside the Aramboly gate.

March towards Trevandrum.

On the 17th the army commenced its march for Trevandrum, the Travancore capital. The only resistance they met with was on the morning of the same day at a village where they had to cross the Susendram river, on the further side of which a portion of the Travancore force was posted in a strong position on a high bank. The Travancoreans were routed and dispersed with much loss to them and some to our troops. Nine guns were taken and the large villages of Cotaur and Nagercoil fell into the hands of the English. This was the last action fought and the last blood shed in this brief war. The English marched steadily forward, taking possession in their way of the abandoned forts of Oodagherry and Palpanāvaram, but before they reached the capital an armistice was proclaimed. On the arrival of the troops at the capital it was found that within the Rājā's palace walls an arsenal had been provided containing 140 pieces of serviceable cannon, 14,000 stand of arms, and abundance of ammunition, all which the Rājā was obliged to deliver up to the English. The late Dewan, the author of the rebellion, was speedily traced to the interior of a pagoda with brazen doors, and while the troops were breaking open the doors he killed himself. His brothers and six accomplices were taken alive and hanged at Quilon in front of the 12th Regiment, in the murder of the men belonging to which they had participated. Colonel Macaulay, the Resident, had now landed from a vessel of war in which he had some time before made his escape from Cochin when the rebellion broke out. Immediately on his arrival at the capital a new Dewan was appointed and new arrangements made for securing the peace of the country. Whilst the British force was approaching from the eastward through the Travancore lines the subsidiary force at Quilon was by no means idle. Shut up in the heart of a difficult country, with the inhabitants all in arms against them, they had had several severe actions, in which they were invariably victorious. Nevertheless their situation was daily becoming more critical until the news of the capture of the Aramboly lines reached the masses by which they were surrounded, when, giving up every hope of further success, they dispersed in all directions.

Events at Trevandrum.

General Welsh states that those lines had up to that time been deemed impregnable, and that Tippu Sultan in the zenith of his power had been repulsed from them with considerable loss. He adds that it was natural therefore that the report of their capture should at once decide the fate of the kingdom. The capture of the Aramboly lines was a brave achievement and undoubtedly decided the fate of the kingdom, but the General was mistaken in supposing that these were the lines from which Tippu was repulsed. The lines he failed to take were those on the northern frontier between Travancore and Cochin. This event occurred long before in December 1789.

APPENDIX I.

The following particulars are from Shungoonny Menon's History :—

"The Colonel afterwards marched to Trevandrum, and on reaching the neighbourhood, encamped at a place called Pappenecode, when the Maha Rajah sent a deputation headed by His Highness' favourite Ummany Thamby *alias* Marthanden Eravy, who conveyed to the Colonel His Highness' extreme regret at the occurrence of the insurrection created by Dewan Valu Thamby, and of the adoption of measures for the Dewan's apprehension and delivery. Colonel Macaulay arrived in the camp on the 3rd March. Arrangements were made for the apprehension of the minister. A party of Travancore and British officers was despatched in pursuit of the Dalawah, and a reward of (50,000) fifty thousand rupees was offered for his apprehension.

Flight of the Dewan.

"Ummany Thamby, the head of the deputation, was appointed Dewan on the 18th March 1809 with the full concurrence of the British Government, and he at once sent persons in pursuit of the Dalawah. The runaway Dalawah wandered in the jungles about Vallicote in the Kunnathoor district. He was hotly pursued by the officers even here. From this place he came to Munnady, in the same district, and took refuge in a vacant house belonging to a Potty. The servant of Valu Thamby, who wandered in the streets there with his master's silver and gold utensils, was seen by the officers and apprehended, and he revealed to them the Thamby's hiding-place. He then fled to the Bhagavathi pagoda at Munnady with his brother Padmanabhen Thamby and determined to put an end to his existence. He asked his brother to stab him. This the brother refused to do at first, when the Dalawah plunged his own dagger in his bosom. But as the self-inflicted wound did not prove mortal, he cried out to his brother 'cut my neck,' which request the brother complied with, and in one stroke severed the neck from the body. By that time the pursuers reached the pagoda and forced open the door, when they found the lifeless body of Valu Thamby and his brother standing close to it with a drawn sword. The brother was seized and the body removed to Trevandrum, where it was exposed on a gibbet at Kunnammalay for public execration. Lord Minto, the then Governor-General, most strongly condemned this insult offered to the body of such a great man as Valu Thamby.

Death of the Dewan.

"The deceased Dalawah's brother Padmanabhen Thamby was hanged on the 10th of April, in the presence of the 12th Regiment at Quilon, on the supposition that he took part in the assassination of Surgeon Hume, and also in the most cruel and inhuman act of the drowning at Pullathurthee of a detachment of the 12th Regiment.

"Ummany Thamby Dewan was dreaded by the relatives of the late minister, and his house was razed to the ground and plantain and castor trees planted thereon.

Fate of the rest of the rebels.

"Most of the relatives were transported to the Maldives, but after going a certain distance stress of weather compelled them to touch at Tuticorin. Some appear to have committed suicide, some died in

APPENDIX I. prison, while the rest were flogged and banished. All these were done by Valu Thamby's successor Ummany Thamby.

"Several of the promoters of the insurrection, chief among whom was Vycome Padmanabha Pillay, the murderer of the Europeans at Poracaud, Alleppey, &c., were punished by being publicly hanged at Quilon, Poracaud and Pallathurthee, the spots where the Europeans were massacred."—p. 349.

Political Results.

Aitchison's Treaties.

The political and financial results of the rebellion appear in Aitchison's Treaties, Vol. V. The Rājā was obliged to pay the expenses incurred by the British Government in this expedition, and a brigade was left at Quilon as a subsidiary force, agreeably to the treaty concluded in November 1795. The debts thus incurred were but tardily discharged, and the British Government were about to assume the internal administration of the country as the only means of insuring their satisfactory settlement when the Rājā died in 1811. The Rājā was succeeded by Latchmi Rāṇi, who, according to the peculiar custom of the family of Travancore, assumed charge of the Government until a male heir was born. She held it till 1814, during which time the British Resident, Colonel Munro. acted also as Minister, and by his judicious measures completely relieved the condition of the country. Latchmi Rāṇi was succeeded by her eldest son, and the country was, during his minority, successfully managed by her sister as Regent, under the counsels of the British Resident.

Shenkōṭṭai.

I subjoin some particulars respecting Shenkotta.

On the cession of Tinnevelly to the British Government by the Nawab of the Carnatic in 1801 it was found that the Nawab claimed the district of Shenkōṭṭai, a portion of Travancore situated to the east of the ghauts, as one of his Zemindaries. It was asserted also that this claim was admitted by the Rajah of Travancore, who had regularly paid peshcush as Zemindar of Shenkōṭṭai to the Nawab's Government.

The Travancore authorities do not admit that Shenkōṭṭai was ever a Zemindary under the Nawab, and the following is Sir Madava Row's statement of the case in his manuscript history. Some of the facts have already been quoted from Shungoonny Menon:—

"Mahomed Yusuf Khan, generalissimo of the forces of the Nawab of the Carnatic, incurred his master's displeasure, in consequence of which by the assistance of the English he was captured and hanged. Travancore having befriended Yusuf Khan, though only as the general of Mahomed Ali, the Nawab in revenge annexed Kaḷakādu and Shenkotta again to the Carnatic.

"But an ambassador, Māṇika Bhaṭṭa, was sent to Madras to the Nawab, and with the assistance of the English succeeded in obtaining the restoration of Shenkotta, not however till Kaḷakāḍu was ceded and the Nawab, flushed with victory, exacted a tribute of 3,000 Vella fanams a year as a compensation to his Government for the restoration of Shenkotta. APPENDIX I.

"This continued to be paid to the Nawab till the Carnatic was ceded to the British. Thereafter the payment was made to them instead, and to this day it is incorporated with, and is a component part of, the subsidy of 8,00,000 rupees paid to the British Government."

It will be seen from the above statement that the only real discrepancy between the two representations relates to the use of one word, the word "Zemindar." Muhammad Yusuf Khan was executed in 1764, so that the relation described above as subsisting between Shenkōttai and the Nawab lasted for 37 years.

APPENDIX II.

ACCOUNT OF THE FLOODS AND PESTILENTIAL FEVER IN TINNEVELLY IN 1810–12.

THERE was a very severe flood in Tinnevelly on the 6th December 1810, "the like of which," Mr. Hepburn the Collector says, "has not occurred within the memory of man." The river bank was breached in many places, and most of the tanks and water channels were breached. 500 houses were carried away in the town of Alvar Tinnevelly. APPENDIX II.

In March 1811 the Collector reports that there had been another very heavy fall of rain for ten days in the end of February. This was a very unusual season for heavy rain and floods. He adds that this unusual rain has rendered the season unhealthy, particularly in the vicinity of the hills and along the sea-coast, where the mortality amongst the natives had been excessive.

On the 6th of April the Collector reports that rain had set in again in March and was continuing till the date of his letter. There was almost continuous rain for nearly three months, in February, March and April. The pestilential fever also had greatly increased and the mortality was frightful. In one village, that of Selvamarudūr, in the Calcaud Taluk (near Edeyengoody) visited by his assistant Mr. Hanbury, 50 houses were found entirely empty, and in every house in the village some had died. In other villages he found that a few of the inhabitants had fled and that all the rest were dead. A peon was sent to a village to make a demand for assessment and found the whole of the village officers and all the respectable inhabitants dead. In many places the grain rotted in the ground for want of hands to reap and gather it in.

Two causes for the fever had been suggested. One was that it arose from exhalations from the salt marshes near the sea, the smell arising from which was very dreadful. The other that it had travelled to Tinnevelly from Coimbatore, Dindigul and Madura, where it was said to have broken out first. The latter was the general opinion of the

APPENDIX II. natives. They said every individual amongst the pilgrims who went to Pulney and other sacred places in that region died on his return to his village. This origin of the fever was confirmed, they thought, by the circumstance that the fever was particularly fatal in the vicinity of the mountains.

A Medical Committee was convened to consider the condition of each of the districts affected by the pestilence. It assembled at Bhavaný 8th May 1811. All that they could do was to prescribe the use of such preventives and such remedies as would naturally suggest themselves. They could not make the pestilential air wholesome, and the natives generally would be found too poor and too much attached to custom to avail themselves of most of the recommendations. The Committee recommended that the natives should build better houses, that the floor of their houses should be raised above the ground, that they should sleep on cots, with mattresses of twisted straw and coverlets, that they should clothe themselves more warmly, that they should use a sort of sandal for the feet, that they should not go out in the morning till the heavy fogs had been dispelled by the sun, and that they should eat better food. Amongst the remedies they recommended the only febrifuge was the bark of the Nim or Margosa.

In Dindigul the number of persons who fell victims to the pestilence in the course of nine months was not less than 34,000. Another authority estimates the number at one in thirteen of the population, but the calculation seems hardly reliable, seeing that in some places half the population were said to have died. In Madura the worst of the epidemic was before May in 1811. The epidemic, however, broke out again with great violence in 1812, and in the town of Ramnad, during the three months between December 1812 and February 1813, one in six were reported to have died.

Letters from Mr. Hepburn, the Collector, to the Board of Revenue, in 1811.

"2. The epidemical disease which forms the subject of these letters first became of sufficient importance in the month of February to attract attention and to impede the usual regularity of the collections. At first it was, however, principally prevalent in the Streevilliputtūr District, which joins the taluks of Madura and lies near the hills, the course of which it followed to the southward, where it has since prevailed very universally. Soon afterwards it broke out in the vicinity of the sea-coast and committed great ravages in the Punjamahl and Calacaud Taluks. To enable the Board, however, the better to trace its progress, I have the honor to enclose a small sketch of the province with the different taluks marked out, which will make the subject more easily understood.

"3. When the Medical Committee which is ordered here shall have investigated the subject they will no doubt, with the aid of the science which they possess, be able to account satisfactorily for the mortality which has occurred; yet it is to be apprehended that the principal cause of it is to be looked for in the very uncommon circumstances of the season. The Board recollect the great destruction of houses reported in consequence of the inundation in December last, and the loss of huts was still greater. After that fall of rain the weather still continued hot and close, in the early part of the nights in particular, attended with very heavy dews towards morning. The heat of the early part of the night indeed caused many of the natives who had houses to sleep in the open air, by which they became exposed, while their bodies were still hot, to the chilling damps towards morning, which in all probability was the cause of the fever which succeeded, and of those whose houses had been destroyed many were obliged to do so from having no shelter to cover them. The rain soon after commenced and continued for three months, and generally the people were found totally unprovided against it; and to such as had no houses was added the misfortune of worse than ordinary food, as they often could not dry their grain to convert it into rice, having no place to preserve it in from the rain, in consequence of which they were deprived of almost every comfort they are in the habit of enjoying. That these causes operated in a considerable degree appears from the mortality having been much greater amongst the lower classes of people, particularly toddy-drawers, who live in temporary cabins made of cadjan only, most of which were destroyed in the monsoon, than amongst the better description of the inhabitants who live in good houses.

"4. Whether in addition to these causes the disease was infectious and imported from Madura and Dindigul it is impossible for me to say. The natives have a strong impression that it was, which certainly seems in some degree confirmed by the mortality amongst the pilgrims who have returned from Pulney in the Dindigul District; but to decide the question requires the exercise of a professional knowledge, which can only be expected from the report of the Medical Committee upon the subject. At first the disease was very rapidly fatal. The patient was seized with it on one day, had often a sort of fit or convulsion the second day, and generally died on the third. If he survived the ninth day he generally got over it, but was left in a state of great debility from the fever, which lasted from a fortnight to a month afterwards. At first the return of the fever was diurnal, but afterwards it only recurred once every other day, and in the cases where it proved fatal was often attended with a bloody flux. Such is the account which I have been able to obtain of this awful visitation, and whether the opinions formed are correct or not will hereafter be seen from the report of the medical men soon expected here. I can however say with great truth that they have been stimulated by the greatest interest and anxiety in the subject and that they have occupied my best attention.

"5. Within these last ten days the land winds have set in, which hold out the most anxious hope that the change of weather will produce an alleviation of the disease; as yet it is still however represented to be very prevalent, and although there are instances of speedy deaths from it, yet I hope that there is room to think the general features of it are beginning to change, and that of those taken ill the number of deaths is smaller, although the patients are still left in a state of great weakness from the wasting of a long-continued periodi-

APPENDIX II. cal fever, which renders them unable for a length of time to attend to their usual duties and occupations; and from the protracted nature of the disease, it is frequent that the whole numbers of a family are to be found in one or other of the stages of the disease. The season is also still very extraordinary, as the land winds which in general blow with considerable violence are remarkably mild with frequent lulls and a heavy thick oppressive atmosphere. Had there not been a very violent squall, although of short duration, on the 29th ultimo, the state of the weather is such as to give rise to the apprehension that the whole will conclude with some violent convulsion of nature.

"6. On enquiring of the people whether such a calamity was ever experienced here before, they state that they remember a very unhealthy season about thirty-four years ago, but that its effects were not so general nor so fatal as in the present instance. This assertion is corroborated by a passage in Orme's *History of Hindustan*, in which the Board will find it mentioned in paragraph 2nd, page 201, old edition, that in the month of March 1757 a very unusual fall of rain had taken place in the province of Tinnevelly, which lasted for two days, and in addition to the damage done to the crops, had brought on an epidemic sickness which carried off numbers of the inhabitants by sudden deaths. The whole description, which is of some length, bears a strong resemblance to the present season, only that the calamity was not of the same extent. If two days rain, however, at that time could produce the effects recorded, some estimate may be formed of those arising from three months of such frequent and equally unseasonable rains.

"7. As before stated the disease was first reported in February to be so general in the district of Strivaleputtur as to cause considerable interruption to the collections. It was then however principally confined to the villages near the hills, in which it prevailed so generally that the peons could not go to demand the revenue, most of those who had been in the villages near the hills being laid up by the fever. To the end of February the fever still continued in this district and had spread all over it on the 26th March; the Tasildar reported that in many instances the crops were left uncut upon the ground for want of people to reap them, and that from the number of those whose business it was to collect and remit the revenue being sick great interruption was at present experienced in the collections.

"8. From Strivaleputtur the disease followed the course of the hills to Tenkashee, which has suffered in a very severe degree from it, as also the intermediate pollams shown in the accompanying sketch. Towards the end of February or beginning of March it had become very prevalent, and in the course of that month the Tasildar reported the number of deaths in the cusbah was from 10 to 15 daily, and in the other villages in proportion, and that many people had left the district for fear of the infection. He also represented that the crops were left standing on the ground for want of people to cut them, and that there were not people enough who were free from fever to attend the sick and burn the dead, and if he sent his peons to demand the revenue they generally found the people in a state rendering them entirely incapable of attending to their concerns. Of all the taluks this one has suffered most in proportion to its population from the fever. APPENDIX II.

"9. In Brummadaspuram the people were represented to have been rather sickly since the month of November last, but the epidemical fever does not seem to have made a very alarming progress till the beginning of March. Since that time the Tasildar represents the people to have suffered much, and he mentions many of the villages where there are not people enough to attend the sick and to burn the dead. The Board will observe a village of the name of Kuddyum in this neighbourhood. In this village, which was a very fine one, it is computed that about a thousand people have been carried off by the fever. Of these there were forty families of Brahmans, of whom twenty-six are entirely swept away, eight have deserted, and of the others about one half of the numbers of each family are dead.

"10. In Sharrinmadavy the fever was later in commencing, and no representations of its having reached a serious height were made till the beginning of April. A great many people have had the disease, but as far as can be learnt the mortality does not appear to have been so great as in some of the other districts.

"11. In Nellumbalam, with the exception of the town of Tinnevelly, the disease does not appear to have commenced so early as in the vicinity of the hills. In the month of April, however, it was represented as very generally prevalent, most of the people being sick and many having died. In the town of Tinnevelly, as before reported, the deaths are estimated for a considerable time to have amounted to fifteen or twenty people a day. The town is still unhealthy, but the cases of sudden death are decreased, as is also the number of casualties.

"12. In the districts of Vedoogramem, Streeviguntam, Gungundam and Alwar Tinnevelly the disease has been much less destructive than in the others, although there has been a considerable degree of sickness, which has incapacitated the people from attending to their business.

"13. It has already been stated that the disease early began to make its appearance on the sea-coast. How this is to be accounted for it is difficult to say, unless it arose from that part of the country having suffered much from the inundation in December and the houses of the people not being so good or durable as in the interior. There are also a great number of toddy-drawers who reside in huts made of cadjans only on the coast, most of which were destroyed in the monsoon and the people left exposed. Many of the salt marshes were also overflowed in the monsoon, the exhalation from which is very offensive. The mortality therefore all along the coast to Cape Comorin has been very great, and the district of Calcaud being bounded by the hills upon the other side has from these two causes suffered most severely from the fever. The Tasildar mentions many villages which are nearly depopulated, and almost all his peons have been sick. In addition to these misfortunes the small-pox has lately made its appearance in the Punjamahl Taluk, but it has not yet done much mischief.

Appendix II. This disease is probably imported from Travancore where I have been informed it is now raging, but it does not appear that the fever which has committed such ravages here has extended itself to that country, where the seasons are remarkable for their regularity.

"14. The taluk of Shankaranainarkovil is the only one which now remains to be noticed, and although surrounded by those parts which suffered most severely from the fever, it is extraordinary that till near the end of April it was only experienced in a comparatively slight degree and the deaths very few. On the 22nd of that month, however, it was represented as having become very general, and that a number of people were dying suddenly as in the other districts where it first broke out. The last accounts state it still continues.

"15. The above is a statement of the progress of the disease in the different parts of the province, as reported to me by the public officers and ascertained as correctly as possible from the best information which it has otherwise been in my power to collect and in compliance with the Board's orders. Instructions have been sent to endeavour to ascertain as near as possible the actual number of people who have fallen victims to this calamity. There has not yet, however, been time for a compliance with these orders from the state in which the people are whose duty it is to furnish them, and also from the dislike which the people of this country have in general to all enquiries of this nature, and they consequently evince much unwillingness to furnish any information respecting it. Independent of these circumstances it is to be apprehended that any account recorded just now would be liable to inaccuracy, as in many places where the fever began the people left their villages until the disease should subside. As soon, however, as any return is obtained which can be depended upon, the Board shall immediately be furnished with it."

APPENDIX III.

TINNEVELLY NATIVE AUTHORS.

App. III. The Pāṇḍya country, especially as was natural Madura itself, the capital of the country and the abode of its kings, abounded in authors. It might with equal propriety be said to have abounded in poets, almost every ancient Tamil composition having been in verse. Madura became celebrated in Tamil literary circles for its so-called "college." This college, however, was not a teaching institution, but an association of poets, who gave their *imprimatur* to works they considered classical by giving the writer a place on their board, which was literally a board, viz., the board on which they sat when they met, represented afterwards to have been a miraculous diamond bench capable of expanding and contracting. The name for this college, Sangam (Sanskrit), has the same meaning as the Latin *collegium*, viz., an association or society of learned men. Tradition says that there were three such colleges at Madura at different times, and that

Madura College.

it was to the last of them that Tiruvaḷḷuvar, the celebrated author of the Kuraḷ, was admitted. Another of the accepted poets was the author of the Nālaḍiyār. Tiruvaḷḷuvar (a name which means the sacred Paraiya priest) is esteemed the prince of Tamil poets; but having been a Paraiya, it was not without a miracle wrought in his favour that he was allowed a place on the much-coveted bench. All this passes current freely in popular tradition, but it is impossible now to ascertain how much truth these legends contain. It is the less necessary for our present purpose to endeavour to ascertain this, seeing that none of the great writers of that time is said to have belonged to Tinnevelly. It is true that Tinnevelly boasts in the possession of Agastyar-malai, the place to which the great rishi Agastya, styled "the Southern Sage" and "the Tamil Sage," retired after having not only invented Tamil grammar but the Tamil language itself, and also that works are still extant—grammars and books of medicine, alchymy, and mystic theology—which are commonly attributed to him. When I have mentioned, however, that all this is related and believed without a particle of evidence in its favour, and against every conceivable probability, I think I have done enough.

Agastya.

A considerable number of Tamil compositions of some degree of merit are attributed on sufficient evidence to persons who are known to have belonged to Tinnevelly, but there are only four of these which could fairly claim a place in a history of Tamil literature.

Nammāḻvār.

I. The first and probably the oldest of these is a portion of the great Vaishṇava composition called the great Prabandham or Tiru-vāy-moḻi, the words of the Sacred Mouth. The whole work contains 4,000 verses, 1,000 of which are attributed to a native of Tinnevelly. This was Nammāḻvār, one of the twelve Āḻvārs or disciples (Āḻvār means one who profoundly humbled himself) of Rāmānuja Āchārya, the founder of the Srī-vaishnava or Visisht-ādvaita school of Hindu theosophy. The Brahman adherents of this school are called in the Tamil country Aiyangārs. The age of the Āḻvārs is not certainly known, but it must have been subsequent to the age of their master Rāmānuja, who flourished about the beginning or middle of the 12th century A.D. The Tinnevelly Āḻvār gave his name to Āḻvār Tirunagari, a place called also, but erroneously, Ālvār Tinnevelly. The oldest name of this place is Kurugūr or Kurugāpuri. In later times the name which I have found in inscriptions is Tenkarai (the South-bank, equivalent to the English Southwark), a name which survives as the name of the taluk in which this place is included. It was called by this name in contradistinction to Srī-vaikunṭham, a still more considerable town on the northern bank. Āḻvār Tirunagari, the name by which it is now called, the meaning of which is the holy city of the Āḻvār, is one of the principal Vaishnava holy places in Tinnevelly, with a population of 5,600. The real name of the Āḻvār of this place is said to have been Jaḍakōpa, a common name now amongst Vaishnavas, and his father is said to have been one Kari

Āḻvār-tirunagari.

App. III.

Māran, a scion of the Pāṇḍya dynasty. Māran means Pāṇḍyan. Nammāḻvār means our Āḻvār, and this title is said to have been conferred upon him by Vishṇu himself, as a mark of special confidence and favour. Though only one in twelve of the Āḻvārs, his share in the hymns of the great Prabandham was one part in four.

Translation of the Mahābhārata.

II. The second important composition attributed to a native of Tinnevelly is the Tamil poetical translation of the Mahā-bhārata, or at least of the greater part of it, which is believed to have been written at Srī-villiputtūr, by a Vaishnava Brahman called Sārva Bhauma[1] Aiyangār. From the name of the place to which he belonged he is commonly called Villiputtūrār. Possibly at the time the poem became famous Srī, sacred, had not been commonly prefixed to the name of the place. At present if the Srī were omitted, the name would not be recognised. The poet is sometimes called an Āḻvār, but this is only out of respect, as the title is also sometimes given to Kambar, the author of the Tamil poetical version of the Rāmāyaṇa. The Tamil Mahā-bhārata is not considered by any means equal in beauty to the Tamil Rāmāyaṇa, which stands, with the Chintāmaṇi and the Kuraḷ, in the very first rank of Tamil poems, but it is considered notwithstanding a very fine composition. Portions of it have frequently been prescribed for the study of candidates for University distinctions.

Srī-villiputtūr.

The date of the author of this work is unknown, but it is never supposed to be very early. Pandits generally suppose that he lived two or three hundred years ago, which seems probable enough and would place him in the age of the Nāyaka rulers of Madura. Villiputtūr means the new town of the bow-man, and of course a legend—several legends indeed—are related to account for this name and explain who the bow-man was. It has received the title of Srī, sacred, on account of its Vaishnava temple, which is a holy place of some celebrity, ranking perhaps with that at Āḻvār Tirunagari. Tirumalai Nāyaka, the celebrated ruler of Madura, had a palace in this place, which is still shown. In the Government Records the name of the place appears as Nāchiyār Kovil, with a population of over 14,000.

Parimēlaḻagar.

III. The third literary character belonging to Tinnevelly whose name claims to occupy a place in the literary history of the Tamil country is a commentator on the Kural called Parimēlaḻagar. I should hardly have thought of placing a mere commentator in this rank, were it not that his *urai* or commentary is considered the first of its kind. According to the opinion of the Tamil people the best of all poems is Tiruvaḷḷuvar's Kuraḷ, and the best of all commentaries is

[1] Sārva Bhauma means possessing the whole world or known throughout the whole world.

Parimēlaḷagar's commentary thereon. The date of this writer is unknown, but he is believed by some to have lived in the Karisal-Ḳāḍu, or black cotton soil country, in the northern part of Tinnevelly. In the Northern Tamil country I have always heard Parimēlaḷagar represented to have been a Brahman, but some Pandits in Tinnevelly —not themselves Shanars—maintain that he was a Shanar guru. Others assert that he was neither a Brāhman nor a Shanar, but a Veḷḷāḷa. App. III.

Nīti-neri-viḷakkam.

IV. Perhaps the latest of the Tinnevelly literary celebrities was the author of the Nīti-neri-viḷakkam, a work consisting of ethical stanzas, arranged more or less after the fashion of the Kural and the Nālaḍiyār. These stanzas have secured themselves a good place in general estimation, but few of them rise to the highest order of originality and merit. They are frequently made use of in University examinations. The author was a Saiva ascetic, a Veḷḷāḷa by caste, called Kumāra-guru-para-Tambirān. Tambirān, his lordship, is the usual title of the head of a Saiva monastery. Our author however was not the head of any monastery, but seems to have had the title conferred upon him as a term of respect. Compare the use of Abbe amongst the French. He is sometimes called also Kumāra-guru-para-Swāmigāḷ. Swāmigāḷ is the honorific plural of Swāmi, lord. Kumāra-guru-para belonged to Srī-vaikuṇṭhaṁ, a well-known town on the northern bank of the Tāmraparṇi. This has always been a place of some importance, and is now the capital of the Tenkarai Taluk. The name by which it is called denotes that it is a holy place amongst the Vaishṇavas. Vaikuṇṭham is the name of Vishṇu's heaven. The population of the place is upwards of 7,000. Kumāra-guru-para-Tambirān is said to have flourished during the reign of Tirumalai Nāyaka, the celebrated king of Madura. If so, he is to be placed between A.D. 1623 and 1659.

Srī-vaikuṇṭham.

APPENDIX IV.

SEPULCHRAL URNS IN TINNEVELLY.

App. IV.

I AM anxious to obtain some information as to the extent of the area within which sepulchral urns, like those to which I am about to refer, are found.

The urns I refer to are large earthenware jars containing fragments of human bones, generally in a very decayed state. They are of various sizes, corresponding with the age of the person whose remains were to be disposed of. The largest I have found was eleven feet in circumference, and the smallest have been between four and five. The shape varies a little within certain limits, so that I have not found any two urns perfectly alike, but the type generally adhered to is that of the large earthen jars (in Tamil kūnai) with which the

Shape of urns.

App. IV.

people in this neighbourhood draw water from wells for their cultivation. The urn is without handles, feet, or cover. It swells out towards the middle and terminates in a point, so that it is only when it is surrounded with earth that it keeps an upright position. The urns do much credit to the workmanship of the people by whom they were made, being made of better-tempered clay, better burnt, and much stronger than any of the pottery made in these times in this part of India. They would contain a human body easily enough in a doubled-up position, if it could be got inside, but the mouth is generally so narrow that this would present some difficulty. One opinion is that the bones were denuded of flesh and separated before they were packed into the urns. Generally decay is found to have advanced so far that theories respecting the mode in which the body was put in can neither be verified nor disproved. Fragments only of the harder bones remain, and the urn seems to contain little more than a mass of earth. In one instance I found the bones partially petrified, and therefore almost perfect, though they had fallen asunder; but this was the large eleven-feet urn referred to above, discovered at Korkai, so that in this instance it was conceivable that the body had been placed in it entire. The skull was nearly perfect—a skull of a low type. At Ilanji, near Courtallum, on opening an urn distinct traces of the shape of a skeleton were discovered. The skull was found resting on the sternum, and on each side of the sternum was a tibia. It appeared clear, therefore, in this case, that the body had been doubled up and forced in head foremost, though it was not clear how the shoulders could have got in. The bones were of the consistence of ochre, and crumbled to pieces when they were taken out. Nothing could be preserved but a piece of the skull and the teeth, which were those of an adult. Dr. Fry, Surgeon to the Resident of Travancore, who was present at the find, pointed out that the molars had been worn down by eating grain, and that the edges of the front teeth also had been worn down by biting some kind of parched pulse. Afterwards, on examining the mouths of some natives, I found their front teeth worn down a little in the same manner, and as they admitted, from the same cause. I have not noticed any trace of the bones in these urns having been calcined. I believe they were not. Cremation, I think, was not then in use.

Mode of interment.

Characteristics of the human remains.

In addition to human bones a few small earthen vessels are found in most of the jars. Sometimes such vessels are arranged outside instead of being placed inside. These vessels are of various shapes, all more or less elegant, and all appear to have been highly polished. At first I supposed they had been glazed, but I have been informed by Dr. Hunter, late of the Madras School of Arts, that what I noticed was a polish, not a true glaze. Whatever it was, I have not noticed anything of the kind in the native pottery of these parts and these times. In many cases the polish or glaze is black, and the decay of these blackened vessels seems to have given rise to the supposition that the bones had sometimes been calcined.

Description of contents.

On the accompanying plate (see *Indian Antiquary* for October 1877) are sketches of five of these little vessels. When these have been shown to natives, they say that one appears to have been an oil vessel, and another a spittoon! The use of the vessel with the lid is unknown. In these times such vessels would be made of bell-metal, not of pottery. We may conclude that the object in view in placing these vessels in the urn was that the ghost of the departed might be supplied with the ghosts of eatables and drinkables, together with the ghosts of suitable vessels for eating and drinking out of, in the other world. Small stones about the size of a cocoanut are generally found heaped round the mouth of the urn, and the discovery of such stones ranged in a circle, corresponding to the circular mouth of the urn, will be found to be a reason for suspecting the existence of an urn underneath.

Native theories.

The natives of these times know nothing whatever of the people by whom this singular mode of sepulture was practised, or of the time when they lived. They do not identify them with the Samaṇas—that is, the Jainas and Buddhists lumped together—about whom tolerably distinct traditions survive, nor does there appear to be anything in or about the jars distinctively Jaina or Buddhistic. There is a myth current amongst the natives, it is true, respecting the people who were buried in these jars, but this myth seems to me merely a confession of their ignorance. They say that in the Trētāyuga—that is, about a million of years ago—people used to live to a great age, but that however old they were they did not die, but the older they grew the smaller they became. They got so small at length that to keep them out of the way of harm it was necessary to place them in the little triangular niches in the walls of native houses in which the lamp is kept. At length when the younger people could no longer bear the trouble of looking after their dwarf ancestors, they placed them in earthen jars, put with them in the jars a number of little vessels containing rice, water, oil, &c., and buried them in a sort of cemetery near the village.

Interpretation of names.

The name by which these urns are called in the Tamil country does not throw much light on their origin. This name assumes three forms. In the Tamil dictionary it is madamadakkattāḻi. A more common form of this is madamadakkan-dāḻi, the meaning of both which forms is the same, viz., the taḻi or large jar which boils over. The meaning attributed to this by some natives is rather far-fetched, viz., that the little people who were placed in them used sometimes to come out of the jars and sit about, as if they had boiled over out of them. The form of this word in use amongst the common people seems capable of a more rational interpretation. This is madamattan-dāḻi, or more properly madōnmattan-dāli. Madōnmatta (Sansk.) means 'insane,' but it is sometimes used in Tamil to mean 'very large,' as in the Tamil version of the Panchatantra, where it is used to denote a very large jungle. The great size of the urn being its principal characteristic, it would seem that the name in use amongst the common people is, after all, better warranted than that which is used by those who are regarded as correct speakers.

People interred not pygmies.

Who the people were who buried their dead in these urns is a problem yet unsolved. The only points that can be regarded as cer-

App. IV.

tain are those which have been ascertained by the internal evidence of the urns and their contents themselves. From this it is clear that the people buried in them were not pygmies, but of the same size as people of the present time. How they were put in may be mysterious, but there is no doubt about the size of their bones. The skulls were similar to those of the present time. The teeth also were worn down, like those of the existing race of natives, by eating grain. In a jar opened by Mr. Stuart, then Acting Collector of Tinnevelly, and Dr. Jagor, of Berlin, at Āditta-nallūr near Pudugudi, a head of millet was found. The grain had disappeared, but the husks remained. In one opened by myself at the same place a small copper bangle was found. Copper is not now used for this purpose.

The unknown people must have lived in villages, the jars being found, not one here and another there, but arranged side by side in considerable numbers, as would naturally be done in a cemetery or burial-ground. They were also a comparatively civilized people, as is evident from the excellence of their pottery, and the traces of iron implements or weapons which have sometimes been found in the jars. The conclusion from all this which seems to me most probable is that they were the ancestors of the people now living in the same neighbourhood. If this were the true explanation, it is singular that no relic, trace, or tradition of such a mode of sepulture has survived to the present day. And yet, if we were to adopt the supposition that they were an alien race, it would be still more difficult to conjecture who they were, where they came from, and why they disappeared. Whoever those people were, judging from the rites of sepulture prevailing amongst them, I think it may be regarded as certain that they were not 'Hindūs;' that is, that they were not adherents of the Brahmanical religion commonly called Hindūism. If so they must have lived at that early period when Brahmanical Hindūism was as yet unknown, or at least when it had not yet become the religion of the country. This supposition would carry the urns back to a high antiquity, possibly even an antiquity higher than the Christian era.

Not Hindūs by religion.

I have myself seen these urns both in the Tinnevelly and Madura Districts and in Northern and Southern Travancore, that is, on both sides of the Southern Ghāts, and I am anxious to ascertain in what other districts of India they are found. If the area within which they are found can be accurately traced, some light may be thrown thereby on their history.

APPENDIX V.

EXPLORATIONS AT KORKAI AND KĀYAL.

Appendix V.

I quote here, in confirmation of statements made in various places in the body of the work, an article which appeared in the *Indian Antiquary* for March 1877.

Korkai identified.

"I visited Korkai once many years ago, and, though my visit was a hurried one, yet from what I saw, and from the inquiries I made, I

APPENDIX V.

came to the conclusion that Korkai (in Tamil properly Kolkai, euphonized into Korkai), though now so insignificant, was to be identified with the Κόλχοι of the Greeks, which Lassen had identified with Kīḻakarai, a place on the Ramnad or Madura coast. The Greeks came to Κόλχοι to purchase pearls, certainly soon after the Christian era, probably many years before, and represented it as the headquarters of the pearl trade between Cape Kumārī and the place they called Κῶρυ, properly Kōṭī, now Rāmeśvaram, which was also an emporium of the same trade. It must have been regarded as a considerable place at that time, seeing that from its name they called the Gulf of Manar the Kolchic Gulf. This was the Korkai to which all native traditions pointed as the cradle of South Indian civilization, the place where the three brothers Chēran, Chōḻan, and Pāṇḍiyan were said to have been born and brought up, and from whence they set forth to form dynasties and kingdoms,—or, as might more readily be admitted, the place where the rule of the Pāṇḍyas commenced, and from whence they afterwards migrated to Madura. The meaning of the name Korkai is 'an army, a camp.' The interest of this identification was heightened by the conclusion at which I arrived at the same time, that an insignificant place called Old Kāyal, about halfway between Korkai and the sea, was to be identified with the Cael of Marco Polo, the most important city and seaport on the eastern coast of India during the Middle Ages. (See Colonel Yule's *Marco Polo.*) The sites of two famous places were thus discovered in the same neighbourhood, and a glance at the geology of the neighbourhood disclosed the reason why each had been abandoned in turn. Both places are situated on the delta of the Tāmraparnī,—Korkai within five, Kāyal within two, miles of the sea,—and each was originally on the sea-coast. As the silt accumulated in the sea near the mouth of the river, or as the land rose, or from both causes, Korkai was found at length to be too far inland for the convenience of a seaborne trade, and Kāyal (meaning a 'lagoon opening into the sea') rose in its stead on the sea-shore, and attained perhaps to still greater dimensions. Kāyal carried on an immense direct trade with China and Arabia, the evidences of which—broken pieces of China and Arabian pottery—are found lying all over the open plain on which the city stood. In time, however, through the continuous operation of the same causes, Kāyal came to be too far from the sea; and accordingly, shortly after the Portuguese arrived on the Coromandel Coast, they abandoned Kāyal, and established themselves instead at Tuticorin, which has ever since been the principal seaport of Tinnevelly, there being no river near to silt up the harbour and roads. It would seem as if Korkai, though probably never so important an emporium of trade as Kāyal, must at one time have been nearly as large. This is proved by the relics of pottery, &c., scattered about the country for miles, and especially by the circumstance that places, such as Akkasālai ('the mint'), which are now at a distance from Korkai, are ascertained, by the inscriptions I have found on the walls of the temples, to have been portions of Korkai originally.

Kāyal.

Retirement of the sea from both places.

APPENDIX V.

Excavations at Korkai.

"Whilst in Korkai and the neighbourhood I employed ten or twelve coolies for four days to make excavations here and there, under the superintendence of one of my assistants; whilst it was made the duty of the choir boys—much more a pleasure to them than a duty—to examine every shovelful of the earth that was thrown up, to see whether it contained any objects of interest. The Collector of the district kindly sent me a peon, to let the people of the place see that nothing illegal or improper was going to be done, and in return I sent him a list of the articles found, though unfortunately they were of no particular interest.

Geology of Korkai.

"The geology of the place seemed to me more interesting than its antiquities. The whole of the country in this neighbourhood is included in the delta of the Tāmrāparnī, the great river of Tinnevelly; and this place is situated in the last formed portion of the delta, lowest and nearest the sea, so that the mode in which the delta was formed, which is doubtless more or less the mode in which all deltas have been formed, could be easily studied. The upper stratum is composed of stiff alluvial clay, which had been brought down by the river and deposited in the bed of the adjacent sea. Every portion of this alluvium contains sea-shells in great abundance,—not merely sea-shore shells, but deep-sea shells, such as the *chank* and the pearl oyster. So abundant are they that in places where the surface of the ground has been washed away by rain, and cultivation has not been carried on, the white shell-covered surface glitters almost like water in the moonlight, and in some places as you walk along the roads, especially near Māramangalam, the shells go crackling under your feet, as they would by the sea-shore when the tide is out. This being the last formed portion of the delta, the alluvial stratum is very shallow. The average depth cannot be more than six feet, and at the bottoms of tanks I have found it no more than three. Underneath this I invariably found a layer of grit-stone (called by the people 'salt-stone'), rarely more than a foot in thickness, composed of the larger grains of sea-sand, such as lie on the surface, mixed with comminuted shells. This had evidently been the surface of the ancient sea-bed, for underneath I invariably came upon beautiful white sea-sand in smaller grains, containing great quantities of unbroken shells. Doubtless the grit-stone had been formed by the infiltration of the alluvium from above. I found it impossible to ascertain the depth of the sand, or what it rested on, for after digging into it for a few feet the hole always got filled with water, and the water flowed in so fast that baling out was useless. Strange to say, some of the shells I found in this ancient sea-bed retained a portion of their original colour.

Recent appearance of shells.

One in particular—a *Conus*—looked as if it had been alive only a few years ago. What makes this so remarkable is that this portion of the delta must have been inhabited at least 2,500 years ago, and it must have been many ages earlier when the deposition of the alluvium commenced.

No traces of the Greeks.

"I hoped by making excavations in Korkai and the neighbourhood to find some traces of the Greeks, but in this I was doomed to be disappointed. The ancient level of the village is about eight feet below its present level, which of itself is a proof of great antiquity. When the diggers reached this depth they invariably found traces of human habitations, shreds of Indian pottery, &c., but nothing of the nature I hoped to find. On the surface we found two Singhalese copper coins (I conclude them to be Singhalese from the management of the drapery), but the inscriptions were quite obliterated. I also found two images of Buddha, sitting, in his usual attitude of contemplation. One of them was out in the fields, the other in the village. I suspected that the latter was worshipped, though it was known to belong to a different religion. The people strenuously denied this, but one morning when I happened to pass I saw a garland of flowers which had been placed by some person round its neck. The person who did so evidently thought that if ever Buddha got his head above water again, he had a chance of being remembered for good! The most interesting things that were found were three of those mysterious sepulchral urns which have hitherto puzzled everybody. The natives know nothing about them, and the common opinion amongst Europeans is that they pertained to a race which died out, but of which no relic remains except these urns. The urns are made of a peculiarly good variety of the ordinary pottery of the country, but there are always some little vessels found inside, some of which are beautifully shaped, with a polish or glaze which the potters of these days cannot imitate. Two of the urns I found contained no bones, but only traces of bone-dust; but one, a monster urn, 11 feet in circumference —unfortunately found broken—contained a complete set of entire human bones, including a perfect skull. The circumstances in which this urn was found were very interesting. The people to whom it belonged had dug down through the alluvial soil of the delta and the grit-stone till they came to the white sea-sand, and in this they had deposited the urn. The grit-stone had then partially reformed all round, and I found the cavity of the skull filled up with grit-stone. All the bones were more or less petrified. The notion invariably entertained by the natives of these days is that the people buried in these urns were a race of pygmies, but the bones found in this urn were admitted by the natives who were standing about when it was opened to be those of a full-grown man of the usual size. Strange to say, a deputation of women came to my tent one day for the purpose of seeing the bones.

Image of Buddha.

Sepulchral urns.

Petrified human bones.

"I visited Old Kāyal (Marco Polo's Cael) twice, and set my excavators at work for a day in a place about two miles from the present village, which represents only the western boundary of the ancient city. At a depth of three feet beneath the present surface they came on the *chunammed* floor of a house, but found nothing of importance. The extent of the site of Kāyal was so great that it would take a month, instead of a single day merely, to explore it properly. I found, however, the whole surface of the ground, literally for miles, covered with evidences of the perfect truth of Marco Polo's statements respecting the trade of the place, confirmed by those of the Muhammadan historians. According to those statements, Kāyal was

Explorations in Kāyal.

APPENDIX V.

China and Arabian pottery.

frequented by great numbers of vessels from the Arabian coast and from China—(*junks*)—in one of which latter Marco Polo himself arrived; and accordingly I picked up everywhere on the open plain broken pieces of China porcelain of all qualities, and broken pieces of Arabian pottery. I could easily, if I had chosen, have collected a cart-load, but the pieces had been broken again and again by the plough and the feet of bullocks, so that, though the material in each case was obvious enough, all trace of the shape of the article had disappeared. Old Kāyal, or what remains of it, is now inhabited almost exclusively by Labbīs (native Muhammadans) and Roman Catholic fishermen.

"The people of these parts, as generally throughout India, have not the remotest notion of the object Europeans have in view in searching for antiquities. Whatever we may say, they think our real object is to endeavour to discover hidden treasures; and this they consider a very risky business, for all hidden treasures are in the custody of demons, who will not allow them to be rifled with impunity. At Korkai, before my explorations commenced, many of the people expressed an earnest hope that I would not make any excavations near any temple or image, because, although very likely there might be treasure underneath, the demons in charge would be so enraged that they would destroy the village outright. I assured the people that I would take care not to come near any temple or image, and I scrupulously kept my word. My old friend M—— of Ārumuga-mangalam professes to have received a dreadful fright some years ago from the demons that watch over hidden treasure, when he helped the then Collector of Tinnevelly, Mr. Puckle, to make explorations near Kāyal. The night after the first day's exploration a she-demon appeared to him in a dream, and asked him in terrible tones how he dared to meddle with her treasures. In the morning when he awoke, he found—dreadful to relate—that his feet were fastened round the back of his neck in such a way that he was unable to loose them without assistance! I need scarcely add that no further part in the exploration was taken by him. I wanted him to tell me the story; but he was afraid, I suppose, I should laugh at him, and so I failed; but he told it quite gravely to my assistants, and has told the story so often that he evidently believes it himself now. Even Europeans, it seems, are not quite so free from danger as they suppose. Many years ago there was a Collector of Tinnevelly, it is said, who determined to dig for the treasure which was believed to have been hidden in a certain place by a woman who intended to make use of it in some subsequent birth, and which for the time being, of course, was under the custody of demons. He was warned that something dreadful would happen, but, being a European, he did not care. He pitched his tent near the place, and the whole of the first day was occupied by himself, his peons, and his coolies in digging. At length, as night drew on, they came to a carefully built stone receptacle; and, justly concluding that this was the place where the treasure was hidden, the Collector set a watch over it and went to sleep in his tent, with the intention of opening the stone receptacle the next morning. The next morning

Superstitious fears.

Wonderful occurrence to an explorer.

came, and the Collector found himself, not in his tent, but in bed in his own bungalow many miles away at Palamcotta; the tent was found pitched at the other side of the river, and of the excavations that had been made the previous day not a trace remained!"

Discovery of Arabic Coins.

Some years ago a considerable quantity of Muhammadan gold coins was discovered in Tinnevelly near an old road leading from Kāyal. So far as appears all the coins—which with one exception are Arabic—belonged to the 13th century A.D. and probably therefore were brought to India by Arab merchants some time before Marco Polo's visit in 1292. They were discovered by coolies engaged in digging the southern channel leading from Pudugudi, at the southern end of the Srīvaikunṭham anicut, in the direction of Tiruchendūr. The nearest village to the spot was Tentirupati or Tentirupērai, the nearest town Āḷvār Tirunagari. The channel was being carried through a road when the vessel containing the coins was discovered several feet beneath the surface. Kāyal lies to the north of the Tāmraparṇī near the sea, and this place lay to the south some distance inland, but as the road under which they were found led from Kāyal to Kāyalpaṭṭaṇam and Kulasēkharapaṭṭaṇam, places where Arab merchants resided and traded even then, I think we are warranted in connecting the find with Marco Polo's Kāyal. Doubtless the treasure was buried in the hurry of some alarm of robbers or local war, and we may conclude from the owners never having returned and taken it away that the alarm proved only too well founded, and that the owners lost their lives as well as their treasure.

I here quote the account of the discovery furnished to the Board of Revenue by Mr. R. K. Puckle, Collector of the district, on the 25th October 1873:

"On the 25th December (1872) last a gang of labourers while engaged on cutting a channel connected with the Strivaiguntam Anicut Project came upon a large copper pot filled with gold ingots and coins. The pot was of large size, capable of holding six Madras measures of grain, and from the marks inside it must have been filled with treasure.

"2. The probable value of the treasure is estimated at a lakh of rupees.

"3. The labourers divided the spoil and made off with it, but the matter soon became public and the Tahsildar succeeded in recovering Rupees 8,000 worth of coin and ingots. This was mostly recovered from a little girl who ran away from her house with a chatty which fell, broke, and scattered the gold in front of the officials who were coming to search.

"4. The rest was quickly buried or melted down, and all traces of it were lost. I am told, however, that the share of one of the labourers, which he deposited with a kavalgar, who afterwards denied having received it, was worth 900 rupees, so, as there were twenty labourers besides headmen to share the spoil, the find must have been very extensive.

Appendix V.

"5. On hearing of the discovery I notified the course to be pursued under the Act, but nothing was given up. The treasure recovered was deposited with the Civil Court, and the case was inquired into after due notification. The Court has decided, as per proceeding enclosed, that the terms of the Act were sufficiently observed and that the treasure should be restored to the finders.

"6. This treasure was buried in the sandy tract between the coast and the large town of Alwartirunagari, some fifteen miles from the mouth of the Tambrapurni. It was found near an old avenue leading inland from what was once the city of Kāyal, and this treasure was probably buried some hundreds of years ago.

"7. The coins are principally Arabic, but one is European. This, as far as can be ascertained, is a coin of Joanna of Castile, A.D. 1236. Some of the Arabic coins are still older: one bears the impress of the Mahomedan year 71, and another bears the name of Sultan Salaudeen, who may be the Saladin of history."

I here add the description of the coins sent to the Madras Government Museum by Mr. Puckle, kindly furnished to me by Dr. G. Bidie, Superintendent of the Museum.

"The coins are 31 in number, and the inscriptions are in Arabic or Kufic, with one exception, viz., that of a coin of Peter of Aragon, the legend on which is Latin in Gothic character. All the Kalifat coins, with the exception of nine, have been deciphered and belong to the 13th century. So of course does that of Peter of Aragon, it being after 1276. There is a doubt about some of the dates, but none are apparently later than 1300."

INDEX.

A.

B.

C.

D.

E.

F.

G.

L.

PAGE

M.

N.

O.

P.

Q.

R.

S.

T.

U.

V.

W.

X.

Y.

Z.